Negotiating Water Rights

Negotiating Water Rights

Edited by

BRYAN RANDOLPH BRUNS
RUTH S. MEINZEN-DICK

IFPRI

INTERNATIONAL FOOD POLICY RESEARCH INSTITUTE

INTERMEDIATE TECHNOLOGY PUBLICATIONS 2000

Intermediate Technology Publications Ltd,
103–105 Southampton Row, London WC1B 4HH, UK

© International Food Policy Research Institute 2000

A CIP catalogue record for this book is available from the
British Library

ISBN 1 85339 484 X

Typeset by Line Arts, Pondicherry
Printed in India by Chaman Enterprises, New Delhi

Dedication

In memory of H.L. Joep Spiertz, 1940–99
for his lasting contributions to the study of water rights.

Contents

List of Tables

List of Figures

List of Maps

Foreword

Many societies have a saying that 'water is life.' No resource is more important than water for food production, human health, local livelihoods, and the wellbeing of ecosystems. Yet with rising populations and demands for water from all sectors—agriculture, industry, domestic water supply, and even environmental conservation—there is scarcity and competition for water, even in countries and regions where water may seem abundant.

Water rights are fundamental to the outcome of this increasing competition for water, whether that competition is between farmers in an irrigation system, between irrigation systems, or between irrigation and other sectors. Currently, irrigation accounts for over 70 per cent of water withdrawals worldwide, and even more in many developing countries. In many cases, water is being reallocated from agriculture to other areas or uses. The question of how the customary rights of existing water users are acknowledged, and whether new allocation patterns are imposed or negotiated with the users, will have a major bearing on rural livelihoods as well as food security.

For many years there has been recognition on the part of researchers and policymakers alike that secure property rights over natural resources are fundamental to giving people incentives to manage those resources sustainably. But attention to water rights has lagged behind attention to tenure of land and tree resources. Researchers have found it difficult to study rights that are attached to a mobile resource like water, while policymakers, realizing the vital importance of this resource, have tended to claim state 'ownership' of water and have been reluctant to recognize the rights of different types of users.

This volume addresses these gaps in understanding and in policy approaches to water rights. It presents a broader view of water rights than conventional interpretations of state law, acknowledging instead that there may be many different bases for claims on water. It shows that water rights are not static but nearly as fluid as the resource itself, subject to negotiation and change. It draws together the work of researchers and grassroots practitioners who have been involved in water allocation.

The case studies in this volume demonstrate the wide variety of water rights, conflicts, and outcomes. They highlight the importance of involving users directly in negotiations over water rights. Such participation is not merely a desirable add-on, but necessary for water allocations to be accepted and implementable. Several of the case studies demonstrate that involving local people in negotiations improves the productivity, as well as the equity, of water distribution.

Yet achieving constructive, negotiated distributions and redistributions of water rights can be a difficult undertaking. The stakes are high: competition for water can lead to violent conflict because peoples' lives and livelihoods are at stake. Achieving positive outcomes from competition requires explicit attention to water rights, and in many cases, reconceptualization of the nature of rights and rightholders. It also requires strengthening the capacity of both government agencies and user groups to negotiate. This volume provides both broad principles and specific examples of how this can be achieved.

Meeting the challenges of equitable water allocation is a formidable task. It calls into question both issues of economic production and fundamental values. But as water becomes more scarce, these issues must be addressed. It is my hope that this book will provide fresh insights for policymakers, practitioners, and researchers and that it will inspire them to take up these challenges by working with the users who have the greatest stake in water allocation.

Per Pinstrup-Andersen
Director General
International Food Policy Research Institute

Preface

Irrigation has long been a local activity in many locations around the world. In such cases, irrigation systems, usually of small or modest scale, have been constructed and operated by collections of local people operating within established, or newly created, forms of social relationships commonly used to mobilize labor, assemble capital, and apportion the results of group investment following acceptable rules.

In this manner, cultivators from the valleys of northern Laos to the tributary creeks of the upper Rio Grande in New Mexico physically constructed the apparatus for water diversion and socially constructed locally recognized and locally defensible access to the appropriated water. These rules of access emerge from ongoing negotiations that both rest on and contribute to the complex cultural ideas and meanings by which people connect with one another and with their natural habitat. The rich complexity of these water access rules as well as their shrewd adaptation to the changing circumstances of the immediate surroundings are each detailed in this book's contributions.

With equal resolve, states nearly everywhere have moved to encompass these local water societies into government systems, thus transforming them into appendages of the national irrigation bureaucracy. Almost inevitably, this transformation has altered locally constructed rules of access to water, often producing state water rights that are a mere parody of the original access rules. Frequently referred to as the process of formalizing water rights, these rights almost always are less attuned to the particularities of place and time; therefore they are less 'fair' in local terms and typically less defensible and secure, given local resources and experiences. Local access rules are reconstructed, sometimes negotiated, as rights within the state's legal system. Moreover, such transformations usually are imposed by the state rather than negotiated with the parties. In short, as Sengupta notes in his chapter, traditional irrigation systems no longer exist in traditional settings.

When local irrigation systems and state irrigation bureaucracies are entangled—now the case almost everywhere as issues of water scarcity and quality expand—how should customary rules of access to water be treated in the new local-state entity? What actions should local water users take to defend their sometimes long-standing arrangements against new claims? What should the state do to respect actions taken locally while also trying to balance contemporary needs and opportunities? As suggested in the title of this book, the editors believe the answer lies in negotiating and in water rights.

A major contribution of this volume is to document how frequently negotiation has been the methodology applied by water users on the ground and to demonstrate the successful outcomes that have occurred. But we also learn that negotiation is an approach underemployed by the state, though it may have much to contribute as we move toward increasingly competitive water use situations.

The second part of the answer, water rights, raises more questions for future consideration. As I understand the suggestion, it is for state and local actors to give customary rules of access, through negotiation, the accoutrements of state-guaranteed water rights. That is, to get along in the modern state, traditional water access rules should be dressed up as state-sanctioned water rights.

It is an appealing and potentially powerful solution and one in step with the late 20th century discussions of human rights worldwide, the role of markets in allocating all sorts of goods, as well as the notion of universal and standard principles of behavior.

But there are three questions that require examination as this water rights approach is executed:

One—how can state legal processes formulate water rights laws that sufficiently capture the nuances, conditionality, and resilience of customary water access practices?

Two—what are the minimal capabilities (judicial, executive) that a state must have to ensure that state water rights will serve local people and their water needs adequately?

Three—are there modern institutional forms other than water rights that a state could use to protect local irrigation investments while also providing opportunities for the future for all citizens?

In this book the reader will find much on which to build as water users, policymakers, and researchers continue searching for better solutions to the world's increasingly complex water problems.

E. Walter Coward, Jr.
Ford Foundation

Acknowledgements

Much of this book grew out of discussions and panel presentations at conferences of the International Association for the Study of Common Property, in Bodo, Norway in 1995, Berkeley, California in 1996, and Vancouver, Canada in 1998. We are indebted to the ideas and enthusiasm of colleagues working on the challenges of managing common pool resources, looking at the opportunities for self-governance, and exploring possibilities which often lie outside familiar dichotomies of state and local, government and market, or public and private.

This book would not have been possible without the generous support provided by the Ford Foundation. Several of the chapters report on research earlier supported by the Ford Foundation, including those by Nyoman Sutawan; Ujjwal Pradhan and Rajendra Pradhan; Ganjar Kurnia, Teten Avianto, and Bryan Randolph Bruns; and the Northern New Mexico Legal Services. Ujjwal Pradhan, Suzanne Siskel and E. Walter Coward, Jr. arranged a grant to the International Food Policy Research Institute, which helped fund editing and other costs. John Ambler had earlier supported research on water rights in India and Nepal using a legal pluralism perspective and involving researchers from Wageningen Agricultural University in the Netherlands. The Ford Foundation has also been a major donor for the conferences of the International Association for the Study of Common Property, where most of the papers were originally presented.

Our work here builds on earlier interests in irrigation and social change developed while studying Development Sociology at Cornell University. E. Walter Coward, Jr., Norman Uphoff, Randolph Barker, Milton Barnett, Gilbert Levine, and other colleagues created a stimulating intellectual community, combining theoretical and practical study of irrigation and water resources management. Linkages with Joep Spiertz and Franz von Benda-Beckmann at Wageningen Agricultural University, and Keebet von Benda-Beckmann at Erasmus University have enriched our understanding of water rights.

This book is part of broader research programs on water resource allocation, and on property rights and collective action, at the International Food Policy Research Institute (IFPRI). IFPRI supported preparation of the manuscript, supplementing the Ford Foundation grant with additional resources. Beverley Abreu and William Whichard provided essential support for word processing and administration. Anna Knox assisted with bibliographic research.

We have benefitted from many suggestions by the chapter authors, and from other friends and colleagues who read and commented on portions of the manuscript, including Wouter Lincklaen Arriens, William Bloomquist, Anna Knox, Claudia Ringler, Mark Rosegrant, Hugh Turral, Robert Yoder, and Wray Witten. Comments from reviewers, including William Easter, Sandra Archibald, Nanda Abeywickrema, and an anonymous reviewer for Sage stimulated us to clarify and focus the discussion. Responsibility for any remaining errors and omissions lies with us.

Bryan Bruns would like to thank his mother, Jean Bruns, for proof-reading an early draft manuscript. His wife, Pakping, and children, Natapong, Lily and Robin, provided motivation (and interruptions, mostly welcome).

Ruth Meinzen-Dick would like to thank IFPRI colleagues for helping her think through ideas, and Carroll, Laura, and Kevin Dick for their understanding and encouragement.

Bryan Randolph Bruns   Ruth S. Meinzen-Dick
Chiang Mai, Thailand   Washington D.C., U.S.A.

1

Negotiating Water Rights: Introduction

RUTH S. MEINZEN-DICK
and BRYAN RANDOLPH BRUNS

'... *on one occasion 22 persons, including myself, destroyed the rice fields, bunds and diversion weirs of the Yampalis to punish them for stealing water.' (from Chapter 7)*

'*The men have betrayed us.... The day of the allocation we came too late, because we were not informed ... they said that the plots would not have been enough for all women.... Therefore they had decided to allocate to the chiefs of the extended households. Our brother had already selected our plots. But he does not know the good sites and he selected a bad site. We could not do anything.' (from Chapter 3)*

'*My channel neighbors get water from small streams, springs or drainage from other fields, in addition to the channel. My field doesn't have access to any other sources of water but the channel; therefore, I must take extra water now and then.' (from Chapter 2)*

Water rights are not just an analytical abstraction. People depend on water for their life and livelihood; people also get killed fighting over water. Around the world, competition for water is increasing, among irrigators and between agriculture, industry, urban water supply and other needs. Conflicting claims challenge the social institutions which mediate access to water.

The unifying thesis of this book is that negotiated approaches are essential to equitably and efficiently allocating water in the face of emerging demands. This chapter introduces themes which run through the cases presented in later chapters. Farmers maneuver among multiple forums to protect and enhance their claims to water, employing different normative repertoires of law and custom, navigating contexts of legal pluralism. Government investments to develop water resources usually restructure water rights in ways which may be counter-productive unless changes are carefully negotiated. One of the most important directions for improving allocation is recognizing and enhancing capacity for user self-governance of water as a common property resource. Reforms in irrigation institutions have already taken significant steps to incorporate farmer participation and devolve management responsibility to water users, but water rights need to be more clearly negotiated. Growing competition for water intensifies already urgent needs to improve institutions for water allocation.

Authors in this book draw on two broad streams of thought, one dealing with property rights, especially common property, and another dealing with institutional reform in irrigation and water resources. Subsequent sections of the introduction expand on these conceptual currents: legal pluralism, water rights, common property, participation in irrigation, and competition for water, after which the final section outlines the plan of the book.

Understanding Legal Pluralism

This book draws on a perspective markedly different from conventional treatments of water (or other property) rights, which often seek to identify a single system of water rights, usually based on interpreting statutory laws and government regulations. Instead, it starts with the perspective of people's experience with water access and control, in which individuals draw upon a range of strategies for claiming and obtaining water. In this, concepts of legal pluralism are valuable, because instead of focusing only on state law they emphasize that multiple legal and normative frameworks coexist.[1] Government, religious, and customary laws, development project rules, and unwritten local norms may all address who should receive water, from which sources, for what purposes.

Even within statutory legal systems, differing federal, provincial, and local laws regulate water. Nor are any of these necessarily well-integrated 'systems' which are internally consistent. Spiertz (Chapter 6) and Sengupta (Chapter 5) emphasize how, in Bali and Bihar, different government agency offices (and officers) have different records and varying interpretations of the pertinent regulations.[2] Different levels of government may conflict. The U.S. Supreme Court's 1912 *Winters* decision upheld Native American rights to water, bringing about a clash between federal and state principles in water allocation, many aspects of which are still unresolved. None of these legal frameworks are static, but all change over time. Social practice often differs significantly from any of the normative systems which are conceived to regulate or justify behavior.

Unfortunately, many treatments of water rights use an overly narrow, legalistic interpretation that overemphasizes statutory rights laid down in government law books. Such an approach is exemplified by statements such as 'there are no water rights here.' This assumes that the formal rights and rules are the only relevant definition of rights. This typically reflects a lack of information about the wide variety of water rights systems, and ignorance of how water is actually allocated in local areas. Legal pluralism argues that understanding water rights needs to start from the local perspectives of those who use water, their daily experiences, the meanings through which they conceive of water and rights, and the options they have available for acquiring water and defending their access to this vital resource.

As an approach, legal pluralism goes beyond dualistic opposition between 'formal state law' and 'local customary law' to look at the tensions and contradictions within and between interacting repertoires. While formal laws are important, they frequently fail to coincide with people's own perceptions of water rights and the ways in which water has been managed at the local level. Despite the power of nation-states, their capacity to enforce their will is constrained by many factors, not least by the dynamics of the agencies and agents through whom they work, and by the power of other social forces, particularly where state reforms challenge entrenched interests. Dealing with local customs alone is also not realistic, because these take place in an environment of state laws, however remote these may sometimes seem. Local or 'customary' rules rarely exist in isolation from state legal history, but instead are complexly intertwined. As a result, recommendations based on statutory rights alone—or on customary practices alone—do not adequately address the combination of technology and institutions[3] which might contribute to improving water allocation, in practice.

A heritage of colonial law and subsequent state legislation overlays evolving local practices in most of the cases from South Asia, Indonesia and Africa in this book, creating various kinds of legal pluralism. In the United States, New Mexico state law explicitly acknowledges rights descending from earlier Spanish and Mexican law, but as Chapter 13 describes, whether and how courts recognize traditional rights may depend on the ability of local people to articulate and defend their rights. The kinds of interactions emphasized by legal pluralism also show up in how environmental conflicts have been contested at the federal and state level in the United States, in courts and in legislatures, and on the ground within local communities. Environmental interests, seeking to protect instream flows and aquatic habitats, have used various legal bases, including the public trust doctrine[4] and appeals to community values to challenge longstanding water rights of irrigation districts and mutual companies (Ingram and Oggins 1992; Koehler 1995). Negotiation has added important alternative forums in many of these cases.

While overlapping legal repertoires may pose complications and barriers to understanding by outside analysts, they offer opportunities to maneuver for those who are directly involved. Those who wish to take water can base their claim on one or another legal framework, or appeal to different authorities, depending on where they have the strongest case—a process referred to as 'forum shopping.' Courts are only one of many forums in which disputants may pursue their interests, and may be inaccessible, incompetent, corrupt, or incapable of effecting solutions. Not only may disputants shop among forums, but outsiders, judges, politicians, bureaucrats, clerics, or local leaders may also intervene in disputes over water, out of a sense of 'justice' or to pursue their own interests, as seen in the cases from Sri Lanka (Chapter 3), Bihar (Chapter 5), Bali (Chapter 6), and Nepal (Chapter 7).[5] This interplay between different legal or normative repertoires, forums, and authorities creates a canvas of problems and opportunities for negotiating water rights.

Reconstructing Water Rights

State intervention, to build irrigation works or regulate water resources, usually reconstructs local water rights in various ways. Water rights are often implicitly embedded in physical infrastructure, so that even approaches to improving irrigation system performance seen as purely 'technical' affect water rights (Hecht 1990). Efforts by cities and industry to obtain more water and restrict competing users introduce new pressures to control access to water. Increased education improves the capacity of at least some local people to challenge or manipulate the legal-bureaucratic tools through which states regulate water resources, stimulating attempts to integrate local practice with state legal principles. In many countries, local roles in governance of water resources are being enhanced by devolution of increasing responsibility and authority to local governmental units. All these processes bring further pressures for change, wanted or unwanted, in institutions for water allocation.

Understanding Rights

In this volume we look at water allocation as a negotiated process, not something that can be simply deduced from technical specifications, economic analysis, or legal exegesis. Negotiation involves interaction between different claimants, not unilateral decisions made in isolation. The process continues over time, not just in a single meeting. Negotiation is used here in a broad sense. It includes sitting around a table to craft an agreement, formal trading arrangements, as well as less visible struggles over access to water, as local people comply with or contest the ways in which state agencies or other users acquire and distribute water. It includes not only engaging in dialogue, but also abstention, obstruction, resistance, and sabotage (Colburn 1989; Scott 1985). Negotiation is a continuing process, influenced—but not fully determined—by changes in rules and laws (clearly illustrated in Guillet's case from Spain in Chapter 8). Agreements may mark major milestones, but usually lead to further negotiation about how the agreement is to be worked out in detail, how to monitor compliance and respond to violations, and whether to revise agreements.

At the heart of this is the allocation process, which is defined as deciding who should receive how much water (Uphoff 1986). Conceptually, allocation is distinct from the task of distribution, which is defined as delivering water in accordance with allocations. In practice, problems with allocation frequently surface during distribution, showing how far this may diverge from allocations formally specified by agency regulations or traditional procedures. These divergences may, in turn, become the basis for modifying the allocation, as seen in Vermillion's case in Chapter 2.

Property rights to any resource are much more than a title on paper: they are essentially a relationship between people that shapes the use of natural resources (F. von Benda-Beckmann 1995).[6] Different systems of water rights are not exclusive, but overlapping: different sets of rules may apply at different places and times, or may be appealed to by different parties. A single user rarely has full 'ownership' rights to control, use, and dispose of the resource purely as she or he sees fit. Rather, it is useful to think of a bundle of rights, with different users and stakeholders having the right to use water for a certain purpose, or subject to various types of conditionality.[7]

Different rights may apply at different levels of the system, as in Chapter 9, with water in the rivers or main canals controlled by the state, water in the secondary distribution system below a certain turnout being common property of a group of users, and individuals having rights over water in tertiary systems or groundwater below their land. In this volume we are primarily concerned with rights at two levels: the rights of a group of users to water, and rights of individuals within the group.

Water rights are a basis for a claim on the resource. Water rights include formal rights embodied in official titles, permits and seasonal irrigation schedules, less formal rights based on customary patterns, and rights implicit in social norms and local practices. A customary pattern of receiving water for 12 hours a day during periods of shortage is seen by users as a water right just as valid as a permit specified in liters per second. Where a temporary brush dam allows water to flow through, downstream users may feel they have a right, which is violated when upstream users install a concrete dam to divert the entire flow. A norm that certain types of people cannot be denied access to water for drinking or watering animals may carry as much weight, in practice, as an abstraction right registered with a government agency.

There may be multiple bases for claims, even for the same resource. The two most widely recognized underlying bases for claims are based on ownership or possession of land along rivers, streams, or over aquifers (riparian rights),[8] and claims based on historic water usage (prior appropriation). These have received greatest attention in the literature on formal water rights, as they are widely found in England, Spain, and their former colonies (including the Americas and Australia). Scott and Coustalin (1995) show that even within England there have been shifts back and forth over time in the strength of each of these bases of claims. However, a myopic focus on only riparian and prior appropriation rights, or attempts to force all other types of water rights into one of these forms, has too often blinded researchers and policymakers to the variety of water rights. Membership in a community or group may provide sufficient basis for a claim on water, especially for domestic or livestock uses. Investment in water control infrastructure provides a basis for claims on the water in farmer-managed irrigation systems, as well as in systems constructed and managed by the government.

These different bases for water rights have implications for management of the resource. For example, prior appropriation rights are often conditional upon 'beneficial use,' which means that those who hold rights have no incentive to reduce their water consumption, because that means giving up part of their right. Formal riparian rights typically limit the ability to transfer water to users in other locations. The development of tradable water rights, separating rights to water from rights to land and making them transferable, is fundamental for the emergence of water markets, which are receiving increasing policy attention in attempts to improve the efficiency of water allocation, as discussed in the final chapter.

Investment in water conveyance infrastructure serves as a basis for shares in the system in many farmer-managed irrigation systems, including the Indonesian *subaks* described in Chapter 2 and 12, Nepali *kulos* (Chapter 7), or Philippine *zanjeras* (Lewis 1980). Share systems developed through farmers' collective investments link rights and responsibilities. Members of a *subak*, *acequia*, or joint tubewell group share the cash and labor contributions required to keep the system functioning, often in direct proportion to their shares in the water (Yoder 1994). Over time, the shares may be sold or passed down from the system's original builders to their heirs. Sutawan's (Chapter 12) and the Northern New Mexico Legal Services' (Chapter 13) cases provide examples of how such systems have evolved.

Reviewing the evidence from many farmer-managed irrigation systems, as well as systems with varying degrees of external intervention, Coward (1986) concludes that the process of investing together to build irrigation infrastructure creates strong bonds among farmers. These bonds form the social capital essential for the sustainable management of these systems. Thus the property rights created by collective action and held in common by the members provide a 'social glue' (Coward 1986, 1990).

Most external interventions to construct or 'improve' irrigation systems do not have as much initial user investment, nor do they provide users with such clear rights. Rights 'bestowed' on people may not be treated in the same manner, or create the same sense of individual and collective responsibility. Thus, Coward (1986) advocates indirect investment strategies for external intervention (for example, providing loans and technical assistance to user groups, who would then undertake the investments and the responsibility to pay for them). External interventions often erode existing rights, and either expand the rights of the state or strengthen new claimants to the resource. Several cases in this book show how this can happen: van Koppen's from Burkina Faso (Chapter 3), Brewer's from Sri Lanka (Chapter 4), and Pradhan and Pradhan's from Nepal (Chapter 7).

'Public,' i.e., government, investment (often with external donor funds), together with concerns over public trust, are often stated as reasons for state reluctance to define water rights for individual farmers or groups of users. Valid questions are raised about why some farmers should capture the benefits of state investment as well as a stronger share of water resources. However, even where governments build and operate large scale irrigation systems, these often turn out to be overlaid on existing local schemes, whose transformed institutions persist in powerfully influencing how water is distributed. Even in 'new' schemes serving previously unirrigated land, government regulations regarding water allocation may be more flouted than obeyed, as head-enders abstract more than their allotted share, local influentials exert power, villagers bribe agency personnel, farmers sabotage gates, and opportunists irrigate lands beyond the official command area (Chambers 1988; Wade 1987). Even where transfers of land are formally forbidden, fields, together with their accompanying water rights, are often rented, mortgaged, leased, and sold extralegally (Chapter 11). Therefore local customs and practice strongly influence water allocation even in 'government-managed' irrigation schemes.

While the state has a legitimate role in managing overall water resources, the failure of agencies to adequately discuss, negotiate, and reach consensus on how rights and responsibilities will be shared has serious repercussions for the sustainability of management improvements, as seen in Sengupta's case from Bihar, India (Chapter 5). If outsiders have constructed the system and it is treated as public property, local users have little sense of responsibility for its upkeep. Many projects mention giving users a 'sense of ownership,' but this may not be enough without real ownership acknowledged by users and outsiders. Furthermore, ownership of only the tertiary distribution infrastructure (such as watercourses) has little value without upstream points that offer some control over water (Hunt 1990).

Rehabilition or system improvement projects have often had unintended consequences for water rights. Sutawan (Chapter 12) shows how the new division structures that the Bali Irrigation Project placed in *subak* canals affected the shares of water among members, while building new headworks that served more than one *subak* led to new water sharing arrangements between *subaks* (see also Spiertz, Chapter 6). Similarly, government 'assistance' to irrigation in Burkina Faso (Chapter 3), Sri Lanka (Chapter 4), and Nepal (Chapter 7) became the basis for new claims on the resource. Farmers in the existing scheme frequently oppose any development that takes water away from them, asserting a strong claim to water rights.

In the Kirindi Oya case (Chapter 4), the government acknowledged the prior rights of the farmers in the old area to receive at least as much water as in the past. However, attempts to spread the additional water captured by the new reservoir meant that the new areas received less intensive irrigation than the old. The result is an unequal distribution of water between the two areas that may appear inequitable to some.

Rights, Equity, and Power

Definitions of equity, like definitions of rights, are contestable. To what extent should they consider existing rights and the past investments of farmers (or their ancestors)? How much scope is there for government investments to create new assets for the poor, even if this challenges the control of existing élites? Pradhan, et al., (1997: 130) ask: 'How do we strike a balance between respecting the rights of existing rights holders and the claims of those who are excluded? And who is to decide these issues?'

Sometimes those making new claims are much poorer than current irrigators. In other cases, the state may make claims, to serve its own projects, or as representative of broader social interests, for water supply, environment and other needs (as illustrated in Chapter 8). Reallocating water may promise potential gains in both efficiency and equity, at least from the perspective of some. Competing claims often have a strong foundation, so for both practical and moral reasons negotiation of water rights may require more than just legitimizing one set of existing local claims.

While negotiations may contribute to solutions, these take place among parties with very unequal power, especially where state agencies are involved. Factories in West Java have more economic and political clout than farmers (Chapter 11). Owners of deep tubewells for irrigation have more wealth than most handpump owners in Bangladesh (Chapter 10), or than water purchasers in Pakistan (Chapter 9). Poor Hispanic farmers with small plots irrigated by *acequias* have less economic, social, and political status than Anglo resorts and developers in New Mexico (Chapter 13). Men, especially the *chef de terre*, had better political connections and social standing than traditional women irrigators when the projects in Burkina Faso began (Chapter 3).

This is not to say that the less powerful will be passive bystanders. They may make their demands heard through appeals to agencies, protests, and agitations. They may also sabotage the physical or institutional structures, either actively or through passive resistance.[9]

But cases in this book from New Mexico (Chapter 13) and Burkina Faso (Chapter 3) point to ways in which asymmetries between claimants can be reduced, so that there is less need for recourse to resistance. In both cases, restructuring the process of applying for (or defending) water rights and more effective dissemination of information to the disadvantaged groups helped them maintain their rights. Northern New Mexico Legal Services' role as an advocate of the *acequia* owners shows the potential role of external actors in affecting the balance of power. Politicians attempt to affect the balance of power in the cases from Nepal (Chapter 7) and Sri Lanka (Chapter 4), though the outcomes do not always favor the disadvantaged.

The institutions through which water rights are negotiated and renegotiated have a critical influence on the possibility of generating equitable and efficient solutions to conflicts, or increasing confusion, rigidity, inefficiency and inequity. In contexts where agriculture is usually the main user of water, the outcome depends to a great extent on how water rights are defined and negotiated among farmers, and between farmers and other users.

Governing Common Property

State action to regulate water, forests, fisheries and other resources may support or undermine user self-governance. Much of the literature on common property has illustrated the conflicts which have occurred when states assert control over resources previously managed at the local level, and the ways in which ignorance and disruption of local management institutions contributes to the degradation and destruction of resources (e.g., Bromley and Cernea 1989; Jodha 1992; Lawry 1990; Richards 1997; Shepherd 1991). In this way, efforts to assert state ownership of water rights may enhance or neglect the social capital of institutions which have already developed at the local level (illustrated by Sengupta's case from Bihar in Chapter 5). State action may help to foster self-organization, for example through legislation which empowers user organizations and by providing independent technical advice (Bloomquist 1992). Other negotiation forums may also play a critical role, as discussed in the concluding chapter.

Much of the literature on common property resource management has sought to demonstrate that self-governance has been and still is feasible, that the postulated 'tragedy of the commons' is neither inevitable, nor even necessarily common.[10] Garrett Hardin's (1968) 'tragedy of the commons' sought to show how rational, self-interested individuals (or households) would overutilize a pasture (or other common pool resource, where each user subtracts from the resource, reducing availability to others). If there were no arrangements for regulation, then each individual would have incentives to keep adding animals to the common pasture long past an optimal level, as they individually gain the benefits from each additional animal, but suffer only a fraction of the collective damage created by overgrazing. Researchers have documented the variety of ways in which users of pastures, irrigation and other common pool resources have overcome obstacles to collective action and sustainably managed the resources (see Baland and Platteau 1996; Bromley et al. 1992; Ostrom 1990). A key distinction emerging from the literature is the difference between an open access resource, where usage is not restricted, and common property resources where access is regulated.

The tragedy of the commons, and more generally the difficulties of collective action, have often been used to justify either direct control by the state, or else division into private property.[11] Analysis of the capacity and conditions for self-governance clarifies the potential of common property resource management as a third option, between state control and privatization.

Researchers on common property have explored how the characteristics of resources affect their management.[12] Pure private ownership is often ineffective and inappropriate for resources where it is difficult or impossible to exclude users, where strong economies of scale encourage natural monopolies and where utilization by one user has major influences (externalities) on others—all characteristics of water resources in many cases. Private tenure, for example tradable water rights, may still be an important part of efficient resource management, if supported by an appropriate framework to regulate the common pool characteristics of the resource, through some combination of user self-organization and state control.

The concept of the tragedy of the commons may also carry invalid assumptions about how resources should be sustainably managed. It is becoming apparent that in complex natural systems, following paths often far from any simple equilibrium, concepts of sustainable yield or carrying capacity may be much more difficult or impossible to apply, in contrast to simpler models dominated by earlier concepts of equilibrium ecology. Raising livestock under arid conditions of uncertainty and fluctuating rainfall may benefit from more sophisticated strategies than simply restricting herds to what could be sustained under average rainfall (Behnke et al. 1993). Drought, fire, landslides and other 'natural disasters' are not necessarily new or unusual events in the longer perspective of ecosystem dynamics. Flooding has been an integral part of the history of river basins, playing essential functions, not the least of which is renewing nutrients. Droughts are a recurring event, even within irrigation systems. Water resource allocation and negotiation of rights needs to encompass not just the flows which might be guaranteed four years out of five, but the larger scope of natural and human dynamics. This constitutes yet another reason why basin water management is unlikely to be simply resolved by a single centralized plan, but needs institutions which can allow allocation to be negotiated and renegotiated in response to dynamic, and often unpredictable, circumstances.

Research on common property is also helping to show the ways in which negotiation of rules for resource use and their enforcement is more ambiguous, contested and richer in meaning than assumed by narrow models of fully-informed, rational individual behavior (North 1989; Ostrom 1990). Resource management involves a continuing process of discourse, not just formulating a one-time agreement. Testing of boundaries, tolerance for errors and flexibility in response to unique circumstances are part of the tapestry of self-organized behavior (Fortmann 1995). Legal pluralism provides a set of intellectual tools for looking at common property resource management, not just in terms of institutional mechanisms, incentives, monitoring, and enforcement, but in terms of contesting claims, conceptions through which meanings are defined and debated.

Formalizing water rights in the face of scarcity can involve a larger role for the state in defining, adjudicating, and enforcing the rights. The tendency of bureaucracies to impose uniform solutions on unique circumstances is often a major source of problems. A key challenge is to enhance agencies' capacity for negotiating customized solutions, and to shift more governance responsibility to institutions capable of greater flexibility, including market mechanisms and self-governance.

Governance goes beyond 'management' to emphasize how the state may authorize organizations to regulate resource use and sanction violations. The *acequia* organizations in Chapter 13 are local government units, with specific powers, distinct from towns or other political subdivisions. However, many of the reforms in irrigation institutions discussed in the next section have not yet created such explicit empowerment for local governance of common pool resources.

Reforming Irrigation Institutions

The infrastructure to provide irrigation represents an enormous investment by governments, donor agencies, and farmers themselves (Rosegrant and Svendsen 1993). Yet the irrigation systems themselves often fail to meet expectations. Water is not delivered reliably or equitably, and not used efficiently. Tail ends of systems receive no water while other portions are waterlogged. Yields are not as high as anticipated, economic returns do not justify the levels of investments made, and the irrigation infrastructure or irrigated lands may not be sustainable. Evidence of problems in irrigation systems appears in a range of technical, agronomic, economic, or social performance indicators (Small and Svendsen 1992).

Improving the performance of irrigation systems has therefore received considerable attention in the past 20 years. Technical interventions provide one means of improving the performance of irrigation systems. Many rehabilitation projects have invested in lining canals, increasing drainage, improving control structures, and even adding management information systems. The Bali Irrigation Project described by Sutawan (Chapter 12) constructed new weirs and proportioning devices in traditional irrigation systems. But experience has shown that physical interventions rarely lead to sustained improvements in performance unless they are integrated with local institutions for irrigation, starting with participation in design. Institutions play a critical role in shaping incentives for users and system managers.

Recognizing the limitations of technical interventions alone, many irrigation rehabilitation projects, as well as broader programs to improve irrigation performance, have included some form of institutional change. Notable examples include the Philippines' reforms of the National Irrigation Authority (NIA) in the 1980s by making it a financially autonomous body (Korten and Siy 1988), with efforts to develop water users' associations and transfer management responsibility to them. Pakistan's On-Farm Water Management Programs from the late 1970s to early 1990s required that farmers form Water Users' Associations (WUA) to get assistance in watercourse lining.

Pilot projects in the Philippines and Sri Lanka demonstrated how increased participation could improve irrigation development and inspired similar efforts in many countries.[13] These efforts used learning processes (Korten 1980) to explore how to most effectively improve participation. Institutionalizing participatory approaches has enhanced agencies' capacity to negotiate with stakeholders. Participation in design has often involved negotiation of the water rights implicit in gates and division structures (Ambler 1990). This experience can guide further efforts to improve institutions for allocating water within and between irrigation systems.

However, time has also shown limitations of organizing farmers as a means for improving irrigation performance, and the need for more fundamental changes. Often, agencies are willing to delegate difficult tasks like distributing water within tertiary blocks and cleaning canals, but much more reluctant to cede genuine authority, or change their internal management to make themselves accountable to WUA. Efforts to organize WUA have been based on a hope that they will perform as well as traditional farmer-managed irrigation organizations, although government-organized WUA often lack the incentives and rights over resources of farmer-managed irrigation systems (Hunt 1989; Lam 1998). The existence of WUA and WUA federations has provided a forum for communication and discussion, but WUA have usually not received any clearer rights to water than existed previously.

Continued frustration with poor performance of irrigation development has led to increased interest in more drastic reforms, going beyond just increasing participation within current institutional structures. This has occurred within a more general context of increased concern for the role local organizations and other institutions of civil society can play in development, shifting away from reliance on bureaucratic agencies as primary instruments for development efforts. One of the most prominent reforms has been to turn over control of entire irrigation systems or parts of systems to local organizations.[14] Small irrigation systems in Indonesia, Nepal and other countries are being transferred to water user associations, while WUA may receive increased responsibility and authority for parts of larger systems. In Africa, structural adjustment reforms have led states to withdraw from state-managed irrigation schemes, often with little or no further support. Programs in Mexico, Colombia, and Turkey have transferred management of larger irrigation systems, covering thousands of hectares, to local organizations, which often have professional staff, vehicles and substantial budgets. In Mexico, formulation of a legal basis for water rights was an explicit part of establishing the institutional basis for irrigation management transfer. However, the irrigation agency continues to operate headworks, even after the transfer of internal scheme operation and maintenance to farmers.

These programs for institutional change share a focus on the formal organizations involved in managing irrigation systems. But institutions are much broader than just organizations. They include markets, social networks, and a range of other, often intangible aspects of society based on shared understandings. Water rights are one of the most critical sets of irrigation-related institutions, along with explicit and implicit rules for system operation. At a recent workshop on experiences with participatory irrigation management in Mexico, Colombia, Argentina, and the Philippines, participants identified the need to clarify water rights and strengthen the rights of WUA as the highest priority 'second generation' issue to be addressed (Svendsen 1997).

We would argue that perspectives of legal pluralism can assist in this process. Instead of assuming that the state holds all rights to water and invites users to 'participate' (often on rather restrictive terms), acknowledging that farmers and other water users have claims to water based on a wide range of criteria can change the dynamic from being a top-down process to one of negotiation among important stakeholders.

Competing for Water

Worldwide, the use of water more than tripled between 1950 and 1990, and is projected to grow by another 80 per cent by the turn of the century (Clarke 1993). Irrigation has been and continues to be by far the largest sector of water consumption, accounting for nearly 70 per cent of water withdrawals worldwide, and over 90 per cent in low-income developing countries (World Bank 1993). Reallocation of water from agriculture is often seen as the best, or the easiest, way to supply demands from other users.

The world economic climate is changing, and along with it water demands. The increases in food production made possible, in part, by expansion of irrigation have led to falling world prices for staple crops such as rice and wheat—the main crops produced on irrigated land (Rosegrant and Svendsen 1993). Moreover, many countries are moving away from policies for domestic self-sufficiency in food production toward reliance on world trade. At the same time industrial production is increasing, and with it demand for water as an input for production. While irrigation is still the largest water user in most countries, the economic returns and political strength of irrigated agriculture have generally declined over time, while other sectors have grown.

Growing populations increase the amount of water needed for domestic use, while migration to cities and rising incomes raise per capita water demands for drinking, cooking, washing, bathing, lawns, and gardens.[15] Municipal water withdrawals are projected to grow by 80 per cent and industrial withdrawals by 84 per cent worldwide from 1995 to 2020. In developing countries, municipal withdrawals are likely to increase by over 150 per cent, and industrial withdrawals more than triple over the same period (Rosegrant et al. 1997).[16] The total effect on water availability for other uses may be much greater, as effluents from domestic uses and factories often pollute remaining water supplies. Furthermore, unlike seasonal irrigation demands, municipal and industrial use require highly reliable water deliveries 24 hours a day, throughout the year. In many cases available water supplies are fully utilized, at least during some periods of the year. Augmenting supplies, through reservoir construction or interbasin transfers, may be precluded by expense or environmental concerns.

As the resource comes under greater pressure, better institutions are needed to allocate and reallocate water between uses and users. Both government agencies and user groups dealing with water have tended to be sectorally defined, focusing exclusively on irrigation, or domestic water supply, or environment. Even within the irrigation sector, allocation between irrigation systems has often been unclear. As long as there is surplus water in the river basin this is not problematic as different users do not interfere with each other. But as overall water use increases, there is interference, not only between surface abstractions along a river, but also between surface and groundwater uses.

Various forms of institutions are being developed to deal with these issues. Sutawan's case study in Bali (Chapter 12) shows the dynamics of the development of federations of irrigation associations along sub-river basins. These irrigation-based institutions are even able to deal with modest amounts of domestic water supply through special allowances. However, the case study by Kurnia, Avianto, and Bruns (Chapter 11) shows how accommodating heavy demands from factories and developers is exceeding the scope of the existing institutions at one site in West Java, resulting in considerable difficulty and ad-hoc arrangements. In northern New Mexico (Chapter 13) all water resources in the state are fully allocated, or even overallocated. One of the pressures for adjudicating water rights comes from urban and industrial interests who want to buy water rights from farmers.

Intersectoral water allocation is not always a case of 'us' against 'them.' The same households may derive part of their income from farming and part from working in factories in West Java, where the textile industry is based in rural areas (Chapter 11). In New Mexico, farmers would like to negotiate to keep the water, and the jobs that it creates, in their communities, even if it moves from agriculture to other types of enterprises (Chapter 13).

The competition for groundwater between domestic use and irrigation in Sadeque's study from Bangladesh (Chapter 10) may seem less of an issue of opposing interests because, at the household level, those with irrigation also need domestic supplies. However, within households, men, women and children have different responsibilities and stakes in irrigation and drinking water. Declining aquifers take water away from shallow domestic handpumps, with access restricted to deeper wells. This change in when and where water is available has differential impacts on various users, with generally negative effects for the poor and many women. Whereas over 90 per cent of households have access to domestic water supplies from shallow tubewells, only a wealthy minority control deep tubewells for irrigation. Such cases show the need to look at water allocation beyond the irrigation sector, and to address the effects of power differences between water claimants.

One institutional approach to water resources reform is the development of water markets. The case studies from Pakistan (Chapter 9) and Bangladesh (Chapter 10) deal with the operation of informal water markets. While water rights are not a central feature of informal markets, tradable water rights are central to the development of formal water markets (Easter et al. 1998; Rosegrant and Binswanger 1994). Even where no formal legal basis exists for transferring water rights, competing users may take the cruder, but effective, approach of buying irrigated farmland and moving its water to meet their needs. Given the magnitude of the pressure for reallocation and the political and economic power of competing interests, the question is not one of whether reallocation will occur, but how. The ways in which reallocation occurs have enormous implications for whether the process flows through equitable, efficient and mutually agreeable channels, or traverses the turbulent rapids of highly adversarial conflict, trickery and expropriation, with attendant risks for those who lose and gain water. The higher value of water in most non-agricultural uses, and potential in agriculture for increasing efficiency and the value per unit of water, create the opportunity for mutual gains, win-win agreements for reallocation, but this cannot be realized without substantial reforms in water rights and other institutions for water allocation.

Plan of the Book

This introduction sets the stage by identifying key issues and concepts, while the case studies illustrate how issues have played out in practice, influenced by a host of contextual factors: water scarcity, level of economic development, legal, social, and economic institutions, the history of each system, and even the personality of particular leaders. This rich variety of contexts offers fertile ground for thinking about how water rights are negotiated and how such processes might be improved.

A summary of key features of each case study is presented in Table 1.1, which also highlights some of the issues found in the

Table 1.1: Characteristics and Selected Key Issues of Case Studies

Chapter	Author	Region, Country	Irrigation Source	Key Issues
2	Douglas L. Vermillion	Southeast Asia Indonesia	surface small-scale *subak*	emerging rights in farmer-constructed system; appeals to various bases for claiming water; need for flexibility.
3	Barbara van Koppen	West Africa Burkina Faso	surface small-scale *bas-fond*	project intervention restructuring rights; stakeholder participation; gender equity.
4	Jeffrey D. Brewer	South Asia Sri Lanka	surface large-scale tanks, reservoir	project intervention restructuring rights; stakeholder participation; old and new rights; role of state in technical advice.
5	Nirmal Sengupta	South Asia India	surface small-scale *ahar pyne*	interaction between state and customary rights; variety of strategies for claiming water; limits of state knowledge; local governance reducing transaction costs.
6	H.L. Joep Spiertz	Southeast Asia Indonesia	surface small-scale *subaks*	legal pluralism; local manipulation of state assistance; limits of state knowledge.
7	Rajendra Pradhan and Ujjwal Pradhan	South Asia Nepal	surface small-scale *kulos*	legal pluralism; access vs. rights to water; variety of strategies for claiming water; local manipulation of state assistance.

	Author	Region/Country	Type/Scale	Issues
8	David Guillet	Western Europe Spain	surface small-scale	demand management; limits of state knowledge, regulatory capacity; local resistance; interacting rights of systems within river basin.
9	Ruth Meinzen-Dick	South Asia Pakistan	groundwater tubewells	difficulty in defining groundwater rights; overlapping rights; informal water markets and social relations.
10	Syed Zahir Sadeque	South Asia Bangladesh	groundwater tubewells	difficulty in defining groundwater rights; competition between irrigation and domestic use; unequal power between different water users.
11	Ganjar Kurnia, Teten W. Avianto and Bryan Randolph Bruns	Southeast Asia Indonesia	surface small-scale	competition between irrigation and industries; variety of strategies for acquiring water; unequal power between different water users.
12	Nyoman Sutawan	Southeast Asia Indonesia	surface small-scale *subaks*	action research to form federations; stakeholder participation; role of outside facilitators; interacting rights of systems within river basin.
13	Northern New Mexico Legal Services	North America United States	surface small-scale *acequias*	role of outside facilitators; stakeholder participation; unequal power between different water users; interacting rights of systems within river basin.

various cases. The cases are predominantly from South Asia and Indonesia. Cases from West Africa, Western Europe, and Western United States show how similar issues arise in other contexts.

The cases are from predominantly small-scale irrigation systems, including both surface and groundwater. Water rights have been less a subject for study in large-scale systems (which also tend to be agency-managed), where the state tends to exert a stronger claim on water rights. Negotiations over rights in larger systems deserve further research. The final chapter of the book discusses research needs, which should obviously cover not just areas included in this collection, but also other areas such as Latin America and East Asia.

Each author highlights a different set of issues that emerge from their studies. Geographic conditions and historical paths shape situations, and the possibilities for improvement. Negotiating forums, courts, markets and other institutions share significant commonalities, but play themselves out in unique ways in each case. The goal of studying these cases is not just to see what general principles may be extracted, but also learning to better navigate the idiosyncrasies of individual locales, searching for solutions which accommodate the specific interests of multiple stakeholders.

The chapters have been arranged to start with cases smaller in scale and scope, farmers dealing with other farmers in a single irrigation scheme, and then expand to include more dimensions of complexity, with government intervention, old and new users, multiple irrigation systems, conjunctive use of groundwater and surface water, competition from other sectors, and explicit interventions to improve negotiation of water rights. To aid the reader, a brief abstract at the start of each chapter outlines the scope and key issues.

We begin with three cases that show how water rights emerge, and may be renegotiated with outside intervention. Vermillion's study (Chapter 2) deals with adjusting water rights to local conditions in a settlement area of Sulawesi, Indonesia, where migrants had recently built their own irrigation system. The case deals with water rights at the micro level of individual farmers' fields, in a situation of socioeconomic homogeneity among farmers.

For Burkina Faso, van Koppen (Chapter 3) describes an outside agency building new infrastructure in already irrigated valleys. In the initial schemes, failure to accommodate the existing land and water rights of women producers had serious repercussions for productivity and equity, but this was corrected in subsequent schemes.

Brewer's study from Sri Lanka (Chapter 4) examines how water rights for ancient and new subunits of an irrigation scheme were adjusted through a process of conflict, trial-and-error, and negotiation. Rights were embodied in seasonal allocation rules and Brewer identifies structural features of allocation rules which made them acceptable to farmers.

The next set of papers seeks to expose the tensions and ambiguities of legal pluralism. Sengupta's study from Bihar, India (Chapter 5) deals explicitly with the role of an under-informed bureaucracy in interpreting 'customary' water rights. The bureaucracy and custom are not homogeneous or static, as seen in the comparisons between colonial and Indian national agencies, between irrigation systems developed under different forms of feudal control, and in changes over time within a system.

Spiertz (Chapter 6) expands on the fundamentals of legal pluralism, and contrasts it with earlier approaches to socio-legal research. He uses a case from Bali, Indonesia to show how outsiders could easily be confused or misled by the complexity of local practices. Conflicting interpretations of rights, rules, and even physical boundaries can coexist, not only between the government and local people, but also between government agencies and between different local groups.

Pradhan and Pradhan (Chapter 7) analyze the range of strategies used by contesting parties in Nepal to gain not just access to water, but legitimated rights. The case examines the process of forum shopping as different claimants use a variety of bases for their claims.

Guillet's case from Spain (Chapter 8) shows that legal pluralism applies also in areas of long-established water rights. The state has had limited capacity to impose new regulations on irrigation communities, who have resisted a range of demand management measures as an infringement of their rights—offering lessons to other countries as they discuss a range of similar policies.

The next two cases investigate the complexities of defining water rights and developing institutions to monitor and enforce use of groundwater, when flows and interactions between users are more difficult to observe. Meinzen-Dick's case from Pakistan (Chapter 9) provides an example of the array of statutory, customary, and normative rights that may apply, and how they affect the operation of informal water markets. In Sadeque's case from Bangladesh (Chapter 10), there are exchanges between domestic water supply and irrigation sources, but effective institutions have not yet emerged to manage the aquifer or allocate water between heterogeneous users.

The theme of intersectoral competition recurs in the case study from West Java, Indonesia by Kurnia, Avianto and Bruns (Chapter 11). Factory owners use a range of legal, quasi-legal, and illegal means to acquire water. Rising demand for water strains existing institutions, including government agencies and user groups, that have been oriented primarily toward irrigation.

In the last two cases, outside groups have sought to catalyze or facilitate negotiations among the various parties, and the chapters offer a first-hand view from those who are involved directly in the process of negotiating water rights. Sutawan's case study of federations of traditional *subaks* in Bali, Indonesia (Chapter 12) exemplifies the process of negotiating water rights in forming federations among *subaks* physically amalgamated to share a new headworks and main canal, and between separate systems along in a river basin. The last case (Chapter 13) tells how Northern New Mexico Legal Services sought to enable poor farmers to take part in water rights adjudications and obtain court recognition of their customary principles for water allocation.

The final chapter explores implications for practice, policy and research. We review options for improving institutional capacity for negotiation and argue that negotiated approaches are necessary in policies reforming water rights. Research and action should focus on four contexts which are of increasing importance for water management: renegotiating rights during project intervention, formalizing water tenure, developing institutions for basin water management, and coping with demands for intersectoral transfer.

Notes

1. This discussion draws upon the work of Griffiths (1986); Merry (1988); Spiertz (1995); Spiertz and Wiber (1996); F. von Benda-Beckmann (1992, 1995); and F. von Benda-Beckmann et al. (1997); and Guillet (1998). In this volume, Spiertz (Chapter 6) lays out the theoretical underpinnings of legal pluralism and applies it to a case in Bali, Indonesia, but other authors use the approach, either explicitly or implicitly.

   Moving from a state-centric perspective on law has profound implications for understanding how water rights are put into practice, and the options which may exist for reforming water allocation institutions. Research on legal pluralism offers one substantial body of existing theory and research which can be drawn upon in understanding local conceptions about rights to resources, disputing in legally complex contexts and the interaction of state and local law. Ideas about the complexity of property rights in local practice do not have to be framed specifically in terms of legal pluralism (e.g., Vandergeest 1997). Similar ideas, stressing the importance of norms, are present in the law and economics literature (Cooter 1997; Ellickson 1991). Some approaches in New Institutional Economics share a related emphasis on private governance rather than state ordering (Williamson 1996).

2. Although they do not always use the language of legal pluralism, a number of studies from other contexts (e.g., 1997 for Kenya; Cruz 1989 for the Philippines; Guillet 1992 for Peru; Nederlof and van Wayjen 1996 for Mexico) show these same principles at work.

3. Following North (1992), it is useful to think of institutions as the 'rules of the game' Coward (1980) provides a clear explanation of the differences between organizations and institutions in irrigation, while Uphoff (1993) gives a range of examples of each.

4. Many countries adhere to some form of Public Trust Doctrine, a principle dating back at least to Roman law, which maintains that the state holds navigable waters and certain other water resources as common heritage for the benefit of the people, and therefore cannot alienate such ownership of the basic resource and concomitant responsibility.

5. Even within the English legal system, Scott and Coustalin (1995) argue that the strengthening of prior appropriation rights in the 17th century was influenced by the royal courts seeking to expand their influence relative to that of the feudal courts, which recognized land-based riparian claims.

6. For evidence on the links between property rights and resource management, see Baland and Platteau 1996; Berkes 1986, 1987; Hanna and Munasinghe 1995; Kurien 1993.

7. Bromley (1991), Schlager and Ostrom (1992), and K. von Benda-Beckmann et al. (1997) discuss bundles or aspects of rights to land, fisheries, water, and other resources.

8. In many government-managed irrigation systems, especially in Asia, having land within designated irrigation command areas is what conveys rights to water.

9. This is illustrated in the book and film *The Milagro Beanfield War* (Nichols 1974) about a conflict over water rights set in New Mexico.

10. Most of the chapters in this book were presented, in earlier versions, at the 1996 or 1998 Conference of the International Association for the Study of Common Property.

11. The 'tragedy of the commons' is one of a family of related problems, which in some formulations have a logically identical structure, including 'prisoner's dilemma,' (Axelrod 1984; Rapaport and Chammah 1965) 'the free rider problem' (Olson 1971; Popkin 1979) and the 'assurance problem' (Ireson 1995; Runge 1986). These formulations clarify the challenges to collective action. Unfortunately, much analysis has focused on pessimistic interpretations of why cooperation should fail, rather than trying to understand the many ways in which successful collective action is organized, overcoming problems. Leadership itself may be a collective good, offering general benefits, but not adequately forthcoming without specific incentives sufficient to motivate individuals to act as leaders (Frohlich and Oppenheimer 1978). A balanced analysis needs to put collective action problems into the context of the problems which constrain centralized command and control approaches and atomistic market processes (e.g., Lindblom 1977).

12. For examples related to water, see Bardhan 1993; Lam 1998; Schlager et al. 1994; Tang 1992; Wade 1987.

13. For discussions of the two pioneering efforts see Korten and Siy 1988; Uphoff 1991. Broader reviews of experience are included in Bruns 1993; Goldensohn et al. 1994; Manor et al. 1990; Meinzen-Dick et al. 1997.

14. For reviews of issues related to turnover or irrigation management transfer (IMT), see Johnson et al. 1995; Turral 1995; and Vermillion 1991 and 1997.

15. In the United States, because of high incomes and recreation preferences, the turfgrass industry (including sod farms, lawns, and golf courses) is a major user of irrigation (Committee on the Future of Irrigation in the Face of Competing Demands, 1996).

16. Rosegrant, Ringler, and Gerpacio's (1997: Table 6) projections for volume withdrawals (in billion cubic meters) are:

Country/ Region	1995				2020			
	Domes-tic	Indus-try	Agricul-ture	Total	Domes-tic	Indus-try	Agricul-ture	Total
Developing	147	170	2,030	2,347	375	531	2,445	3,350
Developed	174	560	664	1,398	204	813	693	1,710
World	322	730	2,694	3,745	579	1,344	3,138	5,060

In percentage terms,, the effect on agriculture is even more pronounced (Rosegrant, Ringler, and Gerpacio 1997: Table 7):

Country/ Region	1995			2020		
	Domestic	Industry	Agriculture	Domestic	Industry	Agriculture
Developing	6	7	87	11	16	73
Developed	13	40	47	12	48	40
World	9	19	72	11	27	62

References

Adams, William M., Elizabeth E. Watson and **Samuel K. Mutiso.** 1997. Water, rules and gender: Water rights in an indigenous irrigation system, Marakwet, Kenya. *Development and Change* 28 (4): 707–30.

Ambler, John. 1990. The influence of farmer water rights on the design of water-proportioning devices. In *Design issues in farmer-managed irrigation systems*, ed. R. Yoder and J. Thurston, 37–52. Colombo, Sri Lanka: International Irrigation Management Institute.

Axelrod, Robert. 1984. *The evolution of cooperation.* New York: Basic Books.

Baland, Jean-Marie and **Jean-Philippe Platteau.** 1996. *Halting the degradation of natural resources: Is there a role for rural communities?* Oxford, U.K.: Clarendon Press.

Bardhan, Pranab. 1993. Analytics of the institutions of informal cooperation in rural development. *World Development* 21 (4): 633–39.

Behnke, R.H., Ian Scoones, and **C. Kervan,** eds. 1993. *Range ecology at disequilibrium: New models of natural variability and pastoral adaptation in African savannas.* London: Overseas Development Institute, International Institute for Environment and Development, Commonwealth Secretariat.

Benda-Beckmann, Franz von. 1992. Introduction: Understanding agrarian law in society. In *Law as a Resource in Agrarian Struggles*, ed. F. von Benda-Beckmann and M. vander Velde, 1–22. Wageningen: Pudoc.

———. 1995. Anthropological approaches to property law and economics. *European Journal of Law and Economics* 2: 309–36.

Benda-Beckmann, Franz von, Kabeet von Benda-Beckmann, and **H.L. Joep Spiertz.** 1997. Local law and customary practice in the study of water rights. In *Water Rights, Conflict and Policy*, ed. Rajendra Pradhan, Franz von Benda-Beckmann, Kabeet von Benda-Beckmann, H.L. Joep Spiertz, S. Khadka, K. Azharul Haq, 221–42. Colombo, Sri Lanka: International Irrigation Management Institute. Proceedings of a workshop held in Kathmandu, Nepal, January 22–24, 1996.

Benda-Beckmann, Keebet von, Mirjam de Bruijn, Han van Dijk, Gerti Hesseling, Barbara van Koppen and Lyda Res. 1997. *Rights of Women to the Natural Resources Land and Water*. Women and Development Working Paper 2. The Hague: NEDA (Netherlands Development Assistance).

Berkes, Fikret. 1986. Local level management and the commons problem: A comparative study of Turkish coastal fisheries. *Marine Policy* 10: 215–29.

———. 1987. The common property resource problem and the fisheries of Barbados and Jamaica. *Environmental Management* 11 (2): 225–35.

Bloomquist, William. 1992. *Dividing the waters: Governing groundwater in Southern California*. San Francisco: Institute for Contemporary Studies.

Bromley, Daniel W. 1991. *Environment and economy: Property rights and public policy*. Oxford, U.K.: Basil Blackwell.

Bromley, Daniel W. and Michael M. Cernea. 1989. *The management of common property natural resources: Some conceptual and operational fallacies*. World Bank Discussion Paper 57. Washington DC: The World Bank.

Bromley, Daniel W., David Feeny, Margaret A. McKean, and Pauline Peters, eds. 1992. *Making the commons work: Theory, practice and policy*. San Francisco, Calif.: Institute for Contemporary Studies.

Bruns, Bryan. 1993. Promoting participation in irrigation: Reflections on experience in Southeast Asia. *World Development* 21 (11): 1837–49.

Chambers, Robert. 1988. *Managing canal irrigation: Practical analysis from South Asia*. New Delhi, India: Oxford and IBH.

Clarke, Robin. 1993. *Water: The international crisis*. Cambridge, Mass.: MIT Press.

Colburn, Forrest D., ed. 1989. *Everyday forms of peasant resistance*. Armonk, N.Y.: M.E. Sharpe.

Cooter, Robert D. 1997. The rule of state law and the rule-of-law state: Economic analysis of the legal foundations of development. *Annual World Bank Conference on Development Economics* 1997: 191–237.

Committee on the Future of Irrigation in the Face of Competing Demands. 1996. *A new era for irrigation*. National Research Council. Washington DC: National Academy Press.

Coward, E. Walter, Jr. 1980. Irrigation development: Institutional and organizational issues. In *Irrigation and agricultural development in Asia: Perspectives from the social sciences*, ed. E. Walter Coward, 15–27. Ithaca, N.Y.: Cornell University Press.

———. 1986. Direct or indirect alternatives for irrigation investment and the creation of property. In *Irrigation investment, technology and management strategies for development*, ed. K. William Easter, 225–44. Boulder, Colo.: Westview Press.

———. 1990. Property rights and network order: The case of irrigation works in the Western Himalayas. *Human Organization* 49 (1): 78–88.

Cruz, Ma. Concepcion J. 1989. Water as common property: The case of irrigation water rights in the Philippines. In *Common property resources, ecology and community-based sustainable development*, ed. Fikret Berkes, 218–39. London: Belhaven Press.

Easter K. William, Mark Rosegrant, and Ariel Dinar, eds. 1998. *Markets for water: Potential and performance*. Boston, Mass.: Kluwer Academic Publishers.

Ellickson, Robert C. 1991. *Order without law: How neighbors settle disputes*. Cambridge, Mass.: Harvard University Press.

Fortmann, Louise. 1995. Talking claims: Discursive strategies in contesting property. *World Development* 23 (6): 1053–63.

Frohlich, Norman and Joe A. Oppenheimer. 1978. *Modern political economy*. Engelwood Cliffs, N.J.: Prentice-Hall.

Goldensohn, Max, Honorato Angeles, Sigit Arif, Gilllian Brown, Upendra Gautam, Kapila Goonesekera, Leo Gonzalez, Helmi, Tariq Husain, A. Saleemi, and K.K. Singh. 1994. *Participation and empowerment: An assessment of water user associations in Asia and Egypt*. Arlington, Virginia: Irrigation Support Project for Asia and the Near East.

Griffiths, J. 1986. What is legal pluralism? *Journal of Legal Pluralism* 24: 1–50.

Guillet, David. 1992. *Covering ground: Communal water management and the state in the Peruvian highlands*. Ann Arbor: University of Michigan Press.

———. 1998. Rethinking legal pluralism: Local law and state law in the evolution of water property rights in Northwestern Spain. *Comparative Studies in Society and History*, 2: 97–117.

Hanna, Susan and Mohan Munasinghe. 1995. An introduction to property rights and the environment. In *Property rights and the environment*, ed. Susan Hanna and Mohan Munasinghe, 3–11. Stockholm, Sweden and Washington, D.C.: The Beijer International Institute of Ecological Economics and the World Bank.

Hardin, Garrett. 1968. The tragedy of the commons. *Science* (162): 1243–48.

Hecht, Robert. 1990. Land and water rights and the design of small-scale irrigation projects: The case of Baluchistan. *Irrigation and Drainage Systems* 4: 59–76.

Hunt, Robert. 1989. Appropriate social organization? Water user associations in bureaucratic canal irrigation systems. *Human Organization* 48 (1): 79–90.

———. 1990. Organizational control over water: The positive identification of a social constraint on farmer participation. In *Social, economic, and institutional issues in Third World irrigation management*, ed. R.K. Sampath and Robert A. Young, 141–154. Boulder, Colo.: Westview Press.

Ingram, Helen and Cy R. Oggins. 1992. The public trust doctrine and community values in water. *Natural Resources Journal* 32 (Summer): 515–37.

Ireson, Randall. 1995. Village irrigation in Laos: Traditional patterns of common property resource management. *Society and Natural Resources* 8: 541–58.

Jodha, Narpat S. 1992. *Common property resources: A missing dimension of development strategies*. World Bank Discussion Paper 169. Washington DC: World Bank.

Johnson, Samuel H., Douglas L. Vermillion, and **J.A. Sagardoy,** eds. 1995. *Irrigation management transfer: Selected papers from the International Conference on Irrigation Management Transfer*. Rome: International Irrigation Management Institute, Food and Agriculture Organization of the United Nations.

Koehler, Cynthia L. 1995. Water rights and the public trust doctrine: Resolution of the Mono Lake controversy. *Ecological Law Quarterly* 22 (3): 541–90.

Korten, David C. 1980. Community organization and rural development: A learning process approach. *Public Administration Review* 40 (5): 480–510.

Korten, Frances F., and **Robert Y. Siy, Jr.** 1988. *Transforming a bureaucracy: The experience of the Philippine National Irrigation Administration*. West Hartford, Conn.: Kumarian Press.

Kurien, John. 1993. Ruining the commons: Coastal overfishing and fisherworkers' actions in south India. *Ecologist* 23 (1): 5–11.

Lam, Wai Fung. 1998. *Governing irrigation systems in Nepal: Institutions, infrastructure, and collective action*. Oakland, Calif.: Institute for Contemporary Studies.

Lawry, Steven W. 1990. Tenure policy toward common property natural resources in sub-Saharan Africa. *Natural Resources Journal* 30: 403–22.

Lewis, Henry T. 1980. Irrigation societies in the Northern Philippines. In *Irrigation and agricultural development in Asia: Perspectives from the social sciences*, ed. E. Walter Coward, Jr., 153–71. Ithaca, N.Y.: Cornell University Press.

Lindblom, Charles E. 1977. *Politics and markets: The world's political and economic systems*. New York: Basic Books.

Manor, Shaul, Sanguan Patamatamkul, and **Manuel Olin,** eds. 1990. *Role of social organizers in assisting farmer managed irrigation systems: Proceedings of a regional workshop held at Khonkaen, Thailand, May 15–29, 1989*. Colombo, Sri Lanka: International Irrigation Management Institute.

Meinzen-Dick, Ruth S., Meyra S. Mendoza, Loic Sadoulet, Ghada Abiad-Shields, and **Ashok Subramanian.** 1997. Sustainable water user associations: Lessons from a literature review. In *User organizations for sustainable water services*, ed. Ashok Subramanian, N. Vijay Jagannathan, and Ruth S. Meinzen-Dick, 7–87. Washington, D.C.: The World Bank.

Merry, Sally E. 1988. Legal pluralism. *Law and Society Review* 22: 869–96.

Nederlof, Marc and **Eric van Wayjen.** 1996. Religion and local water rights versus land owners and state. In *Crops, people and irrigation: Water allocation practices of farmers and engineers*, ed. Geert Diemer and Frans P. Huibers, 73–88. London: Intermediate Technology.

Nichols, John. 1974. *The Milagro beanfield war.* New York: Holt, Rinehart and Winston.

North, Douglas C. 1989. Institutions and economic growth: An historical introduction. *World Development* 17 (9): 1319–32.

———. 1992. Institutions, ideology and economic performance. *Cato Journal* 11 (3): 477–88.

Olson, Mancur. 1971. *The logic of collective action: Public goods and the theory of groups.* 2nd Edition. Cambridge, Mass.: Harvard University Press.

Ostrom, Elinor. 1990. *Governing the commons: The evolution of institutions for collective action.* Cambridge, U.K.: Cambridge University Press.

Popkin, Samuel L. 1979. *The rational peasant: The political economy of rural society in Vietnam.* Berkeley: University of California Press.

Pradhan, Rajendra, K.A. Haq and **Ujjwal Pradhan.** 1997. Law, rights and equity: Implications of state intervention in farmer managed irrigation systems. In *Water rights, conflict and policy*, ed. Rajendra Pradhan, Franz von Benda-Beckmann, Kabeet von Benda-Beckmann, H.L. Joep Spiertz, S. Khadka, and K. Azharul Haq, 93–110. Colombo, Sri Lanka: International Irrigation Management Institute.

Rapoport, Anatol, and **Albert M. Chammah.** 1965. *Prisoners' dilemma.* Ann Arbor: University of Michigan Press.

Richards, Michael. 1997. Common property resource institutions and forest management in Latin America. *Development and Change* 28: 95–117.

Rosegrant, Mark W. and **Hans P. Binswanger.** 1994. Markets in tradable water rights: Potential for efficiency gains in developing country water resource allocation. *World Development* 22 (11): 1–11.

Rosegrant, Mark W. and **S. Renato Gazmuri Schleyer.** 1994. *Tradable water rights: Experiences in reforming water allocation policy.* Washington, D.C.: Irrigation Support Project for Asia and the Near East.

Rosegrant, Mark W. and **Mark Svendsen.** 1993. Asian food production in the 1990s: Irrigation investment and management policy. *Food Policy* 18 (1): 13–32.

Rosegrant, Mark. W., Claudia Ringler, and **Roberta Gerpacio.** 1997. Water and land resources and global food supply. Paper presented and the 23rd International Conference of Agricultural Economists on Food Security, Diversification, and Resource Management, August 10–16. Sacramento, Calif.

Runge, Carlisle Ford. 1986. Common property and collective action in economic development. *World Development* 14 (5): 623–35.

Saleth, R. Maria. 1994. Groundwater markets in India: A legal and institutional perspective. In *Selling water: Conceptual and policy debates over groundwater markets in India*, ed. M. Moench, 59–71. Gujarat, India: VIKSAT, Pacific Institute, Natural Heritage Institute.

Schlager, Edela and **Elinor Ostrom.** 1992. Property rights regimes and natural resources: A conceptual analysis. *Land Economics* 68 (3): 249–62.

Schlager, Edella, William Bloomquist, and **Shui Yan Tang.** 1994. Mobile flows, storage, and self-organized institutions for governing common-pool resources. *Land Economics* 70 (3): 294–317.

Scott, A., and **G. Coustalin.** 1995. The evolution of water rights. *Natural Resources Journal* 35 (4): 821–979.

Scott, James C. 1985. *Weapons of the weak: Everyday forms of peasant resistance.* New Haven, Conn.: Yale University Press.

Shepherd, Gillian 1991. The communal management of forests in the semi-arid and sub-humid regions of Africa: Past practice and prospects for the future. *Development Policy Review* 9 (2): 151–76.

Small, Leslie, and **Mark Svendsen.** 1992. A framework for assessing irrigation performance. IFPRI Working Paper on Irrigation Performance No. 1. Washington, D.C.: International Food Policy Research Institute.

Spiertz, H.L. Joep. 1995. State and customary laws: Legal pluralism and water rights. *FMIS Newsletter* 13: 1–7.

Spiertz, H.L. Joep and **Melanie G. Wiber,** eds. 1996. *The role of law in natural resource management.* The Hague, The Netherlands: VUGA.

Svendsen, Mark. 1997. Second generation issues of privatized irrigation. In *Water, economics, management and demand,* ed. Melvyn Kay, Tom Franks, and Lawrence Smith, 409–19. London: E & FN Spon.

Tang, Shui Yan. 1992. *Institutions and collective action: Self-governance in irrigation.* San Francisco, Calif.: Institute for Contemporary Studies.

Turral, Hugh. 1995. *Devolution of management in public irrigation systems: Cost shedding, empowerment and performance.* London: Overseas Development Institute.

Uphoff, Norman T. 1986. *Improving international irrigation management with farmer participation: Getting the process right.* Boulder, Colo.: Westview Press.

———. 1991. *Learning from Gal Oya: Possibilities for participatory development and post-Newtonian social science.* Ithaca, N.Y.: Cornell University Press.

———. 1993. Grassroots organizations and NGOs in rural development: Opportunities with diminishing states and expanding markets. *World Development* 21 (4): 607–22.

Vandergeest, Peter. 1997. Rethinking property. *Common Property Resource Digest* 1997 (41): 4–6.

Vermillion, Douglas L. 1991. *The turnover and self management of irrigation institutions in developing countries*. Colombo, Sri Lanka: International Irrigation Management Institute.

————. 1997. *Impacts of irrigation management transfer: A review of the evidence*. Colombo, Sri Lanka: International Irrigation Management Institute.

Wade, Robert. 1987. *Village republics: Economic conditions for collective action in South India*. Cambridge, U.K.: Cambridge University Press.

Williamson, Oliver E. 1996. *The mechanisms of governance*. New York: Oxford University Press.

World Bank. 1993. *Water resources management*. World Bank policy paper. Washington, D.C.: The World Bank.

Yoder, Robert. 1994. *Locally managed irrigation systems: Essential tasks and implications for assistance, management transfer and turnover programs*. Colombo, Sri Lanka: International Irrigation Management Institute.

2

Water Rights in the State of Nature: Emergent Expectations in an Indonesian Settlement

Douglas L. Vermillion

This study examines how a socially recognized and predictable pattern of water rights and allocation emerged from a process of trial and error with water allocation and negotiations in a resettlement area in North Sulawesi, Indonesia. Balinese farmers in two newly developed irrigation systems recognized that the traditional rule of water allocation that divides water in proportion to the area served was a simplistic first approximation. Through interpersonal exchanges a set of socially recognized criteria emerged to justify certain farmers in taking more than proportional amounts of water, 'borrowing water,' in response to diversity among fields in soils, access to secondary water supplies, distance from the headworks and other factors. A decision tree model uses field observations of water distribution over two seasons to assess criteria used for modifying distribution. The criteria which the farmers used to adjust flows constituted a second approximation for more equitable water allocation among farmers.

Introduction

This study analyzes the emergence of locally defined water rights among Balinese settlers in two newly developed irrigation systems in North Sulawesi, Indonesia.[1] Two farmer-built irrigation systems located in a recently deforested resettlement area provide the setting for examining the origins of water rights and cooperation, before the activities of the state became a significant factor in the irrigation systems.

With rising populations and diversifying economies, competition for water is rapidly intensifying in many developing countries, especially in Asia (Arriens et al. 1996; Seckler 1996). At the same time, due to financial pressure and management failure, many countries are devolving management of irrigation systems to local farmer organizations (Johnson et al. 1995). These changes have brought about widespread interest in how to create farmer organizations that will cooperate in sharing water (EDI 1996; Meinzen-Dick et al. 1997). They have also renewed interest in developing formal water rights and markets in developing countries (Pradhan et al. 1997; Rosegrant and Binswanger 1994).

These changes point to the need to better understand what makes cooperation possible, the processes whereby locally valid water allocation principles emerge, and to what extent local groups have the ability to solve problems of resource allocation. This paper provides insights into the basis for cooperation by examining the origins of common property rights among people sharing a scarce resource in a newly settled environment.

Michael Taylor's (1982, 1987) theoretical analysis of the origins of cooperation and community in a 'state of anarchy' (i.e., without the coercive role of the state) identified shared beliefs or norms, direct social relationships among people, and repeating reciprocity as the key elements of cooperation. Normally, these features exist only in relatively small groups where direct, personal interaction is possible. Schofield states that the main theoretical problem for explaining the rise and maintenance of cooperation is:

> ... the manner by which individuals attain knowledge of each others' preferences and likely behavior ... the problem is one of

common knowledge ... what is the minimal amount that one agent must know in a given milieu about the beliefs and wants of other agents to be able to form coherent notions about their behavior and for this knowledge to be communicable to the others? (Schofield 1985, 12–13)

Macpherson's (1978) sociological theory of property posits that rights to resources are the outgrowth of social relationships. Rights are based upon a socially recognized justifying theory about who has entitlements in or to things. They are, in essence, common expectations about how people relate to each other vis-à-vis resources. Rights to resources are shaped by social institutions but evolve through social interactions and the interplay of contending interests—all of which (not to mention the physical environment) are subject to constant change. Following Ostrom (1992), this paper considers social rules to have both a cognitive and behavioral aspect. They are not rules unless to a significant extent they are practiced (as rules-in-use) by a common group.

Combining the these points about cooperation and property, the primary concern of this study is to examine the process whereby common knowledge about water rights emerges among farmers who are learning to share water in a new environment. This includes an examination of the extent to which common conceptions about water rights shape the actual behavior of farmers in obtaining water for their fields. This will uncover the principle of equity that underlies the emergent water rights.

The problem is analyzed by answering a series of questions:

- What is the nature of the process whereby common conceptions about water rights emerge among farmers?
- What is the justifying theory (à la Macpherson) that differentiates individual water rights among farmers?
- To what extent do the farmers' conceptions about water rights determine their behavior and its outcomes?
- How does water allocation respond to fluctuations in water supply and demand?
- What are the equity implications of this process?

Balinese Transmigrants in the Dumoga Valley

The two irrigation systems in this study are located in the villages of Mopugad and Werdi Agung in the Dumoga Valley of North Sulawesi, Indonesia. The Dumoga Valley is a major government transmigration area. It is located one degree north of the equator at an elevation of 170 meters. Map 2.1 shows the location of the Valley in Indonesia. The Valley has 30,000 hectares of arable land surrounded by steep mountains. Average annual rainfall is 1,937 millimeters, with a bimodal and monsoon pattern. Soil types range from alluvial soils of sandy clay to clay of basaltic and volcanic origin. Farmers in both systems are transmigrants from Bali. Differences among farmers in landholdings and wealth are small relative to more established agricultural settings elsewhere. Farmers in both systems produce two rice crops per year. Average yields for rice crops during the study period (1982–83) generally varied between 3 and 6 tons per hectare.

The Mopugad system is a 28-hectare river diversion system located on the sloping northern rim of the valley. It was built by farmers in 1977. Water is diverted from a small river by a 1-meter high concrete weir, built with 150 sacks of cement that were contributed by the 30 original farmers whose land allocations happened to be within the service area of the system. Farmers designed and constructed the weir and network without external assistance. The most educated among them was the secretary of the *subak* (or irrigation society) who held a high school degree. The weir was still in its original sound condition in 1983. The irrigation water supply is dependent on fluctuating stream flows and can be rather erratic and unpredictable. The Theoretical Relative Water Supply (TRWS) for the system varied between 0.6 and 2.5 during the two seasons studied. Theoretical Relative Water Supply is the ratio between water supply (effective rain plus irrigation supply) to potential water demand (estimated potential crop evapotranspiration plus water conveyance loss—see Levine 1982).

The system in Werdi Agung was first built in 1970 and served 50 hectares. In 1980, it was incorporated into block 18, an area in the middle of the 5,500-hectare Kosinggolan irrigation system that was built by the government. Originally, water was diverted from a small

Map 2.1: Location of Dumoga Valley, North Sulawesi, Indonesia

river on the southern rim of the valley. But after the main canal of the Kosinggolan system cut across the path of the traditional supply canal, the Werdi Agung area began receiving water from the government built canal. The Werdi Agung 'subsystem' experienced relatively less fluctuation in its water supply than did Mopugad, because its source, the Kosinggolan main canal, was regulated. However, it also experienced periods of scarcity; its TRWS varied between 0.7 and 1.7 during the two seasons studied.

The Mopugad and Werdi Agung systems are approximately 12 kilometers apart. Farmers in both systems were resettled under the Government's transmigration program, which allocated 2 hectares of land per family. Hence, differences among farmers in landholdings and physical capital are minor. Most farmer families own 2–4 hectares of land. Because of the geographic quota system of the program, farmers in both systems originated from various places in Bali. The villages of Mopugad and Werdi Agung are not natural or indigenous groupings but are amalgams of Balinese from different parts of Bali and even include some Christians amongst the dominant Hindus.

Staking Claims

Considerable literature exists on the traditional Balinese *subak*, much of which depicts the *subak* and the broader Balinese social order to be in a state of well-adapted cultural and ecological equilibrium.[2] Little information exists, however, about social organization and resource management in Balinese settlements outside Bali (see Davis 1977; Vermillion 1986).

The researcher came to the field sites aware of the literature on the remarkably elaborate Balinese system for managing irrigation. Traditionally, it is based primarily on proportional allocation of water according to land area served, subject to occasional adjustments made for variations in soil and other factors (see Geertz 1980). The expectation was of finding something similar to Bali, though perhaps a little crude because of the newness of the irrigation systems.

Preliminary interviews with farmer leaders indicated that service area proportionality was indeed the basic rule for water allocation among farmers' fields. But the first several inspections of both systems revealed something else going on in practice, that appeared to be more than a little crude. Downright anarchy seemed to be the rule. There was an apparent rampant disregard for the traditional *tektek*, or *temuku*—a wooden log cut out so as to divide water proportionately. It was frequently undercut, blocked, circumvented by breaches or just pulled out and tossed aside. Every day the whole configuration of water division and tampering was different, even though the current official rule was continuous flow with proportional allocation to fields. The first observations seemed to confirm the views of local officials of the agriculture and irrigation departments—that the farmer organizations were not yet 'functional' and water distribution was anarchic.

Given the apparent gap between rules and practice, it was necessary to make a detailed examination of both rhetoric and behavior relative to water allocation in order to determine whether this was a situation of loosely structured 'anarchy' or whether there was a deeper structure that was not readily apparent on the surface. Inspections of all canals, from head to tail, in both systems were made three times per week during the first season. During the second season, two inspections per week were sufficient in order to document the pattern of water distribution in effect. For each inspection a record was made of how the water was actually divided. Interviews were held with *subak* leaders and farmers encountered in the field in order to elicit farmers' perceptions and rationale for how water was being divided.

In both Mopugad and Werdi Agung, membership in the *subak* (or renting water and maintaining channels as a tenant) established a right to a standard share of water based on the size of the irrigated field. Membership was granted to all those who owned land in the irrigated service area and who helped build the system originally. The *subak* formally established shares. A 'standard share' or division refers to the socially designated proportion of the total water supply that is based solely on the relative land area served by a channel or field outlet. The *subak* decided that this would be the best and simplest basis for allocating water in the beginning. Because farmers built the system, the government had no role in the allocation of shares. The *subak* makes no permanent changes in shares unless there is a significant change in the amount of rice land irrigated, or unless some more permanent exception to the land size basis for a division emerges, due to some extreme physical condition.

Subak authorities reported only three official cases in both systems of permanent enlargement of the water share. The one case in Mopugad concerned a small plot near a ravine that had high water infiltration rates and did not receive any drainage from neighbors. The two cases in Werdi Agung concerned plots next to gullies that had exceptionally high infiltration rates. Each of the systems had one case of a farmer who petitioned *subak* authorities to enlarge the permanent allocation beyond the standard share because of unusually high seepage rates. In both instances the requests were denied since *subak* leaders judged that the farmers had failed to create an adequate hardpan floor in their rice basins due to poor plowing practices.

In both systems, farmers frequently altered the standard proportional division of water by temporarily taking extra amounts of water (or 'surplus shares'). 'Surplus shares' refers to a share of water taken at a given point of time that exceeds the 'standard share' based on land size proportionality. Farmers used the following methods to alter the standard division:

- Widen one's intake;
- cut a breach or hole in the channel bund that runs alongside one's field in order to bring extra water onto one's field;
- block the channel below the intake to one's channel or field in order to divert more water onto one's field;
- make a hole below or on the side of the *temuku*, or *tektek*, in order to add to the flow to one's field;
- block the flow into a neighboring channel in order to direct more water into one's own channel;
- close the intake for a channel neighbor's field upstream; and
- redirect the drainage from a neighbor's field, which normally enters a canal, into one's own field (making use of, for instance, a small aqueduct, crafted from bamboo or wood).

In the vast majority of cases, this activity was done informally and unilaterally by farmers when they happened to be at the farm and felt the need or felt justified in taking extra water (or sometimes when they wanted to cut it off). If the farmer who was adjusting the flow happened to encounter another farmer whose field was affected by the action, he or she would typically explain why the farmer needed extra water and that it was only temporary. Farmers in the system held the view that as long as one had talked to the neighbors at the outset of the season about the general timing of planting and one's justifications for borrowing extra water sometimes, one need not seek permission each time before doing so during the season.

Normally, the water taker would not return the water division to the standard division. It was considered the responsibility of each water user to visit their field regularly and inspect and help control the division of water. Farmers told me more than once, 'Whoever goes to the field often gets the water.' Farmers indicated little respect for those who were too lazy, or so busy opening and working land elsewhere, that they did not go to their irrigated field often enough to control the water situation. So it was left to those affected by the adjustments to return the situation to 'normal' when they came to their field.

In their incidental discussions about water distribution, farmers emphasized flexibility, tolerance, and experimentation. This was a response to both the newness of the environment and ancient cultural norms. At the time of the study, many fields were still new and farmers were still creating the hardpan or, in some cases, were gradually expanding the area of their field that was irrigated. Farmers were still learning about micro-level variations in physical conditions and farming practices among their fields and themselves and they preferred, in this early stage, a temporary and tentative approach, rather than a permanent and official approach, to deal with the physical and technical diversity among fields.

The notion of *rukun* is prominent among Balinese. This is both a norm of solidarity and a civic process of 'mutual adjustment,' that has as its purpose 'the creation and maintenance of order' (Geertz 1980: 48, 84). When asked what they thought of this or the act of 'stealing' water, farmers would normally refer to it as 'borrowing' water (*pinjam air*) and express the importance of flexibility, give and take (*baku tarik*) and patience with one's channel neighbors, who were referred to as 'friends' (*teman* or *kawan*). Farmers often admitted that there was reciprocity; they themselves 'borrowed' water from a farmer who happened to be 'borrowing' water from them at the time of the interview.

Kesadaran (understanding) and *sabar* (patience) were considered the proper response to water taking. More than once, farmers were observed inspecting an altered division of water that was not in their favor and then leaving the alteration in place. Patience was not only a virtue, it was also an investment meant to invoke a patient response from others in the future when one might need to borrow extra water.

Malu (social shame), not formal sanctions, was the primary motivation for limiting excessive water taking, to avoid making a scene in front of others and limiting the amount of problem solving that had to be dealt with through formal channels. Farmers were apt to say such things as, 'As long as my field is wet, the water is enough,' to convey the impression that their demand for water was, in fact, only modest. These norms emphasized moderation in a learning environment characterized by frequent mutual adjustments to physical differences among fields. Acts of 'borrowing' were meant, in part, to test the degree of tolerance of one's channel neighbors towards one's assertion of a right to a temporary surplus share of water.

Only a small fraction of these acts of 'borrowing' extra water evoked complaints that were taken to the *subak* leadership. Fines for first time offenses of water theft were relatively low; they went up for subsequent offenses.

So, the mostly informal process of 'mutual adjustment' of the division of water can be understood as a dynamic response to a recurring problem of allocating a resource in a new environment where there was considerable micro-level diversity and incomplete knowledge among farmers regarding each other's field conditions and differential levels of demand for water. It was a process of trying to measure the appropriateness of one's standard or surplus share of water against that of one's neighbor, largely by taking extra water as needed, waiting to observe the response of those affected, and when encountering a channel neighbor, attempting to persuade him or her that one should have a right to take a surplus share. The farmer asserting this 'right' would then appeal to some justifying criteria, hoping that neighbors would accept it. The tentative and incomplete knowledge among farmers necessitated that adjustments to the standard share be tolerated and be done on a temporary basis, until perhaps in the future, when things would be clearer and more permanent adjustments could be granted officially.

Emergence of a Justifying Theory

Through regular occurrences of farmers 'borrowing' extra water and frequently engaging in interpersonal persuasion, debates, and negotiation, farmers gradually developed a commonly recognized set of justifying criteria for augmenting their supplies beyond the standard proportional share. The criteria gradually became socially recognized less through formal decision-making than through interpersonal assertions and the decentralized reciprocities between experimental assertions and tolerant or intolerant responses.

Particularly in the early years, the range of rhetoric exceeded what later became socially acceptable criteria for asserting a surplus share. The following are a few examples of exchanges observed, with a note after each indicating whether the criteria stated were socially accepted or rejected:

- The water in my field seeps through my sandy soils very quickly, so I need to take extra. *(Accepted)*
- My channel neighbors get water from small streams, springs or drainage from other fields, in addition to the channel. My field doesn't have access to any other sources of water but the channel; therefore, I must take extra water now and then. *(Accepted)*
- My field is at the tail end of the channel. A lot of the water that is supposed to come to my field disappears on the way, so sometimes I have to go upstream and redirect extra water to my field. *(Accepted)*
- I am constructing new rice terraces and need extra water to soften and level the hard, virgin ground. *(Accepted)*
- I need to have a fish pond to raise enough money to send my children to school. I have to take extra water for the pond, but it all goes back into the channel anyway. *(Accepted)*
- Since I drain all of my water back to the channel, it doesn't matter whether I borrow extra water for my paddy field, because it all goes back to be used by my friends downstream. *(Rejected)*
- Since the channel cuts through the middle of my field and prevents me from getting full production, I should have a right to

take extra water to increase my production and make up the
difference. *(Rejected)*

- The channel I receive water from cuts through the middle of
  my upstream neighbor's field, so it is easy for him to always be
  taking extra water. So I have to take extra water to make up the
  difference. *(Rejected)*

Through a gradual process of experimental assertion, validation
and rejection, the clash of rhetoric was gradually distilled to a limited set of justifying criteria that was generally recognized as acceptable rationale for asserting rights to a surplus share. Whether or not
application of the criteria in a particular case was acceptable was, of
course, another matter.

At this early stage of development of the irrigation systems, when
hardpans were still under formation, area irrigated within fields was
still changing, and knowledge about each other's field conditions
was incomplete, farmers preferred a tentative approach. The justifying criteria only applied to temporary acts of borrowing extra water
and only insofar as the actions, in the aggregate, did not prevent
others from receiving their standard shares.

The somewhat ephemeral 'surplus share' was approximated through
temporary acts of borrowing extra water. Although the justifying
criteria came to be socially accepted, and probably served to reduce
the range of rhetoric and level of chaos that otherwise might have
prevailed without it, debate and tolerance testing continued over
application of the criteria to specific cases and the frequency with
which extra water was 'borrowed' by certain farmers.

The process of creating 'rights' evolved through the following
steps:

- Adoption of a preliminary, simple allocation rule (around which
  further refinements could be negotiated);
- individual and ad hoc assertions and claims to extra water
  above the simple allocation rule;
- social acceptance or rejection of the assertions and claims;
- emergence of common expectations about who had valid rights
  to take extra water above the standard allocation rule; and
- possible eventual formalization of the expectation into a right
  to a permanent surplus share.

Extent of Compliance with the Justifying Theory

This section turns to an examination of which farmers in the two systems regularly asserted their right to a surplus share of water and the extent to which this behavior fit the local model of justifying criteria.

During participant observation, the author saw indications of opportunism among water users. Nevertheless physical inequalities, such as relative soil infiltration rate, channel position, the availability of alternative water sources, or forms of land use with high water demand (such as new terracing or keeping fish ponds) were clearly at the hub of the rhetoric about water allocation. We will now see to what extent the 'justifying theory' was reflected in practice.

The first step was to identify irrigated plots in each system whose farmers 'borrowed' water frequently in comparison with fellow water users. It was not possible through observation, informant accounts, or farmer interviews to obtain reliable quantitative information about how often each farmer took extra water during a given season or other period. However, key informants could readily make a categorical comparison between farmers who 'often' or 'did not often' take extra water. Extensive data from participant observation was used to validate or correct categorizations by informants. The categorizations were found to be consistent from season to season.

Taking extra water 'often' was defined as taking water above and beyond the standard proportional division on a regular basis (i.e., more frequently than just during peak water demand periods). To 'not often' borrow water meant to borrow water only during intermittent, high demand periods, if at all.

Maps 2.2 and 2.3 are, respectively, maps of the Mopugad and Werdi Agung systems which indicate the channels and farm parcels in each system. Farm parcels are shaded to distinguish parcels whose farmers borrowed water 'often' and 'not often.' As can be seen, the habitually frequent 'borrowers' do not group together in either the upper or lower reaches of the channels, in either system. Factors other than mere channel position are clearly involved in the predisposition to take extra water often or not, relative to one's channel neighbors.

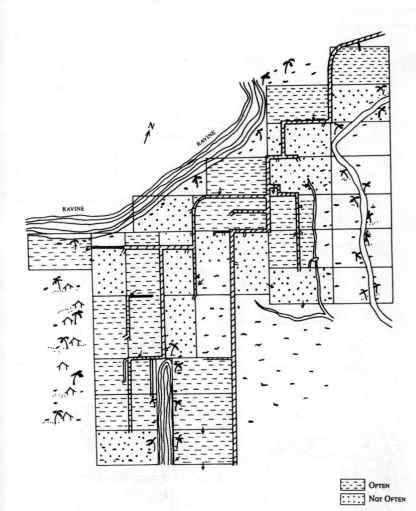

**Map 2.2: Parcels Which Frequently Added Water Beyond
the Standard Share, Mopugad**

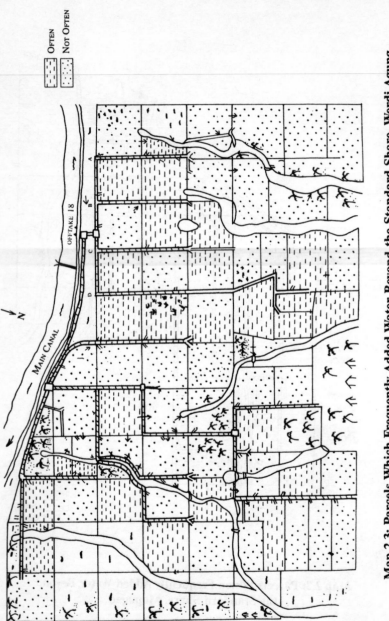

Map 2.3: Parcels Which Frequently Added Water Beyond the Standard Share, Werdi Agung

Based upon key informant interviews and personal observation, it was possible to construct models that represented the configuration of locally accepted justifying criteria for taking extra water, plus certain disincentives. Somewhat surprisingly, the models were basically the same in both systems. They are presented in the form of decision tree diagrams.

Testing the Model in Mopugad

Figure 2.1 shows the model for Mopugad. The three factors on the left are the primary justifying criteria identified by farmers. The first criterion is whether or not the infiltration rate on one's field is significantly higher than the average infiltration rates on other fields in the system. The second criterion is whether or not one's field is in the lower end of the channel (defined here as the lower third of the channel). The third criterion is whether or not the field, during the period of observation, had a form of land use that had a particularly high water demand (for example, land leveling, new terracing, or fish ponds).

There are two additional factors that act as disincentives for taking extra water. The first is where a parcel depends more on non-channel sources of water—such as, neighbor's drainage, groundwater recharge, or other surface sources—than on the channel. The second disincentive to taking a surplus share is where a farmer passively obtains extra water through the frequent borrowing practices of an upstream neighbor. The method used by the neighbor to augment water supply tends to direct additional flow to one's own field as well.

In Mopugad, 20 of the fields met at least one of the justifying criteria and 14 did not. Of the 14 fields not meeting even one of the criteria, 10 of them did not take extra water 'often,' as the model predicts. However, the behavior of four of the 'often' cases could not be explained by the model. They did not fulfill any of the justifying criteria in the model and yet were frequent takers of surplus shares. These were parcels A1, B1, C1 and, M6.

Sixteen of the 20 cases that met the justifying criteria did not have either disincentive and pursued a pattern of taking extra water relatively often. Four of the 20 cases were constrained by disincentives and did not take surplus shares. Of the four that were constrained

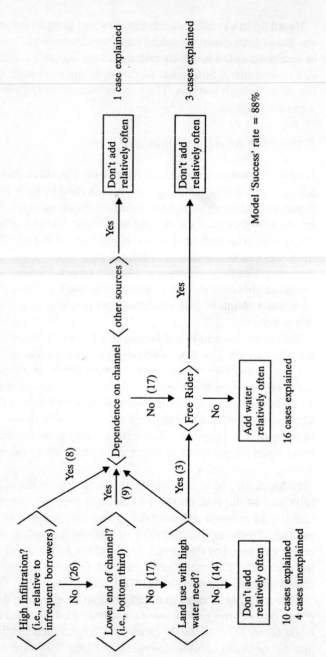

Figure 2.1: Model of Justifying Criteria to Exceed Standard Water Share, Mopugad

34 cases

High Infiltration?
(i.e., relative to
infrequent borrowers)

Yes (8)

No (26)

Lower end of channel?
(i.e., bottom third)

Yes
(9)

No (17)

Land use with high
water need?

Yes (3)

No (14)

Don't add
relatively often

10 cases explained
4 cases unexplained

Dependence on channel

other sources

Yes

Don't add
relatively often

1 case explained

No (17)

Free Rider

Yes

Don't add
relatively often

3 cases explained

No

Add water
relatively often

16 cases explained

Model 'Success' rate = 88%

by disincentives, one had low dependence on the channel and three were downstream from other frequent 'borrowers.' The model 'explained' the borrowing patterns of 30 of the 34 plots, or 88 per cent of all farmers.

Testing the Model in Werdi Agung

The model for the Werdi Agung system is given in Figure 2.2. Eighteen cases lacked any of the justifying criteria and 14 of these did not often borrow water. The remaining 57 cases fulfilled at least one of the justifying criteria. Nineteen of these had little dependence on the channel as a source of water, and did not borrow water often. This reflects the prevalence of groundwater recharge and alternative water sources that exist in the lower portions of the system. This is in contrast to Mopugad, which generally lacks return flow lower in the system. Six others were downstream from other borrowers, and did not often borrow water themselves. Of the 32 cases that had incentives but no disincentives, 25 were frequent borrowers, as the model predicts, but seven were not. The model successfully explains the relative borrowing patterns of 85 per cent of the farmers.

Of the 11 unexplained cases in Werdi Agung, seven met the justifying criteria and had no disincentives but still did not often take extra water. Two of these, Z1 and A2, had high infiltration rates but were at the top end of channels, where the flow is relatively high and reliable. Most of the unexplained cases were not those who frequently took extra water without justification, but those who did not often take extra water, despite so qualifying relative to the justifying criteria.

In Mopugad, four cases (A1, B1, C1 and M6) or 12 per cent, were frequent borrowers who did not meet any apparent justifying criteria. In Werdi Agung, four cases (F2, J2, K1, L2) or 5 per cent, were frequent borrowers who did not fulfill apparent justifying criteria, as specified in the model. So, 85 to 88 per cent of the cases observed are either farmers who frequently take extra water and qualify to do so under the justifying criteria or farmers who do not take extra water and do not qualify under the justifying criteria.

Clearly, farmers in the two systems considered the traditional standard share system based on land area proportionality to be only a first approximation of an equitable allocation of water. Except for

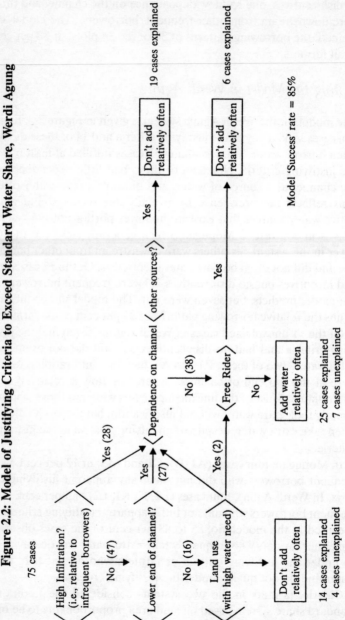

Figure 2.2: Model of Justifying Criteria to Exceed Standard Water Share, Werdi Agung

75 cases

High Infiltration?
(i.e., relative to
infrequent borrowers)

No (47) → Lower end of channel?

Yes (28)

No (16) → Land use
(with high water need)

Yes (27)

Yes (2)

Don't add
relatively often

14 cases explained
4 cases unexplained

Dependence on channel ⟨ other sources? ⟩

Free Rider

No (38)

Yes

Don't add
relatively often

19 cases explained

No

Add water
relatively often

25 cases explained
7 cases unexplained

Yes

Don't add
relatively often

6 cases explained

Model 'Success' rate = 85%

a few cases of abuse, farmers in both systems were, through inter-action with their environment and channel neighbors, gradually forging a 'second approximation,' that was a customized response to the inherent and unique variations throughout the systems.[3] The principle was thus not one of simply delivering equal amounts of water to each farmer proportional to land, but of equitable distribu-tion adjusted according to needs, as influenced by supply from other sources and demand caused by porous soils and other factors. The essence of the local theory was to provide a fair allocation of water among farmers taking into account (insofar as was practically possi-ble) inherent differences in soils and access to water.

Mutual Adjustment During Two Seasons

This section analyzes the informal mutual adjustment of the stan-dard division of water related to the fluctuating conditions of water supply and demand during the two seasons.

In Mopugad, in the first season (from June to September) land preparation and transplanting was staggered because of water shortages and also to facilitate the use of exchange labor among farmers. Two weeks after transplanting the Theoretical Relative Water Supply (TRWS) dropped below 1.0. Farmers of parcels C9 and D3 requested a formal rotation, which began thereafter. The intensity of informal alteration of the standard division escalated considerably while the TRWS stayed below 1.0, and soils were cracking in the fields in the lower reaches. After week eight, the TRWS continued to decline, and the *subak* decided that the full flow of water for the entire system would be allocated to single par-cels for twelve-hour turns, starting in order of need and request. The *subak* head, secretary, and treasurer took turns guarding the water at night. This arrangement continued, although with numer-ous exceptions, until well into the ripening phase, when pre-harvest drying began.

During the second season, transplanting was staggered over a longer period than in the first season. After a period of abundance, by week eight the rains tapered off and the TRWS began another gradual decline. The *subak* agreed to keep the standard division intact overnight and allow borrowing to be arranged interpersonally during the daytime. Despite the high frequency of borrowing and the tensions among farmers, it was felt that direct arrangements between farmers would work as well as or better than formal rotations arranged through the *subak*. By the ripening phase, eight members had been fined for water theft. This was the first time the *subak* levied any fines for water theft. The fines were set at half the established rate of about U.S. $2.50 for first infractions because of the difficult economic condition imposed by the drought.

In the Werdi Agung system, water was adequate during the land preparation period in the first season. Soon after transplanting, the TRWS began to decline. When it dropped below 1.0 in the seventh week, numerous complaints emerged about water scarcity and an upsurge in water borrowing occurred. After week nine, the TRWS rose and remained above 1.0 until pre-harvest drying began. During the last five weeks of the season, mice and birds became a serious problem and this kept more people than usual in the fields, to scare them away. Having more people continuously in the fields may have discouraged some water theft during this time. Partial blocking of channels and field inlets were more common during this period than complete blocking and other more brazen methods frequently observed when fewer people were in the fields. This suggests that some of the 'borrowing' activity was not socially acceptable and such behavior was inhibited when a lot of people were in the fields.

In the second season, when continuous flow irrigation proved inadequate for land preparation, farmers decided to rotate the full flow for a channel to individual plots for 20-hour turns. After three weeks, nearly all the farmers had finished transplanting and the system reverted to the standard division with continued interpersonal borrowing.

The intensity of alteration activity, measured by weekly averages of all alterations in the standard division of water that were observed during each field inspection, was correlated with weekly values for TRWS. Generally, declines in TRWS prompted a rise in alteration activity, and vice versa. In Mopugad, for both the first and second seasons, the correlation coefficient for the relationship between alteration intensity and TRWS was .35. There was no significant correlation between alteration intensity and TRWS in Werdi Agung.[4] This was mainly due to pervasive return flow within the system and supplemental water sources, that served to moderate the need for farmers in the tail and middle areas to seek extra water by manipulating the division of channels.

Implications of the Adjustments for Equity

We now turn to the question of what were the implications for equity of the informal practices of adjusting the standard division of water. Specifically, 'did the patterns of regular alteration of the standard division of water result in more or less equity than would be the case if the standard division based on service area proportionality was implemented strictly?'

One way to address this question is through examination of the total number of occurrences of each type and location of observed alteration in the standard division of water, based on observations of the water distribution over two planting seasons. This documents the directions of net gains and losses of water distribution among parcels as a result of the patterns of adjustments.

In Mopugad the net effect of channel division alterations is in the direction of sending extra water to the lower end of channel C. This is where the largest group of parcels that had the lowest relative water adequacy (i.e., the lowest proportion of inspections with water covering the sample parcels) are. Of the five channel division points in Mopugad, three of them were found to have a net effect of directing extra water toward fields with relatively lower levels of water availability (as measured by the proportion of field inspections for which sample fields had standing water on them).

In Werdi Agung, alterations of six of the eight channel division points had a net effect of directing extra water towards fields with relatively less water available. So, the pattern of alterations at the level of channel division points is also in the direction of counteracting or moderating inequalities in water availability that exist within the system.

A similar examination of field-level alterations showed that, in Werdi Agung, as in Mopugad, there is a discernible tendency for alterations at the field intake level to counteract the water related inequalities imposed by the physical characteristics of the system. These inequalities are not necessarily simple head–tail differences, but also include variations in soils and return flows.

Conclusion

In contrast to communal, highly programmed images of the Balinese *subak*, in the Mopugad and Werdi Agung systems in north Sulawesi the proportional water shares rule was routinely altered through ad hoc competitive acts of 'borrowing' extra water by a large number of the farmers in each system. What might appear to the casual observer as anarchy was in fact a socially validated pattern of individual adjustments to the standard allocation of water. The 'state of nature' observed in this study was neither complete communal harmony nor brutish opportunism. It was somewhere between Rousseau's (1762) and Hobbes' (1651) depictions of the state of nature, and could perhaps best be characterized as a social struggle for balance between justice and enterprise.

Through numerous temporary acts of taking extra water and negotiating among farmers, a commonly accepted set of 'justifying criteria' gradually emerged at the group level. In the aggregate, without central coordination, these disparate actions resulted primarily in counteracting the inherent inequality in landform within the systems.

Interpersonal interaction among water users in the two study systems is primarily a second approximation for allocating water, following the first approximation of the share-based division of water. The traditional rule of farm-area-based proportional allocation of water was found to be only a starting point in the search for equity in an environment characterized by considerable micro diversity among farms in access to different sources of water, soil porosity and location along canals. In a setting riddled by pronounced inequalities among fields but not among farmers, the set of justifying criteria and informal interactions among farmers created a more equitable and socially acceptable pattern of water allocation than would have resulted from strict reliance on area-based proportional allocation of water.

These results provide insights into how cooperation and water rights emerge. They also provide rationale for making some suggestions about how management transfer and organizing farmers should be done. The key elements of cooperation in this study were:

- Relative social homogeneity among a relatively small group of farmers;

- motivation of farmers to avoid social conflict in a setting with numerous cross-cutting social pressures to avoid conflict;
- existence of a standard (if incomplete) allocation rule to structure and simplify negotiation and problem solving;
- a forum for frequent, interpersonal interaction among farmers to exchange information and requests, which acted to build common knowledge about physical differences and identify valid justifying criteria for adjusting the standard allocation rule; and
- a process of reciprocal give-and-take, that encouraged tolerance, experimentation, and information sharing among farmers.

The study suggests that group objectives, at this small-scale, can often be achieved through interpersonal interaction without centralized information processing and control. At the level of interaction among 30 to 50 farmers, water distribution is more an art than a science. A state presence is not needed, nor do water user associations need to function, or be trained to function, as mini-bureaucracies with elaborate and standardized administrative procedures. Elaborate standard organizational structures should not be imposed from above, especially before farmers have had experience with self-management.

To a significant extent, time and local experience with problem-solving should be precursors to organizational structuring and formulation of water rights. Perhaps the more complex the environment and uncertain the decision-making, the less structure should be imposed at the beginning of management transfer or projects to organize water users associations. And, conflict mediating arrangements are needed in order for interpersonal interaction to produce common knowledge and cooperation.

The study also implies that efforts to monitor and evaluate the performance of water users associations should avoid the 'bureaucratic fixation with means' typical of many benefit monitoring and evaluation methods. Number of meetings held, percentage of farmers attending meetings or formal organizational structure should not be seen as ends in themselves. Rather, emphasis should be given to measuring management outcomes in terms of equity, efficiency and productivity, although local processes may continue to escape the understanding of outsiders.

Notes

1. This study is based on field research conducted by the author between 1982–83. The study employed semi-structured group and key informant interviews, sample surveys, repeated inspection of canal networks and water discharge measurements through two seasons (June to September 1982 and December to April 1983).
2. See for example, Boon 1977; Geertz 1980, 1972; Gladwin 1977; Grader 1960; Lansing 1987; Liefrinck 1969.
3. See Vermillion 1989. This paper examines the adjustments made by farmers to their irrigation infrastructure to make it more compatible with the micro-level diversity which was not adequately incorporated into the network as designed by engineers.
4. Correlation coefficients were only -0.10 and -0.05 for the first and second seasons, respectively, and were not significant at the .90 level.

References

Arriens, Wouter Lincklaen, Jeremy Bird, Jeremy Berkoff, and **Paul Mosley**, eds. 1996. Towards effective water policy in the Asian and Pacific region, Volume I: Overview of issues and recommendations. In *Proceedings of the regional consultation workshop, May 10–14, Manila, Philippines*. Manila, Philippines: Asian Development Bank.

Boon, James. 1977. *The anthropological romance of Bali, 1597–1972: Dynamic perspectives in marriage and caste, politics and religion*. Cambridge, U.K.: Cambridge University Press.

Davis, Gloria Jean. 1977. Parigi: A social history of the Balinese movement to Central Sulawesi, 1907–1974. Ph.D. diss., Stanford University, Stanford, Calif., U.S.A.

EDI (Economic Development Institute of the World Bank). 1996. *Handbook on participatory irrigation management*. Washington, D.C.: Economic Development Institute of the World Bank.

Geertz, Clifford. 1972. The wet and the dry: Traditional irrigation in Bali and Morocco. *Human Ecology* 1: 23–39.

———. 1980. *Negara: The theatre state in nineteenth century Bali*. Princeton, N.J.: Princeton University Press.

Gladwin, Christina Horn. 1977. A model of farmers' decisions to adopt the recommendations of Plan Puebla. Ph.D. diss., Agricultural Economics, Stanford University, Stanford, Calif., U.S.A.

Grader, C.J. 1960. Irrigation system in the region of Jembrana. In *Bali, studies in life, thought, ritual*, 267–88. The Hague, The Netherlands: W. van Hoeve.

Hobbes, Thomas. 1651. *Leviathan*. New York: Collier Books edition, 1962.

Johnson, S.H., Douglas L. Vermillion and **J.A. Sagardoy.** 1995. *Irrigation management transfer*. Selected papers from the International Conference on Irrigation Management Transfer, September 20–24, 1994, Wuhan, China. FAO Water Report 5. Rome: International Irrigation Management Institute and Food and Agriculture Organization of the United Nations.

Lansing, Stephen J. 1987. Balinese water temples and the management of irrigation. *American Anthropologist* 89: 326–41.

Levine, Gilbert. 1982. *Relative water supply: An explanatory variable for irrigation systems*. The Determinants of Developing Country Irrigation Project Problems Project Technical Report No. 6. Washington, D.C.: U.S. Agency for International Development.

Liefrinck, F.A. 1969 [1886]. Rice cultivation in northern Bali. In *Bali, further studies in life, thought, ritual*, 3–73. The Hague, The Netherlands: W. van Hoeve.

Macpherson, C.B., ed. 1978. *Property: Mainstream and critical positions*. Toronto: University of Toronto Press.

Meinzen-Dick, Ruth, Meyra Mendoza, Loic Sadoulet, Ghada Abiad-Shields, and **Ashok Subramanian.** 1997. Sustainable water user associations: Lessons from a literature review. In *User organizations for sustainable water services*, ed. Ashok Subramanian, N. Vijay Jagannathan, and Ruth Meinzen-Dick, 7–87. World Bank Technical Paper Number 354. Washington, D.C.: World Bank.

Ostrom, Elinor. 1992. *Crafting institutions for self-governing irrigation systems*. San Francisco, Calif.: ICS Press.

Pradhan, Rajendra, Franz von Benda-Beckmann, Keebet von Benda-Beckmann, H.L.J. Spiertz, Shantam S. Khadka and **K. Azharul Haq**, eds. 1997. *Water rights, conflict and policy*. Colombo, Sri Lanka: International Irrigation Management Institute.

Rosegrant, Mark W. and **Hans P. Binswanger.** 1994. Markets in tradable water rights: Potential for efficiency gains in developing country water resource allocation. *World Development* 22 (11): 1613–25.

Rousseau, Jean Jacques. 1762. *The social contract*. New York: E.P. Dutton edition, 1950.

Schofield, Norman. 1985. Anarchy, altruism and cooperation: A review. *Social Choice and Welfare* 2: 207–19.

Seckler, David. 1996. *The new era of water resources management: From 'dry' to 'wet' water savings*. IIMI Research Report 1. Colombo, Sri Lanka: International Irrigation Management Institute.

Taylor, Michael. 1982. *Community, anarchy and liberty*. Cambridge, U.K.: Cambridge University Press.

————. 1987. *The possibility of cooperation*. Cambridge, U.K.: Cambridge University Press.

Vermillion, Douglas L. 1986. Rules and processes: Dividing water and negotiating order in two new irrigation systems in North Sulawesi, Indonesia. Ph.D. diss., Cornell University, Ithaca, N.Y., U.S.A.

————. 1989. *Second approximations: Unplanned farmer contributions to irrigation design*. ODI/IIMI Irrigation Management Network Paper No. 89/2c. London, U.K.: Overseas Development Institute.

3

Gendered Water and Land Rights in Rice Valley Improvement, Burkina Faso

BARBARA VAN KOPPEN[1]

It is widely assumed that local gender and class hierarchies are the major obstacles in achieving equity. However, skewed expropriation and vesting of new rights exclusively in the local male élite or male heads of households may result from how a development agency structures local forums and determines title criteria. This chapter analyzes negotiations on water and land rights under externally supported construction of water infrastructure in southwest Burkina Faso, West Africa. The project used the concept of the unitary household to legitimize expropriation of women's rights to rice land. Initially the local forum was dominated by the male élite and paid male construction workers. At later sites, local male leaders took the initiative to include women, who farmed almost all the rice land, with better outcomes for productivity, as well as equity.

Introduction

For most water infrastructure development, external agencies provide technical expertise and bear most of the construction costs. Too little attention is paid to how intervention processes define users' rights to the water conveyed by the newly constructed or rehabilitated infrastructure. It is too often assumed that users' rights start to count only after construction, when the scheme is to be handed over to users. This ignores the social and legal dimensions of the identification, design and construction phases and the steering role of external agencies in these matters (Benda-Beckmann et al. 1996).

Between 1979 and 1993, *Projet de développement de la riziculture dans la province de la Comoé*, or in short *Opération Riz* (OR), improved ten small rice valleys covering a total of 1,100 hectares in Burkina Faso, (formerly Upper Volta) West Africa. In each valley, or *bas-fond*, OR expropriated land and water rights and reallocated rights to the improved resources. OR intervened in a production and tenure system that was almost exclusively controlled by women: rice cultivation in the *bas-fonds*. Men controled production in the uplands.

Initially the project endowed men with resource rights. This gap between local reality and the agency's approach illustrates how projects can skew prevailing gender relations, as many authors have pointed out (Benda-Beckmann 1991; Carney 1988; Hanger and Morris 1973; van Koppen and Mahmud 1996). The project's usage of the alien concept of the unitary household[2] implied women's exclusion as rights holders, ignoring intra-household production relations and gendered division of resource rights. Only gradually did title criteria and allocation procedures crystallize in a way that better served productivity and equity. This chapter presents this learning process, to provide insight on ways to vest water rights in priority target groups and the effects on productivity, equity and poverty alleviation. In later schemes women producers received rights. The male local élite and other men refused to continue questioning women's existing power as the agency had done. This contradicts the common assumption that the male local élite and men in general have all the power and always use this power to appropriate substantial project benefits at the expense of women. The agency's gender approach, rather than local class and gender hierarchies, appears as the main explanatory factor for women's loss of land and water rights.

Field research in Burkina Faso studied OR activities through 1993. Interviews were conducted with female and male rice producers, male and female local authorities and administrative authorities,

Comoé Province

Map 3.1: Map of Burkina Faso: Comoé Province

project field officers and sociological, agronomic and technical project staff, project management, and expatriate assistants. Project archives at the project's head office in Banfora and at the office of the Delegation of the Commission of the European Community in Ouagadougou were also studied.[3]

The next section describes the social organization of production and resource tenure. The following section shows how during project identification and formulation, the external project initiators took important decisions regarding these resource rights. In the first two schemes, the project management imposed household-based allocation, with negative consequences for productivity and equity. In the next two schemes, field officers, local farmers, and village élites invented practices for producer-based allocation that respected former resource rights. These practices then crystallized to become the standard project procedure. The final section presents the lessons learned and implications for construction and rehabilitation projects elsewhere.

Local Socio-legal Organization of Production

Gendered Farming System

Agriculture is the main source of income in Comoé Province. As in much of sub-Saharan Africa, the farming system is dual, 'both husbands and wives are full-time farmers but their agricultural production is separate, although there is an intricate system of exchanges and interdependencies between the two production systems' (Ministère de l'Agriculture et d'Elevage 1991; Safiliou 1988).

Gently rolling hills divide the landscape into uplands and valleys. Rainfed maize, millet, sorghum, fonio, sesame, groundnuts and cotton grow on the uplands. Groundnuts and cotton are the most important cash crops. In upland agriculture, male household heads dominate land tenure and decision-making. They mobilize the labor of their women and children, and control the harvests. Women and young men cultivate small upland plots on their own account.

In the valleys, or *bas-fonds*, inland swamp rice is cultivated during the rainy season. Annual rainfall is 1,000–1,200 millimeters. These *bas-fonds* are depressions subject to shallow or deep flooding with runoff and rising subsoil water sources. This naturally available water cascades from field to field along the valley slopes. At plot level farmers open or close small earthen bunds and ditches to store or drain water.

Women manage more than four-fifths of all rice plots, and control the harvests. Younger women combine their own rice production with labor obligations on their husbands' upland fields. Older women of all ethnic groups dedicate themselves full-time to rice cultivation, which is their primary source of income. In this region, as in many West African societies, women in their mid-forties are 'liberated' from their obligations to work on their husbands' fields when their children are old enough to fulfill labor obligations. From then onwards they must provide for themselves.

Rice cultivation is labor-intensive. Women mobilize the labor of their unmarried and married daughters, mothers and maternal aunts, as well as unpaid and paid working groups and individual laborers. The labor contribution of male relatives to women's rice plots ranges from 0 to 3 per cent of total labor time required (van Koppen et al. 1987). Two-thirds or more of all women cultivate at least two plots (OR 1991). The total rice area cultivated per woman varies between 0.17 hectare and 0.34 hectare or more (OR 1991; C. Ouedraogo 1978; E. Ouedraogo 1990). There are also households in the villages surrounding the *bas-fonds* in which no woman cultivates rice. This proportion varies between one-third and three-quarters of the households (OR 1980c).[4]

Rice is consumed and sold. It is the preferred food for ceremonies, guests, and gifts. If men in Comoé need rice, they usually must buy it on the market or from their wives. In half of the *bas-fonds*, men own less than 1 per cent of the plots. In the other half, male ownership may reach 14 per cent. Most men who have rice plots are older land chiefs or family chiefs, who use the rice for their ceremonial obligations and for visitors. Their wives do the work. For the occasional man who cultivates rice himself, rice is a second crop. 'If one sees a man going down into the *bas-fonds*, one knows he has finished upland cropping.'

The only exceptions to this pattern of women dominating rice cultivation are some 50 men of the N'Gon Dioula living in a provincial town. In the 1940s, the scarcity of fertile dry lands in the locality pushed these men to cultivate rice. The women of this ethnic group are traders rather than farmers. Rice as a woman's crop is quite widespread in West Africa. It is reported among the riverine Gambian ethnic groups (Carney 1988; Dey 1984), the Kusasi of northeast Ghana (Dey 1984; Whitehead 1981) and the Senoufo in south Mali (Doucouré et al. 1996). Rice cultivation by both men and women occurs in other places such as Sierra Leone (Richards 1986).

Land and Water Tenure

As in most West African countries, land, whether uplands or *basfonds*, belongs to 'a large family, with many members who died, some who are alive and innumerable members to be born' (Bachelet 1982). The first clan that comes into a region assumes the authority of land chief (in French: *chef de terre*; in Dioula: *dugukolontigi*). Anyone can clear fallow upland or *bas-fond*, including newcomers, but the land chief concerned has to give formal permission for the use of this new land. Usually the chief grants permission because 'you cannot deny people to feed themselves and their children.' Use of land strengthens the users' claims on the land over the years and generations. However, these proprietors are not allowed to transfer or sell land to people outside the group.

Among most communities in the Comoé Province land inheritance is still matrilineal, so land stays within the mother's clan over the generations. In Dioula, this is called *basirafè*, which literally means 'in the way of the mother.' Sons inherit uplands from the brothers of their mothers, while daughters inherit their mothers' plots in the *bas-fonds*. Nowadays matrilineal inheritance is slowly changing towards patrilineal inheritance, especially in the uplands and among the Senoufo.

In local tenure, land chiefs have a certain authority on land issues, and in the *bas-fonds* on water issues as well. They permit newcomers to occupy unused land, but they cannot take land back or redistribute the land of these new cultivators, because by doing this 'one would go against the will of his father' (C. Ouedraogo 1978). Land chiefs represent the group's interests towards third parties and within the group. Land chiefs primarily function as administrators (Le Roy 1982: 55). They are informed about initial land clearance and later transfers over the generations of all families in their area. In these oral societies there is no registration other than in the memories of the land chief.

Land chiefs may intervene in land disputes, which are primarily inheritance issues. In the *bas-fonds* they may intervene in water disputes. Water management conflicts arise, for example, as neighboring plot owners enlarge their own cultivable area, encroaching bunds from both sides to the point of collapse. The need to stock water may conflict with a downstream neighbor's need for water. Downstream neighbors may suffer from excess drainage, or face the problem of sand and weeds floating in with the drained water. In land or water conflicts the parties try to find solutions themselves. This is promoted by the rule that if intervention is needed, both parties must pay, even the party judged to be in the right. Another rule stipulates that if there is no solution, the land will be taken away from both parties.

Land chiefs play a central role in several socio-religious customs, making sacrifices, giving the sign to start rice cultivation, and fixing totem days on which no one may use a hoe. As recognition of the authority of the land chief, the land users in his or her area give the chief some 10 per cent of their harvest. They also work on the chief's rice plots for one or two days a year.

Land chiefs governing uplands are always men. However, in the *bas-fonds*, women of the clan, married daughters, sisters or the daughters of the sisters of male land chiefs, often carry out the function of land-cum-water authority. In some villages a taboo may even prohibit male chiefs from going down into the *bas-fond* during the cropping season. 'This would cause inundation's and make cultivation impossible; a sacrifice would be needed to repair the damage,' reported a female chief. Only the slaughtering of animals is strictly forbidden for women chiefs, 'because women give life.' Male chiefs may also act as the main representative of the group for outsiders.

Women's Land Rights

As rice cultivators, women have land rights in the *bas-fonds*. Women obtain plots in three main ways: via maternal relatives, via the husband's family and via the land chief. These three modes of acquisition were present more or less equally for 177 studied plots of 80 women in four *bas-fonds* (E. Ouedraogo 1990; Somé 1991).

Mother's Lineage: Women's Ownership Rights

In this case the rice plot passes from mother to daughter without interference of male kin or land chiefs. 'You do not have money, so the rice plot is your treasure to give to your daughter.' Usually the eldest daughter who has worked longest with the mother inherits the plot, and she divides the land with her younger sisters. This inheritance system assures women of the labor force of their daughters, and assures daughters of their future land rights. Women keep these plots even in case of divorce, during illness when the plot is fallow for several years, or despite non-fulfillment of labor obligations on the land chief's field (Somé 1991). In some cases, a woman works an inherited rice plot as far off as 10 kilometers from her marital residence.

Husband's Lineage: Women's Use Rights

If there are no plots in the matriclan to inherit or if a woman marries far away, she can obtain a rice plot via her husband's family, especially when she is older. In these virilocal societies, women go to live with their husband at marriage. Not only must her husband agree to the land allocation but so must her husband's mother, sisters and aunts. Generally husbands prefer that their wives grow rice, rather than their sisters who 'are going to feed another family.' However, men do not support their young wives' land requests if women's own productive activities would jeopardize their labor obligations on men's upland fields. Most wives obtain life-long use rights, but in case of divorce they cannot take the plot to 'feed another man.' There are exceptions on this rule especially when the divorce is at the husband's initiative (Van Etten 1991).

Request to the Land Chief: Establishing New Rights

The growing population density increasingly leads women to ask the land chiefs for permission to occupy unused land in the *bas-fonds*. Women go themselves, or mothers negotiate with a land chief on behalf of their daughters (Van Etten 1991). In several villages and ethnic groups, husbands accompany their wives or brothers accompany their sisters, when they go to make a formal request for land. According to a male land chief 'nowadays women should not bother their husbands anymore and address themselves directly to the land chief.' Elsewhere, however, it may be impossible for women to obtain a plot without the husband's formal request to the land chief. This is the case in a village studied by Somé (1991). Here women need the approval of both their husbands and the male land chief. This particular land chief allocates at best one small plot because 'if women get more land they are not going to work properly on their husbands' fields.' Divorced women can hardly acquire land, and one of them complained that 'the land chief does not have as much confidence in women as he has in men.'

In principle, requested plots become the property of the clan who asked for it. In some parts of the Comoé Province, families can still vest new permanent rights to land acquired via the land chief. Elsewhere in the province, land chiefs increasingly prevent people from establishing longer term use rights by allocating land for only one to four years. The land chief quoted above takes plots back 'without even giving a valid reason.' All 20 women interviewed, including the wife of the land chief, were critical of the land chief saying that he took too long to answer a request for a plot of land, imposed the choice of site and asked for excessive crop shares. He considered land under his authority as private property, which he lent to others for strict compensation. This behavior led at least two of the women interviewed to prefer that the state come and manage the *bas-fond*, as in the neighboring schemes of OR (Somé 1991).

So, in local land and water tenure, women have had independent access to land in the *bas-fonds* without interference of husbands and land chiefs under matrilineal inheritance. These male authorities or relatives might even not know the location of the plot. Access to rice lands via in-laws requires the husband's mediation. This allows him partial control over his wife's labor. If the land chief mediates access to land, he may enrich himself and hamper women's timely cultivation and long term rights.

Project Identification and Formulation

Opération Riz aims to improve rice production and producers' incomes. It constructs two types of partial water control infrastructure. A central drain in the *bas-fond* provides quick evacuation of the floods, with storage and irrigation facilities for dryer periods in the cropping season. Bunds built along contour lines, together with soil leveling, improve spreading of peak floods, and water retention in drier periods. The project provides high yielding crop varieties, fertilizers, credit, and marketing facilities. Training is given on infrastructure operation and maintenance, and on cultivation practices. Users are organized in two-tier water users organizations, the 'Rice Organization Units' (*Unités de Groupement Rizicole*) and 'Rice Organizations' (*Groupements Rizicoles*).

The project began in January 1979, and as of 1998 was still continuing. Burkina Faso and the European Community provide financing. France and the Netherlands contributed technical assistance during the period studied, that is from 1979 to 1993. Table 3.1 shows the characteristics of the schemes built from 1980 to 1993.

Technical Planning

A French engineer carried out the technical identification and formulation study. He selected eight *bas-fonds* covering a total of 1,000 hectares, for project intervention during four years. His rough physical designs took only hydro-technical aspects into account (Faye 1978). He had little contact with local people (C. Ouedraogo 1978). The proposed technical plans were all incorporated in the official project document (DCCE 1978).

Legal Planning

Statutory law No. 29–63/AN of 1963 'allows the state to intervene at any time in the rural areas according to the criteria of its own development policy and ... to reserve for the state parts of the land object of improvements' (H. Ouedraogo 1986: 165–66). Under this law, state endorsement of the site selection implied the formal decision to expropriate all local resource rights in that area and reallocate the improved resources on a tenancy basis. On this legal basis, OR decided to expropriate the land and reallocate lifelong tenancy rights according to new plot boundaries.

Even after technical improvement, the hydrological conditions within a scheme would still differ substantially. The plot location, for example higher or lower on the slope, would strongly influence

Table 3.1: Characteristics of Schemes Constructed by OR from 1980–93

Number	Scheme	Size (hectares)	Year of Construction	Total Producers	Percentage Women	Title Criteria
1.	Tanion	188	'80–83	1,371	?	Household
2.	Dakoro	45	'80–81	235	56*	Household
3.	Moadougou	106	'83–84	339	96	Producer
4.	Niofila	101	'83	562	82	Producer
5.	Badini	130	'84	420	86	Producer
6.	Kawara	226	'84–85	1,142	93	Producer
7.	Sobara	54	'85–86	331	93	Producer
8.	Badini aval I	76	'91	390	79	Producer
9.	Badini aval II	124	'92	645	80	Producer
10.	Lomangara	40	'93	203	89	Producer
Total		1,090		5,638	85	

Source: DCCE 1990; OR 1997
Note: * Source Groesz 1992

the availability of water. In this natural environment, rights to a specific plot are land-cum-water rights. The new rights to the improved land would also be land-cum-water rights in that they link to the rights to operate the new infrastructure. Moreover, they would imply membership in the water users' organization and access to other services from the project.

Title Criteria

The physical design proposed uniform new plots of 0.25 hectare, without further justification. With one plot per beneficiary, the total number of beneficiaries was planned to be 4,000. The project document stated that these 4,000 plots would be allocated to 'the women who already cultivate rice in the *bas-fonds* that are to be improved' (DCCE 1978: 7). This decision was based upon the productivity and equity considerations expressed in the two sociological studies during the formulation phase (C. Ouedraogo 1978; *Société Africaine d'Etudes de Développement* [SAED] 1978).

The reports pointed out women's existing role in rice cultivation and the willingness women expressed to adopt new practices. The sociologists stated their doubts about the willingness of male family heads to spend their efforts in labor-intensive rice cropping when they already cultivated profitable cash crops like groundnuts (SAED 1978, 41). Allocation to women was expected to be the outcome 'if the mode of allocation would be left to the villagers' (SAED 1978: 42).

The SAED study tried to assess whether this technically defined number of 4,000 beneficiaries would match local reality. The only 'respectable' concepts and empirical data available at this time were 45 interviews with family heads and demographic data of the National Institute of Statistics and Demography of 1975. These data allowed estimating the number of women rice cultivators, the number of extended families and the number of nuclear families.

One scenario in the study adapted technology to social reality. It calculated that by reducing the plot size from 0.25 hectare to 0.15 hectare, all women rice cultivators could receive a plot. The other scenario adapted social reality to technology. It calculated that with allocation to the extended family, or the so-called family farm (*exploitation familiale*), there would be an excess of plots. If all nuclear families (*ménages*) received a plot, the 4,000 plots would not be sufficient. So the sociologists started with demographic concepts on the household and nuclear household. Then, they simply assumed that this demographic concept fully overlapped with the social organization of agricultural production by assuming some unitary family or nuclear family farm. As seen in the former section, this does not match reality in which household members control their own intra-household production unit, and do not cultivate 'as a family.' The next step was to consider this assumed unit of production as a legal entity, represented by one person, the male head. This representative would be vested with resource rights. They thus defined the legal entities that would fit an engineer's decision to design 4,000 plots of 0.25 hectare.

Procedures

The identification and formulation phases paid little attention to procedures to identify the 4,000 rice cultivators and to expropriate and reallocate the land-cum-water rights. The SAED study formulated a general recommendation that 'a committee elected by the population should be created to follow the project's progress, assist in plot allocation and mobilize people's participation' (SAED 1978: 44).

The rights that would be expropriated were ignored. According to the SAED, male land chiefs should be contacted because 'rice land is not inherited,' and '*bas-fonds* for rice cultivation are the 'property' of the land chief who allocates plots to those who request [it]' (SAED 1978: 20). The project document follows this biased interpretation (DCCE 1978: 3). The other sociological report recognized the existence of women's vested rights via matrilineal inheritance, but only in half the *bas-fonds*. Elsewhere it was stated that 'almost everywhere the management of rice plots is assured by men, who distribute to women, and by women who cultivate' (C. Ouedraogo 1978). This trivialized women's vested land rights. It ascribed forms of 'traditional' control over rice land to both husbands and male land chiefs which they never had in reality. Lack of time, lack of competence in agrarian law, and lack of contacts with women rather than with male authorities, contributed to this misconception.

Household-based Allocation

Local Forums and Expropriation

In 1979, OR started schemes A and B simultaneously. The emphasis was on construction. Expropriation of land and the mobilization of labor were the agenda at the interface between project officials and local people. This strongly influenced who was included in the communication network established by the project engineers, technicians and, male field workers for regular negotiations, or in other words, who was included in the local forum for decision-making on project matters. These were male land chiefs, village authorities, and administrative village representatives. The male élite assisted during further technical design and construction. They mobilized male construction laborers. Up to 200 laborers were mobilized by them per day and were well paid. They also managed maintenance funds.

This élite readily put women's rice lands at the disposal of OR. According to the women, the project and this élite had given them the idea that women would receive a plot on the day of distribution. In both schemes, the project also organized the women rice cultivators into extension groups of some 15 to 20 members. These women's networks were separate and only for agronomic tests on farmers' plots, agricultural demonstrations, and extension.

Allocation Procedures and Criteria

In 1980, the project's expatriate management, an engineer and agronomist, initiated demographic surveys 'to evaluate the total population concerned, to get an idea about the number of men and women cultivators in the *bas-fonds* in order to proceed to a more rational redistribution of plots after the construction' (OR 1980a: 7).' The questionnaires were addressed to the male household heads. They asked detailed questions on the agricultural activities of each active family member on the 'family' field and on individual fields, including rice plots, and asked whether 'the family' had rice land in the *bas-fond* to be improved or wanted to have an improved plot. The field officers also visited the nearby tax offices to copy the lists of all households (Groesz 1992: 20). In 1980, the project management commented as follows on the findings in scheme A:

An estimation of the population was made to know the number of families cultivating in the *bas-fond*. It was found that 191 families cultivate a plot in the *bas-fond*, and that 791 persons also cultivate an individual plot. On this basis, one could reasonably allocate 0.25 hectare to each family and 0.125 hectare to those who cultivate an individual plot (OR 1980b).

The project management interpreted the survey data wrongly by assuming that, in addition to the 791 cultivators (741 women and 50 men) in 191 families the 'family' as such would cultivate another 'family rice plot.' This imaginary production unit was sufficient basis to introduce a new category of potential title holders: male family heads. Just before cultivation in the new scheme would start in 1981, the project management made a decision on the title criteria that categorically excluded women:

Information and sensitization meetings on the land distribution and cultivation requirements have been held in scheme A in the presence of the village chiefs, land chiefs and authorities. Unanimously it was decided that one or more plots would be allocated to the family heads according to the number of active members (OR 1981b).

We proceeded to a survey of active members per family in order to guarantee an equitable allocation.... Contacts were laid with the individual farmers concerned. It appeared that they agreed with any form of distribution. Therefore, allocation will be based upon the number of active members (OR 1981a).

The 'individual farmers' were this class- and gender-biased forum, upon which the project management had depended to reach the construction targets. Evidently, these men endorsed a project's proposal which would provide them with a type of control over *bas-fond* land they had never had before. In addition to the wages for construction, men's cooperation with the project was rewarded with land titles.

Scheme B was smaller. The number of farmers (484), almost exclusively female rice cultivators, already outnumbered the number of plots foreseen (360) (OR 1980c). In this scheme, household-based allocation was explicitly justified as a solution to a distribution problem: only one plot per household would be allocated. This one plot would be allocated to the male head. So the project categorically ignored women's own demands for plots, because [*sic*] there were too many women for the land. At the same time, a new category of title holders was introduced: male household heads. Furthermore, among the 484 new plot holders were 75 men who had not had any relation with the scheme before, neither did any of the women in their households cultivate in the *bas-fond*, nor did they have a plot themselves (Groesz 1992: 47; OR 1982).

Land Distribution

In reality, on the day of land distribution no demographic list was used. Plots were allocated on the spot to any local man who presented himself. The project's field officer had formal responsibility, but the land chief of that portion of the *bas-fond* closely 'witnessed' the process. Although some less important land chiefs complained they had lost land, rumors prevailed that land chiefs gave land to their own family and 'even allocated plots to babies.'

Women in scheme A felt 'the men have betrayed us.' The two sisters of the most important land chief in scheme B commented as follows:

> Our brother, the village chief, and the people from the project said to us that there would be a list of the women wanting a plot. We thought that each woman would select her own plot. The day of the allocation we came too late, because we were not informed. Part of the plots had already been allocated. Then they said that the plots would not have been enough for all women, because many women would have wanted plots, including those who had no plot before. Therefore, they had decided to allocate land to the chiefs of the extended households. Our brother had already selected our plots. But he does not know the good sites and he selected a bad site. We could not do anything. The chiefs of the families divided the plots they had got. First they took a part for themselves, and the rest they divided in small parts for the older women in their family. We have never seen a list.

For years OR had no idea of the actual number of rice cultivators, and estimates in the reports fluctuated considerably. One report even claimed that the plots had been allocated 'in alphabetical order' (SNV 1984: 19). Only much later did OR recognize the effects of household-based allocation on productivity and equity.

Effects on Productivity and Equity

Three studies (Groesz 1992; OR 1987a, b; E. Ouedraogo 1990) showed that the earlier predictions about allocation to men had been valid. Both in scheme A (E. Ouedraogo 1990: 11–12) and scheme B men did not abandon their upland food and cash crops to start working in the schemes, but let their wives cultivate the land. However, their new rights enabled them to increase their control over the harvest.

> In scheme B ... plots were allocated to family heads. The latter have divided those among their women after taking a portion for themselves. Thus the women cultivate half or two-thirds of the plot for the man and they themselves have only a small portion which gives them very little in comparison with the charges they bear. The need to revise their status is felt. The women want to be owners of the plots they cultivate, which would motivate them much more (OR 1987b: 8).

Out of 95 plots in scheme B studied by Groesz (1992) 44 per cent belong to men. Only on 10 per cent of these plots did the men provide some labor, which was minimal. However, 94 per cent of the rice harvest from these plots is put in men's granaries, and so is under men's control. In one interview a woman strongly disagreed when her husband called his plot the 'family' plot, the expression introduced by OR, instead of the local expression 'man's plot' (Groesz 1992).

Among 58 women who worked in the rice fields in scheme B, Groesz (1992) reports that: 28 per cent had not received any land from their husbands but were obliged to cultivate his plot; 26 per cent received some land of their own from their husbands and 21 per cent from other relatives, especially brothers. Only 7 per cent, all widows, had succeeded in negotiating their own plots directly with OR on the second day of land distribution. But other widows had been less successful on that day, and did not obtain land via relatives either. Nineteen per cent of the women interviewed had inherited the plots in the decade since the allocation, or obtained their plot otherwise.

Allocation to men has strengthened men's control over rice plots vis-à-vis their sisters as rice land inheritors. All improved plots of men in scheme B would go to their sons. Mothers would still pass on their plots to both sons and daughters, but the preference for a son as inheritor increased, especially when the daughter's marital home was at some distance (Groesz 1992).

This increasing inequity and women's exploitation depressed production at the plot and scheme level. According to Groesz' (1992: 41) observations, women's plots were better maintained than men's. Although no further comparative data are available, it is plausible that the motivation for women to provide labor for rice, which they do not control, is limited to the minimal culturally defined labor obligations.

Although men as formal plot holders were responsible for infrastructure maintenance, most of them did nothing. The male village élite in schemes A, B and C used the maintenance fund to repair a school, a road, and a prefect's office. Money quickly disappeared (scheme B), or was said to have been used for the land chief's pilgrimage to Mecca (scheme C). Field officers could not retrieve the money, even with the prefect's help. Only in one part of scheme A, where a competent male leader was elected, was the money kept safe. Recently, political rivalries forced him to leave office.

Inadequacy of the infrastructure further frustrated mobilization for operation and maintenance of the earlier schemes. Overdimensioning of the central drain, inadequate leveling and earthen constructions unable to resist floods 'spoiled the *bas-fond*' to the point that cultivators wished the project 'to fill up this bad hole and leave.' One can wonder if women would have accepted such design had they had been involved in construction work (Dey 1984). In 1988 parts of scheme A were rehabilitated.

OR did not yet recognize these negative effects when it continued the next schemes. Other factors induced a change.

Change Towards Producer-based Allocation

In schemes C and D the project started with a similar bias towards the male élite. The crucial difference was that OR contacted the local authorities long before construction. Project field officers, local male authorities and women rice cultivators used this time to develop criteria and procedures that fitted production and equity considerations of both local people and the project.

Scheme C

Conforming to the earlier approach, OR contacted the male élite to inform them about construction plans and the proposed land alloca-tion to both men and women. This was in 1981, two years before construction was to start.

> In the meeting the land chiefs expressed their amazement that they had never been contacted for the construction of this infra-structure. The village authorities asked whether the survey would only concern the women cultivating in the *bas-fond*. Mr. ... answered that a survey would be held among both men and women which would allow allocating the plots more equitably (OR 1981c).

After several meetings between the project, prefect, male village chiefs and land chiefs, the local chiefs 'invited the women, because rice is a woman's affair,' as one male land chief explained. So the local forum expanded to include women. Many men still benefitted from the project's wage employment and the élite misused the maintenance funds, but women played a major role in the negotia-tions on the land-cum-water titles. A women leader summarized these negotiations as follows.

> The field officer registered all women per quarter. Some men asked for plots because the field officer said that if it succeeds everybody will have rice. But men do not like the work of rice. Some abandoned it and left it to their women. If you do not work you cannot take the benefits. During the land distribution women negotiated their own plots while men observed, because the women cultivate. For the collective maintenance work men help because everybody eats the rice.

No demographic survey and tax lists were compiled in this scheme. Although the project had allowed men to apply for land, only 4 per cent of the new title holders are male (DCCE 1990). The central drain has slightly improved water management. Women carry out the maintenance work.

Scheme D

In scheme D the first contacts were established in 1980, while construction was only to start in 1983. Immediately after the project began, the field officer took the initiative to contact the land chiefs and register the plot users. In two villages they were almost exclusively women, but the opposite was found for the N'Gon Dioula. This obvious and rapid inventory of rights holders made the demographic survey superfluous. Although such surveys were still conducted in scheme D, they were never used. Women participated during the land distribution in the *bas-fond*. After allocation of plots to former title holders, new producers obtained plots. The large majority of them were women.

The physical infrastructure changed from scheme D onwards because of the negative experiences with the central drains and irrigation facilities in the first two schemes. The project started to construct bunds according to the contour lines, which resemble the existing infrastructure. This technique hardly requires new centralized organization for scheme operation and maintenance. Costs per hectare are only one-eighth as high as for the former system (SNV 1984). The massive wage employment offered to men also disappeared.

The Crystallized Procedure

This new approach, developed by the field officers, village authorities and farmers, crystallized further in the three schemes that followed from 1984 to 1986. From 1987 onwards, OR gradually formulated these tested practices into a consistent procedure of expropriation, allocation of rights, and stipulation of obligations (*cahier des charges*). The first three schemes in the second phase of OR, from 1990 onwards, applied the procedures and made further refinements. Now this written project regulation structures the interactions between project and villagers, and between project, prefects, and other administrative authorities.

The elements are the following:

- **Information for all concerned.** Public meetings inform village authorities, administrative authorities and all current rice cultivators about the project's proposals for construction, expropriation of land, reallocation, rights and obligations for future plot holders and future project assistance for crop intensification, operation and maintenance and users' organization.
- **Registration of current plot holders.** Field officers inventory current plot holders in the field. They register name, sex, age, quarter or village, ethnic group, liberated or non-liberated woman, number of plots cultivated, and plots held in neighboring schemes that have already been improved. In the field or later, the names are checked with the land chiefs. In order to accommodate women's collaboration on one plot, OR increasingly accepts the individual registration of and plot allocation to all different workers on one plot, like mother and daughter.
- **Registration of new applicants.** Once all former plot holders can obtain plots, remaining plots are allocated to any new applicants. Interested candidates register with the field worker. OR decides on plot sizes, how many new requests can be satisfied, and so to what extent the 'have-nots' benefit from the intervention. The little information available shows that most new applicants are women. Male requests might come from the land chiefs. Where fertile uplands are scarce, other men are increasingly applying and cultivating rice (OR 1997).
- **Placement and land distribution.** Rice cultivators from the same quarter or village are placed in the same portion of the improved *bas-fond* for social cohesion. Further plot selection is at random. On the days of distribution, plots are distributed according to lists of rights holders and topographical maps. A committee of project staff and male village and administrative authorities supervises the process.

In general women rice cultivators accept this drastic change in land-cum-water rights, especially those who gain in the redistribution of land. However, former land holders still find it difficult to shift to another site, where others have buried their sacrifices, and to see their own claims on a site that were built over the generations vanish. Efforts to return to the old site immediately after land distribution, or whenever the new rights holder stops cultivating, are

reported occasionally. On the other hand, the crop shares that cultivators give to the land chiefs are decreasing. Evidently, land chiefs
regret this erosion of their traditional power (E. Ouedraogo 1990;
SAED 1988).

Before the project, most women cultivated two plots or more.
The project has a uniform rule that rice cultivators can benefit from
only one plot. It is appreciated that less time is needed for travel
(c.f. Groesz 1992). A disadvantage, however, is that cultivation risks
are not spread anymore. In order to avoid risks some cultivators
have started or continue to cultivate plots in unimproved local *bas-
fonds* (E. Ouedraogo 1990).

Conclusion

External support for irrigation infrastructure development does not
merely introduce technical expertise and funds for new physical
infrastructure. It also introduces title criteria and procedures which
steer negotiations on land and water rights. Once the moment of
handing-over the scheme to the users is reached, important stages
in the expropriation of former rights and the allocation of new
rights have already passed. The effects of different procedures on
production and equity under similar physical infrastructure became
clear in *Opération Riz*.

During the identification phase, design decisions for site selection
entailed the formal expropriation of all former claims on water
flows and land, without the claimants even being aware of this decision. The assumption that former cultivators would automatically
become the new title holders eased smooth project approval by the
funding organization. At the local level, negotiations took place in
forums composed of those whose participation was solicited by the
project. In the first schemes, the project solicited people's participation primarily for rapid construction. The male political élite and
well-paid construction workers were effective in arranging expropriation and construction. Initial promises that former rights holders
would become the new rights holders facilitated land expropriation.
However, the men in the local forums later endorsed the project's
proposal to allocate the new resources to men. Introducing the foreign concept of the unitary household, represented by a male household head, solved the problem of distribution of scarce resources by

simply excluding more than half the potential claimants along gender lines, and generational lines as well.

When the mode of people's participation was left to the participants, local forums emerged which took productivity and equity considerations into account. The forums included current and potential
producers. Existing rights were recognized. This procedure actually
took less time overall.

Male farmers in the Comoé Province in Burkina Faso have little
interest in rice cultivation and in land-cum-water rights in *bas-fonds*.
If they had been more interested, then women's loss of resource
rights and the shift from production for their own income to unpaid
labor provision on men's fields might have remained as unnoticed
here as it still is in many similar construction projects and titling
programs worldwide.[5] Nevertheless, the lessons learned by OR have
the following implications for construction projects elsewhere:

- Early inclusion of resource-poor women and men in the local
  forums, at the interface of the project and the community, is
  pivotal for their improved access to water and for poverty alleviation. In a sense, the first step to become a rights holder is to
  be a member of the forum which negotiates rights. Water users'
  organizations for operation and maintenance evolve out of
  these early forums. Agencies strongly steer the composition of
  these forums. So, inclusion of the resource-poor depends primarily on agency efforts. Incorporation of local registration
  arrangements may actually save time.
- Any technical design intrinsically entails the expropriation of
  water rights or land-cum-water rights (see Dey 1990). Expropriation and compensation need to be arranged in time, with
  effective participation of those who may lose existing rights.
  On the other hand, opportunities to include resource-poor
  smallholders without former access to water and irrigable land
  in the new arrangements can be considerable, provided these
  new potential rights holders participate in the local forums.
- Title criteria and other aspects of the new rights, and the procedures for implementation, need to have crystallized sufficiently
  before the investments in construction are carried out. This is
  even more evident in projects in which water rights are vested
  on the basis of participation in the investments in infrastructure,
  either by providing labor or cash for construction (Coward 1986).

- Negotiations on the legal dimensions of any designed infrastructure need to be public and transparent. Engineers should adapt the design to the desired water rights rather than implicitly imposing changes in water flows and rights by a so-called 'technical' design.
- The concept of the unitary household is inadequate to analyze agricultural production relations. Actual production units, and rights and obligations of individual producers within households, must be recognized. Most decision-making on infrastructure construction, operation and maintenance needs to be organized in multi-tiered organizations with forms of representation. However, the interests that male household heads represent may well go against the interests of other household members. Forms of representation should emerge from open discussions with both men and women. The same holds true for representation by authorities in class or ethnic hierarchies.

Intervention practitioners and policymakers increasingly recognize the need for users' participation and organization in construction projects. They should act on the understanding that negotiations on resource rights are at the heart of such participation, from the first plans for collective investments onwards.

Notes

1. I am grateful for the generous support of all contributors to the research. The responsibility for the opinions expressed is mine. The citations of the French project documents are all my translations.
2. The unitary model of the household assumes that all members of the household have common objectives and will pool all resources (see Alderman et al. 1995). There is a growing body of literature for Africa, Asia and Latin America which challenges this concept as a model to explain behavior (see Agarwal 1994; Deere and Léon 1997; Jones 1986; Quisumbing 1996; and Safiliou 1988).
3. For more details on the study, see van Koppen 1998.
4. Very few comparative data on land productivity of women's and men's rice plots are available. They do not indicate a systematic difference (CRPA, 1990; OR 1992).
5. For a review of how privatization and titling programs have often led to women losing control over land, particularly in Africa, see Lastarria-Cornhiel (1997).

References

Agarwal, Bina. 1994. *A field of one's own. Gender and land rights in South Asia.* Cambridge, U.K.: University Press.

Alderman, H., P. Chiappori, L. Haddad, J. Hoddinott, and **R. Kanbur.** 1995. Unitary versus collective models of the household: Is it time to shift the burden of proof? *The World Bank Research Observer* 10 (1) (February): 1–19.

Bachelet, Michel. 1982. Titulaires de droits fonciers coutumiers. Chapter 4 in *Encyclopédie Juridique de l'Afrique. Tome 5: Droit des biens*, ed. A. Bourgi. Abidjan: Les Nouvelles Editions Africaines.

Benda-Beckmann, Keebet von. 1991. Development, law and gender skewing: An examination of the impact of development on the socio-legal position of women in Indonesia, with special reference to the Minangkabau. In *The socio-legal position of women in changing society*, guest editors, LaPrairie and Els Baerends. *Journal of Legal Pluralism and Unofficial Law* 30&31: 87–120.

Benda-Beckmann, Keebet von, Mirjam de Bruijn, Han van Dijk, Gerti Hesseling, Barbara van Koppen and **Lyda Res.** 1996. Women's rights to land and water. Literature review. The Hague: The Special Program Women and Development, Department of International Cooperation, Ministry of Foreign Affairs, The Government of The Netherlands.

Carney, Judith. 1988. Struggles over land and crops in an irrigated rice scheme: The Gambia. In *Agriculture, women and land. The African experience*, ed. Jean Davison, 59–78. Boulder, Colo.: Westview Press.

Coward, Walter E., Jr. 1986. State and locality in Asian irrigation development: The property factor. In *Irrigation management in developing countries: Current issues and approaches*, ed. Ranjan K. Sampath and Kenneth C. Nobe, 491–508. Proceedings of an Invited Seminar Series sponsored by the International School for Agricultural and Resource Development (ISARD), Studies in Water and Policy Management, No. 8. Boulder, Colo. and London: Westview Press.

CPRA (Burkina Faso, Ministère de l'Agriculture et de l'Elevage. Direction des Etudes et de Planification, Centre Régional de Production Agropastorale de la Comoé et Projet Planification Rurale). 1990. Niveau d'application des thèmes techniques. En relation avec quelques charactéristiques socio-économiques des exploitation agricoles. Campagne 1989/1990. Rapport final. Banfora, Burkina Faso: Centre Régional de Production Agro-pastorale.

Deere, Carmen Diana, and **Magdalena Léon.** 1997. Women, land rights and the Latin American counter-reforms. Paper prepared for the presentation at the XX International Congress of the Latin American Studies Association (LASA), April 1979, Guadalajara, Mexico.

DCCE (Délégation de la Commission des Communautés Européennes en République de Haute Volta). 1978. Proposition de financement. Développement de la riziculture dans l'Organisme Régional de Développement (ORD) de la Comoé. 4ème Fonds Européen de Développement, Bruxelles.

———— 1990. Proposition de financement. Opération Riz (Phase II). 6ème Fonds Européen de Développement, Ouagadougou.

Dey, Jennie. 1984. Women in rice farming systems. Focus: Sub-Saharan Africa. Women in Agriculture 2. Women in Agricultural Production and Rural Development Service. Human Resources, Institutions and Agrarian Reform Division, Food and Agriculture Organization of the United Nations, Rome.

Dey, Jennie 1990. Gender issues in irrigation project design in Sub-Saharan Africa. Contribution to the International Workshop Design for Sustainable, Farmer-managed Irrigation Schemes in Sub-Saharan Africa. Department of Irrigation and Soil and Water Conservation, Wageningen Agricultural University, the Netherlands.

Doucouré, Defoer, Ahmadi and **De Groote.** 1996. Amélioration de la productivité du riz de bas-fond au Mali Sud. Papier présenté au séminaire sur l'aménagement des bas-fonds au Mali, Octobre 1996. Institut d'Economie Rurale Centre, Sikasso Mali. Régional de Recherche Agronomique-Sikasso, Equipe Systèmes de Production et Gestion de Ressources Naturelles et Programme Bas-Fonds.

Faye, Bernard. 1978. Expertise sur les aménagements rizicoles de l'Organisme Régional de Développement de la Comoé, Février 1978. Bureau pour le Développement de la Production Agricole, Paris.

Groesz, Nelleke. 1992. Dakoro, la plaine perdue? Een analyse van de motivatie van vrouwen om te investeren in de rijstproductie en de cultuurtechnische infrastructuur: Het project Opération Riz Comoé, Burkina Faso. MSc Thesis Department of Irrigation and Soil and Water Conservation, Wageningen Agricultural University, the Netherlands.

Hanger, Jane and **Jon Morris.** 1973. Women and the household economy. In *Mwea: An irrigated rice settlement in Kenya*, ed. Robert Chambers and Jon Morris, 209–37. Munchen: Weltforum Verlag.

Jones, Christine W. 1986. Intra-household bargaining in response to the introduction of new crops: A case study from North Cameroon. In *Understanding Africa's rural households and farming systems*, ed. Joyce L. Moock, 105–23. Boulder, Colo.: Westview Press.

Lastarria-Cornhiel, Susanna 1997. Impact of privatization on gender and property rights in Africa. *World Development* 25 (8): 1317–34.

Le Roy, Etienne. 1982. Caractères des droits fonciers coutumiers. Chapter 2 in *Encyclopédie Juridique de l'Afrique. Tome 5: Droit des biens*, ed. A. Bourgi, 39–47. Abidjan: Les Nouvelles Editions Africaines.

Ministère de l'Agriculture et d'Elevage. 1991. Participation de la femme dans les projets de développement agro-pastoral: Strategies et moyens d'integration. Rapport du séminaire national, July 1991. Ouagadougou.

OR (Opération Riz, Organisme Régional de Développement de la Comoé, Ministère du Développement Rural, République de Haute Volta). 1980a. Rapport annuel d'activités du 1er Avril 1979 au 31 Mars 1980 du Cellule Vulgarisation-Formation. Banfora, Burkina Faso.

———. 1980b. Rapport d'activities du 1er Janvier 1980 au 31 Mars 1980. Banfora, Burkina Faso.

———. 1980c. Rapport d'activities du 1er Mars 1980 au 30 Juin 1980. Banfora, Burkina Faso.

———. 1981a. Rapport trimestriel du 1er Janvier au 31 Mars 1981. Banfora, Burkina Faso.

———. 1981b. Rapport semestriel nr. 4, April 1981. Banfora, Burkina Faso.

———. 1981c. Proces Verbal de la Réunion à Moadougou le 21 Avril 1981. Banfora. Opération Riz, Organisme Régional de Développement de la Comoé, Ministère du Développement Rural, République de Haute Volta, et Bureau pour le Développement de la Production Agricole 1982. Opération Riz, Avril 1981–Mars 1982. Rapport de Synthèse. Banfora, Burkina Faso.

OR (Opération Riz, Organisme Régional de Développement de la Comoé, Ministère du Développement Rural, République de Haute Volta). 1982. Eugène Millogo. Rapport d'activités du mois d'avril 1982. Dakoro. Cited in: Groesz, Nelleke. 1992. Dakoro, la plaine perdue? Een analyse van de motivatie van vrouwen om te investeren in de rijstproductie en de cultuurtechnische infrastructuur: het project Opération Riz Comoé, Burkina Faso. MSc thesis Department of Irrigation and Soil and Water Conservation, Wageningen Agricultural University, The Netherlands.

OR (Opération Riz, Organisme Régional de Développement de la Comoé, Ministère de l'Agriculture et d'Elevage, Burkina Faso). 1987a. Evaluation de la participation des organisations des producteurs à l'exécution du projet. Rapport des journées de reflexion des 26 et 27 Février 1987. Banfora, Burkina Faso.

OR (Opération Riz, Organisme Régional de Développement de la Comoé, Ministère de l'Agriculture et d'Elevage, Burkina Faso). 1987b. Rapport des rencontres avec les structures organisationnelles sur l'évaluation de leur participation à l'exécution du Projet, Mars 1987. Banfora, Burkina Faso.

OR (Opération Riz, Centre Régional de Production Agro-pastorale de la Comoé, Ministère de l'Agriculture et d'Elevage). 1991. Recensement sur la situation foncière avant aménagement Lomangara, Badini Aval I et Badini Aval II. Banfora, Burkina Faso.

OR (Opération Riz, Projet de Développement de la Riziculture dans la Province de la Comoé). 1992. Suivi Agronomique Campagne 1991/1992. Analysed by N. Groesz and P. van Bronswijk. Unpublished.

OR (Opération Riz, Centre Régional de Production Agro-pastorale de la Comoé, Ministère de l'Agriculture et des Ressources Animales). 1997. Rapport Annuel Janvier–Décembre 1996. Banfora, Burkina Faso.

Ouedraogo, Crys. 1978. Etude sur les plaines aménagables de Banfora. Mars–Avril et Avril–May 1978. Délégation de la Commission de Communautés Européennes en République de Haute-Volta, Ouagadougou.

Ouedraogo, Edith. 1990. Etude socio-économique concernant les exploitants(es) touché(es) par le projet 'Opération Riz Comoé.' Projet Opération Riz Comoé, Ministère de l'Agriculture et de l'Elevage et Association Néerlandaise d'Assistance au Développement, Ouagadougou.

Ouedraogo, Hubert. 1986. Le droit de la terre et les enjeux du développement. Approche comparative des transformations foncières au Burkina (ex-Haute Volta). Thèse pour le Doctorat de 3e cycle en droit. Université de Paris, Pantheon-Sorbonne. Sciences Economiques-sciences humaines-sciences juridiques et politiques, Paris.

Quisumbing, Agnes. 1996. Male-female differences in agricultural productivity: Methodological issues and empirical evidence. *World Development* 24 (10): 1579–95.

Richards, Paul. 1986. *Coping with hunger.* London: Allen and Unwin.

Safiliou, Constantina. 1988. Farming systems and gender issues: Implications for agricultural training and projects. Ministry of Agriculture and Fisheries, The Netherlands and International Agricultural Center.

SAED (Société Africaine d'Etudes de Développement), République de la Haute Volta et Fonds Européen de Développement. 1978. Etudes socio-économiques des plaines rizicoles dans l'Organisme Régional de Développement de la Comoé. Juin 1978. Ouagadougou.

SAED (Société Africaine d'Etudes de Développement), Ministère de l'Agriculture et de l'Elevage, Projet Opération Riz. 1988. Etude socio-économique pour l'exécution de la phase II du projet 'Opération Riz Comoé.' Ouagadougou.

Somé, Jacquéline. 1991. Survey Women and land tenure in Gouéra. Banfora, Burkina Faso. Mimeo.

SNV Burkina Faso. 1984. SNV-project verslag over de inzetten bij het project Operation Riz 1979–1984. Ouagadougou.

van Etten, Jacobijn. 1991 Field notes, MSc Thesis. Department of Irrigation and Soil and Water Conservation, Wageningen Agricultural University, The Netherlands.

van Koppen, Barbara. 1998. *More jobs per drop: Targeting irrigation to poor women and men.* Amsterdam: Royal Tropical Institute.

van **Koppen, Barbara** and **Simeen Mahmud**. 1996. *Women and water-pumps: The impact of participation in irrigation groups on women's status*. London: Intermediate Technology Publications.

van **Koppen, Barbara, Jacquéline Somé, Awa Gnanou, Kadiatou Hié, Fatoumata Koné, Dogotié Sauratié, Marie Somda, Mariam Tiéba, Perpétue Traore, Dambo Zamba**. 1987. Champs personnels des femmes dans la Province de la Comoé, Etude socio-économique. Bureau Economie Familiale Rurale de l'ex Organisme Régional de Développement de la Comoé. Banfora, Burkina Faso.

Whitehead, Ann. 1981. I am hungry, mum: The politics of domestic budgeting. In *Of marriage and the market*, ed. Kate Young, Carol Wolkowitz, and Roslyn McCullagh, 88–111. Whitstable, UK: CSE Books.

4

Negotiating Seasonal Water Allocation Rules in Kirindi Oya, Sri Lanka

JEFFREY D. BREWER

This case examines how local allocation rules were negotiated in the government-managed Kirindi Oya system in Sri Lanka. The system encompasses an ancient tank irrigation system with established rights, and a new irrigation system with recent settlers. The system uses negotiated seasonal planning, an allocation system suited to irrigation systems with storage capacity, a single dominant crop, and variable water supplies. From 1991 to 1994, major and dramatic conflicts—including physical assaults, damage to the system, threats of court cases, and interventions by politicians—arose over water allocation. Attempts to solve these conflicts led to the development of more acceptable local allocation rules. Analysis of this process allows identification of key structural features that make rules acceptable to farmers.

Introduction

Seasonal and annual fluctuations in water supplies make allocation of irrigation water problematic, and aggravate the potential for conflicts inherent in the management of any natural resource. One means for allocating irrigation water found in South Asia is negotiated seasonal planning. In seasonal planning for irrigation, farmers and officials meet before every season to allocate the available water to desired or assigned crops. Normally when water is in short supply, it is allocated to only part of the irrigation command area. Seasonal planning allocation has been well documented in Sri Lanka for farmer-managed systems (Leach 1961) and for government managed systems (Murray-Rust 1983). Similar negotiated systems are found in Tamil Nadu (Brewer et al. 1997; Sakthivadivel et al. 1995) and elsewhere in southern India. Virtually all of these irrigation systems are storage systems dominated by rice.

Seasonal planning would seem to be sensible for systems with storage facilities where the water supply is quite variable, as in Sri Lanka and southern India, and where it is dominated by a single crop. Managers and farmers can adjust the area to be irrigated to fit the water supply to ensure that enough water will be available for the preferred crop. However, adjustment of irrigated area means that some farmers do not get water for their land. Seasonal planning systems thus have a built-in potential for conflict.

This paper follows Uphoff (1986) in the use of the term 'allocation' to refer to the assignment of rights to use water. It distinguishes allocation from the actual delivery of water to users. Conflicts over irrigation matters are so common that Uphoff (1986) and Coward (1980) define conflict management as a fundamental aspect of irrigation management. However, most reported conflicts are not over allocations but rather over in-season deliveries (e.g., de los Reyes 1982; Merrey 1986; Wade 1987; and many others). Conflicts over allocations tend to be matters for court cases at long intervals rather than direct confrontations every season. Conflicts over allocations are most likely to occur when fundamental conditions change.

Many irrigation systems have successfully operated for many years under seasonal planning allocation without serious disruption. In these areas, equity is an important value; in a single crop system equity is often interpreted as availability of equal amounts of water for each piece of land. To provide equity, many groups have invented means of ensuring that all farmers get water. One such means is a land tenure system with landholdings distributed so that all are affected equally when part of the command is cut off (e.g., Leach 1961). Other means include seasonal reallocation of land so that all farmers get a portion within the irrigated area (e.g., de Jong 1989),

and allocation of water to farmers in different years (e.g., Palanisami 1984).

Seasonal planning does not necessarily provide equity. For example, prior to 1984 in the Gal Oya Left Bank system in Sri Lanka,
tail-end farmers rarely got water in the drier (*yala*) season (Murray-
Rust 1983). A similar situation holds today in the Sathanur system
in Tamil Nadu (Sakthivadivel et al. 1995). In some south Indian irrigation systems, differences in water availability are legally recognized by the classification of land into double cropped land, single
cropped land, and other land types. These situations may not cause
conflicts if those who get poorer irrigation service accept the poorer
service because of lesser prior investment or for other reasons.
Thus, for allocation through seasonal planning, prevention of conflict requires negotiation of local allocation rules for dealing with
water shortages. Negotiation processes are quite varied and are
likely to differ significantly between farmer-managed and government-
managed irrigation systems.

The data in this paper come from studies carried out by the International Irrigation Management Institute (IIMI) in Kirindi Oya
between 1986 and 1994.[1] Most important for the present study was
an Asian Development Bank-funded participatory action research
study (IIMI 1995a) carried out between 1991 and 1994 by IIMI in
collaboration with government agencies. A goal of the participatory
action research was to devise appropriate allocation rules, but
events overtook plans and IIMI intervention played only a small
part in negotiating an acceptable system of allocation rules.

This paper focuses on the negotiations; Brewer et al. (1993) and
IIMI (1995a) discuss the underlying technical issues more thoroughly.
The next section provides background information on the Kirindi
Oya irrigation system. A detailed description of negotiation and
conflict over water allocation from 1991 to 1994 follows. Key elements
which contributed to acceptability of new allocation rules are then
analyzed, along with a brief discussion of more general implications.

The Kirindi Oya Irrigation System

Basic Features

The Kirindi Oya System is a partly new irrigation system fed from
the Kirindi Oya (*oya* means 'river' in Sinhala) in southeastern Sri

Lanka (Map 4.1). The system is the largest in the Kirindi Oya basin, and the furthest downstream. Elsewhere in the basin are several smaller irrigation systems, and some upstream farmers pump from the river. The area receives about 1,000 mm of rain annually. There are two farming seasons: the *maha* season from October through February when the northeast monsoon brings heavy rains providing about 70 per cent of annual rainfall, and the *yala* season from April through August when the southwest monsoon brings light rains.

The core of the Kirindi Oya system (Map 4.2) is the Ellegala system serving a command of 10,000 acres. During the 19th century, the Ellegala Diversion was constructed in the Kirindi Oya to feed five ancient and previously independent tanks (small reservoirs). All of Ellegala is planted with rice during the *maha* season. In the past, only a portion of Ellegala could be planted with paddy during the *yala* season; the rest was fallowed or planted with other crops. The average annual cropping intensity in Ellegala is estimated to have been 150 per cent before the construction of the Kirindi Oya system.

The present Kirindi Oya system was created by damming the Kirindi Oya above the Ellegala Diversion to form the Lunugamvehera Reservoir. The Right Bank and Left Bank Main Canals from the reservoir irrigate 13,000 acres of New Areas upstream of the Ellegala tanks; two-thirds of New Areas are in the Right Bank. About 5,100 farming families have been settled in the New Areas. Construction of the Kirindi Oya system took place from 1978 through 1990. The Lunugamvehera Reservoir and the main canals were completed in 1986; the first water issues from the reservoir were made in April 1986. Water for Ellegala is now conveyed through a feeder channel from the Left Bank Main Canal to the Kirindi Oya where it is picked up by the Ellegala Diversion.

Water Shortage

Kirindi Oya is a water short system. The initial appraisal estimated that the average annual inflow to the reservoir would be 318,000 acre-feet, enough for a 200 per cent annual cropping intensity for 20,000 acres of New Areas in addition to 10,000 acres in the Ellegala system (ADB 1977). A 1986 restudy of streamflow data lowered the estimate to 255,000 acre-feet; this lowered the expected annual cropping intensity to 170 per cent (ADB 1986). Using data on actual inflows to 1993, IIMI's analysis showed that annual inflow

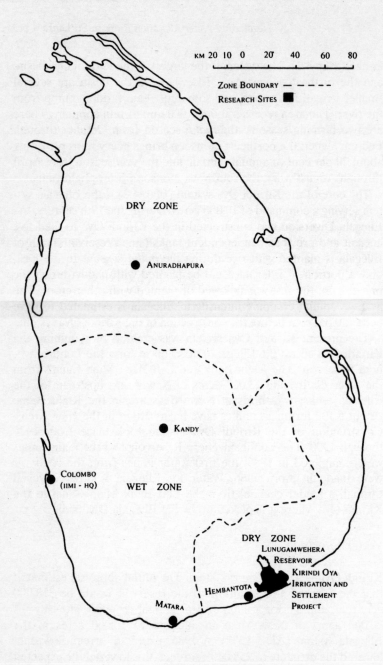

KM 20 10 0 20 40 60 80

ZONE BOUNDARY — — —
RESEARCH SITES ■

DRY ZONE

● ANURADHAPURA

● KANDY

● COLOMBO
(IIMI - HQ)

WET ZONE

DRY ZONE
Lunugamwehera
Reservoir
KIRINDI OYA
IRRIGATION AND
SETTLEMENT
PROJECT

HEMBANTOTA ●

MATARA ●

Map 4.1: Kirindi Oya System

averaged only 234,800 acre-feet. Also, IIMI calculated that the 75 per cent probable annual inflow was 136,400 acre-feet (IIMI 1995a), indicating great variability. The water shortage is partially explained by rainfall lower than the long-term averages (IIMI 1995b). Other water resource development within the basin has also contributed to the shortages. This water shortage led to the abandonment of much of the planned development; only 13,000 of the planned 20,000 acres of New Areas were developed.

Even in the 1970s, the planners of the Kirindi Oya system were aware that there would not be enough water for irrigation if the whole system was planted with paddy. The plans assumed that significant areas would be planted with other, less water-loving crops. Paddy was and is the farmers' preferred crop under irrigation because of an assured market and relatively low risk. Non-paddy crops suited to Kirindi Oya include low-value, relatively low-risk crops such as mung beans and cowpeas, and high-value, high-risk crops such as chillies and onions.

Participatory Reforms in Operation and Maintenance

The central government Irrigation Department planned and oversaw construction of the Kirindi Oya system. Until 1990, Irrigation Department personnel operated and maintained the system down to the tertiary canals ('field channels'). Water distribution and maintenance in the tertiary canals was and is the collective responsibility of the farmers. Research on earlier irrigation management in the Kirindi Oya scheme, even before its expansion, painted a picture of rampant water theft, inefficient water management, and failure to develop effective rules to organize irrigation (Harriss 1977, cited in Ostrom 1990).

Since 1978, Sri Lanka has experimented with giving farmers greater responsibilities in irrigation management (Brewer 1994; Uphoff 1992). In 1984, a participatory management program was created for larger irrigation schemes. Under this program, farmer organizations were created for secondary canal commands (usually 200–300 acres) and a Project Management Committee (PMC) was created for each scheme. A PMC consists of farmer representatives from the farmer organizations and officials from the relevant government agencies. Kirindi Oya was brought into the participatory management program in 1986. Fifty-nine farmer organizations were created. Ellegala and the New Areas were considered separate schemes, hence two PMCs were created: one for Ellegala and one for the New Areas. Since 1990, operation and maintenance of most secondary canals ('distributary channels') have been formally handed over to the farmer organizations.

Water Allocation Principles and Mechanisms

In Sri Lanka, all surface water legally belongs to the government. Water is allocated to government irrigation systems by building the system. Farmers often take water for irrigation by building tanks, such as the five Ellegala tanks, or by digging wells. No permission is required and there is little attempt to plan water resources development. Most farmer-built tanks are tacitly or officially recognized by the government as public irrigation systems.

There are no commonly accepted legal or customary 'water rights' for apportioning water *between* irrigation systems in Sri Lanka. No law exists for this purpose other than a simple assignment of all water rights to the government. Even in the well-known 'tank cascades' where several small-farmer built and operated systems share a single source of water (Madduma-Bandara 1985) there are no recognized rules for division of the water among the tanks (Samad 1995; see also Jinapala et al. 1996).

By both custom and law, irrigation water is allocated to areas within irrigation commands through seasonal planning. Until 1994, the law specified that seasonal decisions were to be made by 'cultivation meetings' of all farmers within the command. Local administrative officials called meetings prior to each season. In Kirindi Oya, because there were too many farmers (over 9,000 when fully developed) for a single meeting, seven cultivation meetings were called each season: one for each of the five Ellegala tanks plus one each for the Right and Left Banks in the New Areas.

Underlying water allocation for irrigation are two generally recognized principles. The first is that of equity of water distribution. Equity is defined as ensuring that every farmer gets water in proportion to landholding within the command. Second, the Irrigation Department and other government officials give priority to standing crops over those not yet planted.

Under the participatory management approach, seasonal planning is a primary duty of the PMC for each scheme. However, until 1994, to reconcile PMC seasonal planning with the law, cultivation meetings were called to ratify PMC decisions. In Kirindi Oya, however, neither the cultivation meetings nor the PMCs dealt with the whole of Kirindi Oya, so they could not allocate water among the various subsystems. Consequently, until 1991, neither played a part in the seasonal allocation process. From *yala* 1986 through *yala* 1991, seasonal allocation decisions were made by the Project Coordinating Committee, a government committee created to coordinate the various activities of the Kirindi Oya construction and settlement project. There were no farmer members in this committee.

Water Allocations: 1986–91

When the Kirindi Oya system was planned, Ellegala farmers were assured that their access to irrigation water would not be impaired. This guarantee appears in vague form in project documents and was given orally by government officials. The existence of this guarantee was publicly recognized by all officials and by the Ellegala farmers, although the exact details were unclear. Many Ellegala farmers claimed that they were guaranteed water for 200 per cent cropping intensity because the original project plan projected 200 per cent cropping intensity for the whole scheme.

Map 4.2 shows the areas allocated water for each season from *yala* 1986 through *maha* 1993–94. This clearly shows that Ellegala was favored. Till 1991, all of Ellegala was allocated water for paddy crops every season except *yala* 1987, when there was an extreme water shortage (Merrey and Somaratne 1988). From *maha* 1986–87 through *yala* 1991, Ellegala had an average annual cropping intensity of 183 per cent.

On the other hand, until 1991, water was allocated to the whole of the New Areas during three seasons only: *maha* 1987–88, *maha* 1988–89, and *maha* 1990–91. In *maha* 1990–91, a portion was allocated water for non-paddy crops rather than paddy. From *maha* 1986–87 through *yala* 1991, the New Areas were allocated water for an average annual cropping intensity of only 95 per cent (the potential command increased from 10,600 acres to 12,200 acres before the 1989 season). Within the New Areas, rough equity was maintained by rotating *maha* water allocations among different parts.

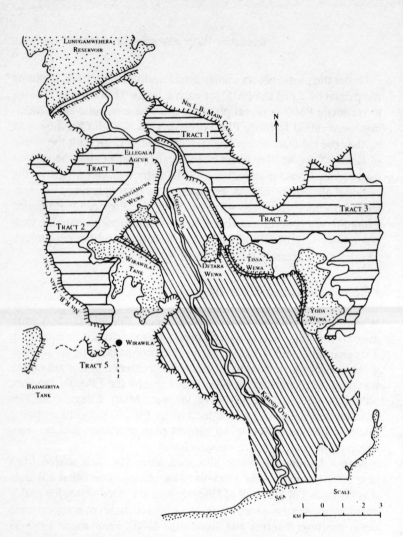

KEY

 FLAT ALLUVIAL PLAIN (EIS) OLD

UNDULATING RESIDUAL PLAIN (NIS) NEW

⊔⊔⊔⊔⊔ MAIN CANAL

⊔⊔⊔⊔⊔ BRANCH CANAL

TANK/RESERVOIR

- - - - - TRACT BOUNDARY

**Map 4.2: Water Allocations in Kirindi Oya: 1986–94
(area in acres)**

Surprisingly, there were no major conflicts among farmers between 1986 and 1991 despite the inequitable allocations. On the one hand, government authorities tacitly recognized Ellegala's claimed priority, on the other, the New Area farmers were not organized to protect their interests. One result was that many New Area farmers illegally rented out or abandoned their allotments; in some areas, over half of the allotments were worked by persons other than the official settlers.

Negotiation and Conflict Over Water Allocation: 1991–94

Recognition of Need for New Water Allocation Rules

By 1990, the need for improved water allocation practices was apparent to most farmers and concerned government officials. Government officials desired greater equity. The government wanted to provide New Area farmers with opportunities to cultivate in order to ensure a good return on its investment in the system (Nijman 1992). Despite considerable government efforts, relatively few farmers had adopted non-paddy crops. It was felt that a better seasonal allocation strategy was necessary to promote non-paddy crops. Also, IIMI's (1990) report on Kirindi Oya identified the need for improved allocations. These various concerns drove attempts by the government to revise the allocation rules.

The Project Management Committee: Maha 1991–92

Based on a recommendation from IIMI, in May 1991 the government combined the two existing PMCs into one and created three subproject committees, one for Ellegala, one for the Right Bank, and one for the Left Bank, to support the PMC. The new PMC was recognized, at least by most agency officers, as the legitimate decision-making body for seasonal allocations.

The single PMC was welcomed by the New Area farmers, since for the first time, it gave them a voice in seasonal allocations. Ellegala farmers were suspicious that it would curtail the priority access to water that they had enjoyed since 1986. At first, Ellegala farmer representatives attended the PMC meetings only as observers.

In its first season, the new PMC made an important innovation. In September 1991, before the *maha* season began, the PMC allocated water to all of Ellegala but allocated water only to portions of the New Areas. *Maha* rains were considerably heavier than expected and in December 1991 the PMC allocated water for paddy to the portions of the New Areas not previously allocated water. Actual cultivation began in these areas in December and January and extended into May; that is, into the *yala* season. The late *maha* cultivation thus took some portion of the *yala* inflow.

Crop Failure in Ellegala: Yala 1992

Ellegala farmers realized that late *maha* cultivation could deprive them of water for *yala* cultivation. The Ellegala farmer representatives began to take direct part in PMC deliberations to protect their interests. Beginning in January 1992, Ellegala farmer representatives consistently requested allocation of water for paddy for all Ellegala in *yala* 1992.

Maha rains stopped in early January 1992 and no rain fell in February or March. By March, people all over Sri Lanka were talking about drought. In 1990, in response to IIMI's studies, the government had appointed a subcommittee consisting of senior officers from the Irrigation Department, the Irrigation Management Division, IIMI, and other agencies, to propose a technically sound allocation policy. The subcommittee made its first recommendations in January 1992. The PMC first took up *yala* water allocations in its meeting in March. Because of differences of opinion about water availability, decisions were postponed for the beginning of the rains.

Following the beginning of the rains in mid-April, the PMC held a series of meetings at which the Irrigation Department consistently warned about water shortages in view of the lack of rain and the late *maha* cultivation. When the April PMC meeting failed to allocate water to all of Ellegala, a large group of Ellegala farmers held a rowdy demonstration at the office of the chief resident engineer demanding the immediate issue of water. As a result, the PMC decided, over the objections of Irrigation Department officials, to issue water for paddy to all of Ellegala. Irrigation Department officers explained the risks to meetings of farmers in the areas where cultivation had not already begun. Some farmers said later that they were persuaded that the risks were too high, but the Farmer Representatives pushed them to cultivate in order to maintain their priority for water allocations during *yala*.

In early May, the late *maha* crops in the New Areas were completed successfully. However, *yala* rains were lighter than usual and failed totally in mid-June. The issuing of water was stopped in early July to protect domestic water supplies. Ellegala farmers protested through political channels and got another 3,000 acre-feet of water released, but releases were stopped for good in late July. The result was a loss of about three-fourths of Ellegala's 1992 *yala* crop to drought. One consequence was that there was wholesale change in the farmer representatives from Ellegala.

Conflicts in the New Areas: Maha 1992–93

In May and June 1992, farmer representatives rejected the new allocation rules earlier proposed by the government-appointed subcommittee. In June, they offered an alternative set of proposals aimed at allowing cultivation in all of Kirindi Oya every season. These proposals were considered unrealistic by specialists. To reconcile the subcommittee proposals and the farmer proposals, a technical committee of local level government officials and IIMI researchers was constituted. The technical committee's first recommendations were presented to the PMC in July 1992. Despite objections, the PMC accepted the recommendations. Under the plan, it was decided that all of the Left Bank and parts of the Right Bank were to be authorized water for non-paddy crops rather than paddy.

From August onwards, opposition to the seasonal plan grew among farmers in the tracts allocated water for non-paddy crops. During August, an 'independent' farmers' organization was formed in the Left Bank and part of the Right Bank with the support of a local government officer, the divisional secretary. He chose to act as the leader of a faction of the farmers, apparently to increase his influence among those farmers. At the September PMC meeting, a farmer representative from the Left Bank complained that local officials answerable to the divisional secretary were removing barbed wire and fence posts from the area. Since fences are essential to protect non-paddy crops from animal incursions, this action was an attempt to prevent farmers from cultivating non-paddy crops. In early October, a meeting of farmers and officers with the central government secretary dealing with irrigation failed to resolve the problems. Most cultivation meetings in October accepted the PMC plan, but the Left Bank cultivation meeting ended without a formal decision because of opposition to non-paddy crops. Despite the opposition, the November PMC meeting finalized allocations as previously proposed.

Those opposed to the allocation plan then turned to politicians. The 'independent' farmer organization persuaded a local politician to appeal personally to the minister for irrigation. A PMC meeting was convened in late November on the minister's orders. At the meeting, the farmer representatives from the protesting areas requested water for paddy, but were opposed by other farmer representatives so the PMC made no changes in the allocations.

A meeting of a Member of Parliament (MP) from the district and the leaders of the 'independent' farmer organization then named a delegation of three farmers to meet with the minister for irrigation. At this meeting, some Left Bank farmers who supported the planting of non-paddy crops were physically assaulted. The delegation met with the minister in the capital during the first week of December. The minister agreed to issue water for paddy to the Left Bank and part of the Right Bank on 20 December if plowing was completed by that date. Very little plowing was completed by 20 December. When the Irrigation Department tried to deliver water only to the plowed fields, they were harassed and threatened by angry farmers. Water delivery to Ellegala was blocked by farmers to get more for the Left Bank tracts and other gates and regulators were taken over by farmers.

The MP called a meeting of official farmer representatives and representatives from the 'independent' farmer organization on 23 December. Those at the meeting demanded water for paddy from 26 December. Selected farmer representatives and the chief resident engineer of the Irrigation Department met the minister for irrigation on 25 December. On the engineer's advice, the minister ordered the issue of water for paddy for the protesting areas from 27 December. Water was released on that date.

Non-paddy crops had been planted in over at least 650 acres of land; in most cases, these crops were simply plowed under. Many farmers later claimed and received compensation from the government for the loss of these crops. Paddy was planted in the protesting areas by the end of January and harvested in May. The *maha* paddy crops all turned out well. However, the *maha* season extended into May and required the use of inflow from *yala* rainfall.

Non-paddy Crops in Ellegala: Yala 1993

In January 1993, the technical committee analyzed probable water supplies and concluded that there would not be enough water for 100 per cent paddy in Ellegala, let alone in the New Areas, partly because *yala* inflow was needed for the late *maha* paddy crops in the New Areas. The technical committee then met with Ellegala farmers to inform them of the water shortage so they could make an informed allocation decision. The PMC considered the *yala* plan in March. The Ellegala PMC representatives requested that the Irrigation Department officers explain the situation to the Ellegala farmers.

At a meeting of the Ellegala farmer representatives, Irrigation Department officials explained that the estimated water available for Ellegala during *yala* would—after subtracting water reserved for late *maha* paddy cultivation and *yala* non-paddy crop cultivation in the New Areas—be enough for no more than 4,450 acres of paddy or for 2,370 acres of paddy and 6,175 acres of non-paddy crops (for a total of 8,545 acres). Farmer representatives from two tanks argued that before the construction of the Lunugamvehera Reservoir their tanks had had priority in times of scarcity and therefore their tanks should have water for paddy. Supported by Irrigation Department officials, other farmer representatives forced agreement that water should be shared among the five tanks in proportion to their command areas. The meeting accepted the Irrigation Department's proposed plan for paddy and non-paddy crops. The farmer representatives then discussed with the farmers under each tank which portions should be planted with paddy, which with non-paddy crops, and which fallowed. Because of numerous disagreements among the farmers, the plan was not completed until the first week of May.

During this season, the area under paddy exceeded the planned area by only 10 per cent, but only 65 per cent of the area allocated water for non-paddy crops was actually planted. The paddy turned out well but the non-paddy crops did not, largely because late planting led to pest and disease problems. At the end of the season, however, the Lunugamvehera Reservoir was effectively empty.

The seasonal allocation process in *yala* 1993 stood in sharp contrast to the process in *yala* 1992. Not only was the decision very different—it was the first time that there was agreement on widespread planting of non-paddy crops—but also the process itself was less confrontational and problematic. In large part this was a result of lessons learned in 1992; one was that the farmers should trust the Irrigation Department's predictions of water availability.

During the season, several prominent Ellegala farmers continued to argue that Ellegala should have rights to water for two full paddy crops per year. The Ellegala Subproject Committee consulted a lawyer about suing the government to establish those rights but then dropped the matter when they concluded that they would not be able to get government support for their claim.

Resistance to Political Interventions: Maha 1993–94

The events of *maha* 1992–93 in Kirindi Oya—including the claim for damages to non-paddy crop crops—generated a great deal of concern both locally and at the level of the central government. The national Parliament appointed two MPs to investigate the issue. The MPs held public meetings with farmer representatives and local officials: at one meeting, the farmer representatives directly asked the MPs not to interfere, but to leave the seasonal decisions to the PMC.

The technical committee developed revised recommendations to deal with problems such as those that arose during *maha* 1992–93. The major revision was the adoption of the idea that it would be assumed at the beginning of the season that the season would be a 'dry' *maha* season for which only two-thirds of the New Areas would get water for paddy while the remaining third would get water for non-paddy crops. If, by the end of December rains were good, the PMC could then authorize late *maha* paddy cultivation in the area previously authorized water for non-paddy crops. These recommendations were presented to a meeting of farmers in July 1993.

After the meeting, the proposed seasonal plan was discussed by various groups of farmers, including a meeting held by the divisional secretary who had led opposition during the preceding year. Opposition to the technical committee's proposals was channeled through the legally recognized farmer organizations rather than through the independent farmer organization of the preceding year, showing that those opposed felt they would be more effective working through the government-recognized structure. A group of New Area farmers developed two proposals to permit cultivation of the whole of Kirindi Oya. With help, these farmers worked out detailed calculations of water requirements to show that these plans would be feasible. These proposals were written up in a report and signed by the president of the Right Bank Subproject Committee.

At the regular September PMC meeting, both the technical committee plan and the Right Bank Subproject Committee proposals were discussed. Because of the differences, the PMC did not decide on a seasonal plan. Two MPs from the area attended this meeting, the first such direct interest by politicians. At a second PMC meeting a few days later, the technical committee's proposal was adopted. The technical committee plan required initial allocation of water for rainfed non-paddy crops in one zone in the New Areas. The PMC decided that the Left Bank should plant rainfed non-paddy crops. A decision about allocating water for a late *maha* paddy crop in that area would be made in January.

After this meeting, some Left Bank farmers appealed to the minister for agriculture; not to the minister for irrigation who had been burned by his intervention the previous year. The minister for agriculture requested the director of irrigation to intervene; the director of irrigation asked for a special PMC meeting in November. At the meeting, an early issue of water to this area for paddy was opposed by everyone except one farmer representative from the Left Bank. Another farmer representative from the Left Bank said that issuing water for paddy would damage the non-paddy crops planted in his tract. The PMC then sent a letter to the director of irrigation opposing the early issue of water and noting that the water situation would be reviewed in January. In addition, the letter stated that the decision should be left to the PMC.

Rains were heavy and by the December PMC meeting it was apparent that there would be water for a late *maha* paddy crop in the Left Bank. At the December meeting, the Irrigation Department announced that several persons, including a prominent municipal counselor from the Left Bank, had requested the immediate issue of water for paddy to the Left Bank. The counselor had encouraged farmers in part of the Left Bank to plant paddy with the rains to strengthen their claim to water issues for paddy. At the PMC meeting, the farmer representatives from the Left Bank said that they preferred delaying water issues for paddy until the harvest of the non-paddy crops. The PMC decided that water for a late *maha* paddy crop would be issued on 15 February.

The municipal counselor, later joined by two monks and eight farmers, then went on a hunger strike at the Lunugamvehera Dam. He demanded that: (*a*) the Left Bank be given the same priority rights as Ellegala, (*b*) water for paddy be issued immediately to the Left Bank, and (*c*) the leaders of the farmer organizations be changed. He got little support because farmers knew they would get water for paddy anyway. The fast ended two days later, after a visit from an MP.

Demands from politicians led to a series of PMC meetings in January. These politicians apparently hoped to establish that they had the power to change the PMC decisions, thus making themselves local power brokers. At the first meeting, two MPs asked that the date of water issue to the Left Bank be moved forward but farmer representatives opposed the request to prevent damage to the non-paddy crops. At the second, another MP asked for the immediate issue of water for paddy to the Left Bank; the PMC again did not agree. At another PMC meeting, the municipal counselor requested that water be issued on 20 January to the Left Bank. This request was opposed by some Left Bank farmer representatives and was turned down.

A cultivation meeting for the Left Bank was held on 24 January. At the meeting, farmers from one portion of the Left Bank unanimously asked for water to be issued for paddy beginning mid-February while farmer representatives from another portion asked for water to be issued immediately. Some farmers, supporters of the municipal counselor, physically assaulted the subproject committee president when he proposed issuing water on 10 February. It took the police to disperse the crowd. The meeting ended without a decision. Afterwards, members of the subproject committee publicly protested the assault while an MP intervened with the police to protect the assaulters.

A PMC meeting on 25 January proposed 10 February as a suitable day for commencing the issue of water. At a PMC meeting on 10 February, it was decided that water would be issued from 25 February on the recommendation of the Left Bank Subproject

Committee; 25 February was the day on which water finally started being issued.

Outcome of the Conflicts and Negotiations

The dramatic events between 1991 and 1994 constituted negotiation of improved local allocation rules for Kirindi Oya. The negotiated set of rules can be succinctly outlined as follows:

- The Project Management Committee is the authority for making seasonal plans, including water allocation decisions.
- Ellegala is to be allocated water for 100 per cent paddy cultivation during the *maha* seasons and is to receive priority for the *yala* seasons, but is only guaranteed enough water for 70 per cent cultivation.
- During periods of water shortage, about two-thirds of the New Areas are to be allocated water for paddy cultivation during *maha*; farmers in the remaining portion are encouraged to plant rainfed non-paddy crops. However, the portion of the New Area not allocated water for paddy will be allocated water for a late *maha* paddy crop if *maha* rainfall is sufficient. During the *yala* season, the New Area zone that received water only for non-paddy crops during the preceding *maha* has priority.

There now exists greater equity in that the New Areas are to be allocated a greater portion of the water. However, Ellegala still gets priority based on its prior use of the water. While Ellegala farmers lost absolute priority and the New Area farmers won increased rights to water, all compromised. The events of *yala* 1993 and *maha* 1993–94 showed widespread acceptance of the revised rules among the farmers, in part because many farmers, particularly farmer representatives, learned a great deal about water availability in the Kirindi Oya system.

The events of *maha* 1993–94 also showed that there remains very strong opposition by farmers in part of the Left Bank to growing non-paddy crops during *maha*. Investigations have shown that the soils in this area are poorly adapted to non-paddy crop cultivation during heavy rains. From *yala* 1994 through *yala* 1995, higher rainfall meant that there was no water shortage and no reason to challenge the rules, but the rules evolved during the 1991–94 period adequately handled the situation during the drier seasons of *maha* 1995–96, *yala* 1996, and *maha* 1996–97. However, in June 1997, Left Bank farmers took control of the sluice of the Left Bank Main Channel in order to take water for paddy cultivation during *yala* 1997. They protested that they had not had the opportunity to plant for two seasons. The period of conflict and negotiations is not yet over.

Key Elements of the Negotiations at Kirindi Oya

Causes of the Conflicts

The conflicts reported here were built into the design of the Kirindi Oya system. The basic problem was conflict between Ellegala and New Area farmers over rights to water in a situation of water shortage. The Ellegala farmers claim to priority rights rested on the government's assurances that their water supply would not be decreased. Their claim to water for 200 per cent rice was based not on history or custom but on the government's plans for the Kirindi Oya system. Unless the Ellegala farmers' claim to absolute priority was accepted by New Area farmers, conflict was certain. New Area farmers might have accepted the Ellegala priority if it had been strongly supported by the government. The government could not afford to support Ellegala's claim since acceptance would probably have led to abandonment of parts of the New Areas in which the government had invested money borrowed from the Asian Development Bank. The resulting conflicts and negotiations were adaptations to the basic intervention: building the Kirindi Oya system.

One question is whether resolution of the conflicts might have happened without crop losses, assaults, etc. Such events might not have happened if the government agencies had taken stronger measures to define and enforce a policy without direct consultation with farmers. This approach would likely have delayed farmer acceptance of the resolution. Instead, by channeling the conflict through the PMC, direct farmer involvement probably assured a quicker development of an acceptable set of rules, but at some cost.

Roles of Government Officials, IIMI, and Politicians

In intervening in water allocation in Kirindi Oya, government officials had three goals: (*a*) to distribute the water more evenly among all farmers for greater equity and to ensure that construction and settlement of the Kirindi Oya system was a good investment, (*b*) to establish a clear set of rules accepted by the farmers that would make allocation decisions predictable and easy to make, so as to prevent anarchy and crop losses that reflect badly on agency performance, and (*c*) to establish cultivation of non-paddy crops as a regular practice. To achieve these goals, government officials primarily acted as expert advisors to the Project Management Committee and to farmer representatives. The officials did not act as mediators. Only one official, the chairman of the Project Management Committee, tried to act as a mediator because of his position on the PMC. IIMI researchers acted as advisors to the government agencies and thus contributed directly to the proposals for new allocation rules.

The officials largely succeeded in achieving the first two goals. However, the strong rejection of non-paddy crops by some farmers shows that they have had only partial success with the third goal. This is not surprising; IIMI investigations suggest that no available non-paddy crop is significantly more profitable than paddy, but all non-paddy crops have higher risks and require more labor. Many farmers would have been interested in adopting bananas but these were ruled out by the government because of the problems of irrigating a 9–12 month crop in a system designed for rice.

Politicians played two roles: mediators and advocates. The minister for irrigation attempted to act as a mediator in *maha* 1992–93, but refused to do so later. The two MPs who investigated the problems in 1993 did so on orders from Parliament so that Parliament could help solve the conflicts. These activities were mandated by the politicians' official responsibilities. All other politicians acted as advocates for one group of farmers or another. On the whole, the involvement of politicians was more destructive than constructive. None of the politicians effectively achieved his goals.

Structural Factors in Acceptability of the Rules

The various proposals differed in their acceptability to farmers. The major reasons were, of course, how well the proposals served the interests of each group of farmers. In addition, some structural features of the proposed rules themselves were important.

Flexibility

Farmers wanted to be sure that they could benefit from normal or heavier than usual rains. The needed flexibility was achieved with the adoption of the concept of a late *maha* season. This idea made it possible for farmers and system managers to wait until late in the season, when most of the rain has fallen, to finally decide how much land could be irrigated for paddy. This idea originated in the PMC during *maha* 1991–92 but was not proposed as an official rule until 1993.

Simplification

Given the number of contending groups of farmers—not only Ellegala farmers but also subgroups of New Area farmers—reaching a seasonal allocation decision can be difficult, as was clearly shown by the various decisions postponed by the PMC. A decision is easier to reach if the persons involved only have to decide among a few possibilities; thus simplification of the alternatives is helpful. The various government proposals approached simplification. All of the government proposals adopted the idea of subdividing the New Areas into defined zones for rotations. The 1993 technical committee proposal reduced *maha* seasons into two types—wet and dry—and reduced crops to three types—paddy, irrigated non-paddy, and rainfed non-paddy. These simplifications narrowed the choices, thus simplifying decisions.

An Acceptable Decision-making Authority

Having the unified Project Management Committee responsible for seasonal allocation decisions made the decisions more acceptable to farmers, because they had some input. Government officials accepted the PMC's authority because of the government's participatory management policy. During the events of 1991–94, the PMC's authority was challenged by groups of farmers who did not like the decisions. The challenges included the creation of the 'independent' farmer organization, and the various appeals to politicians during *maha* 1992–93 and *maha* 1993–94. All of these challenges failed because of support for the PMC by other farmers.

A Source of Technical Advice

The Irrigation Department's role in providing advice to the PMC but not attempting to make decisions was important. Many farmers gained considerable respect for the Irrigation Department's advice on water availability. This respect gave many farmer representatives greater confidence in the rules and in the ability of the PMC to make good decisions.

Generalizing the Lessons of Kirindi Oya

The structural features of the Kirindi Oya seasonal allocation rules that contribute to their acceptability—flexibility, simplicity, participation by farmers in decision making, a respected source of technical advice—are found in many successful irrigation water allocation systems. Like seasonal planning, most irrigation water allocation mechanisms adjust allocations to water availability. For example, share systems that define allocations as portions of available flow make such adjustments automatically. In some government managed irrigation schemes, system managers are responsible for these adjustments. Similarly, most allocation system rules are relatively simple and clear.

However, in many government managed irrigation systems, allocation decisions are not officially made by farmers, but by system managers not answerable to the farmers. In such cases, farmers are likely to intervene unofficially, sometimes aggravating conflicts rather than resolving them (Brewer et al. 1997).

In Kirindi Oya, devising local allocation rules was a process of negotiation through conflict. Negotiation of rules is likely to be required in new or changed systems even where water allocation is carried out in ways other than seasonal planning. In a new farmer-managed system, farmers might negotiate local allocation rules without the conflicts observed in Kirindi Oya. Peaceful negotiation in a government-constructed system, however, is likely to be much more difficult. Such systems are generally large, and may involve thousands of farmers. Engineers often design the systems without consulting the farmers (Fernea 1963). If, as in Kirindi Oya, the farmers were settlers brought in after system construction began, or if the local farmers are unfamiliar with irrigated agriculture, they may not be able to contribute, even if the engineers want to consult farmers. Conflicts over allocation are likely to be common in the first few years of a government-constructed system. If effective agreement can be reached among farmers, conflict need not continue if the water allocation rules are efficient and adapted to the local situation (c.f. Brewer et al. 1997).

Note

1. The author would like to thank the members of the IIMI Kirindi Oya action research team, especially P.G. Somaratne, Research Officer, who recorded most of the data, and R. Sakthivadivel, Senior Irrigation Specialist, who contributed the most toward the technical analyses.

References

ADB (Asian Development Bank). 1977. *Appraisal of the Kirindi Oya irrigation and settlement project in the Republic of Sri Lanka*. Manila, Philippines: Asian Development Bank.

———. 1986. *Preparation report of Kirindi Oya irrigation and settlement project (Phase II) in Sri Lanka*. Manila, Philippines: Asian Development Bank.

Brewer, Jeffrey D. 1994. The participatory irrigation system management policy. *Economic Review* 20 (6): 4–9.

Brewer, Jeffrey D., R. Sakthivadivel, and **K.V. Raju.** 1997. *Water distribution rules and water distribution performance: A case study in the Tambraparani system*. Research Report No. 12. Colombo, Sri Lanka: International Irrigation Management Institute.

Brewer, Jeffrey D., R. Sakthivadivel, and **P.G. Somaratne.** 1993. Developing a seasonal allocation strategy in a water-short system: The case of Kirindi Oya. Paper presented at Internal Program Review, International Irrigation Management Institute, Colombo, Sri Lanka.

Coward, E. Walter, Jr. 1980. Irrigation development: Institutional and organizational issues. In *Irrigation and agricultural development in Asia: Perspectives from the social sciences*, ed. E.W. Coward, Jr., 15–27. Ithaca, N.Y.: Cornell University Press.

Cruz, Ma. Concepcion J., Luzviminda B. Cornista, and **Diogenes C. Dayan.** 1987. *Legal and institutional issues of irrigation water rights in the Philippines*.

Laguna, Philippines: Agrarian Reform Institute, University of the Philippines at Los Baños.

de Jong, Ijsbrand H. 1989. *Fair and unfair: A study into the Bethma system in two Sri Lankan village irrigation systems.* Working Paper No. 15. International Irrigation Management Institute, Colombo, Sri Lanka.

de los Reyes, Romana P. 1982. Sociocultural patterns and irrigation organization: The management of a Philippine community irrigation system. Ph.D. diss., University of California, Berkeley.

Fernea, R.A. 1963. Conflict in irrigation. *Comparative Studies in Society and History* 6 (3): 76–83.

Harriss, John C. 1977. Problems with water management in Hambantota District. In *Green Revolution?* ed. B.H. Farmer, 364–76. Boulder, Colo.: Westview Press.

IIMI (*International Irrigation Management Institute*). 1990. Kirindi Oya Project, Volume II of final report: Irrigation management and crop diversification. Colombo, Sri Lanka: International Irrigation Management Institute.

———. 1995a. Kirindi Oya Project, Volume II of final report: Irrigation management and crop diversification, Phase II. Colombo, Sri Lanka: International Irrigation Management Institute.

———. 1995b. Kirindi Oya irrigation and settlement project: Project impact evaluation study, Colombo, Sri Lanka.

Jinapala, K., Jeffrey D. Brewer and **R. Sakthivadivel.** 1996. *Multilevel participatory planning for water resources development in Sri Lanka.* Gate Keeper Series No. 62. International Institute for the Environment and Development, London.

Leach, Edmund R. 1961. *Pul Eliya: A village in Ceylon.* Cambridge, U.K.: Cambridge University Press.

Madduma-Bandara, C.M. 1985. Catchment ecosystems and village tank cascades in the dry zone of Sri Lanka: A time-tested system of land and water resource management. In *Strategies for river basin management: Environmental integration of land and water in a river basin,* ed. J. Lundqvist, U. Lohm and M. Falkenmark, 99–113. Dordrecht: D. Reidel Publishing Company.

Merrey, Douglas J. 1986. The sociology of Warabandi: A case study from Pakistan. In *Irrigation management in Pakistan: Four papers,* ed. D.J. Merrey and J.M. Wolf, 44–61. Colombo, Sri Lanka: International Irrigation Management Institute.

Merrey, Douglas J. and **P.G. Somaratne.** 1988. *Institutions under stress and people in distress: Institution-building and drought in a new settlement scheme in Sri Lanka.* Colombo, Sri Lanka: International Irrigation Management Institute.

Murray-Rust, D. Hammond. 1983. Irrigation water management in Sri Lanka: An evaluation of technical and policy factors affecting operation of the main channel system. Ph.D. diss., Cornell University, Ithaca, N.Y.

Nijman, Charles. 1992. *Irrigation decision-making processes and conditions: A case study of Sri Lanka's Kirindi Oya irrigation and settlement project.* Colombo, Sri Lanka: International Irrigation Management Institute.

Ostrom, Elinor. 1990. *Governing the commons: The evolution of institutions for collective action.* Cambridge, U.K.: Cambridge University Press.

Palanisami, K. 1984. *Irrigation water management: The determinants of canal water distribution in India—A micro analysis.* New Delhi: Agricole Publishing Academy.

Sakthivadivel, R., Jeffrey D. Brewer, R. Bhatia, S. Narayanmurthy, and **P.S. Rao.** 1995. *Evaluation of schemes under NWMP-I: Bhadra scheme in Karnataka and Sathanur scheme in Tamil Nadu,* 2 volumes. Colombo, Sri Lanka: International Irrigation Management Institute.

Samad, M. 1995. Influence of institutional structure on agrarian activities in the Thirappane cascade. International Irrigation Management Institute, Colombo, Sri Lanka. Mimeo.

Uphoff, Norman. 1986. *Improving international irrigation management with farmer participation: Getting the process right.* Boulder, Colo.: Westview Press.

————. 1992. *Learning from Gal Oya: Possibilities for participatory development and post-Newtonian social science.* Ithaca, N.Y.: Cornell University Press.

Wade, Robert. 1987. *Village republics: Economic conditions for collective action in south India.* Cambridge, U.K.: Cambridge University Press.

5

Negotiation with an Under-informed Bureaucracy: Water Rights on System Tanks in Bihar

NIRMAL SENGUPTA

The history of system tanks in the Gaya District of Bihar illustrates how rights to traditional irrigation tanks changed as the colonial and post-independence Indian bureaucracy expanded its influence. Bureaucratic ignorance may help perpetuate local rights. However, locally defined rights are far from static 'traditions.' Rights are often contested, both in negotiations between settlements and systems, and through reference to state courts and authorities to establish claims. In water rights disputes, the legal system is more an instrument of harassment than a clear property rights charter. Ultimately, many cases are resolved primarily through self-organization, negotiation among the users outside the ambit of the legal system.

Introduction

Although there exists voluminous literature about the modern Indian legal system, and some about land and forest rights, there is little about rights to other natural resources. In general, the colonial government left most natural resources with poorly defined property rights. In the post-independence years the bureaucracy made great inroads through its different functions, but did not improve much on granting of rights. De facto rights, however, have existed all along. Whenever contested, by private parties or by the government, conflicts and negotiations ensued. The resolutions of these disputes were essentially spontaneous self-organization processes.

In recent years there has been growing attention to local management of common property resources, and a recognition of the potential of farmer-managed irrigation systems. Many indigenous irrigation systems provide good examples of farmer management and are therefore, being studied for learning principles of management. But these studies often overlook the fact that the 'traditional' irrigation systems no longer exist in the traditional settings. Their functions are now conducted in an environment of formal rights defined by the state. In some areas, the bureaucracy is careless and ignorant about the norms, customs and performance records of the spontaneous organizations or may interpret them as static 'customary rights,' a favorite construct of formal law. One section of researchers is blind to such inconsistencies and tends to accept the notion that formal laws actually regulate the irrigation systems. The other section rejects these inadequate legal provisions and tends to treat the traditional systems as if they exist in isolation. Actually, even if misinformed, bureaucratic or legal interpretations always impinge on the local negotiation process, delineating the space for forum shopping as various local parties use the threat of external intervention to reach settlements (see Benda-Beckmann and van der Velde 1992; Spiertz, Chapter 6 in this volume).

This paper describes how farmers negotiate water rights in such a setting. If self-organization processes are possible, the de facto rights are redefined again and again even in traditional systems. In such a case, a rigid concept of customary rights makes no sense. However, some efficient principles may survive over a long period. This chapter brings out the existence of such efficient and sustained principles through a historical case study of how rights to traditional irrigation tanks were negotiated as the colonial and post-Independence Indian bureaucracy expanded its influence. The chapter moves from the macro-level to the micro-level, beginning with an overview of water rights in India, and treatment of indigenous irrigation systems.

It then takes up the example of traditional *pynes* in Bihar, and negotiations in Supi Desiyain Pyne in particular. The final sections highlight the contrast between bureaucratic definitions of rights and the farmers' own conceptions.

Diverse Legal Set-up

There is no single system of water rights in India. One way to introduce the complexity is to list the various systems of rights. A better way is to introduce the evolution of the systems in different regions, which would then help the reader anticipate, to some extent, specific features of the regions.

In pursuance of its mercantile objective, the colonial government defined and protected property rights as private and introduced several legal conventions for markets and contracts. A judiciary independent of the executive institutions of the state and acting as a check on them was created to secure these rights of ownership and use, particularly from encroachment by executives (Washbrook 1981). To implement the law, records of rights and rightholders were necessary. It is from this point that different systems of rights began to emerge in different parts of India. While the mercantile objective and basic administrative set-up was the same, the colonial government experimented with many different models for assigning legal rights over property and adopted different definitions of rightholders in different regions.

There were two major types of revenue settlements in India. In the Permanent Settlement introduced in Bengal and Bihar in 1793, the landlords (called *zamindars*) were the rightholders. Recording of rights consisted of recording the names of *zamindars* and revenue payable by each. For 100 years there were no records of tenants, let alone any property rights to be enjoyed by them. This type of settlement prevented the government from having any concern about the economic system within the jurisdictions of the *zamindars* as long as they were able to pay the fixed revenue. Naturally, relations pertaining to waterworks or other natural resources within the domains of the *zamindars* did not come under the purview of public law in the Permanent Settlement areas.

In the Ryotwari Settlement, introduced in south India in the first half of the 19th century, the British proceeded a step further in establishing private property. Settlements were made with individual tenants. Immediately, when the records of rights were being prepared, it surfaced that no individual could lay claims on the local tanks, woodlots, or grazing grounds. The colonial government declared its ownership over such properties and thus committed itself to their upkeep and maintenance. In a few years this necessitated the induction of engineers in the Revenue Department and ultimately gave rise to the Public Works Department (in charge of irrigation works as well) with numerous personnel and considerable expense, but with dismal performance. This marked the rise of the government-as-provider model.

Later, when the *zamindari* system was established in north India, but not as a 100-year settlement, the government-as-provider role was adopted for increasing revenue. In the original Permanent Settlement areas too, around the close of the 19th century, rights of tenants were recorded after the expiration of the 100-year contract. After independence, the *zamindari* system was abolished thus bringing the whole country under a single land rights system. But the actual state of affairs has not become uniform because of the colossal difference in government knowledge about local resources, consequent upon the different settlement experiences. By around the 1830s, the irrigation department in *ryotwari* areas could produce engineers like Sir Arthur Cotton, who were fairly well acquainted with the technology of the local irrigation works and could take up extension projects. By the 1880s the government could release a complete list of nearly 32,000 tanks existing in *ryotwari* areas (Sengupta 1991). In contrast, in *zamindari* areas at the same time, it was very difficult to find even a reference to these works in the official reports. Even in the 1990s, the similarities between the south India works and those of Bihar are not known to Indian irrigation planners (Sengupta 1993b). How can one talk of rights, when even the principal infrastructure is not known?

Water rights might have also been granted under general legal conventions. Legal experts often state that water rights in India are riparian, following the British system. This is rather wishful thinking. The users do not have any statutory right over the sources. Because of the vagueness of the legal position, the public property concept on natural resources has been upheld at will, by the judicial court or by administrative order. In turn, these case laws often guide local conflict settlements. Another general provision, recognition of customary rights, also has its interface with water resources. The colonial authority was also fully aware that it would be politically and socially cumbersome to administer English or Western law to supplant an already complex set of native rules (Galanter 1989). However, the coding of moral and community obligations in Indian society was restricted to matters such as marital customs, and rarely addressed local natural resources. There were some exceptions (e.g., Coward 1990; Sengupta 1980; 1985), but the quality of records was not always impressive. Customary rights and regulations could also be recorded as improper reconstructs (Benda-Beckmann and van der Velde 1992), serving the interests of the administration even if they took on a distorted meaning. For example, the Madras Compulsory Labor Act, 1858 or Kudimaramath Act, empowered revenue officials to summon farmers for unpaid labor for irrigation works, on the grounds that voluntary communal labor was customary (Sengupta 1991: 69–77).

Current studies on water law sometimes report that there are clearly specified water rights in India. They refer to the numerous Irrigation and Drainage Acts in different regions. These Acts are defined only with respect to irrigation water from government irrigation projects. There is no clear legal position on non-government communal works. Almost any position about the situation of rights on water resources can be substantiated by referring to one or another of the plethora of legal provisions. The totality, however, can only be characterized as a situation where rights are poorly defined, making open access possible, particularly by the government. In subsequent periods, some parts of these resources have been diverted by the government to other uses; on some resources regulatory measures have been introduced, and there are some common pool resources for which the government has assumed the role of provider (Sengupta 1996).

Public control, as recognized in the colonial and modern Indian legal system, has practically curtailed all types of popular initiatives towards investment. This is unlike the United States, where recognition of prior appropriation rights encourages private investment, or Japan, where customary communal and private rights were given statutory recognition in modernizing the legal system in the Meiji Restoration period. A startling story from the modernization of Tambraparni system in the 1870s shows how peoples' initiatives were discouraged to favor the public property rights (Sengupta 1991: 138). When the British engineers decided to construct an eighth *anicut* (weir) on the river, the potential beneficiaries had collected a sum of Rs 30,000 on their own for aiding the construction. The government did not use the local contribution on the ground that the beneficiaries might in future use this as a basis to ask for a reduction of rent. The fund was used instead for building a road.

In the post-independence period social justice has been of much greater concern and institutional designs have sought to break the stranglehold of traditional vested interests. Sometimes in this process, the policymakers have paid too little attention to the pre-existing common property relations and remnants of customary rights.

Recently there has been some serious thoughts devoted to local governance, including management of natural resources. Several Acts have been passed, most notably the 1993 Constitutional Amendment Act promoting Panchayati Raj, the local self-government system. There are also efforts to devolve management responsibility for many irrigation systems to users. Although these recent management transfer programs are extensive, they pay little attention to the rights issue. The Eleventh Schedule of the Panchayati Raj Amendment lists several resources, including water, as spheres of influence of local Panchayats. But no state has as yet defined the ownership and control rights of Panchayati Raj institutions over the subjects included in the Schedule, leaving considerable scope for dispute.

The Irrigation Act on Private Works

Surprising though it may seem, pre-existing irrigation systems survived much better in the *zamindari* areas (Sengupta 1980; Sherrard 1916). On second thought, the very absence of alien and uninformed intervention, as in south India, could let the system continue as before. Throughout the 19th century, the government had no need to worry about the indigenous irrigation works in Bihar. After repeated severe famines in different parts of India, the colonial government took up irrigation works as a protective measure and set up an Irrigation Commission in 1901. The Commission observed that the *ahar-pyne*[1] irrigation under the *zamindari* system, unlike its counterparts in south India, was not in a bad state, so much so that

Gaya, the major district served by this type of irrigation, remained practically immune to famines throughout the 19th century (India 1903). There was no necessity for protective works. However, there had been some deterioration which the Commission identified as due to the partition of *zamindari* estates. Mainly because of this the commission recommended an Irrigation Act.

However, there was no great alarm. The government moved in a very casual manner. By 1911, an Irrigation Works Bill was drafted, but it was not proposed immediately, on the ground that the Survey of Gaya, which had started in the same year, would produce valuable additional information for drafting the Bill on a more sound basis. Survey and Settlement operations in Gaya District were completed in 1919. Subsequently, in 1922, the Irrigation Works Bill was proposed in the Legislative Assembly. In contrast to the government, the landlords acted swiftly and fought tooth and nail against the Bill. The original provisions made in the Bill were drastically changed by the Select Committee and further diluted in the debate in the Legislative Council. A reluctant government and a determined opposition produced the first ever Irrigation Act in Bihar (Bihar and Orissa Private Irrigation Works Act 1922) in such a diluted form that it remained practically ineffective.

The Irrigation Act was drafted with the conviction arising out of the philosophy of the Permanent Settlement that the *zamindars* construct, maintain and allocate water from irrigation works, as everything else in their domains. As a remedial measure, therefore, the civil servants were asked to play the same role should the *zamindars* fail. The Act empowered the district collectors to step in from what was basically a wrong premise, that the *zamindars* played a strong role; but the dilutions required them to be extra cautious before they took a single step forward. During the introduction of an amendment in 1939, it was pointed out that only two chapters of the Act which were applied once in a while were concerned with improvement and repair works of an occasional nature and supplemental provisions, like appointment of irrigation committees and recording of customary rotations (*parabandi*).[2] The provisions relating to regular maintenance or extension were of no use. The collectors were permitted to take up works where financial liabilities were small, and that too, after a lengthy legal procedure establishing that the landlords responsible would not take up those works by themselves. The collector of Gaya noted later:

Several experienced officials have held the opinion that the Act actually hindered the repair of the Irrigation Works, because prior to the Act landlords could be persuaded to undertake repairs, but after the passing of the Act they were provided with strong legal excuses for resisting such repairs (Hardman 1938).

On paper, some irrigation cooperatives were formed. No recording of irrigation rotations (*parabandi*) during this period is known to us.

In the late 1930s, there was some improvement consequent upon the formation of the Indian Ministry under the Congress Party. An amendment (Bihar 1939) was proposed which gave discretionary powers to the collectors, evolved emergency procedures for repair, and made provisions for cost recovery from the others if only one of the co-sharer landlords undertook a repair job. A revolving fund was created for this purpose and was placed at the discretion of the collector. The ministry also initiated a Rent Reduction Settlement in certain parts of the province to account for the fall in prices during the Great Depression and the breakdown or neglect of irrigation arrangements (Williams 1941).

Another regulation was passed in 1940 and following independence a second amendment was made in 1950. These amendments increased the role of the officials vis-à-vis the *zamindars*. Ultimately, the *zamindari* system was abolished in the post-independence period and all authority vested with the government. This Act, still in effect after revisions, empowers the bureaucracy to intervene in indigenous irrigation systems almost in any manner they desire. Later we will study the consequences of this and other legal provisions for the Gaya District, which was, according to the Irrigation Commission (India 1903), immune to famine because of its indigenous irrigation system.

Records of Water Rights in Gaya District

By implication, the Permanent Settlement had granted the *zamindars* paramount rights on all common property resources, including irrigation, within their domains. For a long time the *zamindars* had not felt any need to exercise the sanctioned de jure rights, for they had nothing to gain thereby. Long afterwards, at the height of the peasant movements in the 1930s, the *zamindars'* exaggerated legal standing proved to be an excellent instrument of power. During this time, the *zamindars* often forcibly asserted their legal rights over local tanks and prevented water supply to tenants (Sengupta 1980). These conflicts were ultimately resolved in the political arena and brought about revision of property rights through the abolition of the *zamindari* system.

Customs, including customary property rights, could survive longer within the domains of the Permanent Settlement. The estates were constituted as small autonomous units. Within these units, local regulations and laws could be determined by customs and practices. While administering in a highly personalized form, the estate authorities usually adhered to unwritten local norms and customs. But there were written records too. Tekari Raj, the biggest *zamindar* family of Gaya District, had a much celebrated record, known as the *lal bahi* (red book), showing the rights of the beneficiary villages in all the major *pynes* in his *zamindari*.

Within the provisions of the Permanent Settlement, the modern judiciary could admit civil suits on irrigation rights only at the level of disputes between the *zamindars*. It is likely that the *zamindars* were the ultimate authority in negotiations and civil conflicts over water rights involving tenant farmers. After the expiry of a hundred-year contract, for the first time Acts could be made to protect the tenants. The Tenancy Act created the possibility of judicial mediation in cases of civil disputes between the *zamindars* and tenants on the question of irrigation. However, a record of rights was necessary if the government wanted to mediate.

Initially, officials were of the opinion that the records of rights should be made as elaborate as for land, showing the rights of individual tenants. This is in accordance with the British system of settlement. As work began, difficulties emerged. The final outcome was very different from the principle (Sengupta 1993a). In all the records of water rights prepared during the Survey and Settlement, communities—groups of tenants, either the whole villages or parts of these—were shown as units. It may be recalled that unlike Spanish or U.S. water laws, the British legal system had little provision for communal rights (Sengupta 1985). Understandably the judiciary, trained in British jurisprudence, faced problems while dealing with such records.

Gaya, the most important district from the point of view of private irrigation, happened to be the last district taken up for Survey and Settlement Operations. Thus records of rights over water prepared in this district could not be repeated elsewhere. In the Gaya Settlement Operations, two types of irrigation records were prepared (Tanner 1919): (*a*) the village irrigation record or *fard abpashi,* and (*b*) the general *pyne* record. The first dealt with information regarding irrigation within each village, while the second gave the details of a system which benefitted many villages.

Fard abpashi fell short of a detailed record of rights of individual tenants. Nor was it a document which accurately described the existing indigenous system everywhere. It is a peculiar mixture of the two systems. For example:

Column 7: 'Harvest and area irrigated (approx.)'—did not show the holding-by-holding (or plot-by-plot) details of area irrigated. All it required was that a single hamlet or an identifiable distinct part, if it was an exclusive beneficiary, should be noted. In other words, if there existed a corporate right within the village, that should be shown.

Column 8: 'Method of distribution of water'—was a record of the technological arrangements. As a question of social arrangement, it required only information about whether any permission from the landlord was necessary. Implicitly, the tenants were regarded only as corporate entities and autonomous in function, for there was no inquiry about how they reached their decisions.

The corporate existence of tenants in the matter of irrigation was witnessed so vividly by the recording officials that they decided it would be sufficient to give copies of *fard abpashi* to only one tenant in each of the beneficiary units. Some *jeth raiyats* (senior tenants) were chosen for this purpose, who had no representative status under the state legislation. Such records would be of little help in civil disputes, and one does not come across cases where *fard abpashi* was referred to. Today its existence is practically unknown to both government officials and the farmers, although some can be found in district old record rooms.

In the general *pyne* record the corporate treatment of villages was made explicit. In it, the details of diversion arrangements (e.g., rotational regulations between villages, rights of particular villages to construct checkdams) were noted along with the 'customary' arrangement for repair works. Here, too, there was a tendency to reduce corporate bodies to individuals such as the *amlas* (officials) of *zamindars* or the *jeth raiyats* instead of whole groups. But it also described the division of rights between villages benefitting from a single system and therefore was sometimes referred to in legal suits between villagers on the question of irrigation rights, as described in the case study below.

This abortive attempt in the Gaya Settlement Operations is the lone case in preparation of formal water rights for the users to this day. Otherwise, by default, the government enjoys a paramount right on water resources. In reality, however, the government occupies only a formal authoritative position with respect to indigenous irrigation systems, engaging itself primarily in the development of modern irrigation facilities. The ownership of the existing waterworks is now vested in the government. But no specific policy has been developed, no further Act has been passed, and no systematic division of responsibilities between the government and the irrigators has emerged. Different departments carry out some type of irrigation work occasionally. The state of ignorance that was characteristic of the 19th century has returned once again, after a 50-year lapse. In effect, the village communities have practically regained their autonomy with respect to indigenous irrigation. In the exercise of their autonomy they avail many different methods.

A Case Study: Supi Desiyain Pyne

Gaya District in Bihar is located between the hills to its south and the plains of Ganga to its north. Average annual rainfall is below 1,000 mm. Further, because of the slope, run-off water could drain out quickly (Singh and Kumar 1970). Rice cultivation would not have been possible in this region, but for the indigenous irrigation works known as *ahar* and *pyne*. *Ahars* are above-surface storage tanks providing gravity irrigation. *Pynes* are diversion canals from rivers, primarily used as feeder channels for *ahars*. These are 'system tanks' comparable to better-known cases in south India or Sri Lanka (e.g., the Ellegala system described in Chapter 4 of this volume). But, because of historical ignorance (e.g., India 1966), these have not been identified as the same. An irrigation system originating from river Jamuna is described here.

The river Jamuna runs for about 90 kilometers before it meets the river Dardha. For most of the year the river remains dry. Following heavy downpours in the catchment basin, the river swells up and carries water in rushing torrents. During high floods, the Jamuna carries a flood discharge that is as high as 2,000 cusecs (cubic feet per second). Jamuna has many canals and system tanks. The last one in this series is called Supi Desiyain Pyne (hereafter S.D. Pyne). Its tail end passes through Gaya District and hence maps were prepared for individual pyne systems under the general *pyne* record. Figure 5.1 shows the tail end of the Jamuna river irrigation system.

Figure 5.1: Schematic Map of Supi Desiyain Pyne

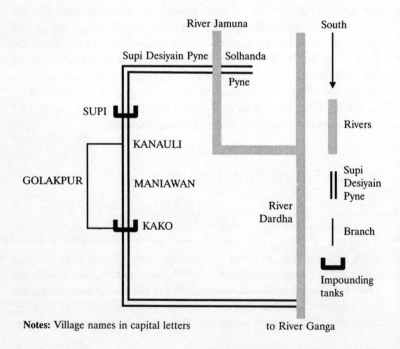

Notes: Village names in capital letters

It is not known when or by whom the S.D. Pyne system was constructed. It may be very old: Kako, the biggest village benefitting from the system, has some antiquarian remains of the 9th or 10th century A.D. According to the general *pyne* record, the S.D. Pyne system and its branches passed through 60 villages and irrigated at least some land in most of these villages. It is difficult to demarcate the exact command area because of the meandering of different *pyne* systems. For example, the S.D. Pyne feeds the tanks at villages Murasa and Maniawan and from each of these tanks a new *pyne* emerges traveling through several villages. The different parts of S.D. Pyne receive surplus water supplies from many other *pynes* including that of the partly completed Uderasthan project. Because of such intertwining, very often it becomes meaningless to identify one *pyne* system as the sole benefactor of a particular area. For administrative or historical reasons, however, separate units have been demarcated. According to the records of the 1920s, the main *pyne* passed through 32 villages and contained as many as 53 outlets (*mohana*). The main channel exists today, though some of its branches are now defunct.

The lower part of the S.D. Pyne, down the Supi *ahar*, is also known as Karua Nala. This is also believed to be a natural watercourse (*nala* = rivulet). It is difficult to distinguish a natural *nala* from an artificial *ahar*; even in this century, artificial channels in this district have become natural drainage lines. However, legal provisions differ depending on whether or not it is a natural watercourse, as discussed below.

Diversion channels beginning from 12 outlets reach other villages and are called *sakhs*. S.D. Pyne has 12 *sakhs* or branches (the term *desiyain* literally means 'with 10 branches'). These branches and their sub-branches reach an additional 28 villages. Often the branches give rise to channels going through other villages. Such channels are called *darsakhs* (sub-branches). The diversion channels which do not leave the villages of origin are called *karha, bhokla*, etc. One should note that the nomenclature has clear bearings on the division of rights. Branches are not necessarily longer than the *karhas*, but because they pass through several villages they raise extra complications in the management of water and therefore, demand separate categorization. The general *pyne* records dealt up to the level of *sakhs* and *darsakhs*. The records show the locations of different fixed outlets (in terms of revenue numbers of the corresponding plots), along with the rights of corporate groups to divert water by permitted types of structures, duration, etc. An idea of the complicated network of S.D. Pyne may be had from the layouts shown in Figure 5.2, prepared from the description of the general *pyne* record for S.D. Pyne. Even a fifth order branch could travel through more than one village, indicating the complicated inter-village coordination necessary for management. When they were functional under the authority of the *zamindars*, the rights must have been clearly defined and disputes settled so as to enable these complicated networks to continue. Most parts of the *pyne* system as complicated as this are now extinct.

Figure 5.2: Network of Supi Desiyain Pyne: A System of Branches Passing Through Several Villages

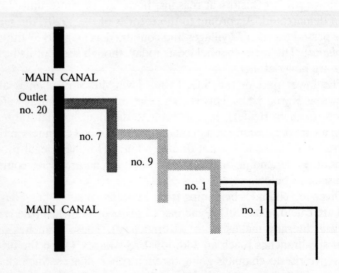

Some of the outlets (seven of the main channel and 12 of the branches and sub-branches) lead to tanks. Thus, the whole system feeds 19 tanks. Although the great majority of the outlets over the whole *pyne* system are used for direct irrigation, together they divert much less water, and benefit a much smaller area, compared to the handful of outlets supplying water to tanks. The 19 villages in which these tanks are located account for more than a half of the total population of all the 60 villages through which the *pyne* system passes. Areawise as well, the tank-owning villages account for more than half of the total geographical area of the 60 villages.

In the following sections, water rights situations are discussed at three different levels: between systems, between settlements, and within a settlement.

Division of Water Rights between Systems

S.D. Pyne shares the water flowing through the River Jamuna with many other *pyne* systems. There was another weir, slightly upstream of the Jamuna, from which the Solhanda Pyne took off. S.D. Pyne therefore received only as much water as was let out in the Jamuna by the beneficiaries of the Solhanda Pyne. Earlier, there was a rotation (*parabandi*) by which Solhanda Pyne was prevented from taking water from the Jamuna every alternate week. Since both systems were included in the estate of the Tekari Raj, a famous *zamindar* of the district, the rotational regulation could be enforced. But after the influence of *zamindars* declined, such regulations were no longer effective. In consequence, since the 1920s, S.D. Pyne received only an irregular and insufficient supply from the Jamuna River. This might be the reason why shortage of water began to be felt in the S.D. Pyne since the 1920s. The common belief, however, was that the catchment area of the Jamuna was shrinking. In its upper reaches more water was flowing towards the Phalgu River. This is quite possible in a country where the watersheds between rivers are not sharply demarcated and slight changes in terrain conditions divert rainwater from one side to another. In the past this might have occurred repeatedly, and water rights would be redefined. Although there may be a range of pre-existing water rights at any point, it is important to recognize that there is no single customary water right.

In the post-Independence period, the irrigation department combined the two intake points and built a masonry weir over the river Jamuna for easier diversion of water into the *pynes* (see Figure 5.1). The departmental staff operate the weir. The water rights of the two systems are not clearly defined, but by convention the weir is opened every alternate week to the left and right sides, supplying the two *pynes* alternately.

In the post-Independence period, a medium-sized irrigation river valley project, called the Uderasthan scheme, was taken up in this area. With an investment of more than Rs 20 million, this scheme included the construction of a diversion structure on the adjacent river Phalgu and distribution of water to benefit a command area of 24,800 hectares. When the scheme was proposed in the 1960s, the Irrigation Department was absolutely ignorant of the potentials of the indigenous system. The layout had not considered the existing *pynes* and had proposed alternate channels. As expected, the department was drawn into numerous litigations over land acquisition, and for several years the project remained half completed. By then, however, awareness about the indigenous systems was growing. One of the chief engineers had even recommended that the local *pynes* be strengthened. By default they were. Since the project could not be commissioned, surplus water from the project drained out through the existing *pynes* in that area, enriching them. This is how Karua Nala started getting more water in the 1970s. However, this is not a secure share: the additional supply may stop once the project is completed. Because the source of the additional supply is so very distant—not only in a geographic sense—from the farmers, they do not even think of negotiation for securing this additional supply.

Lately, an extension program has been sanctioned and partly completed whereby a branch *pyne* (Dharaut Pyne) has partly replaced the old course of the S.D. Pyne. A proposal is under consideration for an inter-basin diversion, costing Rs 180 million. If this is sanctioned, the integrated project will drastically alter the present distribution pattern of surface water among different rivers and *pynes*.

Negotiation between Settlements

The Tenancy Act marked a watershed in the introduction of modern civil law. Before its enactment any civil dispute on water rights would be referred to the *zamindars* for settlement, but since that time laws are referred to wherever problems occur. Supi Desiyain Pyne is one such system where physical problems had already appeared and the Tenancy Act provisions came into use almost immediately. Situations related only to the middle of the system are discussed here.

For reasons discussed in the earlier section, by around the 1920s, the supply of water to the Supi Desiyain Pyne and consequently to the Supi tank decreased (see Figure 5.1). The beneficiaries of the checkdam and diversion (*bandh*) at village Kanauli, who received only the surplus water from the Supi tank, needed more time to fill up their village tank. Naturally, they were reluctant to remove the temporary earthen checkdam letting water flow further downwards through Karua Nala. Villagers downstream who were affected by this came to Kanauli and tried to remove the checkdam by force. There was bloodshed, and not only criminal cases but also civil suits were registered. The villagers of Golakpur, the first of the affected villages, contested the right of the villagers of Kanauli to erect such a diversion.

After prolonged litigation, a verdict was obtained. The court had considered the records of rights (general *pyne* record), but objected to its treatment of a natural watercourse as private property. The entry was declared null and void and the principle upheld was that no one has any right to obstruct the flow of a natural watercourses, which would imply that most of the indigenous irrigation practices were illegal.

However, the award was not executed, thanks to the reluctance of the administrative officials. The villagers of Kanauli were now demoralized, for their opponents, the villagers of Golakpur, could now summon the officials to execute the decision. The defeated party approached the others for a compromise. The villagers of Golakpur too, aware of the seriousness of consequences the villagers of Kanauli would otherwise face, agreed to let them divert water for two days a month. Thus, a new rotational (*parabandi*) regulation emerged, but it was forced to remain out of the jurisdiction of the modern judiciary. Indeed, the verdict forced much of the existing sharing arrangements to remain shy of the judiciary for all of these might be held illegal by reference to the same award.

When a second conflict ensued a few years later down at the Goh Bandh, the contestants had to invent a legally admissible clause. After the Kanauli Bandh case was decided, a shortage of water was felt at the next checkdam (Goh Bandh) site. The villagers of Golakpur now were determined to divert the entire flow to the channel benefitting them. It would deprive the villagers downstream, led by village Maniawan, of water. In the very first year there occurred a violent clash followed by a prolonged litigation which lasted for over

20 years, reaching from the lower to the higher courts. Since the case would be immediately dismissed if the villagers of Golakpur admitted that their *bandh* was on the natural watercourse, they phrased their objection thus: the channel going to Maniawan was the branch (and therefore could be cut off without violating the court award) and the one going to Golakpur was the main *nala* (the natural watercourse). Thus the dispute was now over which one was the true course of Karua Nala. In 1960, Patna High Court gave its decision in favor of Maniawan. Once again there was a mutual agreement between the two villages outside the purview of the civil court, permitting Golakpur to erect such a diversion each alternate week.

Thus by now it was amply clear to all the concerned parties that the norms followed by the judiciary and those required by the irrigators were very different. If at present a party seeks adjudication, it is not for mediation but to harass the opponent and to bring them to terms. This may be seen as an instance of forum shopping, similar in some respects to the case from Nepal described by Pradhan and Pradhan in this volume. The supply of water in Karua Nala has improved since then, particularly after the construction of the Uderasthan Project was taken up. Consequently, such disputes between villages have not been heard of in this area.

In the absence of a useful legal system, the de facto rights are negotiated directly between the stake-holders, but the negotiations cannot occur independent of the law. The law in this sphere is not confined to normative discourse level, so as to have only marginal significance. Instead, it contributes towards determining the real incentives of the agents, not by settlement of rights, but by lending strength to different sides in the negotiations. The explanations of primary (national) property law and the recognition of customary law by local law or administrative orders leave many ambiguities and inconsistent judicial interpretations. Parties in conflict can muster whichever is convenient, but there is always some ambiguity to contest any resolution. In the context of the disputes it is not the legal provisions but the legal procedures which matter more. Transaction costs are so high that court cases are beyond the reach of many. Thus the legal system is more an instrument of harassment than a clear property rights charter. Far from being marginal, the law heavily influences the cost-benefit balance for cooperation and conflict, and favors the competent litigant in the matter of rights on water. It is true that the final award in court cases may go to either side depending on the personal leanings of the mediators. But by then it is not the court awards but the reputations built by the contestants which count more. Thus, the net effect of law is that conflicts linger in civil courts for decades, with manipulative juggling of explanations and a smattering of criminal cases, ultimately being resolved primarily through self-organization by the users outside the ambit of the legal system.

Farmers' Concepts of Water Rights

The farmers' concepts of water rights differ from those of the agencies in many different ways. The following section describes a few, which are by no means exhaustive.

That conflicts are restricted to a part of the *pyne* system is noteworthy. Irrigators do not have much awareness about physical units located beyond 10–15 kilometers. Most of the beneficiaries regard the three parts of S.D. Pyne as different units, so much so that in the second part of the *pyne*, beyond say 15 kilometers from the intake, most people did not refer to the river Jamuna as its source and did not know what kind of diversion structure existed there. Within each part of the system, farmers are uncertain where the water comes from and do not consider the source of supply to be relevant Therefore, the cases of negotiations and conflicts are also restricted within an area about 10–15 kilometers long. Some other researchers (McCay and Acheson 1990) studying other forms of common pool resource, like sea-fishing, have noted similar phenomenon. Community property senses are stronger over sources in the immediate neighborhood, and weaken as distance to the source increases.

Distinct individual rights to water simply do not exist: they are secured only by being a member of a particular corporate group or 'community.' Most members who own land in a particular command area also belong to the same caste and reside in the same hamlet. They have to follow somewhat uniform agricultural and water application practices. These are not demanded explicitly, or even consciously. The very functioning of the system is such that one cannot take advantage of the full benefit if one differs in one or the other of the community attributes.

Among the same caste members residing in the same locality, formal meetings are rarely necessary. Instead, decisions are taken and information circulated in day-to-day interactions. One would note that given the setting, this decision-making process attains the best of both worlds. It is cost-efficient. At the same time, the decisions are not any worse than that in a formal democratic meeting since their requirements and interests are so very similar that everyone may look after every others' interests. But if there is a difference, for example if one member resides in a different hamlet, he would often fail to receive information about the different decisions taken.

This is exemplified in one small command area (Sengupta 1991). Before independence, some parts of this command were owned by an absentee *zamindar*. The estate land was cultivated by his tenants from another hamlet. After independence, the Muslim *zamindar* sold his estate and emigrated to Pakistan. At that time, residents of many other hamlets purchased plots of the estate belonging to this command area. But faced with the problem described above, some of them exchanged their holdings, some others sold those off. By now, all but one of the 35 landowners benefitting from this command area reside in the adjacent hamlet. The transactions have been fully in accordance with the modern law, but the consequence has been reproduction of the traditional community attributes.

Another interesting feature was that equity in water allocation was in-built, not a granted right. The total landholding of each individual in a command was highly fragmented. In consequence, every major landholder who could influence the allocation had interests both at the head and the tail regions of the distributary (Sengupta 1993a). If water available is not sufficient and does not reach the tail end, a part of the command area remains unirrigated, but everyone suffers. Comparable approaches to ensure equitable benefits through constitutive rules are found in other parts of the world. Persistence of fragmentation in many different societies is a well-recorded phenomenon and is not without rationale (Heston and Kumar 1983; McClosky 1975a, 1975b). Under the *bethma* system of Sri Lanka plots are reallocated between families from year to year, giving everyone a piece of good and bad land. Implementation of *bethma*, however, requires negotiation and consent. The case discussed here occurred without a conscious design.

In the above cases, rights on water were defined indirectly, by regulating rights on land and other complementary resources

(Sengupta 1996). By using this approach, the farmers are able to define rights and regulate use of some complex attributes of water resources.

In south India and Sri Lanka, tank beds are besieged with problems. They are encroached by farmers. Desilting has rarely been done. Tank beds are state owned and rights of agricultural use do not exist. In sharp contrast, most parts of the beds of tanks in Bihar are still privately owned and cultivated. These contain excellent subsoil moisture after the rainy season and hence produce very good cash crops during winter. During droughts, the farmers do not use gravity irrigation for command area cultivation. Instead, the tank bed becomes the major rice producing land.[3] When land consolidation operations began in the village, the farmers, after repeated lobbying, finally impressed the consolidation officers with the necessity of not consolidating land owned by each farmer in and out of tank bed, and further, that the size of one's landholding in the tank bed should not exceed half of his holdings in the command area of the same tank.

Once again, this is actually a water right, though defined on irrigation-related land. The two principles together ensure that each farmer has a dominant interest in using tank land as an irrigation source and not encroaching on it for perpetual cultivation. The thousands of tanks of Bihar suffer from many other problems, but not the encroachment problems of south Indian tanks. Also, the farmers have succeeded in more intensive use of village land. Complex and imaginative property rights such as this are indeed essential prerequisites for full utilization of the participation and management capability of farmers. But because of their complexities, officials may fail to understand the logic, even in negotiations.

Probably the practice of tank bed cultivation existed in south India before the government asserted its ownership through Ryotwari Settlement. In some parts it lasted until recently. Ramnathapuram district in Tamil Nadu was an exception within the *ryotwari* tract since it was earlier a *zamindari* settlement. Unlike in the rest of south India, some of the customary practices here continued until the time of independence. One such practice was extensive tank bed cultivation during the dry season. The land in question was not perpetually privately owned as in Bihar. Every year the Revenue Department used to distribute temporary ownership (*patta*) for cultivation of tank beds. Government reports in the 1950s document official objections against the continuation of this practice. After *zamindari* abolition, the engineering wing of the Public Works Department had taken over the tanks from the Revenue Department. They were determined to stop tank-bed cultivation on the plea that the department was not getting enough time to undertake desilting work. To put an end to this practice was not an easy task; the soil produced very good cash crops. For ten years there was a tug of war between the unrelenting farmers and the P.W.D. The Planning Commission recommended a high penalty tax (Sengupta 1991). Finally the government succeeded. But what kind of success was it! To prevent possible problems off-season utilization was forbidden. No amount of negotiation could succeed because the imaginative property rules were beyond the grasp of the technocrats.

Conclusion

In this part of the world the greatest obstacle to effective negotiation between farmers and the bureaucracy is that the latter often have a warped sense of rights. While rights are primarily meant for creating desirable incentive structures (Coward 1985), the bureaucracy tends to view them in terms of regulations or disincentives. In the matter of water rights they are rather quick to attend to the negative side, and unimaginative or reluctant to attend to the positive. Preventive Acts are quickly designed, facilitating processes are not even discussed. In the final analysis this may boil down to a firm conviction that water is a public property. This belief is so deeply rooted that the bureaucracy tends to think of itself as being fully informed about what is good and bad with water. Participation is talked about, but farmers are expected to do what the bureaucracy desires them to do. Negotiations in this setting can have little effect. The prerequisite of a meaningful negotiation is that both parties are willing learners.

This is not to say that leaving matters to the control of local communities is necessarily the answer. A single authority over a territory can facilitate systematic allocation, whereas division of authority into smaller territories may endanger existing networks. It may be recalled that the Bihar and Orissa Private Irrigation Works Act, 1922 was proposed partly because of the problems of maintenance arising out of the partition of *zamindari* estates. The Act empowered the bureaucracy to function as a single authority over the whole system. That the bureaucracy did not address the allocation issue is a different matter.

The challenge today, in the context of policies favoring local governance over natural resources, is to find the appropriate balance between government coordination, and incentives for local management. Although formal laws and regulations may not be followed in practice, they cannot be ignored, as they form an essential part of the context within which local negotiations take place. At the same time, there are a range of systems through which rights have been defined and redefined, though formal law may try to freeze this into a misunderstood snapshot. The arrangements in any irrigation system constantly change—for environmental, institutional, or other reasons. To provide full scope for creative local adaptations to emerge, the state apparatus needs to be flexible in its approaches, based on better information about local conditions.

Notes

1. Pronounced as *paa-in*. This spelling was in use in early English records. Replacement by a modern mode of spelling or by the proper English word (canal) would create some confusion in the following text. Hence, this term will be retained.
2. This local term is more famous as '*barabandi*' or '*warabandi*' used in Punjab and U.P., as well as in the terminology used by the irrigation departments of India. The form, '*parabandi*,' which still survives in Bihar, is found in *Arthashastra*, a public administrative manual written at least 2,000 years ago.
3. This flexible land use pattern is widespread in the drier western India.

References

Benda-Beckmann, Franz von and **Menno van der Velde**, eds. 1992. *Law as a resource in agrarian struggles*. Wageningse Sociologische Studies 33. Wageningen: Agricultural University.

Bihar, Legislative Assembly. 1939. *Proceedings of the Bihar Legislative Assembly, February 13, Discussion on Bihar Private Irrigation Works Act Amendment Bill*. Patna: Government Printing Press.

Coward, E. Walter, Jr. 1985. Property, resistance and participation: The state and traditional irrigation system. Paper presented at 1985 meeting of the Society for Economic Anthropology, April 11–13, Warrenton, Virginia.

————. 1990. Property rights and network order: The case of irrigation works in the Western Himalayas. *Human Organization* 49 (1): 78–88.

Galanter, Marc. 1989. *Law and society in modern India*. Delhi: Oxford University Press.

Hardman, J.S. 1938. Note prepared by J.S. Hardman, I.C.S., Collector of Gaya, Government of Bihar, Revenue Department, Memo No. 3108-R, Patna, 10 April 1938 (handwritten).

Heston, Alan and **Dharma Kumar.** 1983. Persistence of land fragmentation in peasant agriculture: An analysis of South Asian cases. *Explorations in Economic History* 20: 199–220.

India. Irrigation Commission. 1903. *Report of the Irrigation Commission, 1901–1903, Part II (Provincial)*. Calcutta: Government Printing Press.

India. Planning Commission, Committee on Plan Projects. 1966. *Irrigation team all India review of minor irrigation works based on statewise field studies*. New Delhi: Government of India.

McCay, Bonnie J. and **James M. Acheson, eds.** 1990. *The question of the commons: The culture and ecology of communal resources*. Tucson: University of Arizona Press.

McClosky, D.N. 1975a. The economics of enclosures: A market analysis. In *European peasants and their markets*, ed. W.N. Parker and E.L. Jones 73–119. Princeton, N.J.: Princeton University Press.

————. 1975b. The persistence of English common fields. In *European peasants and their markets*, ed. W.N. Parker and E.L. Jones 123–60. Princeton, N.J.: Princeton University Press.

Ostrom, Elinor. 1992. *Crafting institutions for self-governing irrigation systems*. San Francisco: Institute for Contemporary Studies.

Pradhan, Rajendra and **Ujjwal Pradhan.** 2000. Negotiating access and rights: A case study of disputes over rights to an irrigation water source in Nepal. In *Negotiating Water Rights*, ed. Bryan R. Bruns and Ruth Meinzen-Dick 200–221. New Delhi: Vistaar.

Sengupta, Nirmal. 1980. Indigenous irrigation organization of South Bihar. *Indian Economic and Social History Review* 17 (2): 157–89.

————. 1985. Field system, property reform and indigenous irrigation. Paper presented at Second Workshop on Comparative Study of India and Indonesia, Cambridge, Leiden, Delhi and Yogjakarta University Project, October, Leiden.

Sengupta, Nirmal. 1991. *Managing common property: Irrigation in India and Philippines*. New Delhi: Sage Publications.

————. 1993a. Land records and irrigation rights. In *Land reforms in India, Volume 1. Bihar-institutional constraints*, ed. B.N. Yugandhar and K. Gopal Iyer. New Delhi: Sage Publications.

————. 1993b. *User-friendly irrigation designs*. New Delhi: Sage Publications.

————. 1996. Common pool resources, Indian legal system and private initiative. Conference on Law and Economics, Indian Statistical Institute, January 11–13, 1996, New Delhi.

Sherrard, G.C. 1916. Indigenous irrigation works in Bihar and their improvement. *Agricultural Journal of India* 11 (2).

Singh, R.P. and **A. Kumar.** 1970. *Monograph of Bihar*. Patna: Bharathi Bhavan.

Spiertz, H.L. Joep. 2000. Water rights and legal pluralism: Some basics of a legal anthropological approach. In *Negotiating Water Rights*, ed. Bryan R. Bruns and Ruth Meinzen-Dick 162–199. New Delhi: Vistaar.

Tanner, E.L. 1919. *Final report on the survey and settlement operations in the district of Gaya, 1911–1918*. Patna: Government Printing Press.

Washbrook, David. 1981. Law, state and agrarian society in Colonial India. *Modern Asian Studies* 15 (3): 649–721.

Williams, R.A.E. 1941. *Final report on the revised settlement operations under section 112, Bihar Tenancy Act, in eleven sub-divisions of the Patna, Gaya, Shahabad, and Monghyr districts (1937–41)*. Patna: Government Printing Press.

6

Water Rights and Legal Pluralism: Some Basics of a Legal Anthropological Approach

H.L. JOEP SPIERTZ

*The case of irrigation in the Balinese village of Blahpane serves to intro-
duce concepts of legal pluralism. This kind of legal anthropology critiques
and reconceives the relations between law and social behavior. The conceptual tools of legal pluralism can improve understanding of water
rights, starting from the study of local experience amid multiple legal, ritual, and other normative repertoires. A better understanding of the social
significance of law contributes to rethinking development policies and
research on water rights issues.*

Introduction

Since water is of existential importance for human life and organization, water rights are a major issue of ongoing debate, conflict,
negotiation and regulation at the international, interstate, and the
national and regional levels. In many societies, competition for

water, both intersectoral and among parties within certain sectors, such as irrigated agriculture, is endemic. It follows that the conceptualizations of types of water resources, and of rights to use and control them, should be expected to form key elements in any legal system, from the laws of national states down to pre-existing religious or local customary law systems (F. von Benda-Beckmann et al. 1996, 1997; Geertz 1972; Pradhan et al. 1997; Wiber 1992).

Legal Pluralism

A suitable analytical tool for the study of law and human behavior can be found in the concept of 'legal pluralism,' as it has been developed in contemporary legal anthropology. What legal pluralism amounts to, and what its methodological and theoretical merits may be, I will briefly discuss below. What is important to note here is that legal pluralism strongly conveys the notion that, if we want to study water rights in the context of irrigators, engineers and petty bureaucrats on the local levels of water use and management, we have to put aside the conceptualizations of law and society that dominate both legal scholarship and social science approaches. The conceptual framework of legal pluralism is indispensable in view of contemporary water rights policy paradigms which hold that local customary, community-based water rights and organizations for water management should get more attention, should receive recognition or even be re-introduced. It offers tools which can better comprehend how farmers, village leaders, bureaucrats and others live amidst and employ multiple normative repertoires. It aims to explore the different conceptualizations of water and water rights, the functions of water as a natural resource, and the variety of legal statuses attached to water.[1] All these are essential preconditions for any effort to understand or improve water management. Legal pluralism as a tool for understanding law 'in' society makes it its business to explore the relationships between the various legal orders, the types of interest, and the social relationships and practices involving resources in local contexts of social interaction. Research from a perspective of legal pluralism is therefore a prerequisite for recent water policy paradigms, whether they focus on creating property regimes for groundwater control by the state, on bolstering customary law regimes for farmer-managed irrigation systems, or on the possible types and forms of conflict management.

Scope of the Paper

Before going deeper into the problems of water rights and the theoretical and methodological concerns of contemporary legal anthropology, it is instructive to introduce some concepts of legal pluralism within the concrete context of Blahpane, a Balinese village. The complex and contested history of irrigation in this locality illustrates challenges facing those who wish to understand, or modify, water management. Following this case, the second section presents theoretical issues of legal pluralism, showing how the ideas of legal pluralism differ from earlier conceptions and suggesting what legal pluralism means for studying water rights. The third section briefly applies some of these conceptual tools to analyze policy implications on the issues of governance and development, and dilemmas in the field of customary law and water rights. The final section summarizes key points of the legal pluralism paradigm.

The Case of Blahpane

Anyone visiting the island of Bali is easily convinced of the local existence of a very special and powerful organizational structure governing irrigated agriculture. The picturesque sights offered by the island's abundance of obviously well-planned and maintained rice terraces with their intricate patterns of canals, ditches, weirs and water division structures leave little doubt that the *subak*, the famous traditional community irrigation associations of Bali, are very much alive. Local brochures and guides for tourist information similarly convey this message, as do piles of pamphlets, papers, reports, and maps filling the cabinets and bookshelves in many local bureaucrats' and policymakers' offices.[2]

Laws and Institutional Properties as Bargaining Chips

The case of Blahpane shows clearly that realities in the villages and the paddies as well as in the government offices, cannot simply be identified with the structural properties and legal repertoires of Balinese social organization of irrigation and water management.

Local actors negotiate and renegotiate water rights. In the process of forming profitable alliances they use the institutional and legal contexts as bargaining chips. The case affirms that, contrary to the common ideas about rules and behavior, reality cannot be deduced from the normative versions of the valid laws and institutions. It also shows how local actors' representations of reality may be manipulated to make them, seemingly, fit the authoritative institutional repertoires. Similar instances of people manipulating the legal and normative contexts of irrigation can, among others, be found in reports from Nepal (Pradhan and Pradhan 1996) and Sri Lanka (Spiertz and de Jong 1992).

Structuralist and Functionalist Approaches

Data on *subak* are quite abundant, ranging from the first reports of Dutch seafarers in the 16th century to prestigious colonial works describing local customary law.[3] A substantial amount of additional data turns up in contemporary reports on the problems of integrating the local irrigation corporations into the new technological and administrative structures going with government-induced irrigation management programs.[4] Most data on the institutional aspects of *subak*, however, are based on structural-functionalist descriptions and pay little attention to the more empirical issue of how the *subak* laws and institutions relate to actual social practices.[5]

Blahpane Village

Blahpane is a small village in central Bali's district of Gianyar. Although it sits close to the main tourist route from the southern coast to the mountain resorts of the Bangli District, the village of Blahpane is characterized by an atmosphere of remoteness, relative poverty and backwardness, features shared with many inland Balinese villages. By origin Blahpane was a military outpost, guarding the northern border of the fiefdom of Sidan against marauding bands from the mountain principality of Bangli. The habit of the lords of Sidan to switch alliances caused Blahpane to be claimed alternately by the dominant principalities of Gianyar in the west and Klungkung in the east. Colonial intervention in the beginning of this century suppressed petty warfare between principalities and established

Bangli, Klungkung and Gianyar as administrative districts. After this, the Blahpane area was administered first by the District of Klungkung, and later formally incorporated in the District of Gianyar (see Map 6.1).[6]

A Broken Rice Bowl

Blahpane's present village structure reflects its history and geography. Blahpane, its name expressing the equivalent of a broken rice-bowl, counts two residential hamlets of about 500 inhabitants each, separated by a small chasm running north–south. Socially and politically, Blahpane is split in two parts. One part looks to the west, where at a distance of a few miles, the large village of Sidan forms the religious, political and administrative (subdistrict) center. The other part looks south, where the major village of Tulikup forms a similar center (see Map 6.1). Although the Blahpane area is geographically separated from Sidan by several deep gorges, both hamlets of Blahpane are administratively part of the Sidan subdistrict of Gianyar District.[7]

An Administrative and Economic Border-Case

Geographically and administratively an out-of-the-way place, Blahpane is cut-off from the bustling cultural and economic activity of the Gianyar region. Pinned against the Gianyar–Bangli border in the north, the village economy orients itself towards the northern enemies of old. Bangli, however, being a much poorer region than Gianyar, offers little economic opportunity. Social relations with the Bangli villagers are often a bit strained. Means of subsistence in Blahpane mainly revolve around its paddies and house-yards, producing rice and vegetables, coconuts, cloves, and the like.

Subak Gelulung According to the Irrigation Office

Maps and registers of the Gianyar District irrigation offices, dating from 1987–88, show part of the irrigation area of Blahpane as governed by a unit called Subak Gelulung. Gelulung's acreage is assessed to be some 15 hectares, and its leader is reported to be a man called Wayan Dingin.[8] But other entries in the register do not mention Gelulung as a *subak* but as a *tempek*, which would mean that

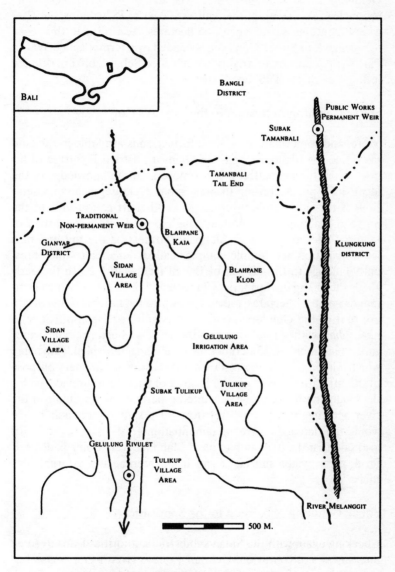

Map 6.1: Blahpane Irrigation Sites

Gelulung is only a sub-*subak* unit.[9] The acreage of Tempek Gelulung
is not clear. At one point the register speaks of 15 hectares, but elsewhere mentions an acreage of 66 hectares. According to this register, Tempek or Subak Gelulung is headed by a farmer called Wayan
Panas and is part of an irrigation unit called Subak Tulikup, situated
in the area of the Tulikup subdistrict.

Subak Gelulung According to the Tax Collector

More, and somewhat different, information is available in the land
tax office for Blahpane's part of Gianyar District. By virtue of his
profession, the tax collector has a more accurate knowledge of the
local situation. According to him, Subak Gelulung is a confederation of the old Gelulung unit and another irrigation unit to the
north of Blahpane. This unit, although located within the district of
Gianyar and consisting of Blahpane farmers, is the tail end of a
large irrigation and temple complex called Tamanbali, which presently belongs to the district of Bangli (see Map 6.1). In the early
1960s the Blahpane farmers of Tamanbali tail-end area, which commands about 31 hectares, joined forces with the farmers of the northern part of the Gelulung area. They established (semi-officially) a
new *subak* with a total command area of 47 hectares, which they
called Gelulung, or, sometimes also Gelulung/Tamanbali (the name
which will be used in the rest of this discussion). The main purpose
of this affiliation was to get the District of Gianyar to provide aid for
the Blahpane farmers. They wanted a permanent weir built in the
river Melanggit, on Bangli territory, at a spot where their intake
would not damage upstream Tamanbali interests. The tax collector
also said that the irrigation units of Blahpane were doing badly, suffering from water shortages and from internal and external conflicts.

Subak Gelulung According to the Subdistrict

Checking again with the Sidan subdistrict authorities leads to some
uneasiness and confusion. Gelulung, one is given to understand, is
indeed the *subak* of the village Blahpane, but there is also a Subak
Gelulung that is part of the Tamanbali complex, and another
Gelulung which belongs to the Tulikup system. But all fall under the
Sidan subdistrict administration. It may seem a bit strange that such

different estimates of the identities and acreages of the local irrigation units would exist both among the various levels of local government and between the local administration and the villagers. It should be noted, however, that this is not so uncommon at all, in Bali as well as elsewhere, especially where units are hydrologically interconnected, with reuse of water (as also mentioned in Guillet's case from Spain in this volume). It would be wrong to see in this merely a sign of a failing bureaucratic grasp and administrative inaccuracy. As I will discuss below, it also signifies the political complexities of local interest management and negotiating water rights.

Local Perspectives

The intricate political complexities of negotiating water rights are reflected in the different versions of the local *subak* territories given by the farmers and their leaders. A visit to Blahpane makes this clear. Coming from the south, one first arrives at the hamlet of Blahpane Klod, the poorer and more backward part of the village. Asking to see the local *subak* leader causes a flutter of discussions among the men who sit passing the afternoon in the shelter of the Klod hamlet community building. Finally a very old man, who may not have seen the paddy fields for long time, can be found to take the responsibility for explaining that in Blahpane there exists no real *subak* at all. The area is just '*natak tiis*,' which means that its landowners are dependent on the drains and seepage of the upstream parts of the Tamanbali complex. Many of them therefore have become sharecroppers in the *subaks* of the Tulikup area. As for Gelulung, that is just part of Tulikup. But then, another, younger man claims that Gelulung is not only part of Tulikup but is also a *subak* in its own right, of which he himself, Wayan Panas, is the leader.

Claims and Counterclaims

This claim by Wayan Panas turns out to be at odds with popular opinion in the northern Blahpane hamlet, Blahpane Kaja. Here, a local farmer, Wayan Dingin, who is also mentioned in the Gianyar registers as the leader of Subak Gelulung, advances quite a different version of the situation. Wayan Dingin proves more than ready to boast of his own *subak* leadership in the Blahpane area, and his father's before him. He claims that in the early 1960s his father, a landowner in the tail end of the Tamanbali system, took the initiative and negotiated a local alliance needed to muster the labor, as well as the financial and political support, for realizing the old ambition of the Tamanbali farmers of Blahpane Kaja: that is, to become independent from the main Tamanbali system in 'foreign' Bangli by persuading the government to build them their own weir in the river Melanggit. Wayan Dingin claims that this alliance of both Tamanbali tail-enders and Gelulung farmers constitutes present Subak Gelulung, of which he is the leader.

Irrigation History and Ensuing Rights

Blahpane Kaja

The northern 30-odd hectares of paddy fields of Blahpane Kaja lie at the tail end of the large Tamanbali irrigation complex, the central and top end of which lies not in Gianyar but in the District of Bangli. According to Blahpane Kaja inhabitants their paddies recurrently suffered severe water shortages caused by bad irrigation management and the unfriendly attitude of the Bangli farmers and *subak* authorities. Memories of past eras of mutual skirmishing and warfare, involving blocking water supplies and accusations of water-theft, did not help much. The situation was all the more intolerable since Blahpane Kaja never failed to fulfill its ritual obligations to the Tamanbali head-system.

Planning a Weir

On the main-Tamanbali territory, at about half a mile, in bird's-eye view, to the northeast of Blahpane, the Melanggit river plunges into deep gorges, becoming inaccessible until it reaches the Klungkung District to the southeast. It had long annoyed Blahpane farmers that Tamanbali irrigation policies kept them cut-off from a major source of irrigation water which direct access to upstream Melanggit would provide. A weir in the Melanggit, at a spot precisely above the precipice where the river water disappears into the gorge would not harm Tamanbali interests, they reasoned. But by a carefully devised system of tunnels and open canals, a (relatively still small) amount of the Melanggit surplus water could be conducted from the new weir to the Blahpane Kaja area, instead of being lost into Klungkung territory. In the early 1960s the political climate appeared favorable for securing government support for such a project, especially since the farmers consented to dig the tunnels and canals themselves.

Negotiating Alliance and Water Rights

In the perception of the Blahpane farmers it was necessary to present the idea of the new weir to the Gianyar authorities as an authentic Gianyar District endeavor. It was important to avoid having the project seen as a rehabilitation of the tail end of the Bangli-based Tamanbali system. Therefore, but also to muster the manpower required for digging the tunnels and canals, the tail-end Tamanbali farmers of Blahpane Kaja contrived to ally with a group of fellow villagers whose paddies were located within the Gelulung irrigation area.

The Gelulung area, lying to the west and south of the hamlet of Blahpane Klod, counts farmers from both Blahpane Klod and Blahpane Kaja. However disputable its precise territory and formal status may be, in one form or another a Gianyar-based irrigation unit called Subak Gelulung is officially registered with the Gianyar administration. This does not apply for the Tamanbali tail end. Since they are considered part of the of the Tamanbali complex, its farmers even have to pay their land tax to Bangli instead of Gianyar.

The Gelulung area, whether or not considered part of Subak Tulikup to the south, was dependent for its irrigation water on a traditional, semi-permanent weir in a rivulet fed only by drainage and seepage, called Tukad Gelulung (see Map 6.1). Therefore many of its farmers were not unwilling to sever whatever ties they had with the Tulikup system and join the Tamanbali tail-end farmers in their effort to get the Gianyar administration support for their project. An agreement was negotiated between them and the Tamanbali tail-enders to the effect that they would construct a division block in the new canal to provide their paddies with one-third of the Melanggit water. But in relation to the Gianyar authorities, it now became the Subak Gelulung, claiming to comprise the whole Blahpane irrigation area, which was presented as the unit applying for support. In order to stress this point, the Gelulung farmers seem even to have arranged a formal split off ritual with Subak Tulikup.

Building the Scheme

Headed by its Tamanbali initiator, the father of Wayan Dingin, Gelulung/Tamanbali succeeded in finding Gianyar administration's support for the new weir in the Melanggit River. It appears that in 1964, the district of Gianyar initiated the construction of the weir. During construction, public works personnel suddenly pulled out. The construction was left for the farmers to complete for themselves, which they did. People maintain that the government's backing out of the project was due to a combination of several factors: the right to collect land tax revenues of the Blahpane Kaja part of the new scheme was not transferred from Bangli to Gianyar; upper Tamanbali was indignant at seeing part of its old *subak* territory breaking away; and the national political upheavals of 1964–65 accompanied a political and ideological swing back to traditionalism, especially in Bali. Another consideration may have been that such investments in an irrigated area of some 47 hectares would have been costly, even taking into account the benefits for the Tulikup area.

Ambiguity in Administrative and Socio-religious Contexts

The new *subak* of Gelulung/Tamanbali comprised of two *tempeks*, one of which was the Blahpane Kaja area at the tail-end of Tamanbali and the other the northern paddies of the Gelulung part of Tulikup. Although they might pretend otherwise, the formation of the new *subak* meant that local bureaucrats had to cope now with three Gelulungs in the area. There was (*a*) Blahpane's new confederated *subak* of Gelulung/Tamanbali—usually called just Gelulung; (*b*) a Gelulung Subak which had formally seceded from Tulikup (but was not perceived as including the Tamanbali tail end); and (*c*) a Gelulung still seen, at least by parts of the administration, as a sub-*subak* of Tulikup.

Another source of confusion, to outsiders anyway, was the fact that, in terms of religious and ritual obligations, the Tamanbali part of Gelulung/Tamanbali was never severed from the main Tamanbali complex. This may have been why the Gelulung/Tamanbali confederation never erected its own weir temple on the Melanggit river bank. Perhaps this would too bluntly identify the area as a new *subak* broken away from Tamanbali. For similar reasons also, discussions

on officially giving a new name to the Gelulung/Tamanbali enterprise remained inconclusive. The reasons given for not building a
proper weir-temple vary from the difficulty of the terrain, lack of
funding, and fear of hurting Tamanbali feelings, to rationalizations
that no temple is needed to worship the gods.

Problems

The new Gelulung/Tamanbali Subak was ill-omened from the start.
It remains a matter of debate whether the absence of a proper weir-
temple might have had something to do with it. Once the new weir
was completed, it did not take long for problems to turn up. They
are the same problems which presently deeply influence irrigation
relations in the Blahpane area. The water supply of the Gelulung/
Tamanbali Subak has remained insufficient. Along the mountain-
slopes, landslides regularly destroy stretches of the open canal. So,
maintenance of the canal involves much labor. A tunnel runs for a
kilometer on the edge of the Tamanbali terrain, and still depends on
the Tamanbali drains. The tunnel has caved in at several places. As a
consequence, there currently is a mood of wariness among the villagers with respect to taking part in *subak* maintenance and repair
work. There are also quiet but unpleasant local rumors as to
whether the tunnel collapse was due to errors by the villagers who
built the tunnel, or was caused by sabotage.

Gianyar District Declines to Help

Wayan Dingin and his friends have filed many requests over the
years with the Gianyar administration, asking for its support for the
improvement and rehabilitation of the canal. The district has turned
down all these requests. As it is understood at the local level in
Blahpane, the present Gianyar authorities' point of view is that the
Blahpane Kaja part of the area belongs to the Bangli-based *subak* of
Tamanbali. Since land tax revenues of Blahpane Kaja never went to
Gianyar, it is up to the District of Bangli to provide support for the
canal, if this is considered necessary.

Farmers Backing Out of the New Legal Construction

Many Gelulung farmers have been disappointed by the meager
results of the joint efforts. They have gradually started to turn their

backs on the Gelulung/Tamanbali association and orient themselves again to a Gelulung as part of the Tulikup system. It is rumored that the government will assist Tulikup in the near future.[10] They appear to have shifted loyalty from Wayan Dingin to his rival *subak* leader from Blahpane Klod, Wayan Panas, who claims to be responsible for the whole Gelulung area. It suits their interests now to refrain from taking part in Gelulung/Tamanbali Subak activities, and to even 'steal' water from their fellow confederacy members to pass on the surplus to their old friends in the Gelulung/Tulikup basin. By this strategy they apparently hope to be seen once more as a part of a Gelulung which is no longer tainted by the blind alley of the Gelulung/Tamanbali affiliation.

Blahpane Kaja Farmers Cling to Their New Found Means of Establishing Water Rights

The Tamanbali tail-end farmers expect nothing from Bangli. They have tried to curb the process of Gelulung/Tamanbali falling apart by staging activities that emphasize the unity of the confederation. The increasing incidents and misdemeanors by their Gelulung/Tulikup partners are not appreciated, but still are mostly left unpunished. If charged by the Sidan authorities with lax irrigation management and failure to maintain cropping regulations, they invariably refer to the water shortages and not to the internal conflicts.

Recently, an affluent resident of Blahpane Kaja donated a plot of land to the corporation to found a temple for the Gelulung/Tamanbali Subak. Such a temple would symbolically prove the *subak*'s existence and unity as a public and religious corporation. Once consecrated, the new temple soon had to be given up as a *subak* meeting place because farmers feared the temple would be profaned by the disputes frequently flaring between Blahpane Klod and Blahpane Kaja members.

Schemes of Meaning

In a sense, the case of the *subak* in Blahpane may be exceptional. Irrigation corporations in Bali do not generally have to cope with all the special problems encountered by the Blahpane farmers. Still, what makes this case so instructive is that it clearly shows that complex sets of cultural and normative schemes of meaning connect people with their natural and social resources. People construe concepts and categories of 'natural resources' through these schemes of meaning. They try to control, exploit, and preserve these 'natural resources' through institutionalized relationships and social practices. The case is instructive also in that it shows how rural people are not simply confronted with a single, unitary legal system—whether consisting of customary *subak* law 'or' official state law—but are confronted with a co-existence and complexity of legal and administrative phenomena. We even saw that similar complexities confront state bureaucrats and project officials as well. This co-existence and also the mutual permeability of different cognitive and normative repertoires is derived from and embedded in a multiplicity of normative and legal systems pertaining to one and the same domain of human life as F. von Benda-Beckmann (1983) puts it. It is to such multiplicities that we refer to as 'legal pluralism.'

Concepts of Legal Pluralism

Over the last 20 years or so it has become a main objective of legal anthropology (that is, the type of legal anthropology I am referring to in these pages) to demystify and to deconstruct the conventional conceptualizations of law in society. It is not my intention here to criticize or diminish the legal science approaches to the social significance of law. It can hardly be denied, however, that conventional legal science approaches, operating, as perhaps they should, from an essentially normative conception of law and society, cannot offer the appropriate tools to understand the actual significance of rights, and their institutional and legal frameworks in social practice.[11] This, *a fortiori*, counts for studies on water rights. Water rights studies have generally not only been dominated by the conventional ethnocentric and legal science dominated perspectives, but have remained relatively scarce as well.

Law and Water

It may seem a truism to mention that throughout history, issues of water rights have formed part of law and legislation, and, by consequence, of legal science and doctrine.[12] Still there exists a relative under-exposure of water law in legal scholarship. To most lawyers, water is a somewhat elusive object if compared with the more self-evident legal dimensions of less fluid matter, such as land. In terms of property for instance, water rights not surprisingly used to be derived from land rights. But the problems encountered in the study of water rights are not caused by the relative marginality of water law alone. Especially if one wants to grasp not only the legal lexicons but also the social significance of water law, one will have to deal with a generic characteristic water law shares with all other laws. This characteristic lies in what is called the 'double-faceted character' of law in society (Cotterrell 1984).

Law and Society

The prototypical legal rule consists of prescriptions or proscriptions, specifying the way people *ought* to behave. As such a law or a body of legal rules can be said to exist as a structural constraint in society. By some 'trick' of thought, however, the role of law as a (mere) structural constraint tends to become equated with social causation (Giddens 1979). Confusion and bias come about because the prototypical legal rule is both a prescriptive norm and a descriptive fact. It is this double-faceted character of law which confuses and biases legal and socio-legal analysis of the significance of law in society. What a legal rule or normative principle does is attach a normative proposition or evaluation to a fact it describes. It is often not realized that such 'legal facts' are not empirical facts. Ownership, for instance, may be a legal fact but not an empirical one, and vice versa. Legal facts are not the substantive descriptions of social practices they are often taken for; they are metaphorical or hypothetical only. Or, as F. von Benda-Beckmann (1983) puts it, they are only situation images. As such, legal rules and institutions are part of the structural properties of society. But whether or why society's descriptive/normative repertoires and actual people's behavior may correspond, remains a very different matter.

The Study of Water Rights

The confusion and bias caused by the double-faceted character of law lies at the background of most studies of water rights, common property approaches included. The habit of mixing up the empirical and the legal has been both reinforced and obscured by the social and cultural prestige derived from a general belief that law is the main source of order in society (Cotterrell 1984; Roberts 1979). In the wake of legal scholarship, not only anthropologists and sociologists, but also public administration scientists and, most notably, economists and agronomists have long neglected to scrutinize more carefully the relations between water law and water rights and water related social practices. The actual social significance of law was mostly assumed rather than empirically researched.[13] Recent water policy paradigms, however, which bring the issue of water rights to the forefront, seem to be triggering a different kind of water rights studies. There is a tendency at least to question the conventional outlook which consigns water rights to the formal legal lexicons and the domain of legal discourse. As is reflected in several chapters in this book, the new concern with water rights does not necessarily take the common assumptions about the social significance of law and rights for granted.

Reconceiving Law and Behavior

Blind spots

Sociology, anthropology, the various agro-economic and political sciences, and other disciplines studying water resource management, seem to have long nurtured a blind spot for the legal and para-legal dimensions of their objects of study. Generally, matters involving law, legislation, and rights have been either seen as irrelevant, or were seen as exclusively belonging to the domain of legal science. Nevertheless, quite contrary to what one would expect, social science's conceptualizations of social institutions, of social rules and human behavior, of common goods and private rights, of conflict and conflict management, have long been dominated by the bias of normative (basically legal) definitions.

Western Bias and Doctrinal Assumptions

The call for deconstruction and reconstruction of the analytical tools for socio-legal research did not come about accidentally. From its very origin legal anthropology has strongly been oriented to problems of comparison. In the wake of colonial domination over non-Western peoples, anthropology of law (or the mixtures of legal and social science which in retrospect can pass for early legal anthropology) started out to identify indigenous social rules and institutions which could qualify as representing indigenous peoples' legal systems. It may not be too surprising that the comparative basis of these efforts was predominantly grounded in Western legal bias and doctrinal assumptions.

Norms and Behavior

Besides a weak comparative basis, most of the earlier studies suffered from a profound bias regarding the interrelationship between society's legal lexicons or normative repertoires, and peoples' behavior. These relationships were mainly seen in terms of one-dimensional causalities, in which the 'living' norms could simply be deducted from behavior, and vice versa. Legal anthropology has not suffered alone from these conceptual weaknesses. Structuralist modes of focusing on social structures and institutions have similarly imprisoned mainstream anthropology and sociology, envisioning actual social practices and relationships mainly in terms of compliance or deviance. This, most contemporary social scientists will agree, is a myopic, lopsided way of looking at what is happening on the ground.

Mystification of Traditional Law

Colonial, and some postcolonial legal anthropology, persistently conceptualized (customary) law and practices in isolation from their wider socio-legal, administrative and political environment. Conceptual rigidity compounds this by preventing perception of, and accounting for, the processes of change within these systems. Such misconceptions have often resulted in mystification and romanticizing of the 'ancient, ingrained rules and practices of indigenous communities, based on stable, equitable, conservation-minded local knowledge.' On the other hand, customary laws and practices have often been vilified and accused of obstructing social and economic change. In this perception, tradition became backwardness; the (falsely) perceived equity of common property regimes became the 'tragedy of the commons'; lineage and extended family claims on property obstructed rational (that is, individualized) exploitation of productive resources, and so on. To a large extent such mystifications and false conceptualizations can be traced to biased ideas about how legal frameworks and social practices relate.

Versions of Legal Pluralism

Searching for more sophisticated ideas of the relationships between law and human behavior, legal anthropology developed the concept of 'legal pluralism' (F. von Benda-Beckmann 1983; Griffiths 1986; Merry 1988; Pospisil 1971; VanderLinden 1989). Legal pluralism was conceived of, at first, as 'the accommodation within national legal systems of a variety of bodies of law, customary, religious, and state law, applicable under specified conditions to the different ethnic, religious, and racial groups' (Sawyerr 1974).[14] To a large extent colonial policies of legal pluralism were rooted in the efforts to provide a legal basis for policies of Western domination and exploitation by the creation of separate social and economic spheres for the indigenous peoples.

The rapid increase of state presence in most domains of social life, especially in the developing countries after their independence, inspired legal anthropologists to come up with another concept of legal pluralism. Legal pluralism became defined now as the coexistence of multiple legal systems pertaining to *one* (a same) domain of social life (F. von Benda-Beckmann 1983). It was recognized, moreover, that there was no sound reason to confine legal anthropologists' concepts of legal orders to the strictly normative lawyer's definitions of legal systems. From a social science perspective which aims at studying the actual social significance of law, lawyer's law should be seen as forming only part of a multiplicity of institutional arrangements and normative repertoires in society. Legal anthropologists, therefore, include in their conceptual framework all instances in which other, officially nonlegal, institutions and normative lexicons are generated and maintained in social life. One speaks in this respect of unofficial law, or self-regulation. At the local levels, citizens as well as staff members of administrative agencies usually have to cope with a plurality of legal bodies or normative repertoires. Besides the norms of state agencies and legal science, versions of religious law, or traditions and various forms of self-regulation may also be part of the local legal universe (see F. Benda-Beckmann et al. 1996, 1997).

Destabilization of the Paradigm of the Centrality of Law

Perhaps the most useful element of such developments has been the destabilization of the deductive view of law as an institution central to social order. Real life experiences with law often do not support this view of the centrality of law (Spiertz and Wiber 1996). Pluralism is a 'condition, thus a way of being, of existing' (VanderLinden 1989) for the individual who in daily life is confronted with several, often contradictory, regulatory orders (Spiertz and Wiber 1996). Contrary to what one might expect, pluralism is not reduced or eliminated by the modern bureaucratic state's attempts at legal 'hegemony' (Griffiths 1986); the state often promotes legal pluralism by its interventionist habit of overregulation. This creates a condition of existence where many people constantly struggle to find their way within the pluralistic legal universe they live in, with its often contradictory, or compounding, norms and institutions.

A Different Perspective on Deviance and Non-Compliance

Another consequence of adopting a perspective of legal pluralism, or rather perhaps legal complexity, has been its impact on legal anthropologists' ideas of the relationship between rules and human behavior. Discrepancies between rules (belonging to whichever domain of society's structural and institutional frameworks) and behavior no longer need to be seen in terms of such one-dimensional categories as deviance or non-compliance, They have to be explained in terms of peoples' options. The same counts for rule-conforming behavior. In view of a complex, multilayered legal universe from which people can be imagined picking their choice, it becomes especially clear that specific social practices and law, customary law, or state law, or whatever structural and cultural properties, should not be analytically conflated (Spiertz 1991).

Water Rights in Local Experience

Shifting from Studying Rules to the Individual

In Blahpane as well as elsewhere, the legal and institutional properties of society are mobilized by local actors in the relevant arenas to gain access to the means of subsistence. However, phenomena like this have been greatly underexposed in legal science dominated approaches to the role of law in society. To study the real position of people in relation to the law requires a different methodological approach from that used in traditional legal studies. The focus has to shift away from law as a codified or customary set of rules, and turn instead to the individual who stands at the intersection point of many different legal domains. Studying the individual requires understanding the social arenas in which (s)he moves (Spiertz and Wiber 1996). Studying the individual means focusing on how enterprising agents, using natural resources, are embedded in several different layers of social organization. These layers include various bodies of cultural tradition, ideas and ideologies, the normative and regulatory institutions (with the attendant concepts of rights), the layers of professional and day-to-day practices, everyday social relationships and actors' interests (see F. von Benda-Beckmann 1995).

Legal Fields

In this effort there is considerable advantage in focusing on 'social loci' rather than on legal systems. As Moore (1978) observes, 'between the body politic and the individual, there are interposed various smaller organized social fields to which the individual 'belongs,' (e.g., professional or residential units) and these are more or less formally organized. In complex societies these fields are linked together and interact in a complex chain. One of the mechanisms by which they do this relates to the way that an individual simultaneously belongs to many different fields. Griffiths (1986) argues that the advantage of this view of the structure of social space is that we are not concerned with 'things' but with 'social loci.' Where such social fields have the power to generate rules and enforce them, we speak of a 'legal field.' However, it is important that these fields not be conceived of as impenetrable entities of an institutional character, but as bounded but permeable ones. They always intersect with other fields of social interest and activities (see Griffiths 1986; Spiertz and DeJong 1992). Much of the rules which average people experience, including rules about where they can live, how they can conduct their business, what social safety nets are available to them, how they get access to water and land, and other important considerations come from just these sorts of fields (see e.g., Wiber 1995).

Law as a Discourse

Legal fields may originate in diverse contexts such as politics, religion, economics, and common interest associations; examples may range from monastic orders to workers' unions, professional societies to veterans' associations, village communities, irrigation units, and bureaucrats' offices as well. Legal fields are potential forces for the generation and maintenance of rules within a small, circumscribed social group. This makes them ideal for the study of the relationship between rules and behavior (see F. von Benda-Beckmann 1988; Griffiths 1986; Merry 1988; Spiertz and Wiber 1996). As we have seen in the Blahpane case, within such legal fields, law is a distinctive manner of 'imagining the real' (Geertz 1983), and as such forms a 'discourse' which people employ under specific circumstances involving the planning for, justification of, or attack on various behavioral options (F. von Benda-Beckmann 1983).

One can clearly observe this, for instance, in the strategic use of the *subak* institutional repertoire in the Blahpane case. In their struggles to obtain, within the new government-built irrigation schemes, the amounts of water necessary for intensifying cultivation with high-yielding varieties, many *subak* corporations became oriented at displaying, at least to the outside world, some of the territorial and formal organizational dimensions of the ideal traditional, socio-religious, *subak* model, as it is known in terms of the local cultural repertoires. This is in spite of the fact that many of the rituals governing the production cycle became irrelevant with the introduction of high-yielding rice varieties. Formerly, the question whether an irrigation association could be considered to constitute a real, traditional *subak* (and not just a subunit or not even that) answering to the prerequisites of the dominant models, may have often been a non-issue. However, given the idioms of tradition that penetrated the language of interaction in the field of public administration, to be recognized as a real traditional *subak*, with its own territorial and personal authority derived from traditional law, became an asset to be guarded jealously.

The Multilocality of Law

In the Blahpane case one can see how law as an instrument of government policy as well as an instrument of local interest management is a double-faced medium. A legal repertoire may have different functions in different settings, such as government offices and village life. Keebet and Franz von Benda-Beckmann (1991) call this 'the multilocality of law.' They argue that it is important for getting a clearer understanding of the social significance of law to question the assumptions that go with saying that law (a law, or a normative framework) 'exists.' The existence of law, at the level of society's normative repertoires, should be analytically distinguished, therefore, from its existence in the social process. Legal repertoires, in a way, just 'hang in the air,' as Franz and Keebet von Benda-Beckmann phrase it, as long as the 'when' and 'where' of their actually becoming a social factor is not concretized, be it in parliamentary debate, courtroom deliberation, administrative decision-making, farmer choices on cropping patterns or whatever (see also Spiertz 1991, 1992). As the Blahpane case demonstrates, on this down-to-earth level of existence a law, or a normative institution can 'exist' very differently, and can mean different things in different localities. In a sense, the *subak* of the Sidan subdistrict administration, or the *subak* of Tamanbali, or the *subak* of Gelulung are not, or better, are only in specific situations, the *subak* of Wayan Dingin. In other words, plurality of law should not only be seen in terms of different normative systems pertaining to one domain of social life, but also in the way in which one legal rule or one institution can manifest itself differently in different levels and contexts.

Contradictory Versions of Local Legal Orders

Legal systems or subsystems are by no means well-integrated wholes, neither within the various government organizations nor in people's economic and social life. Local forms of customary and folk legal regulation are far from unambiguous. There are usually different, and often contradictory versions of local legal orders. They usually have different, and often conflicting, bases of political authority, substantive regulations, and procedural modes to solve problems and contain disputes (F. von Benda-Beckmann et al. 1997). Starting from peoples' daily experience we can also observe various sets of normative systems becoming intertwined in the local processes of social ordering. Such intertwined complexities characterize social, economic and political conditions in most rural areas. They are the daily experience of farmers, bureaucrats and development agents. Legal anthropology teaches researchers in the field of natural resource management, property regimes, and water rights, not to start from the normative oratory of the legal profession, nor from the recitals of local traditional law. Instead, the place to begin lies in people's daily experience regarding their normative environment, with all its ambiguity, variation and contradiction. It explicitly draws attention to what can be called 'the how, and the when and where' of the significance of law in social practice.

Policy Implications of Legal Pluralism

Growing concern about sustainable and equitable use and allocation of natural resources has triggered off new efforts to develop better policies addressing the reconstruction of governance, markets, and civil society in developing countries. While the primary concern is the reconstruction of the economy, legal and administrative elements have, again, become one of the central points of debate. For example, in the World Bank policy statements of the early 1990s on the issue of 'good governance': '...ecological considerations and ... political, and mainly legal-administrative factors, are no longer considered as factors external to the economy, but are brought *into* the economy ... it is through law that the reordered public and private regulatory domains must get their legitimate structure (F. von Benda-Beckmann 1994: 57).'

Governance and Development

In the ensuing debates on the relationship of good governance and economy, it became clear that to the World Bank the issue was not so much the actual relationships between economic, political, and legal factors, but how they 'ought' to be. So, here again, normative considerations predominated. Instead of concern with establishing new scientific insights between economy and governance, the World Bank appeared to be concerned with creating a wider berth for pragmatic maneuvering within the emerging new constraints in the sphere of its activities (F. von Benda-Beckmann 1994: 58), i.e., the statement of principle that 'the rule of law' must become the guideline for legislative, administrative and judicial activities in the member countries.

Reading Catch-all Concepts

The tendency to highlight the normative rhetoric of the 'rule of law' as a resource for the legitimation of opportunistic maneuvering apparently is not confined to local conditions, like those in the Blahpane Subak case, alone. If one looks at the sweeping statements of international development policies from the perspective of the insights that lie at the basis of legal pluralism, such catch-all concepts as 'the rule of law' (Gutto 1982) lose much of their magic. It is not hard to see then that in the Bank's policy statements (World Bank 1991, 1992) normative rhetoric took the place of genuine efforts to analyze the relationship between governance and development. Or, quoting F. von Benda-Beckmann again (1994: 61):

> It is promising that more attention is finally being given to law in the circles of economists, political scientists and development planners. However, the assumptions underlying such attention are disquieting in their simplicity and normative orientation, as well as in their lack of insight into the ways in which legal structures acquire social and economic significance.

The Normative Fairyland vs. Unpleasant Facts

Thus the World Bank selectively took into account the normative principles of the 'rule of law' to accommodate equally normative, economic doctrines of deregulation and privatization directed against government intervention. The different principles were reconciled by a normative manipulation of the linkage between governance and development, which stipulated that the 'rule of law' should not be considered a goal in itself, but 'is only relevant to the extent that it establishes a set of preconditions for development' (World Bank, 1992, as cited by F. von Benda-Beckmann 1994). Legal anthropology, now, can teach us what the mixture of products of grand and undifferentiated rhetorics of wishful thinking which constitutes the 'normative fairyland' (F. von Benda-Beckmann 1994: 59), comes to in social reality. Instead of believing the normative fairyland, we would conceive of it simply as data; as factors in the much more encompassing universe of real life where we are confronted with many unpleasant if not unexpected facts. Among these are corruption, legal insecurity, violations of human rights, economic monopolies, inhuman labor conditions, increasing ecological problems, and many other inequitable consequences of economic change (F. von Benda-Beckmann 1994).

To take one example: corruption. Corruption is a phenomenon that can be seen as one of the clearest indications that strictly legally planned development is a fiction (Mooij 1992). Most development planners still see corruption simply as deviant behavior. They do not usually ask why they should rely on the assumption that officials will conform to what they are expected to do according to the official rules. From a legal anthropological point of view, however, corruption can (should) be analyzed as an instance of legal pluralism; multiplicity and complexity of normative frameworks. The effect of taking the perspective of legal pluralism here might be, at least, a sensitization of development planners, who mostly seem to find it unproblematic to continue thinking in terms of public and private spheres. The analytical conceptualizations of legal pluralism which I explained with the help of the Blahpane case, may help to realize that 'the normative construction of the relationships through which different organizational structures are distinguished and interrelated and divided into public and private spheres, are not identical with actual relationships and practices' (F. von Benda-Beckmann 1994: 62).

The Reach of Legal Pluralism

It can be argued that legal pluralism offers both a good reason and a fitting instrument for looking into issues of property rights and privatization, as well as into the functioning of bureaucracy. Legal pluralism forms both an addition to and a specialization of actor-oriented socio-legal research and policy. The insight that for social studies of the relationships between state and citizens it is not enough to give consideration only to the 'normatively defined, official and public relations that the state "should" have with its citizens' (F. von Benda-Beckmann 1994: 62), makes this clear. The approach we call legal pluralism is indispensable wherever and whenever one directs policy and research objectives at the linkage of governance and development, or governance and equity, governance and livelihood, governance and the protection of common goods, or governance and whatever. It holds true in the case of World Bank policies, as well as common property rights research and activists' conceptualizations. But it also applies to many, seemingly rather mundane, issues like the too broad and, if one comes to think about it, often basically normative concepts we use to conceptualize social structures and institutions. It may go without saying that this counts for the concepts of our trade like rights, ownership, state law, customary law, etcetera. But it also applies to seemingly more neutral concepts, like *subak*, community, boundaries, stakeholders. Often these can also be identified as representing mainly normative definitions of bundles of relationships, which in real life may acquire varying constellations or dimensions of social relations. We only have to take a look at the Blahpane case to see this confirmed.

The Dilemma of Recognizing Customary Law[15]

Narrowing down to water rights and customary law, there is another issue that bears on the implications of the legal pluralism approach for planning policy. In contemporary development policy it is deemed important to involve local people in the processes of change and development intervention as well as take their customary institutions and laws seriously into account. On some occasions in the recent past this has been tried, with questionable success, by the re-introduction of allegedly effective and equitable traditional institutions, like *bethma* in Sri Lanka (see Spiertz and de Jong 1992). But what are the possibilities and problems when one wants to give serious attention to customary law in water rights policies? How can we take current customary rules and practices into account?

Customary Law, Local Law and Inequality

When one talks about taking customary law and practices into account, one usually does so out of the conviction that these norms are an expression of the people's own values, and that intervention and legislation have to avoid measures that would weaken or contradict them. This normative assumption underlies many water policy efforts. Customary law is often taken to be inherently democratic, egalitarian, equitable and therefore deserving support, while state law or government regulations are not. Yet there is ample evidence that in local communities unequal power relationships greatly affect the ways in which water is distributed and managed and the extent to which norms are being followed.

Thus questions that seem not immediately relevant for the study of water rights or the framing of water policy come into focus, such as whether 'the community' is a homogeneous category, who the social, economic, and political élites are, and to what extent social stratification and power positions are supported by customary law. With regards to water rights themselves, we need to ask whether and how water rights differ for different social classes or castes, men and women, original occupants and newcomers. Finally, it is essential to ask who profits from the existing arrangements.

To Recognize Which Customary Law?

It appears that local differences in political and economic power are crucial for our understanding of the question whether, by whom and with how much success decision-making authorities, functionaries of village institutions or state courts, can be mobilized. From legal anthropological research it is known that the powerless have far more difficulty than the powerful in mobilizing law and legal institutions, whether state institutions or other, to defend their interests. Local law thus may not be democratic at all. On the other hand, since local law usually is a mixture of elements from a changing constellation of legal pluralism, it may in some respects be more democratic and flexible than the 'official' repertoires of customary law.

As legal pluralism makes clear, often there is not one generally accepted local law, nor is there is a valid criterion on which to select among the existing versions of local law. Moreover, none of the existing versions may go back to ancient tradition. Finally, incorporation almost inevitably leads to change and distortion. The colonial history has shown that it is exceedingly difficult if not impossible to incorporate customary law into the state legal system without changing it in a fundamental way. This poses a dilemma for researchers and legal advisors who are called upon to provide information on customary law, especially if they are sympathetic to it. To make local law relevant in the court and policy contexts often requires framing them in a language which will be more readily accepted by policy makers, but this involves adapting, changing and even distorting local law. Yet without this, there is a risk that policymakers and judges will not find the research evidence relevant in their own framework. In changing roles from academic scholar to advocate for customary law, the researcher risks becoming a bad scholar; or else he remains a research scholar and risks becoming an unsuccessful advocate. Social science provides little guidance on this essentially pragmatic and political decision (F. von Benda-Beckmann et al. 1996).

Taking Customary or Local Law into Account as Significant Factors

Whatever choice one makes in this dilemma, and however one may value local law and practices, they are facts of social life and have to be taken seriously as such in order to understand people's behavior. As is shown by R. Pradhan and U. Pradhan in their contribution in this volume, in Nepal caste differences as normative principles, in combination with differences in economic wealth and political power, still largely determine access to water and the distribution of water and maintenance activities. Differences in land ownership determine differences in access to water. One may wish these factors were irrelevant and one may not want to take them into account in the sense of accepting or legitimating their normative validity. Yet it is a fact of local law, a factor that very likely will influence the consequences of whatever intervention is proposed.

Taking such factors into account becomes especially important in relation to policy objectives concerned with values such as equitable, efficient, and sustainable use of water. In many parts of the world, research has shown that farmer-managed irrigation systems are more reliable and efficient than government-operated systems. This seems to suggest that local or customary law in this realm deserves support. The examples from Bali and Sulawesi in this volume also indicate that local law may also be a resource in achieving equal distribution of water, but that this is not automatically so. By contrast, research that has been done in Nepal (e.g., Pradhan and Pradhan 1996) shows that however efficient the farmer-managed systems may be, they are notoriously unequal in water distribution. Could it be, then, that in Nepal these systems function more efficiently than government systems precisely because of the political and economic power inequalities shaped by local, or customary, law? 'In the heat of the defense of suppressed people, it is easily forgotten that they may be as much suppressed by their own élites as by government agencies (F. von Benda-Beckmann et al. 1996: 94).'

Reliability and efficiency do not necessarily go hand in hand with equality and justice nor with sustainability. Thinking through realistic possibilities for future developments, one needs an understanding of what the role of local law and practices has been in each of these respects. The paradigm of legal pluralism thus may help to avoid developing an ideal, but somewhat romantic, and totally unrealistic, view of the functioning of customary and local law as an element of formulating policy objectives.

Conclusion

From the 1970s on, after having learned the hard lessons from scores of abortive efforts at socio-legal engineering, legal anthropology began to develop quite a different outlook on the issues of law and society. The comparative study of law in society, the conventional dichotomies of state law versus customary law, the issues of legal rules versus non-legal rules, and the old ethnocentric, legal science dominated, frameworks of analysis became increasingly questioned.

From descriptions of normative repertoires with an eye mainly to identifying their legal character, the main focus of legal anthropology has shifted to trying to understand the actual significance of such repertoires in social practice. Legal anthropologists have moved away from the legal disciplines' boast that law should be conceptualized as representing the ultimate or even the main source of order in society. They take the perspective that law should be seen as only part of a multiplicity of institutional arrangements and normative repertoires in society. Among these one can find law in the sense of state (or lawyers') law, as well as forms of law which are known as religious law and customary law. Recognizing that there exist multiple sources of order in society, it is stipulated, moreover, that there is no scientifically sound reason for legal anthropologists to confine their scope to the phenomena one generally has in mind if one speaks of law. Legal anthropologists include in their conceptual framework all those instances in social life in which other, law-like, normative repertoires are generated and maintained. These are called unofficial law, local law or self-regulation.

In most domains of social life more than one legal, or law-like, system will be relevant. This is called legal pluralism. Legal pluralism means that in many life situations farmers, water users, village headmen, bureaucrats and officials can make use of more than one normative repertoire to rationalize and legitimize their decisions or their behavior. Which specific repertoire, in which specific case, people will orient themselves to, will mostly be a matter of expediency, of local knowledge, perceived contexts of interaction, and power relations. We saw in this paper that irrigation in Blahpane constitutes such a domain of life where plural normative and institutional frameworks apply. Plurality of normative frameworks pertaining to the various domains of social life can be found in any society, from the ladies garment business in New York, as described by Moore (1978), to the irrigation associations in Bihar, as described by Nirmal Sengupta in this volume. For the past 25 years, instances of legal pluralism have been documented, implictly or explicitly, in many studies from all over the world. It has equally been documented that in most cases the coexistence of legal repertoires and institutions lies at the basis of considerable legal insecurity and conflict.

The paradigm of legal pluralism, or legal complexity, has important consequences for the conceptualization of the relationship between norms and behavior. Discrepancies between rules and behavior have to be explained in terms of peoples' options. Legal lexicons and human behavior and decisions should not be analytically conflated. Local people live in a complex legal universe, in which there may be many reasons and many ways to let decision be motivated by legal repertoires other than the official law. 'Locality' has become a key notion of the legal anthropological approach. It means that one should start from the assumption that the relationship between rules and behavior can be studied fruitfully only by looking into real-life situations; real life situations in different time and social space. In this paper I have aimed at giving some examples of what this would mean. In the Blahpane case we have seen how people maneuver, making strategic choices among the available normative lexicons (with their different content, source and basis of validity). We have seen that law is not a mirror of social reality; that legal pluralism may result in contesting claims; or that it may result in self-regulation or 'local law,' which may be quite different from the official repertoires.

We have seen that laws and legal institutions are social resources, which are interpreted, transformed, mixed and selected in real life. They are both constraining and enabling. They may function as an object of exchange, and so become an asset in negotiations, as well as become internalized as peoples' rights or legal principles (F. von Benda-Beckmann et al. 1996). We have also seen that one cannot fruitfully employ the property concepts of the various legal systems as analytical concepts. Even the sophisticated (but normatively informed) diagrams of modalities of water rights, which students of common property rights use to advance, tell us little about the actual behavior or actual relationships of real people.

It appears that, generally speaking, the social significance of normative frameworks (whether these are the products of modern law, customary law or other normative models) is mainly to be found in their functions as both a guideline and a resource for negotiating and exerting social and economic power. There exists a fair amount of case studies (not discussed in this paper), which draw attention to such phenomena as actors' strategic behavior involving both legal forum shopping and legal idiom (language of interaction) shopping as a resource in interest management. At least as important is the need (for well-meaning interventionists in particular) to be aware that the normative reasons people may give for certain behavior (e.g., by reference to custom, tradition, or state law) may not necessarily be the causes for their behavior, even if behavior is in accordance with the law. Realizing this may help to conceive of more realistic development policies.

Finally, as in this paper both the sections on Blahpane and policy implications have demonstrated, it is very useful to draw attention to the fact that legal and other normative frameworks may be more relevant in other spheres of interaction than the one they specifically profess to apply to. In the case of Blahpane, different representations of *subak* boundaries were given in different contexts. Of course, there is a good chance that the insights resulting from legal anthropologists' approach to law and other normative frameworks in society may not always be welcome in technocrats', administrators', and policymakers' circles. The ideas which are linked up with what, by way of shorthand, I have called the paradigm of legal pluralism, question not only the unwarranted assumptions and wishful thinking dominated folklores about the relations between law and behavior. They also concern such deeply rooted concepts as the relations between the state and its citizens, and the distinctions between the public and the private domains. All the same, the paradigm of legal pluralism can offer a forceful contribution to a better understanding of the role of law and ideologies, or the ways of 'imagining the real' (Geertz 1983) in society.

Notes

1. The variety of legal status of water may involve, for instance, whether water is considered to be 'owned' by the state or by specific local communities. See Pradhan and Pradhan (1996), Durga and Pradhan (1997).
2. This is a revised and abbreviated version of the case published before in H.L. Joep Spiertz (1991). The case is based on fieldwork on Bali conducted by the author in 1988 with the support of Wageningen Agricultural University, Department of Agrarian Law.
3. According to available sources (Rouffaer and Ijzerman 1915) it was the fleet-captain Cornelis de Houtman who was among the first to report on the Balinese irrigation system. The voyage by De Houtman to the Indonesian archipelago took place in 1595–97 in the service of the Dutch East Indies Company, which served to surpass the Portugese presence in the archipelago. More extensive reports on Balinese irrigation management and its embeddedness in customary *Adat* law come from Dutch Colonial civil servants, which included engineers and legal scholars. Of these reports written in a period of about 60 years between the colonial incorporation of the island of Bali under direct Dutch rule until Indonesia's Independence in the late 1940s, only some of the most prestigeous works are mentioned here. Liefrinck (1886) and Grader (1939) wrote extensively about the irrigation system in northern Bali, which is in many respects different from other parts of Bali. The late law professor, Victor E. Korn wrote a very voluminous dissertation on almost all aspects of Balinese *Adat* law throughout the island (Korn 1932). After Independence it is Clifford Geertz who for the last several decades has been one of the main sources of scholarship on Balinese social organization, including its irrigation system (Geertz 1959, 1967, 1972, 1980, 1983). It should be noted, however, that, starting with the violent overthrow of South Bali's principalities by the Dutch in the early 20th century, works on the various aspects of Balinese life and culture easily run into the thousands.

4. See, also, the Balinese anthropologist I Gusti Ngurah Bagus (1986) and the social scientists and irrigation specialists I Nyoman Sutawan (1986) and I Gde Pitana (1988). See also Lansing (1987) and Spiertz (1989a, 1989b).

5. Very little research has been done in this respect. For publications, see Sutawan (1986), Pitana (1988), Spiertz (1989a, 1991, 1992), Spiertz and de Jong (1992). For Balinese farmer settlements in south Sulawesi, see Dik Roth (1998).

6. This map is based on the Department of Public Works map 'Peta Lokasi Bangunan Gedung/Kantor Proyek E&P Pengairan Kabupaten Gianyar 1988.'

7. Various aspects of religious organization, remnants of pre-colonial political organization and colonial administration, have blended together in present Balinese village organization to the effect that one cannot speak of villages in the sense of clearly identifiable, all-compassing territorial units. In an administrative sense, Blahpane is one village consisting of two hamlets. In the religious and customary law sense, Blahpane Kaja and Blahpane Klod are two separate villages.

8. The names of individuals in this case are fictional.

9. The Balinese 'subak' is both a territorial unit and a corporation. The Balinese speak of the subak as the 'wet' village as opposed to the residential units which are the 'dry' village (See also Geertz, 1967, 1972). Like the 'dry' village which can consist of more than one hamlet, the subak can be subdivided into sub-units: tempek. As a corporation the main tasks of the subak are irrigation water management, cropping regulation, and sustenance of the religious requirements for successful rice production.

10. Irrigation department maps indicate that the Gelulung/Tulikup system commands two minor (nonpermanent) weirs. These lie in a north–south running rivulet called Tukad Gelulung. Since these are registered as so-called non-public works units, information dries up at this point.

11. One of the most confusing elements of conventional legal scholarship in this respect is that it tends to conflate, in the terms of the scholar Schiff (1981), the 'is' and the 'ought'. It conflates the world as it 'is' and the world as it 'should be.'

12. Through time, lawyers have produced numerous studies on water rights and organizations for water management, and developed doctrines on their legal character and how these should fit into the constitutional and other legal frameworks of the respective countries. Substantial amounts of lawyers' work has been done, for instance, on Californian water laws, on Spanish and Muslim water laws, and on the Dutch semi-community based polders and waterschappen (which, historically, served to protect the land from the sea rather than to irrigate the fields).

Systematic legal works on water rights have remained scarce however. Among the most encompassing recent works on water rights from the perspective of legal doctrine are some books by Chhatrapati Singh (1991, 1992) on water rights and water law in India. As Chhatrapati Singh states in the preface to the 1990 volume: '... (his) work is about the legality of water rights, that is, about its nature, status, functions and sources, and not a sociological account of the status or history of water rights ... the work is about the jurisprudence of this right'.

13. Paraphrasing Clifford Geertz (1983) in his essay on 'fact and law in comparative perspective', it can be said that both legal scholarship and anthropology have generally been more attracted to discovering 'broad principles' in 'parochial facts', than to analyzing how, precisely, the broad principles of social organization and law would relate to the parochial facts of social practices (Spiertz 1990).

14. Sawyerr (1974) gives a number of fine examples of this type of legal pluralism.

15. This section draws on F. von Benda-Beckmann et al. 1996. Readers are referred to that source for a more extensive discussion of the dilemmas involved.

References

Archer, R. 1993. *Markets and good government.* Draft paper, INCI meeting.

Bagus, Ngurah I.G. 1986. Hubungan pura subak dengan pertanian di Bali: Analisis sistemik tentang hubungan pura ulun danau dengan pertanian di Bali Timur. *Research Report.* Denpasar: Universitas Udayana.

Benda-Beckmann, Franz von. 1983. Why law does not behave: Critical and constructive reflections on the social scientific perception of the social significance of law. In *Proceedings of the Folk Law and Legal Pluralism Commission Symposia, XIth International Conference of Anthropological and Ethnological Sciences*, Harold Finkler, compiler, Vol. 1, 233–62. Vancouver, British Columbia: XIth IUAES Congress.

———. 1988. Comment on Merry. *Law and Society Review* 22 (5): 897–901.

———. 1994. Good governance, law and social reality: Problematic relationships. *Knowledge and Policy: The International Journal of Knowledge Transfer and Utilization* 7 (3): 55–67.

Benda-Beckmann, Franz von and **Keebet von Benda-Beckmann.** 1991. Law in Society: From blindman's-buff to multilocal law. In *Living law in the low countries.* Special Issue of *Recht der Werkelijkheid*, 119–39. Amsterdam: VUGA

Benda-Beckmann, Franz von, Keebet von Benda-Beckmann and **H.L. Joep Spiertz.** 1996. Water Rights and Policy. *The role of law in natural resource management,* ed. by Joep Spiertz and Melanie G. Wiber, 77–100. The Hague: VUGA. New Brunswick: Wilfred Laurier U.P.

———. 1997. Local law and customary practices in the study of water rights. In *Water rights, conflict and policy,* ed. Rajendra Pradhan, Franz von Benda-Beckmann, Keebet von Benda-Beckmann, H.L. Joep Spiertz, S. Khadka, and K. Azharul Haq, 221–42. Colombo, Sri Lanka: International Irrigation Management Institute.

Benda-Beckmann, Keebet von, H.L. Joep Spiertz and **Franz von Benda-Beckmann.** 1995. Contesting rights to water in Nepal irrigation: A legal anthropological perspective. In: *The scarcity of water,* ed. by Brans et al., 224–42. The Hague, London, Boston: Kluwer Law International.

Cotterrell R. 1984. *The sociology of law: An introduction.* London: Butterworths.

Durga, K.C. and **Rajendra Pradhan.** 1997. Improvement and enlargement of a farmer managed irrigation system in Tanahu: Changing rights to water and conflict resolution. In *Water rights, conflict and policy,* ed. Rajendra Pradhan, Franz von Benda-Beckmann, Keebet von Benda-Beckmann, H.L. Joep Spiertz, S. Khadka, and K. Azharul Haq, 135–56. Colombo, Sri Lanka: International Irrigation Management Institute.

Foley, S. 1987. Breach of promise—breach of faith: The green revolution in Bali. Research Paper. Centre for Resource and Environmental Studies, A.N.U. Canberra.

Geertz, Clifford. 1959. Form and variation in Balinese village structure. *American Anthropologist* 61 (6): 991–1012.

——— 1967. Tihingan, a Balinese Village. In *Villages in Indonesia,* ed. Koentjaraningrat. Ithaca N.Y.: Cornell University Press.

———. 1963. *Agricultural involution.* Berkeley: University of California Press.

———. 1972. The wet and the dry: Traditional irrigation in Bali and Morocco. *Human Ecology* 1 (March): 23–39.

———. 1980. Organization of the Balinese subak. In *Irrigation and agricultural development in Asia: Perspectives from the Social Sciences,* ed. E. Walter Coward, 70–90. Ithaca, N.Y.: Cornell University Press.

———. 1983. *Local knowledge.* New York: Basic Books.

Giddens, A. 1979. *Central problems in social theory.* London: Macmillan.

Grader, C.J. 1960. [1939]. The irrigation system in the region of Jembrana. In *Bali: Studies in life, thought, and ritual,* ed. Swellengrebel 267–88. The Hague: W. van Hoeve.

Griffiths, J. 1986. What is legal pluralism? *Journal of Legal Pluralism* 24: 1–50.

Gutto, S.B.O. 1982. Kenya's petit-bourgeois state, the public and the rule/ misrule of law. *International Journal of Sociology of Law* 10: 341–61.

Korn, V.E. 1932. *Het Adatrecht van Bali*. Second edition. The Hague: G. Naeff.

Lansing, J. Stephen. 1987. Balinese 'water temples' and the management of irrigation. *American Anthropologist* 89: 326–41.

Liefrinck, F.A. 1969 [1886]. Rice cultivation in northern Bali. In *Bali, further studies in life, thought, and ritual*, ed. Swellengrebel 1–73. Gravenhage. W. van Hoeve.

Merry, Sally M. 1988. Legal pluralism. *Law and Society Review* 22 (5): 869–96.

Moore, S.F. 1978. Law and social change: the semi-autonomous field as an appropriate subject of study. In *Law as process: An anthropological approach*, ed. S.F. Moore, 54–81. London: Routledge and Kegan Paul.

Mooij, J. 1992. Private pockets and public policies: Rethinking the concept of corruption. In *Law as a resource in agrarian struggles*, ed. Franz von Benda-Beckmann and M. Van der Velde 219–40, Wageningen Sociological Studies 33. Wageningen: Pudoc.

Pitana, G. 1988. *Jointly managed subak: Roles of farmers and government in irrigation management in Bali*. Manila: Ateneo de Manila.

Pospisil, Leopold. 1971. *Anthropology of law*. New York: Harper and Row.

Pradhan, Rajendra and **Ujjwal Pradhan**. 1996. Staking a claim: Law, politics and water rights in farmer managed irrigation systems in Nepal. In *The role of law in natural resource management*, ed. Joep Spiertz and Melanie G. Wiber, 61–76. The Hague: VUGA.

Pradhan, Rajendra, A. Haq, and **Ujjwal Pradhan**. 1997. Law, rights and equity: Implications of state intervention in farmer managed irrigation systems. In *Water rights, conflict and policy*, ed. by Rajendra Pradhan, Franz von Benda-Beckmann, Keebet von Benda-Beckmann, H.L. Joep Spiertz, S. Khadka, K. Azharul Haq, 111–34. Colombo, Sri Lanka: International Irrigation Management Institute.

Roberts, Simon. 1979. *Order and dispute*. Harmondsworth: Penguin.

Roth, Dik. 1998. The diverging and merging worlds of subak and water users' association: Balinese irrigators in a Public Works irrigation system in Luwu District, South Sulawesi, Indonesia. Paper presented at the seminar series Water and Politics, Wageningen Agricultural University, February 1998.

Rouffaer, G.P. and **J.W. Ijzerman**, eds. 1915. *De eerste schipvaart der Nederlanders naar Oost-Indie onder Cornelis de Houtman, 1595–1597*. Lindschoten: Verceniging.

Sawyerr, Akilagpa. 1974. Application of law in Tanzania: A 'proper remedy' approach to some problems of legal pluralism. *East African Law Journal* 7: 223–46.

Sawyerr, Akilagpa. 1977. Judicial manipulation of customary family law in Tanzania. In *Law and the family in Africa*, ed. S.A. Roberts, 115–27. The Hague: Mouton.

Singh, Chhatrapati. 1991. *Water rights and principles of water resources management.* London: Sweet & Maxwell.

———. 1992. *Water law in India.* London: Sweet & Maxwell.

Schiff David N. 1981. Law as a social phenomenon. In *Sociological approaches to law*, ed. Adam Podgórecki and Christopher J. Whelan, 151–66. London: Croom Helm.

Spiertz, H.L. Joep. 1989a. De mythe van de Subak: Irrigatie op Bali in rechtsantropologisch perspectief. *Recht der Werkelijkheid* 1: 6–33.

———. 1989b. A legal anthropological research perspective on village and *subak* in Bali. *Antropologi Indonesia/Indonesian Journal of Social and Cultural Anthropology* (47): 76–83.

———. 1990. On broad principles and parochial facts. Conference paper for the International Eidos Seminar, Amsterdam, June 1990.

———. 1991. The transformation of traditional law: A tale of people's participation in irrigation management on Bali. *Landscape and Urban Planning* 20: 189–96.

———. 1992. Between cannibalism and pluralism: On the construction of legal frameworks in irrigation management in Bali and Sri Lanka. In *Law as a resource in agrarian struggles*, ed. F. von Benda-Beckmann and M. van der Velde, 89–109. Wageningen Agricultural University: Pudoc.

———. 1995. State and customary laws: Legal pluralism and water rights. *FMIS Newsletter* 13: 1–7.

Spiertz, H.L.J. and **I.J.H. de Jong.** 1992. Traditional law and irrigation management: The case of Bethma. In *Irrigators and engineers: Essays in honour of Lucas Horst*, ed. G. Diemer and J. Slabbers, 185–202. Amsterdam: Thesis Publishers.

Spiertz, H.L.J. and **Melanie G. Wiber.** 1996. The bull in the china shop: Regulation, property rights and natural resource management: An introduction. In *The role of law in natural resource management*, ed. Joep Spiertz and Melanie G. Wiber, 1–16. The Hague: VUGA Publishers.

Sutawan, Nyoman. 1986. Farmer managed irrigation systems and the impact of government assistance: A note from Bali, Indonesia. Workshop on Public Intervention in Farmer-managed Irrigation Systems, Kathmandu.

VanderLinden J. 1989. Return to legal pluralism. *Journal of Legal Pluralism* 28: 149–57.

Wiber, M.G. 1992. Levels of property rights, levels of law: A case study from the northern Philippines. *Man* (N.S.) 26: 469–92.

Wiber, Melanie G. 1995. Everyday forms of violence: Farmers' experiences of regulation in the Canadian dairy industry. *Journal of Legal Pluralism and Folk Law* 35: 1–23.

World Bank. 1991. *The challenge of poverty. World development report 1991.* Washington, D.C.: World Bank.

———. 1992. *Governance and development.* Washington, D.C.: World Bank.

7

Negotiating Access and Rights: Disputes Over Rights to an Irrigation Water Source in Nepal[1]

RAJENDRA PRADHAN and UJJWAL PRADHAN

This chapter discusses a long-standing conflict between farmers of two neighboring villages in a hill district of Nepal over rights to tap water from a perennial, spring-fed stream. The farmers shop for and use the best strategy they believe is available to them in a specific situation. The strategies include negotiation, litigation, violence, and use of government-aided projects and officials. The strategies they employ depend on the social relations (e.g., power or 'good' or 'bad' relations) between the stakeholders, and the external resources they are able to deploy (e.g., links with powerful government officials) and the legal resources (law, courts, etc.) they have at their disposal. Negotiation is only one of the means used to establish and protect water rights. Stakeholders do not negotiate or dispute over water rights in general but specific types of rights (rights to control and manage, rights to use, prior rights, etc.). The chapter also suggests that it would be useful to differentiate between rights, access, and acquisition of water.

Introduction

Nepal has a long history of irrigation, but until the middle of this century direct involvement of the Nepalese state in irrigation management and development was limited (Benjamin et al. 1994; U. Pradhan 1990). Although the state did construct or finance the construction or repairs of irrigation systems, and managed or supervised the management of some systems, its main contribution to irrigation development was by means of laws and regulations which encouraged and sometimes forced local élites and ordinary farmers, usually tenants, to construct and operate irrigation systems. Legal tradition and weak administration made it possible and necessary for the irrigators to construct and manage their irrigation systems with little interference from state agencies (Benjamin et al. 1994; P. Pradhan 1989; U. Pradhan 1990). The state has increased its involvement in irrigation development immensely over the last four decades. It has rehabilitated and enlarged existing farmer-managed irrigation systems (FMIS), usually with international aid, constructed and managed new irrigation systems (known as agency managed irrigation systems, or AMIS), and enacted new laws, regulations, and policies which have given the state more authority to control and regulate water management and use.[2] Nevertheless, farmers continue to manage their irrigation systems and water resources relatively independent of the state. The irrigation systems discussed in this contribution are examples of such FMIS.

One of the major irrigation management activities is the acquisition of water from water sources such as rivers, streams, and springs. In farmer-managed irrigation systems, the farmers themselves have to acquire water. Whenever possible they divert water from new (uncontested) sources, and if this is not possible they try to acquire water from sources used by others by negotiation, disputing, 'stealing' water on the sly, or forcefully acquiring water, often using political or administrative connections. The farmers are not satisfied with just acquiring water; their long-term goal is to legitimize their access to the water source, that is, to establish rights to the water. In other words, irrigators attempt to get their claims to a share of water from a water source accepted by other users and competitors. Existing users usually employ various strategies such as guarding their water sources, punishing 'water thieves,' negotiation, or going to court, to prevent the new users from acquiring water, and more importantly, from establishing rights to water in their water sources. Or they may allow new users to acquire water but under specific conditions and for a limited time so long as they do not assert rights to the water source.

Many stakeholders are often not happy with the existing constellation of water rights to a water source, either because they have no access to water or access to a smaller share of water than they feel they have rights to, or because water rights relations were imposed on them by government officials, politicians, the courts, or the dominant stakeholders. They attempt to change the existing constellation of water rights relations whenever opportunities are available, such as destruction of intakes due to landslides or floods, rehabilitation and extension of irrigation systems by the state or donor agencies, changes in law, and shifts in the balance of power between stakeholders. It is then not surprising that water rights relations are usually not permanent but provisional and subject to further (and frequent) negotiation and disputing.[3]

The farmers shop for and use what they believe is the best strategy available to them in a specific situation. The strategies they use depend, on the one hand, on the social relations between the stakeholders (such as power, kinship, economic, political, and also whether they have 'good' or 'bad' relations) as well as the external resources (such as connections with powerful officials) they are able to use and, on the other hand, the legal resources they have at their disposal. Legal resources include both law, in the sense of cognitive and normative orders, and dispute processing institutions such as courts, quasi-judicial bodies (District Administration Office, for example), and village councils.

In Nepal, as elsewhere, individuals have access to different legal orders such as state law and state courts, local law, and local dispute processing mechanisms. The coexistence and interaction of different legal orders in a social field (nation state, community, factory, or irrigation organization) is known as legal pluralism (c.f. F. von Benda-Beckmann et al. 1997; Griffiths 1986; Merry 1988). The significance of legal pluralism, for the purpose of this paper, is that stakeholders have the option of using different legal orders or normative repertoires to justify and legitimize their claims. The normative order they choose depends on which legal order they believe best suits their claim at that particular time. Similarly, they have the option of shopping for the forum which they believe is most likely to settle the dispute in their favor (c.f. K. von Benda-Beckmann 1984).

Negotiation and disputes usually operate within the framework of law, even if the stakeholders do not agree on which law or rule is to be used, or interpret the same law differently. However, stakeholders do not always operate within the legal framework; they may use illegal or non-legal strategies such as 'stealing' on the sly (weapons of the weak)[4] or diverting or protecting water by brute force (weapons of the strong). These strategies are often used when they are unable to acquire water or establish or protect water rights by operating within a 'legal' framework. Negotiation then is only one strategy, and not always the most important or useful one, used by stakeholders in pursuit of their interests. It is usually used when the parties have good relations and are willing to compromise and not insist on strict application or interpretation of law.

The term water rights, like property rights, is a broad, encompassing concept which includes diverse kinds and levels of rights (F. von Benda-Beckmann et al. 1997; Schlager and Ostrom 1992; Wiber 1992). In most general terms, 'there is some differentiation between rights to control, regulate, supervise, represent in outside relations, and regulate and allocate water on the one hand, and rights to use and exploit it economically on the other' (F. von Benda-Beckmann et al. 1997: 224). There often are diverse and different level of rights in a specific source, such as ownership rights, rights to participate in decision-making process (including decisions concerning allocation of water), rights to use without rights to participate in decision-making process, rights which may or may not be transferred, rights to use only for a specific season or purpose, senior or junior rights, individual rights and residual rights of community, etc. Concerning water sources, ownership rights, rights to allocate and to use may be held by different stakeholders and may or may not be contested. For example, ownership rights of a spring may be vested in the owner of the land in which the spring is located but neighbors may have rights to use the water for drinking or irrigation purposes.

There is an important difference between having rights to water and being able to actually acquire water by virtue of mere physical access to the resource. Rights 'exist' in the realm of law; they are claims (or interests) which are socially accepted and legitimized by law, whether state or local or both (c.f. Talbot 1997; Wiber 1992).

This is similar to the point made by Schlager and Ostrom (1992) that rights are derived from rules. People who have rights to water may be prevented from acquiring water, and conversely, people without rights may be able to acquire water either by force or by stealth. Acquisition of water is the actual appropriation of water from a source by whatever means; it may be licit or illicit, carried out by those who have rights or do not have rights in the water source, or whose claims are contested. The term acquisition is similar to the term access as used by Talbot (1997: 3–4): 'the freedom or ability to obtain or make use of .... It includes the socially sanctioned and the illicit, the de jure and the de facto, the right as only part of the ability.' But access is still at the level of potential; not all who have access to a water source can actually appropriate water from it. Further, in plural legal situations rights may be differently constituted and different rules may be applicable in different legal orders. Some farmers may claim that they are acquiring water legally from a water source, justifying their action by reference to one interpretation of a law or one legal order whereas other farmers may perceive that action as illegal based on another legal order or a different interpretation of the same law. Claims which are accepted as legitimate (rights) according to one legal order, for example, state law, may not be accepted as legitimate in another, such as local law.

Farmers negotiate, dispute, and use other strategies not so much to establish or protect water rights in general but specific kinds or types of rights. The strategy that the farmers use is influenced by the types of water rights they want to secure or protect and whether they want to secure or protect rights or acquire water or prevent others from acquiring water. These issues feature strongly in the following three cases.

In the first dispute, one village, in response to damage to their diversion weir and physical threat to their lives, filed a case in the courts to protect their rights to a water source, to which they claim exclusive use rights. In the second case, the defendants in the first dispute destroyed the newly constructed gabion diversion weir to lay claims to the water source and also to force negotiation so that they could acquire water. In the third case, an NGO-funded drinking water project was used as a pretext to try to secure rights to use water for irrigation.

The Setting

Satrasaya Phant and Yampa Phant are adjoining villages in the Tanahu District, west of Kathmandu. Five farmers constructed Satrasaya Phant Kulo about 150 years ago to irrigate approximately 9 hectares of land in Satrasaya Phant. The command area was gradually expanded over the years and by 1989 it irrigated 16.72 hectares of land, owned by 45 households. The command area of the irrigation system was increased to 29 hectares, and benefitted 73 households after the completion of the irrigation system rehabilitation and extension project funded by World Bank and implemented by the Department of Irrigation.[5]

Yampa Phant is divided into two parts, the upper part is known as Jaisi Phant and the lower as Baraha Phant. Formerly, each phant (an area with relatively flat land in the hills) had its own canal (Kulo). Jaisi Kulo irrigated fields in Jaisi Phant and Baraha Kulo in Baraha Phant. Both canals were constructed and managed by farmers. Informants were not sure when these canals were constructed but they believe that it was probably constructed around the same time as the Satrasaya Phant Kulo. The original command areas of these irrigation systems are not known but in the Cadastral Survey carried out in 1933 it was estimated that the two canals irrigated 22.75 hectares of land. Another survey carried out in 1972 recorded that the two canals irrigated only 13.08 hectares of land. The irrigated area gradually increased after 1972 when farmers from other villages began buying land and settling in the village, and especially after the canals were rehabilitated and improved as part of the Hill Food Irrigation Development Project (HFIDP) in 1988 and 1989. The two canals were combined to form a single system with one diversion structure and two main branches. It has a command area of 37 hectares and benefits 65 households.

The water source of Satrasaya Phant Kulo is Thulo Andhi Khola, a stream which is fed by Barahi Andhi Mul, a perennial spring, located about three kilometers from the command area and half a kilometer above the intake point of the canal (see Map 7.1). Most of the water in Thulo Andhi Khola is diverted to Satrasaya Phant Kulo, except what seeps through or flows over the diversion structure. The main water source of Baraha Kulo and Jaisi Kulo (now

Figure 7.1: Schematic Diagram of Satrasaya Phant and Yampa Phant

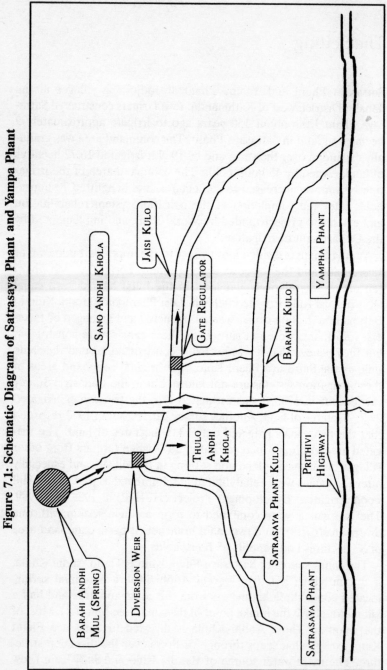

combined into a single system) is Sano Andhi Khola, a small stream which is virtually dry from February until the onset of monsoon in June. Thulo and Sano Andhi Khola join to form Andhi Khola. Baraha Kulo and Jaisi Kulo divert water from Thulo Andhi Khola. The Yampalis have always depended on Thulo Andhi Khola as an additional water source for their rice irrigation, especially if the monsoon is late or there is drought. To be able to utilize water from this stream for their irrigation, especially during the dry months, the Yampalis have to breach the diversion weir of the Satrasaya Phant or block the entrance of the Satrasaya Phant Kulo so that the water flows over the diversion weir.

We do not have any firm evidence about how the two villages shared water from Thulo Andhi Khola in the past. Informants provide contested versions but it appears that when relations between the two villages were good, the Yampalis were allowed to acquire water from the disputed source and when relations were bad, they 'stole' water. The Yampalis claim that they have always tapped water from the disputed source. Some of them even assert that they tapped half the water from the water source. Other Yampalis claim that during their fathers' time, they were allowed to acquire water from the disputed source because relations between the two villages were good on account of a marriage between two élite families in the two villages. Later they required more water for irrigation because they had converted some of their upland fields (*bari*) to irrigated lowland fields (*khet*). They had requested a powerful person in Satrasaya Phant several times to use his influence to convince Satrasaya Phant farmers to allot them a small share of the water from Thulo Andhi Khola but he refused to do so and instead told them that they did not have any rights to the water. They would be allowed to tap the water, but only if the Satrasaya Phant farmers agreed. Satrasaya Phant farmers usually did give them permission to divert the water. Some Satrasaya Phant farmers assert that the Yampalis were never given permission to tap water from their water source and that they (the Yampalis) stole in the past and continue to do so today. However, many Satrasaya Phant farmers do acknowledge that the Yampalis were allowed to use their water source for limited periods. According to some old informants, the Yampalis requested water for their monsoon crop if there was drought. If they were refused permission, the Yampalis usually stole water by breaching the temporary diversion weir. The Satrasaya farmers then repaired the weir and destroyed diversion weirs and the rice fields of the Yampalis to punish them for 'stealing' water. A few informants in their late 70s and 80s recall taking part in such activities when they were young. As one informant recalled, 'I forgot the year but on one occasion 22 persons, including myself, destroyed the rice fields, bunds and diversion weirs of the Yampalis to punish them for stealing water.'

The Yampalis were not too happy about having to depend on the goodwill of the Satrasaya Phant farmers for water. They could steal water but this method of acquiring water was not always successful and moreover they were often punished for it. The Yampalis therefore used different strategies to acquire water and, equally important, to establish rights to use water from this source. The strategies used by the Yampalis varied from negotiation when relations with the Satrasaya Phant farmers were cordial, to using force and stealing water when relations were bad. They also tried to use government and project officials. The Satrasaya Phant farmers negotiated, threatened and punished Yampalis, and filed cases in courts to protect their rights. The following sections describe the strategies used by Yampalis and Satrasaya Phant farmers in three separate disputes: a court case, a dispute over the destruction of the diversion weir, and a dispute over the source of the drinking water project.

The Court Case

Towards the late 1940s, relations between the two villages had deteriorated and the Yampalis had to resort to 'stealing' water to irrigate their monsoon rice crop. Tension between the two villages, specifically the élites, had increased because of a dispute between the Adhikaris of Satrasaya Phant and Hari Prasad Shrestha of Yampa Phant over another issue, not related to water. The Adhikaris were a rich family who owned large tracts of land in Satrasaya Phant. Mr Shrestha was a rich man, who owned much land and also farmed, on contract, a large tract of land in Yampa Phant owned by a powerful Pande family of Kathmandu. It was during this period of bad relations between the two villages that an incident occurred which led to the court case described below.

The monsoon was late in 1952. The Yampalis were worried because they depended on the monsoon rains to flood their fields and until their fields were flooded they could not transplant monsoon paddy seedlings. Delay in monsoon also meant that water discharge in Sano Andhi Khola, their main source of water for irrigation, was very low. The Yampalis felt they had no alternative but to steal water from the disputed water source because Satrasaya Phant farmers would not give them permission to divert water from Thulo Andhi Khola on account of the strained relations between the two villages. When a tenant farmer attempted to breach the diversion weir of Satrasaya Phant Kulo he was caught by a few Satrasaya Phant farmers and fined Rs 5. He reported this incident to Mr Shrestha, his landlord who had probably encouraged him to 'steal' water. The next day, Mr Shrestha, together with a few other farmers, destroyed the diversion weir. By this act they were claiming rights to use water from the disputed source.

As soon as the Satrasaya Phant farmers were informed that the diversion weir had been damaged, they rushed to the site to repair the weir. Mr Shrestha, who was guarding this site with a few Yampalis, tried to scare them away with his rifle but they were not frightened. On the contrary they threatened to kill Mr Shrestha if he used his rifle. Seeing how determined these farmers were, the Yampalis vanished. The farmers then repaired their diversion weir, irrigated their fields, and transplanted rice seedlings.

Satrasaya Phant farmers had successfully defended themselves against the threat to their water source on this occasion. But they were not sure whether they could continue to defend their water source by show of force. They were also not sure when and how the Yampalis would retaliate and negotiation was not possible because of the antagonistic relations between the leading families of the two villages. A few of the leading Satrasaya Phant farmers therefore filed a case against Mr Shrestha and 33 other Yampalis in the court. In seeking the protection of the court, they used state law to protect their water rights.

Within the context of the court, both disputing parties used similar legal rhetoric (state law) to justify their claims. The difference lies in the interpretation of fact and evidence (c.f. F. von Benda-Beckmann et al. 1997: 231). The petitioners put forward two arguments to support their claim to exclusive rights to the water source. First, they asserted that Satrasaya Phant Kulo was older than the canals of Yampa Phant. They were thus claiming rights of prior appropriation in accordance with the extant law. They further argued that the Yampalis had never diverted water from the disputed water source and that there was no written agreement about water sharing. This argument is ingenuous in that in most instances such agreements, if they existed, would have been verbal and not written and signed agreements. The Yampalis, naturally, could not provide written evidence. The petitioners alleged that the Yampalis had damaged their diversion weir and petitioned the court to award them compensation of Rs 100 for the damages.

The Yampalis insisted that they too had rights to use water from the water source. They asserted, though they were not able to provide written proof, that their canals were older than Satrasaya Phant's and that it was well known to everyone that they had been sharing water from the disputed source. They maintained that they did not damage the diversion weir; all they did was to acquire water they had traditionally diverted from the water source.

Two state laws are relevant here. First is the provision in the Chapter on Land Reclamation in the National Code which deals with the rights and obligations of irrigators.[6] Briefly, the provision states that prior appropriators have first rights to water from the source. In normal circumstances, this means that diversion weirs may be constructed upstream of the existing intake structures only if water supply to the existing downstream canals is not adversely affected. The petitioners used this law to justify their rights to deny the defendants access to water from the water source. The defendants used the same law to argue that they have rights to the water source because they appropriated water before Satrasaya Phant farmers. They had allowed the petitioners to construct a diversion weir above their intake structures on the condition that water supply to their canals would not be affected.

The second state law is based on court decisions. The courts have repeatedly upheld rights of persons to continue using resources such as water or land if they can prove that they have been using the resources from 'previous times', even if they do not own or have 'rights' to the resource (Khanal and K.C. 1997). This law is relevant mainly in the courts or with quasi-judicial bodies such as the District Administration Office or the Village Councils. The petitioners claimed that the defendants had never used water from the disputed source whereas the defendants asserted that they had been using about half the water discharge from 'previous' times and therefore have rights to divert water from the source.

The court gave its decision four years later. The court ruled (*a*) that the water should be used as per previous practice (*sabik bamo-jim*); (*b*) that the defendants should pay compensation of Rs 100 to the petitioners; and (*c*) that the defendants should not destroy the diversion weir without the court's permission. The defendants appealed against the decision in the court of appeal which upheld the decision of the lower court. The Supreme Court also upheld the decisions of the lower courts.

In the post-trial stage of court cases, the decision has to be implemented in the social field where the dispute originated (K. von Benda-Beckmann 1985). In the local arena, court decisions may not be implemented or implemented only partially, or differently than intended by the judges because state law may not be as significant as local law or social and power relations. Further, the disputants may interpret the court decision differently. In this case, the decision relating to compensation was not contested by the litigating parties. The Yampalis acknowledged that they had damaged the diversion weir and they were willing to pay compensation as demanded by the petitioners. As the case described below shows, the Yampalis did not always follow the court's ruling that they should not destroy the diversion weir without the court's permission.

The first part of the court decision was equivocal: 'water is to be used as per previous practice or use (*sabik bamojim*)' whereas the moot point was whether the Yampalis had been using water regularly from this source in the past and therefore had rights to continue diverting water. The court threw the ball back into their own court, that is, the disputing parties were to resolve this question themselves. The disputants did not agree on the interpretation of this part of the decision and were unable to marshal resources to have their interpretation upheld. Both parties continue to claim that the court decision was in their favor and use the court decision as a rhetoric to justify their actions and claims.

Outside the court context, some Satrasaya Phant farmers are willing to concede that the Yampalis did divert water from the disputed source but they were careful to point out that it was only under specific conditions and with permission. In other words, they did not concede that Yampalis had rights to water from the source. Similarly, a few Yampalis admitted that they probably never shared water equally (and did not have rights) but that they were allowed to acquire water for specific periods when they had good relations with the Satrasaya Phant farmers.

The Supreme Court decision did not resolve the conflict. The Yampalis continued to 'steal' water from the disputed intake by breaching the diversion weir while they waited for suitable opportunities to secure rights to water from the disputed source. The Satrasaya Phant farmers organized themselves better to protect their water source. They took turns to guard the diversion weir, especially at night, during the rice season (P. Pradhan 1989: 20). They later hired a water contractor whose duty, among others, was to patrol the diversion weir. Animosity between the two villages on account of the court case made it difficult for them to negotiate a settlement.

Dispute over the Construction of the Permanent Diversion Weir

In 1989, as part of the Satrasaya Phant Kulo rehabilitation and enlargement project mentioned earlier, the brushwood diversion weir was replaced with a gabion structure. The new diversion weir was more difficult to breach and allowed less water to seep through than the old one and made it more difficult for the Yampalis to acquire water. The Yampalis were not informed, much less consulted, about the construction of the weir. They could not prevent the construction of the weir either by negotiation with the Satrasaya Phant farmers, given the hostility between the two villages, or by appealing to higher authorities because they could not prove that they had rights to the water source. Moreover, the construction of the gabion weir was part of the World Bank project, which had been sanctioned by and implemented by the Department of Irrigation, allegedly due to the lobbying efforts of a Satrasaya Phant farmer who had influential contacts in Kathmandu.

Given the limited options available to them, the desperate Yampalis did not take recourse to judicial or quasi-judicial process but resorted to a strategy used elsewhere in Nepal to both claim and protect water rights (Pradhan and Pradhan 1996; Pradhan et al. 1997b): they damaged the diversion weir. The Yampalis could have gone to court to have the construction work stopped but they had very little legal grounds to do so, especially after the previous court case. They could have gone to quasi-judicial officials such as the chief district officer but state officials usually supported development projects, especially government projects. As far as the Yampalis were concerned, they had once again asserted their claims to rights to water from the disputed source. By demonstrating their willingness to use force, they hoped to get the Satrasaya Phant farmers to negotiate a compromise.

The Yampalis later tried to negotiate with their adversaries, suggesting that they would pay for the construction cost of the diversion weir provided it was destroyed. The Satrasaya Phant farmers did not agree to the suggestion but they repaired the damaged gabion structure. The disputants did not pursue the matter further.

In this dispute, the Satrasaya Phant farmers used the opportunity provided by the state-aided project to construct a more permanent and stronger diversion weir and to reinforce their claims to exclusive rights to the water source. As has been observed by others (Ambler 1990; K.C. and Pradhan 1997) one way to protect or augment water rights is by constructing better physical structures which are more difficult to damage and allow less seepage of water. Physical structures also provide material proof of water rights.

The two parties did not attempt to negotiate before or during the construction of the diversion weir or before the Yampalis damaged it because of the bad relations between them. They negotiated after the fact, as it were, but could not reach a compromise. The Yampalis had strategically suggested that they would pay for the cost incurred in the construction of the diversion dam if they were allowed to use this intake to irrigate their fields. But the Satrasaya farmers were not taken in by this stratagem. Had they agreed, after a few years of licitly using the source, the Yampalis could have claimed in court that they have been legally using this water source and demand rights to use water from this source as per previous practice (*sabik bamojim*). The Satrasaya farmers were in a strong position to ignore the demands of the Yampalis because the structure was being constructed by the Department of Irrigation. The government would come down heavily on anyone who damaged or destroyed government aided 'developmental' structures, especially those funded by foreign donor agencies (see Pradhan et al. 1997b).

Another reason is that the court had ruled earlier that the Yampalis should not destroy the diversion weir without the court's permission.

Although the Yampalis were not able to establish rights to water from this source, they were able to acquire water when they needed it for irrigation. Perhaps emboldened by the lack of retaliatory action against them for damaging the diversion weir, they continued to 'steal' water and awaited a suitable opportunity to establish their claim. A drinking water project provided them with such an opportunity.

Dispute over the Source of Drinking Water

In 1992 the Yampalis received a grant from the Tanahu District Red Cross to install pipes to supply drinking water to their village. They planned to use Barahi Adi Mul, a perennial spring, for the project because it was the most reliable water source of water in this area. The problem was that the Satrasaya Phant farmers claimed exclusive rights to Barahi Adi Mul, the water source for Thulo Andhi Khola, which in turn was the water source for Satrasaya Phant Kulo. It is not clear whether the Yampalis informed or discussed with the farmers of Satrasaya Phant their plan to use this source for their drinking water project. The Satrasaya Phant farmers claim that they were not informed whereas the Yampalis claim that they had discussed their plan with the chairman of the Satrasaya Phant water users committee. In any case, as related by informants from Satrasaya Phant, they forcefully prevented the Yampalis from digging and laying pipes. The Yampalis reported this incident to the District Red Cross office and later filed a complaint against them with the District Administration Office (CDO) and the District Police. The Yampalis present a less adversial version. They claim that after informing the chairman of the Satrasaya Phant water users committee and laying 100 meters of pipe they received a letter from the committee requesting them to stop work until they held a discussion. The Yampalis stopped work and requested the CDO, the DSP, the chairman of the DDC and officials of the Red Cross to mediate.

A few days later these officials, accompanied by Yampalis, visited Satrasaya Phant to settle the dispute. These officials suggested that the Yampalis should be allowed to use water from the disputed source for the drinking water project, after considering the needs of irrigation of Satrasaya Phant. Satrasaya Phant farmers at first did not agree with this suggestion, however, under pressure from the officials they agreed to allow the Yampalis to tap their drinking water from the disputed source but on the condition that they did not break the diversion weir to irrigate their fields. The Yampalis, however, did not agree to this condition because, as one informant put it, '...for us irrigation is more important than drinking water. We would rather use the Barahi Andhi Mul source for irrigation than for drinking water.' They therefore used another water source for their drinking water project and continued to divert water ('illicitly') from Thulo Andhi Khola for irrigation.

In this dispute, the Yampalis used a clever strategy to try to establish rights in the disputed water source. The Yampalis, emboldened by the grant given to them by the once powerful Red Cross, patronized by the royal family, used this opportunity to lay claims to the disputed water source by tapping it for their drinking water project. They had hoped that by establishing rights to use water from this source for drinking water, they could later establish rights for irrigation. However, on this occasion too the Satrasaya Phant farmers were not taken in by the strategy, nor were the officials. For these officials it was important that the project was successfully completed and a law and order situation resolved. If this meant that the disputed water source was to be used for the project, they could 'persuade' the Satrasaya Phant farmers to allow the Yampalis to do so. At the same time, they had to take into consideration the fact that Satrasaya Phant farmers had been using this water source for irrigation and that they had prior rights to the water. The Satrasaya Phant farmers were willing to grant them rights to acquire water from their water source but only for the drinking water project in exchange for which the Yampalis would have to stop stealing water for irrigation. The mediation effort was not successful because the Yampalis did not want to give up their claims to use the water source for irrigation.

Discussion and Conclusion

The Yampalis have been trying for over 75 years to establish rights to use water from the disputed water source. The strategies they used to acquire water and to establish water rights ranged from negotiation to force to the use of development project and administrative officials. Although the Satrasaya Phant farmers succeeded in preventing the Yampalis from establishing water rights in the disputed water source, the Yampalis continue to claim that they have rights to a share of the water. One way in which they have expressed this claim is by 'stealing' water from the disputed water source.

One of the common but illicit ways of gaining access to and acquiring water from disputed water sources is by stealing (Pradhan and Pradhan 1996; Pradhan et al. 1997a). This strategy is often used when negotiation and other strategies fail. In many cases, the 'water thieves' have been able to secure rights to acquire water and in some cases even to have a say in water allocation and other decisions (see Pradhan and Pradhan 1996). However, the 'water thieves' do not always succeed in establishing rights to use water; and sometimes, as in the case discussed in this contribution, they may be able to acquire water but are punished for it. In the past Satrasaya Phant farmers reacted strongly to water 'stealing' by the Yampalis. They punished them severely for this, in their eyes, illegal act. Later they guarded the diversion structure to prevent further theft, especially during the crucial monsoon months. Satrasaya Phant farmers, however, were more lenient, especially when relations were cordial, to the Yampalis' requests for water so long as they did not assert that they had rights to it and diverted water only for a specified time. The Yampalis were thus given access to water, more specifically, they were given permission to acquire water but under strict conditions.

By allowing the Yampalis to 'acquire' water, Satrasaya Phant farmers, at least temporarily, have been able to avoid disputing and guarding their water source and to protect their rights to control, allocate, and distribute water. By not asserting their claims, the Yampalis are able to acquire the water they need from the disputed source, peacefully, confidently, and without hindrance. From their perspective, they have been able to acquire only part of the supply of water to which they have rights. In the future they may be able to establish rights to use water from the disputed water source, that is, rights acknowledged by Satrasaya Phant farmers.

Another method of asserting claims to water sources used in the present case and elsewhere in Nepal, is by use of force, more precisely by destroying diversion weirs (Pradhan and Pradhan 1996; Pradhan and Pradhan 1997). Physical structures such as diversion weirs are visible means of asserting and protecting water rights. Permanent structures block diversion by farmers whose claims are not accepted. Destruction of diversion weirs is usually a desperate act by the farmers who feel that the structure is not only a symbol of the denial of their claims, but equally, which makes it more difficult for them to acquire water (by stealing for example). We must not think that such destructions are always acts of resistance by the weak. This could be the case in the second dispute when the Yampalis damaged the new gabion diversion weir, but not so when in the first dispute the Yampalis damaged the brushwood diversion structures and then threatened the Satrasaya Phant with a rifle. Such acts usually lead to escalation of disputes and deterioration of relations.

The court is usually not a strategy, at least not the first strategy, the farmers use to protect or establish water rights. This is not only because of the time and expense involved but also because they are not sure how the court will decide. Equally important is that court decisions have to be implemented in the social field where the dispute originated. Here more important and significant than court decisions and state law are local law and social and political relations. It is difficult to implement court decisions without massive state backing, all the more so when the disputants are of relatively equal standing. In the first dispute, the equivocal decision given by the court made it difficult to resolve the conflict and implement the decision. Perhaps the judges knew only too well that such disputes are best left to the disputants to resolve in their own ways.

The second and third disputes indicate how external intervention (government-aided rehabitation and extension project and Red Cross-funded drinking water project), with all that these imply in terms of support from state officials, provide opportunities for stakeholders to attempt to alter or reinforce existing water rights relations (see Pradhan et al. 1997a). In the second dispute, Satrasaya Phant farmers, aided wittingly or unwittingly by the Department of Irrigation, were able to buttress their claims to exclusive rights to the water source by constructing a diversion weir which was stronger and leaked less than the brush wood structure. This made it even more difficult for the Yampalis to acquire water (even by stealing), not to speak about establishing rights. Here, the Department of Irrigation possibly helped Satrasaya Phant farmers ignore state law.

In the third dispute, the Yampalis took the initiative in using the opportunity provided by the drinking water project to attempt to establish rights to a share of water from the disputed water source for drinking water purposes which they planned later to use for irrigation. Their strategy did not work because Satrasaya Phant farmers as well as the officials were aware of their subterfuge. Had the officials been more persuasive, they could have helped Yampalis establish rights to water from the disputed source.

In the disputes discussed in this paper, negotiation did not seem a viable strategy to establish and protect water rights because both parties did not budge from their claims. The two villages do not seem to have made much efforts at negotiating. Even when relations between the two villages were very cordial, the Yampalis were not able to secure rights to water from the disputed source.

It is important to note that the supply of water to their fields was not the major reason why the Satrasaya Phant farmers consistently refused to accept the Yampalis' claims to rights to tap water from the disputed water source. There was more than sufficient water supply in the water source for both disputing villages, as can be seen from the fact that (a) Satrasaya Phant still had abundant water when they allowed Yampalis to divert water when relations with them were good or when they stole water; and (b) the command area of Satrasaya Phant Kulo was increased by nearly 75 per cent using the same water source. The main reason why Satrasaya Phant farmers were not willing to grant the Yampalis rights to a share in the water was that they wanted to retain control over the water source and to allocate water as they pleased.

The Yampalis were not satisfied with being able to acquire water either with permission from Satrasaya Phant farmers or by theft; they wanted to ensure a guaranteed supply of water for their monsoon paddy crop by establishing rights to use water and also to control water allocation. Faced with the failures of their strategies to get their claims accepted by Satrasaya Phant farmers, they were realistic enough to seek ways which would make it possible for them to acquire water sufficient for their monsoon paddy crop while they awaited another opportunity to establish water rights.

In this chapter we have argued that negotiation is only one strategy among others, and not always the most useful or successful one, used by the farmers to establish or protect water rights. Negotiation seems to work mainly when relations between the disputants are good or, to put it differently, good relations are conducive to negotiated settlement of disputes. Other strategies are more effective in situations of bad, adversarial relations. The strategies used depend not only on the relations between the disputants but also the resources (power, connections, legal, etc.) available to them and the type of rights sought to be established or protected. The strategy used also depends on whether the objective is to establish or protect rights or to gain access and acquire water (or prevent others from gaining access and acquiring water). Negotiation is more likely to be used and succeed when the issue of water rights is put aside or transformed into the issue of acquisition of water. It is much more difficult to reach a negotiated settlement on water rights issue than on the issue of water acquisition.

Notes

1. This paper is based on a research entitled 'Study of Water Rights in Nepal' carried out by the International Irrigation Management Institute, Nepal office and Legal Research and Development Forum (FREEDEAL), Nepal in 1994 and 1995. Fieldwork for this part was carried out mainly by Durga K.C. The project was funded by the Ford Foundation. We would like to thank editors Ruth Meinzen-Dick and Bryan Bruns as well as the reviewer of this book for useful suggestions.
2. For a review of water related laws in Nepal see Khadga 1997 and U. Pradhan 1995.
3. For such frequent conflicts in Nepal, see Benda-Beckmann et al. 1997; U. Pradhan 1990; Pradhan and Pradhan 1996; Pradhan and Pradhan 1997; K.C. and Pradhan 1997; Shukla et al. 1997.
4. This term is derived from Scott 1985, which he used to describe the 'everyday forms of resistence' by peasants.
5. See Durga and Pradhan 1997; Pradhan et al. 1997b for a discussion of conflicts and disputes before, during, and after this project.
6. This section of the National Code has been discussed by Pradhan 1990 and Benjamin et al. 1994 among others.

References

Ambler, John. 1990. The influence of farmer water rights on the design of water-proportioning devices. In *Design issues in farmer-managed irrigation* *systems*, ed. Robert Yoder and Juanita Thurston, 37–52. Colombo, Sri Lanka: International Irrigation Management Institute.

Ansari, N. 1995. Accomplishment and progress of ILC pilot project. In *Improving support services to farmer managed irrigation systems in Nepal*, 43–51. Kathmandu: Research and Technology Development Branch and International Irrigation Management Institute.

Benda-Beckmann, Keebet von. 1984. *The broken staircase to consensus: Village justice and state courts in Minangkabau.* Dordrech, The Netherlands: Foris.

———. 1985. The social significance of Minangkabau State Court decisions. *Journal of Legal Pluralism* 23: 1–68.

Benda-Beckmann, Franz von and Keebet von Benda-Beckmann. 1996. A functional analysis of property rights, with special reference to Indonesia. Paper presented at the CERES/CPS workshop on Property Rights and Economic Development in South-East Asia and Oceania. Wageningen, The Netherlands, November.

Benda-Beckmann, Franz von, Keebet von Benda-Beckmann, and H.L. Joep Spiertz. 1997. Local law and customary practices in the study of water rights. In *Water rights, conflict and policy*, ed. Rajendra Pradhan, Franz von Benda-Beckmann, Keebet von Benda-Beckmann, H.L. Joep Spiertz, S. Khadka, and K. Azharul Haq, 221–42. Colombo, Sri Lanka: International Irrigation Management Institute.

Benda-Beckmann, Keebet von, H.L.J. Spiertz, and Franz von Benda-Beckmann. 1997. Disputing water rights: Scarcity of water in Nepal hill irrigation. In *The scarcity of water. Emerging legal and policy responses*, ed. E.H.P. Brans, E.J. de Haan, A. Nollkaemper, and J. Rinzema, 224–42. London: Kluwer Law International.

Benjamin, Paul, Wai Fung Lam, Elinor Ostrom, and Ganesh Shivakoti. 1994. *Institutions, incentives, and irrigation in Nepal.* Burlington, Vt.: Associates in Rural Development.

Griffiths, J. 1986. What is legal pluralism? *Journal of Legal Pluralism* 24: 1–50.

K.C., Durga and R. Pradhan. 1997. Improvement and enlargement of a farmer managed irrigation system in Tanahu: Changing rights to water and conflict resolution. In *Water rights, conflict and policy*, ed. Rajendra Pradhan, Franz von Benda-Beckmann, Keebet von Benda-Beckmann, H.L. Joep Spiertz, S. Khadka, and K. Azharul Haq, 135–56. Colombo, Sri Lanka: International Irrigation Management Institute.

Khanal, Bishal and Santosh K.C. 1997. Analysis of Supreme Court cases and decisions related to water rights in Nepal. In *Water rights, conflict and policy*, ed. Rajendra Pradhan, Franz von Benda-Beckmann, Keebet von Benda-Beckmann, H.L. Joep Spiertz, S. Khadka, and K. Azharul Haq, 47–62. Colombo, Sri Lanka: International Irrigation Management Institute.

Merry, Sally, E. 1988. Legal pluralism. *Law and Society Review* 22 (5): 869–96.

Pradhan, Mahesh. C. and **Rajendra Pradhan.** 1997. Disputing, negotiating and accommodating as means to acquire and protect water rights: A case study of conflicts in Dang. In *Water rights, conflict and policy,* ed. Rajendra Pradhan, Franz von Benda-Beckmann, Keebet von Benda-Beckmann, H.L. Joep Spiertz, S. Khadka, and K. Azharul Haq, 157–72. Colombo, Sri Lanka: International Irrigation Management Institute.

Pradhan, Prachanda. 1989. *Patterns of irrigation organization in Nepal.* Colombo, Sri Lanka: International Irrigation Management Institute.

Pradhan, Rajendra and **Ujjwal Pradhan.** 1996. Staking a claim: Law, politics and water rights in farmer managed irrigation systems in Nepal. In *The role of law in natural resources management,* ed. H.L. Joep Spiertz and Melanie G. Wiber, 61–76. The Hague, The Netherlands: Vuga.

Pradhan, Rajendra, Franz von Benda-Beckmann, Keebet von Benda-Beckmann, H.L. Joep Spiertz, S. Khadga, K.A. Haq, eds. 1997a. *Water rights, conflict and policy.* Colombo, Sri Lanka: International Irrigation Management Institute.

Pradhan, Rajendra, K.A. Haq, and **Ujjwal Pradhan.** 1997b. Law, rights and equity: Implications of state intervention in farmer managed irrigation systems. In *Water rights, conflict and policy,* ed. Rajendra Pradhan, Franz von Benda-Beckmann, Keebet von Benda-Beckmann, H.L. Joep Spiertz, S. Khadka, K. Azharul Haq, 111–34. Colombo, Sri Lanka: International Irrigation Management Institute.

Pradhan, Ujjwal. 1990. Property rights and state intervention in hill irrigation systems in Nepal. Ph.D. diss., Cornell University, Ithaca, New York.

———. 1994. Farmers' water rights and their relation to data collection and management. In *From farmers' fields to data fields and back,* ed. J. Sowerine, Ganesh Shivakoti, Ujjwal Pradhan, Athutosh Shukla, and Elinor Ostrom. Kathmandu: International Irrigation Management Institute and IAAS.

Schlager, Edela and **Elinor Ostrom.** 1992. Property-rights regimes and natural resources: A conceptual analysis. *Land Economics* 68 (2): 249–62.

Scott, James C. 1985. *Weapons of the weak. Everyday forms of peasant resistance.* New Haven, Conn.: Yale University Press.

Shukla, Athutosh, Narayan R. Joshi, Ganesh Shivakoti, Rabi Poudel and **Narayan Shrestha.** 1997. Dynamics in water rights and arbitration on water right conflicts: Cases of farmer managed irrigation systems from East Chitwan. In *Water rights, conflict and policy,* ed. Rajendra Pradhan, Franz von Benda-Beckmann, Keebet von Benda-Beckmann, H.L. Joep Spiertz, S. Khadka, and K. Azharul Haq, 173–94. Colombo, Sri Lanka: International Irrigation Management Institute.

Talbot, R. 1997. Theorising access. Forest profits along Senegal's Charcoal Commodity Chain. Draft Manuscript.

Wiber, Melanie G. 1992. Levels of property rights and levels of law: A case study from the northern Philippines. *Man* (N.S.) 26: 469–92.

8

Water Property Rights and Resistance to Demand Management in Northwestern Spain

DAVID GUILLET

The current political discourse in Spain concerning demand management versus supply augmentation for water resources neglects the previous historical experience. Efforts to manage demand antedate the current debate, beginning over a hundred years ago with the 1879 Water Law. Farmers resisted the implementation of demand management measures, perceiving them as an attenuation of their rights to water. However, until the death of Franco opened up political space, resistance was localized and hidden. Lacking formal channels, farmers resorted to informal, evasive actions to circumvent formal rules or procedures, negotiating 'informal adjustments' or 'working arrangements.' While local resistance has continued and remained highly effective, farmers now find new channels at the regional and national levels to articulate resistance to demand management.

Introduction

Faced with increasing water scarcity and the need to maintain or increase irrigated agricultural production, states are increasingly intervening in local water management. Until recently, external intervention took the form of supply augmentation. This strategy has been sharply criticized, however, for the high and increasing financial, economic, and environmental costs of dams and other large-scale water works. As a result, observers now advocate the management of demand. This entails recognizing the economic value of water and introducing policies that induce consumers to internalize the scarcity value of water. Policies to implement demand management range from charging or levying administrative fees for the amount consumed, to assessing punitive costs for wastage, to water markets.

These questions are particularly relevant in Spain, a semi-arid country where irrigation plays an important role in agriculture. Spanish irrigation systems have an extraordinarily long history dating back, in many instances, to the Roman and Islamic presence. They use a variety of flexible and approximate forms of water distribution, including allocation by proportionate shares and increments of time (Al-Mudayna 1991; Butzer et al. 1985; Olcina Gil and Morales Gil 1992). The large-scale, long-canal systems of Valencia, Murcia, Orihuela and Alicante in eastern Spain have been extensively studied and are commonly cited in the institutional analysis literature as examples of successful long-term, robust common pool regimes (Glick 1970; Maas and Anderson 1978; Ostrom 1990: 69–82). The numerous small-scale irrigation systems located on the slopes and upper valleys of the mountain chains that cut across the country, such as those in the Orbigo Valley of northwestern Spain, have received much less attention.

Since the late 19th century, the Spanish government has intervened vigorously in water policy, beginning with a comprehensive water law in 1879 (Naylon 1973; Ortega Cantero 1984; San Miguel 1993). The 1985 Water Law, which overruled the 1879 Water Law, created a public domain over all water resources. Today, a national water plan is emerging from public debate prior to its enactment into law. Many demand management measures are being debated in this process. Due to the economic crisis of the early 1990s, farmers interpret pressures to manage demand through new, more efficient irrigation technologies and consumption-based taxation as additional costs at a time when production costs are already high and commodity prices low or falling (Guillet 1997).

The reigning historical consensus on the impact of the 1879 Water Law is that the state has exerted a protagonist role in exploiting surface water, albeit one that could only be implemented after the creation of watershed management authorities in 1926. This perspective influences the current debate on the National Water Plan by concluding that state efforts to manage demand are the modern answer to traditional water management that lacks measures to foster water savings. However, this view is in need of reassessment. Demand management measures had actually been included in the 1879 Water Law but were not implemented because of local, largely hidden, farmer resistance. Unable to increase the amount of irrigable land by implementing these measures, the state embraced a protagonist role in increasing the supply of water. Farmers have continued to resist demand management measures till this day, but in the post-Franco era, this opposition takes on a public, interest-group form.

At the core of the resistance to demand management is the perception of a breach of the farmer's contract with the state, an attenuation of their ancient and hard-won rights to water. Local law, steeped in local knowledge and practice, played a key role in the evolution of these rights.[1] Customary laws determined the contractual terms, including the rights of exclusivity and transferability, that governed the use of irrigation water. Local law lowered the costs of the state legal system by providing precedents for the codification of law and the judicial system. Where property rights specified by state law proved unworkable in practice, it was local law that allowed property rights to water to function by adapting some of the previously cumbersome specifications of the central government to local conditions. The state accepted this customary law out of pragmatic recognition of its efficacy.

The resistance by Spanish farmers to the demand management of an earlier era has implications beyond those of redressing a historical inaccuracy. Similar farmer-managed irrigation systems, characterized by unmeasured water use, water available on demand at no or minimal cost, and poorly specified, flexible and, at best, approximately measured water rights are found throughout the world. The World Bank estimates that 85 per cent of the world's irrigated area relies on small-scale, gravity-flow canal systems managed by farmers (World Bank 1992). These farmer-managed irrigation systems average less than 40 hectares in size and in many countries number in the thousands (Mabry 1996: Table 1.1 pp. 5, 6).

Policymakers would profit from close examination of this historical case to address the issues of equity and efficiency largely ignored in an almost hagiographic discussion of demand management. In Peru, for example, legislators proposed a new water law which would implement a market-based system of freely tradable water rights (ECLAC 1997) in a country that, like Spain, has at least a thousand-year tradition of farmer-managed irrigation (Mitchell and Guillet 1994). Implementing a system of freely tradable water rights in countries like Peru raises serious questions of the equity and efficiency of water use in these systems and may prove impractical due to technical reasons and farmer opposition, as found in Spain (Guillet 1999; Trawick 1997).

This paper analyzes these issues in the context of farmer-managed irrigation systems in the Orbigo Valley of northwestern Spain over the last 100 years.[2] In the first section, a short history of these irrigation systems is presented. An analysis of the demand management features of the 1879 Water Law and subsequent legislation follows. The concluding section details the reaction of Orbigo farmers to the implementation of the 1879 Water Law.

Presas of the Orbigo Valley

In the upper Duero Valley, fast-flowing rivers descend the geologically young Cantabrian-Asturian mountains and provide easily diverted water to irrigate fertile alluvial terraces called *riberas* and *vegas*. In the narrow, cold, upper valleys of the mountains, individual villages traditionally tapped rivers to irrigate pastures. On the lower slopes and valleys, several villages joined to construct and manage irrigation systems. Over 500 of these small-scale systems are legally recognized today under the provisions of Spanish water law and many more are organized informally, the immense majority with less than 200 hectares of irrigated land (Díez Gonzalez 1992: 44).

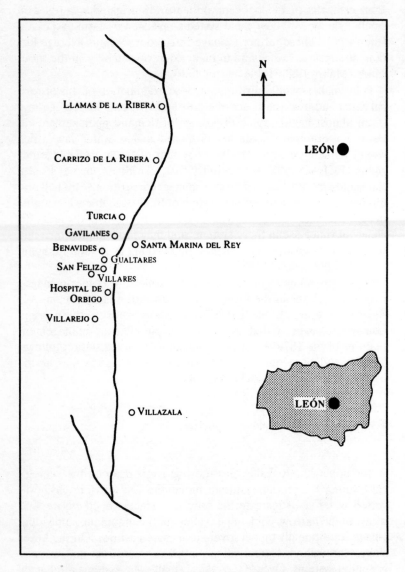

Map 8.1: The Orbigo Valley of Northwestern Spain

These systems were created during the repopulation of the Duero Valley in the 9th through the 12th centuries when small groups of Christian settlers, monasteries, and royalty settled the area following the expulsion of the Muslims. During the latter part of the period, municipalities formed quasi-corporate irrigation associations called *presas* to construct dam and canal systems to divert water from the Orbigo River. *Presas* obtained a concession from the state, or contracted with upstream holders of riparian rights, for access to water and rights-of-way. In certain instances, however, court rulings to protect prior rights, or contracts for the reconstruction of the dam and main canal by the *presas*, specified the size of the opening (*bocatoma*) of the diversion canal. Along the course of the canal, from the offtake point to the point of diversion to municipalities, *presas* considered the hydraulic infrastructure of the dam and main canal jointly owned, and the water transported through it a public good.

The *presas*, in turn, allocated water to municipalities on the basis of proportionate shares, units of time, and, occasionally, according to crops irrigated. In this way, *presas* adroitly lowered the transaction costs of contracting for water. These settings lent themselves to 'transactional modes' based on reputation, trust, and reciprocity. Municipal councils developed a rich body of customary law based on local knowledge and practice to regulate the distribution and use of the water diverted from the main canal. While usually tacit and unwritten, customary water law occasionally found voice in municipal charters and, later, ordinances. Once diverted from the main canal to a municipality, water was considered communal property. Municipalities, in turn, distributed water to the fields according to a traditional linkage of water and landownership. Simple queuing mechanisms were used when water was ample and a system of turns, combined with a lottery in some instances, when water was scarce (Guillet 1998).

Customary water law developed in concert with the elaboration of a uniform seven-volume legal code in the second half of the 13th century, *Las Siete Partidas*. The structure of water property rights enshrined in the *Partidas* was more appropriate for the slow flowing, high volume rivers of the great plateaus of Old Castile. Therefore, the municipalities had to adapt the rights to the geologically young, wide, and flat beds of the Orbigo River. The property rights attached in the *Partidas* to water mills, for example, were heavily influenced by the practice in the central tablelands of Spain of locating them directly on rivers. Landowners were given the right to construct mills on their own land as long as they did not obstruct the existing rights of downstream mill owners. The fluvial geomorphology of the Orbigo, however—like most of the fast flowing and annually flooding rivers of the upper Duero basin—did not allow for the permanent installation of mills in the river bed. In the Orbigo Valley, mills were incorporated into new or existing canal irrigation systems based on diverted river water. This created a multitude of problems between irrigators and mill owners. As a result, municipal councils routinely attenuated the private rights of landowners to construct mills as specified in the *Partidas* and regulated their use. These regulations became incorporated into concessions for mills and local law. Local law, steeped in local knowledge and practice, stepped into the breach to adjust property rights to these realities (Guillet 1998).

Presas, and their member villages, also endowed excess water and return flows with specified rights of exclusivity and transferability in formal and informal contractual relationships among *presas*, between *presas* and municipalities, and between municipalities and end-users. The founders of the *presas* designed their hydraulic infrastructure to reuse return flows from upstream systems and rights to these flows were recognized in local customary law. Bestowing limited forms of property rights over excess water contradicted its status in the *Partidas* as an inalienable, free good. In this environment of scarce water, however, rights to excess water reflected its de facto value. Ownership of excess water was not allocated homogeneously, however, but varied in the degree to which the flow could be ascertained. Where the flow was highly variable and thus not fully predictable, for example, it was treated as the free good defined in the *Partidas*.

The normative ordering of local legal systems, central to enforcement and dispute resolution, contributed to a *presa*'s ability to assign rights to water and formulate efficient allocation rules. Local law coexisted in a dialectic relation with central or state law rather than remaining separate. Local and state law differed considerably in procedure. State law was normative in its uniformity, completeness, and generalizability, and was embedded in lengthy and costly procedures. Local law, in contrast, was ad hoc, pragmatic, and free to achieve quick and inexpensive resolutions. Informal, arbitrated agreements were predominantly oral, although scribes recorded final agreements. Traditional usages and customs informed judgments; recourse to written law was infrequent. Arbitrators, chosen for their expertise in the issue at hand, had recourse to flexible remedies. State law only selectively intervened in the definition and defense of property rights, by providing contract guarantees, a definition of certain property rights, and a system of state courts for their defense. Thus, much of the definition and defense of property rights occurred locally.

State Intervention in the Specification of Water Rights

The modern era of state intervention in demand management can be traced to the 1879 Water Law.[3] This law was enacted in a spirit of reform and the hope that expanded and more efficient irrigation would solve many pressing rural problems (Gómez Mendoza 1992; Orti 1984). It was considered a model of progressive water policy at the time. Pressures to grant new concessions of water to expand irrigated area motivated the inclusion of provisions for demand management. Existing irrigation systems were felt to harbor much waste and inefficient water use. The Water Law addressed these goals through a blanket prohibition on the wasteful use of public water (Article 204), new corporate management bodies, and an orderly and rational procedure for determining the availability of surplus water for new uses (Article 190).

To 'avoid quarrels and litigation' (Article 5, Model Ordinance), the Water Law created new corporate management bodies, called irrigation communities (*comunidades de regantes*). This step enabled irrigators sharing a water source to obtain permanent rights to the water and to transform quasi-corporate *presas* into fully corporate, legally recognized, irrigation associations. A model ordinance appended to the Water Law was followed in the subsequent organization of irrigation communities. Article 241 of the Water Law facilitated the organization of central syndicates from irrigation communities sharing the water of a river. This introduced a new level of organization above the irrigation community.

The procedure (Articles 191, 192, Water Law) for determining the availability of surplus water established standard measures for water volume in cubic meters per second for new concessions (Article 152, Water Law) and liters per second for irrigation communities (Article 74, Model Ordinance). The location and extent of irrigated land also had to be specified in a standard measure of hectares (Article 152, Water Law). The direct measurement of water volume required the installation of volumetric measurement devices. The Water Law empowered the minister of public works to force long-standing water users lacking these devices to install them at their own expense and to assume the costs of the measurement of their irrigated area (Article 152, Water Law).

Article 8 of the Model Ordinance held that the rights and obligations of irrigators should be computed in proportion to the water they use. Water use could be measured by the:

> employment or the quantity to which they have claim, or the quantity of water which they consume, or to the extent of the land which they irrigate or have right to irrigate, as well as to the amounts which they contribute to the outlay of the community.

This provision represented a retreat from the direct measurement of consumption as determinant of rights and obligations. Given the high costs of directly measuring consumption, in particular the costs of volumetric measuring devices, indirect measures were much more feasible.

Irrigated area came to assume great potential importance because the Model Ordinance specified a series of rights and obligations for irrigators that varied by the size of the irrigated area. Rights included access to water and voting representation in the general assembly and syndicate of the irrigation community. In irrigation communities with several member municipalities, like the Orbigo Presas, Article 58 of the Model Ordinances specified that the representation was governed by the number of hectares of irrigated land each municipality contributed to the total irrigated area of the irrigation community. This same principle also delimited the proportionate representation of each irrigation community in a central syndicate. Irrigated area further determined the obligations of individual irrigators and municipalities in terms of their respective contributions in cash, labor, and kind to the construction and maintenance of physical improvements and tariffs paid to watershed authorities.

While the law gave irrigation communities and syndicates an active and legitimate role in water management, on the one hand, it also took away power by allowing mayors, provincial governors, and the minister of public works to exercise authority in certain areas. These areas were those in which the state chose to grant individuals discretionary power rather than rely on inflexible rules. For example, depending on the situation, the mayor (Article 178), provincial governor (Article 181), or minister of public works (Articles 182 and 185) could be charged with authorizing uses for water. Similarly, the minister of public works was empowered with determining the volume of the concession of an existing irrigation system that lacked one, and requiring the installation of measuring devices if necessary.

The 1879 Water Law continued in force for over one hundred years, until it was replaced by a new water code in 1985. In 1926, watershed management bodies, called *Confederaciónes Hidrográficas*, were established (Cano García 1992). These bodies have helped rationalize water use in large watersheds and regularly intervene between the state and irrigation communities. The 1985 Water Law was aimed at correcting deficiencies of the earlier law and at making water policy consistent with the decentralized regional autonomy created in the post-Franco era. The law reconceptualized watershed authorities, expanding their geographical range, increasing their authority, giving them new powers, and modifying their governing, administrative, and planning bodies. Watershed authorities were empowered to intervene directly in local irrigation and put pressure on irrigation communities and syndicates to conform to a regional hydrological plan. The 1985 Water Law also reflected the European Community's environmental concerns in establishing water quality standards and minimum water levels to maintain biotic diversity in rivers (Guillet 1997).

State Intervention in the Orbigo Valley

Looking at how these efforts at legal reform played out in practice in the past illustrates some of the dialectical relationship between state and customary law. In the Orbigo Valley, farmers in the town of Hospital de Orbigo triggered a first ruling based on the 1879 Water Law through an application for a concession of 100 liters per second of water to construct a new irrigation system (see Map 8.1). If granted, this would have been the first new concession in several centuries on the Orbigo River. It set into motion a major rethinking of how the water of the river was distributed. A well-connected teacher in a progressive, experimental school in the town, the Fundación Sierra Pambley, organized the project and used his social and political contacts to promote the application. Downstream villages fought it bitterly. The public works agency decided to put an end to the legal wrangling and to allow the concession to go forward. In December 1895, it ordered 'that the irrigation systems of the Orbigo River be regulated so that each village takes no more water than it needs and those villages form irrigation communities with their regulations, rules, syndicates, and *junta de riegos.*' The provincial governor granted the concession in June 1896, and a royal decree confirmed it the following December. In April, 1902, Hospital de Orbigo became the first irrigation community formed in the *ribera* under the 1879 Water Law.

The ripples from Hospital de Orbigo spread up and down the *ribera*. In December of 1904, the village of Villarejo applied for a concession of 85 liters per second of water to irrigate 570 hectares of land. Lower villages and towns immediately opposed the application arguing that it would negatively affect their prior rights to Orbigo water. Villarejo countered this by citing provisions in the 1879 Water Law requiring each municipality to install measuring devices and to determine the quantity of water it used. In May 1905, the head engineer of Leon province ruled in the case. He declared that the conflicting claims of villages and towns highlighted a longstanding problem of waste, anarchy, and inequity in the distribution of Orbigo water. He agreed to install measuring devices, to distribute water by irrigated area, to normalize the unspecified concessions of municipalities, and to review Villarejo's request in accordance with state water law. If 85 liters per second of water remained after downstream municipalities' consumption was accounted for, Villarejo's application would be granted. Ultimately, suggested the engineer, the solution to the problem of the Orbigo River rested in the implementation of the order of the director of the public works agency of December 15, 1895, to monitor water flow to each municipality and organize irrigation communities.

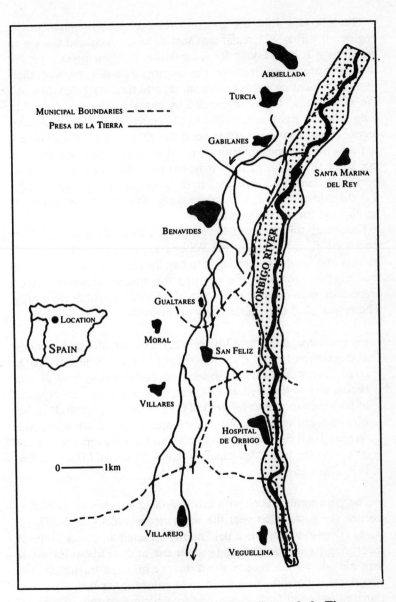

Map 8.2: Municipal Boundaries of the Presa de la Tierra

The following July, the governor took action to implement the engineer's ruling. A circular was sent to nine towns and villages in the Orbigo Ribera asking for information on their procedures for drawing water from the river, the quantity of water involved, their titles documenting rights to this water, and their irrigated area. All the villages and towns responded by citing generalized claims to long-standing rights originating in old concessions and royal privileges. These documents, responded the villages and towns, did not indicate the volume of water diverted from the river and they did not know the extent of their irrigated area. No documents to support their claims were provided to the governor. Hospital de Orbigo was the sole exception: it had already supplied the information in its application for a concession.

Faced with this response, the governor exercised the discretionary power afforded him under the Water Law. In April 1906, he asked mayors and local water officials to pay for the costs of determining the irrigated area and of measuring the volume of water in their respective municipalities. Municipal officials resisted vigorously. The response of one municipality is illustrative:

> the municipal council of Villarejo agrees unanimously to request authorization from the Civil Governor of the Province to charge large landowners (*terratenientes*) the extraordinary levy of four thousand two hundred and eleven pesetas to meet the expenses of flow measurements (*aforos*) of the Orbigo river water. It is they who will receive the benefits of the appraisal. Otherwise, various *vecinos* [legal residents], who don't own landed property, will end up paying the levy (Municipal Archives, Villarejo. Minutes 1906–1910 folios 16–17).

The government faced with this resistance was forced in 1908 to assume the costs. That year the watershed authority of the Duero River (División Hidráulica del Duero) initiated a project to install measuring devices and regulate water use in the Orbigo Presas. In his rationale for the project the director expressed frustration. For one, it was impossible, he argued, to monitor the expansion of unauthorized irrigated land. According to Article 8 of the 1879 Water Law, after 20 years of continuous use, these illegal extensions became legal. In not one case of this kind was the flow of water specified. Moreover, villages and towns were wasting water by useless irrigation and inundating pastures and roads. Upstream users were diverting excessive water, leaving downstream fields dry. The state found itself in a bind. While new concessions were obviously necessary to meet the growing demand for irrigation, no one knew how much water was already assigned by the existing concessions. This raised the distinct possibility of granting a request for which water was not available or denying others for which surplus water existed.

During the project, the question of the calculation of the flow of existing irrigation came up. The project, apparently for the first time, calculated the irrigated area of each village and town. Once the irrigated area was obtained, the volume of the concession was specified by assigning one liter per second of water to each irrigated hectare. In commenting on this procedure, the project engineer defended the setting of a figure which he felt was excessive for the mixed cultivation of tubers, legumes, and cereals. Many parts of the Orbigo bottom lands, he argued, had loose, porous subsoils which allowed water to infiltrate rapidly, and so required a greater volume of water for irrigation than more water retentive subsoils. The prevailing practice of furrow irrigation compounded the problem, leading to considerable wastage and water loss. However, he said, setting a figure in line with accepted optimum requirements for the mixed cultivation of tubers, legumes, and cereals would reduce the flow to villages and towns. It would create hostility and unrest: 'a decision to suddenly restrict the water flow that each measuring device lets in, to that strictly necessary for the cultivation requirements of crops in a zone would certainly cause serious displeasure and challenges to public order' (Ministerio de Obras Publicas. 1918/20).

The engineer was referring to the very real loss of traditional water rights Orbigo farmers would experience if a more stringent formula were implemented. Since the constitution of their *presas*, Orbigo farmers were accustomed to allocating the water their villages received from the main canal when and however they wanted. Any reduction in flow would be perceived as a de facto loss of rights to water. The engineer was concerned that farmers would not resign themselves to such a loss, and would resist. The implied threat of social and political disturbances is a very strong theme in his commentary.

There was reason for the state engineer to be concerned, given a history of episodic, localized, and occasionally violent conflicts over water. In his 1951 novel, *La invisible prisión*, for example, Luis

Alonso Luengo drew on his father's stories to weave a subplot surrounding the murder of a villager from San Feliz by a farmer of Hospital de Orbigo for cutting off its water (Alonso Luengo 1951: 65–83).[4] His father, Paulino Alonso y Fernández de Arellano, a lawyer, was hired as a syndic in 1926 by the then newly created watershed authority of the Duero River, Confederación Hidrográfica del Duero (CHD) to help organize irrigation communities along the Orbigo and Tuerto Rivers. When the Central Irrigation Syndicate of the Barrios de Luna Dam was founded in 1952, he was elected its first president. Alonso y Fernández de Arellano was extremely knowledgeable in the history of agrarian unrest in the *ribera* and a primary source of information for CHD officials on the social, economic, and political situation.

While archival documents and novels oriented to a literate élite were largely inaccessible to Orbigo farmers, events such as the murder in Hospital de Orbigo were the stuff of a lived oral history. Virtually every dam, water mill, sluice gate, and secondary canal has been at one point in time a flash point in the Orbigo Ribera, and most are the subjects of a still remembered history. To take an example, a small dam in the village of Gualtares, diverting water from the main canal of the Presa de la Tierra to the villages of Villares, Villarejo, and Hospital de Orbigo, has been the subject of heated disputes since the mid-15th century. When the Presa de la Tierra was organized into an irrigation community in the mid-1940s, a major dispute erupted over it again. It was only resolved following its dynamiting and intervention by the provincial governor to help negotiate a settlement.

When it came time to assign funds, the project engineer argued that the state would benefit by gaining access to excess water to generate new concessions and should assume the costs of the project. The measurements began in 1911 and were finished in 1912. The final report appeared in 1923 and called for the installation of permanent measuring devices at each diversion dam on the river. The extreme instability of the river and annual flooding forced costly reinforcement of the banks of the river with ramparts. The project was reviewed again in 1923 but the measuring devices were never installed.

In the years following Hospital de Orbigo's application for a concession, Orbigo Presas were slowly organized into irrigation communities. The challenge Veguellina mounted led to its own organization as an irrigation community in 1903, followed by Presa Grande (1910), Presa Cerrajera (1924), Presa de la Tierra (1945), and Villanueva de Carrizo (1948). The real boom in irrigation community organization occurred after the Barrios de Luna Dam, on the Luna River, upstream of the Orbigo, became operational in 1952. Seven were organized from 1955 to 1974, and the remaining *presas* were formalized, by 1975.

In their organization into irrigation communities, the use of total irrigated area as indirect measure of consumption changed the way Orbigo Presas functioned. The Presa de la Tierra, which diverts water off Orbigo River to irrigate land in Benavides, Gualtares, San Feliz, Villares, Moral, Hospital de Orbigo and Villarejo is illustrative. The *presa* was granted a permanent right by the Chancellery of Valladolid in the 16th century to take water off the river within the municipal borders of the town of Santa Marina del Rey and bring it to lower villages and towns by way of a canal (Guillet 1998). This privilege was used to establish its claim for a permanent concession to water when the *presa* was organized into an irrigation community in 1947. To calculate the concession, state engineers applied the formula of one liter per second of water for each hectare of irrigated land.

The use of total irrigated area to determine the number of representatives possessed by each member village or town redistributed power within the new irrigation community. Before its transformation, the *presa* was governed by a rather weak and amorphous board made up of irrigation judges from each village or town. Historically, the water judge from Villares was the 'first among equals' and represented the Presa de la Tierra to outsiders. This fact, together with other evidence, suggests that Villares and Villarejo were the original founders of the *presa* (Guillet 1998: 52–53). At the time of its reorganization in 1947, Villares and Villarejo were each represented by two irrigation judges. Benavides and Hospital de Orbigo on the other hand, had one each. When representatives were named to the new managerial board during the organization of the irrigation community, Benavides and Hospital de Orbigo were each given an additional representative and Villares and Villarejo each lost one, based on their respective total irrigated areas. The reassignment of representatives gave the towns of Benavides and Hospital de Orbigo a much greater voice over other member villages and weakened Villares and Villarejo.

This potential shift in power was countered in an adroit working arrangement. Informal succession rules were instituted to ensure that each village and town retained its traditional historical position in the new power structure. These unwritten rules hold that the president of the irrigation community always comes from Benavides, the president of the syndicate from Villarejo, and the secretary from San Feliz. Such succession rules are consistent with historical facts. Benavides, historically the seat of the feudal lord, the Conde de Luna, and possessing high economic status as a regional marketing town, entered the *presa* originally in exchange for the rights of way it granted downstream villages to bring the main canal through its municipal boundaries. It gained the right to name the president of the irrigation community, a symbolically important position but one not engaged in day to day water management decisions. Villarejo, at the tail end of the main canal, was one of the original founders of the *presa*. By controlling the presidency of the syndicate, the key managerial position, it maintains its original historical status of founder and the power to keep downstream users from being affected adversely by upstream users.

The obligations of each municipality to the *presa* came under fire next. Introducing irrigated area as the denominator of a village or town's contribution to infrastructure wrought havoc with ancient contracts, dating to the construction of the *presa* and its later expansion, specifying the terms of the relations between a village or town and the *presa*. Under the water law, the irrigated area of each municipality governed its contribution in labor, cash and kind to infrastructure, to the annual reconstruction of the dam, maintenance of the main canal, and physical improvements to *presa* infrastructure. Beyond a certain point, upstream villages did not contribute to downstream infrastructure. The issue was debated fiercely during initial meetings of the community. It was eventually resolved through direct intervention by the provincial governor in the negotiations.

Specifying the concession of each village or town in liters per second per hectare provided a new goal in the political arena: a numerical target for municipalities who felt that they were not getting a fair share under existing flexible mechanisms of allocation. They began to petition for infrastructure improvements so that they received what was specified for them in the new concession to the Presa de la Tierra.

Lastly, the Duero watershed authority levied tariffs based on the total irrigated area of the new irrigation communities. As the titular owners of water rights, irrigation communities were billed each year for the tariffs. Yet, villages and towns received water from the irrigation community and then distributed it to their irrigators. Irrigation communities billed municipalities, in turn, for their proportionate share of the tariffs based on their total irrigated area. Villages and towns, in turn, minimized real costs by renting harvested fields as pastures and using the proceeds to pay water fees. They were able to do this through local customs requiring landowners to open up their fields to communal pasturing after harvest. In addition, they expected irrigators to participate in work parties, *hacenderas*, to maintain municipal irrigation infrastructure and to contribute to the village or town's share of the upkeep of the dam and main canal.

The manner in which tariffs were levied in conjunction with water distribution practice created a potential free-rider problem. Farmers frequently farmed land outside their own village or town, because of the scarcity of nearby land or because their spouse brought in land on marriage. From the perspective of a village or town one who farmed land within its borders but did not live there was considered a *forastero* or outsider, in contrast to a *vecino*. Water rights were attached to land no matter where the landowner lived. Free-riding could occur when a farmer claimed water for land in a municipality other than one's own and failed to contribute labor, cash, and kind to the maintenance of irrigation infrastructure. To resolve the problem, villages and towns charged *forasteros* an extra fee added to the normal tariff calculated for a *vecino*. While not entirely legal, the state acquiesced out of a pragmatic concern for the collection of fees.

The final report of the project to regularize irrigation on the Orbigo River advocated implementing the provision of the 1879 Water Law regarding the formation of a central syndicate of the *presas* sharing the water of the river. The idea lapsed until the construction of the Barrios de Luna Dam on the Luna River, upstream of the Orbigo, neared completion. In 1952, the Central Irrigation Syndicate of the Barrios de Luna Dam (Sindicato Central de Riegos del Embalse de Barrios de Luna) was created. The dam became operational in 1956 and reduced significantly the seasonal inundations and periodic and catastrophic flooding that had plagued the *ribera*. The Central Syndicate charged a *Junta de Explotación* with scheduling and coordinating the release of water from the dam and now meetings to coordinate its distribution for irrigation are held weekly during the irrigation season. During the meeting, data are provided on the inflow, outflow, and present capacity of the dam. The meeting then shifts to the setting up of turns for the villages. Representatives of irrigation communities, usually presidents of the respective Syndicates, attend the meeting and, in turn, communicate the schedule to their members. The meeting is chaired by a representative from the Duero watershed authority. The Central Syndicate also provides a tribunal for the resolution of disputes within and between irrigation communities.

The experience of negotiation and accommodation between the Presa de la Tierra and the state was replicated with minor variations in other Orbigo Presas upon their organization into irrigation communities. The use of an indirect measure of water consumption was a key axis on which these negotiations continued. Tariffs were imposed on the Presa de la Tierra with little outcry as the irrigation community passed the burden of collecting them from end-users to villages and towns. While the Central Syndicate implemented proportional voting rights in its governing board, irrigation communities often ignored them in instituting succession rules. Succession to office within irrigation communities often diverged completely from regulatory guidelines and was adjusted informally to fit historical experience. Ancient formulas governing the obligations of villages and towns to the *presa* were altered. In some instances the civil governor exercised discretionary power to force an accord; in others, a tacit, informal agreement reoriented relations. In still others, working arrangements were included in the ordinances. Changing flexible, proportionate water rights to fixed volumes provided opportunities for villages and towns to improve their positions. Finally, the organization of the Barrios de Luna Syndicate further helped coordinate the allocation of water on a wider scale.

Conclusion

In Spain, the public debate currently opposing demand management to an earlier policy of supply augmentation is historically inaccurate.

It reifies the consensus in Spanish agrarian history of the state as protagonist in water policy, enshrined in the 1879 Water Law and facilitated by the 1926 legislation establishing watershed authorities. The history of water policy subsequently became one of documenting the construction of massive dams and the expansion of irrigated area. The shift to demand management in the 1990s is a response to the high economic and environmental costs of the earlier policy.

As has been argued here, however, the 1879 Water Law contained an explicit agenda of demand management. While the state was willing to assume a protagonist role and expand irrigable area, it lacked the funds during a period of economic crisis. Saving water cost relatively little in comparison, and represented the only viable strategy for expanding irrigable area. The measures invoked in the 1879 Water Law, standardization of water measurement, direct and indirect measurement of water consumption, and linking provision costs and water access to the amount of water consumed, are today recognized principles of demand management.

If these measures had been fully enacted in the Orbigo Ribera, traditional water rights of *presas* would have been attenuated. The 1879 Water Law empowered state officials with the ability to force water users lacking flow measuring devices to install them at their expense and to assume the costs of measuring their irrigated area. Orbigo farmers were able to thwart the implementation of these measures. Municipalities resisted entreaties by the civil governor to supply information on their water consumption and, when the information failed to appear, refused to assume the expenses of obtaining the data. When the state initiated a project to install measuring devices and control demand, reengineering costs were discovered to be very high. Lacking the resources to implement direct measurement of consumption, the state adopted an indirect measure of irrigated land. The acceptance of an uncomfortably high figure of one liter per second per hectare reflects the state's fear of the unrest that a more 'realistic' figure would have generated among Orbigo farmers.

Orbigo farmers had to wait until the death of Franco and a new constitution in 1978 for access to formal channels to articulate their resistance to demand management. Until then, they took evasive actions to circumvent formal rules and procedures, negotiating 'informal adjustments' and 'working arrangements' with provincial officials and watershed authorities. They were surprisingly successful in this regard. In the hundred years since the 1879 Water Law, *presas* have been organized into irrigation communities and have secured permanent concessions to water, while maintaining traditional forms of allocation and distribution including constant running water in main canals, allocation by time and proportional distribution to villages and towns, and on-demand distribution by villages and towns to farmers of the water necessary for irrigation unless scarcity forces the imposition of turns. This was accomplished without Orbigo farmers contributing to the payment of the costs of installing water measurement devices, the radical modification of ancient formulas of the costs and benefits of membership by villages and towns in *presas*, the delimitation of water flowing into main canals, or the direct measurement of the consumption of water.

Spain today appears to be in a retreat from full implementation of demand management among farmer-managed irrigation systems. The parallels with the earlier response of farmer resistance to demand management described here are significant. Local water management has been kept relatively intact. The state has only selectively intervened in the question of property rights, continuing to leave much of their definition and defense to occur locally. As before, the state accepts systems of local law and governance out of a pragmatic recognition of their efficacy. The results speak for themselves. While suffering from the demographic changes affecting rural Spain, aging and out-migration, the Orbigo Ribera continues to have some of the highest agricultural yields and the highest population densities in Castile and Leon (Cabo Alonso et al. 1987). Access to water is an essential part of this livelihood system.

Notes

1. See Guillet 1998 on the interaction of state and local law in the evolution of property rights in northwestern Spain. This chapter is a revised and expanded version of material contained in Guillet 1997, used with permission of Frank Cass & Co. Ltd.
2. This material is based upon work supported by the National Science Foundation under Grant No. DBS 92122134.
3. An English translation of the law can be found in Hall 1886.
4. Additional information was provided by Luis Alonso Luengo.

References

Primary Sources

Archivo de la Comunidad de Regantes de la Presa de la Tierra (ACRPT).
Archivo General de la Administración. Alcala de Henares (AGA).
Ministerio de Obras Publicas. División Hidráulica del Duero. 1913. Proyecto de ordenamiento y modulación de las zonas de regadío del río Orbigo. Sección comprendida entre el origen del rio y La Bañeza.
——. 1918/20 Archivo General de la Administración. Caja 18.314 Topogr. 24/50 Informe.
Municipal Archives, Villarejo. 1910. Minutes 1906–1910 folios 16–17.

Secondary Sources

Al-Mudayna. 1991. *Historia de los regadíos en España* (1931). Madrid: Ministerio de Agricultura, Pesca y Alimentación.
Alonso Luengo, Luis. 1951. *La invisible prisión*. Madrid: Editorial Biblioteca Nueva.
Butzer, Karl W., Juan F. Mateu and **Elisabeth K. Butzer.** 1985. Irrigation agrosystems in eastern Spain: Roman or Islamic origins? *Annals of the American Association of American Geographers* 75: 479–509.
Cabo Alonso, Angel, Domingo J. Sánchez Zurro and **Fernando Molinero Hernando.** 1987. *Geografía de Castilla y León*. Vol. 4. La actividad agraria. Valladolid: Ambito Ediciones S.A.
Cano García, Gabriel. 1992. Confederaciónes hidrográficas. In *Hitos históricos de los regadíos españoles*, A. Gil Olcina and A. Morales Gil, coordinators, 309–34. Madrid: Ministerio de Agricultura, Pesca y Alimentación.
Díez Gonzalez, Florentin-Agustin. 1992. *La España del regadío y sus instituciones básicas*. Madrid: Gráfica 82.
ECLAC (Economic Commission for Latin America and the Caribbean). 1997. *Progress in the privatization of water-related public services: A country-by-country review for South America*. Santiago: ECLAC.
Gil Olcina, A. and **A. Morales Gil,** eds. 1992. *Hitos históricos de los regadíos españoles*. Madrid: Ministerio de Agricultura, Pesca y Alimentación.
Glick, Thomas F. 1970. *Irrigation and society in medieval Valencia*. Cambridge, Mass.: Harvard University Press.
Gómez Mendoza, Josefina. 1992. Regeneracionismo y regadíos. In *Hitos históricos de los regadíos españoles*, A. Gil Olcina and A. Morales Gil, coordinators, 231–62. Madrid: Ministerio de Agricultura, Pesca y Alimentación.
Guillet, David. 1997. The politics of sustainable agriculture in Europe: Water demand management in Spain. *South European Society and Politics* 2: 97–117.

Guillet, David. 1998. Rethinking legal pluralism: Local law and state law in the evolution of water property rights in northwestern Spain. *Comparative Studies in Society and History* 40 (1): 42–70.

Guillet, David. 1999. Water demand management and farmer managed irrigation systems in the Colca Valley of southwestern Peru. In *Globalization and the rural poor in Latin America: Crisis and response in campesino communities* ed. W. Loker, 137–54. Boulder, Colo.: Lynn Rienner Publishers.

Hall, William Hammond. 1886. *Irrigation development: History, customs, laws and administrative systems relating to irrigation, watercourses and waters in France, Italy and Spain*. Sacramento, Calif.: James J. Ayers, supt. state printing.

Maas, Arthur and **James Anderson.** 1978. ... *And the desert shall rejoice: Conflict, growth and justice in arid environments*. Cambridge, Mass: MIT Press. Reprint edition with corrections Malabar, Fla: R.E. Krieger, 1986.

Mabry, Jonathan B. 1996. The ethnology of local irrigation. In *Canals and communities: Small-scale irrigation systems*, 3–30. Tucson: University of Arizona Press.

Mitchell, W.P. and **D. Guillet,** eds. 1994. *Irrigation at high altitudes: The social organization of water control systems in the Andes*. Arlington, Va.: Society for Latin American Anthropology and the American Anthropological Association.

Naylon, J. 1973. An appraisal of Spanish irrigation and land-settlement policy since 1939. *Iberian Studies* 2 (1): 12–19.

Ortega Cantero, Nicolás. 1984. Las propuestas hidráulicas del reformismo republicano: del fomento del regadío a la articulación del Plan Nacional de Obras Hidráulicas. *Agricultura y Sociedad* 32: 109–289.

Orti, Alfonso. 1984. Política hidráulica y cuestión social: orígenes, etapas y significados del regeneracionismo hidráulico de Joaquin Costa. *Agricultura y Sociedad* 32: 7–107.

Ostrom, Elinor. 1990. *Governing the commons: The evolution of institutions for collective action*. London, U.K.: Cambridge University Press.

San Miguel, Marta. 1993. El agua en el edad moderna: Pragmatismo y desgaña. *Revista del Ministerio de Obras Públicas y Transportes* 411: 48–58.

Trawick, Paul. 1997. Water privatization in the Andes: An indigenous alternative to the proposed reforms. Paper delivered at the 96th Annual Meeting of the American Anthropological Association, Washington D.C., November 19–23.

World Bank. 1992. *World development report 1992: Development and the environment*. Washington D.C.: World Bank and Oxford University Press.

9

Public, Private, and Shared Water: Groundwater Markets and Access in Pakistan

RUTH S. MEINZEN-DICK

*Determining water rights in Pakistan is complex, with canal water chang-
ing from state to common to individual property as it moves from the
main system to farmers' fields. Overlaid on this system is the growing use
of groundwater that is pumped and owned by those who can afford to
invest in tubewells. Groundwater markets, through which tubewell owners
sell water to other farmers, have become the major means of access to
valuable groundwater resources for those who do not have wells. Nevertheless, tubewell water purchasers, especially small and younger farmers,
do not have full access rights: they are frequently denied access when
water or energy supplies are scarce. Joint tubewell ownership provides an
alternative means of access to groundwater for small farmers, with a
stronger right to groundwater than water purchases. This paper examines
the implication of pluralism in water rights for the operation of groundwater markets in Pakistan, with particular reference to their impact on
equity, agricultural productivity, and incomes.*

Introduction

The rights to surface and groundwater in Pakistan are part of complex and overlapping physical, as well as legal systems. Canal water changes from state property in the main delivery system, to common property of a group of farmers on a watercourse, to individual property as it moves on to farmers' fields, and on to an open access resource as it percolates into the aquifer. Complexity is further increased by the growing use of groundwater, captured and pumped by those who can afford to invest in tubewells. Once lifted, groundwater can also be public, private, or common property (depending on whether wells are owned by the state, individual farmers, or groups of farmers), though in practice, most is controlled by private well owners.

Groundwater markets, through which tubewell owners sell water to other farmers, have become the major means of access to valuable groundwater resources for those who are unable to purchase wells. There has been growing attention to the spontaneous emergence of groundwater markets in South Asia, especially India and Bangladesh (see Moench 1994; Shah 1993; Wood and Palmer-Jones 1990). These are informal markets involving the short-term sale of a given quantity of water, not formalized markets involving the sale of water-use rights over a longer term (Easter et al. 1998). These groundwater markets are not regulated by the state, and the making and enforcing of contracts is up to the users.

While most analysts agree that groundwater markets improve the productivity of agriculture, there has been considerable debate regarding the equity implications. In Bangladesh, groundwater markets have been embraced as a way of expanding access to groundwater among very small farmers, and even of enabling groups of landless laborers or women to purchase pumps, provide water, and so benefit from groundwater resources (Kahnert and Levine 1993). In India, some authors (e.g., Barah 1992; Janakarajan 1994) have argued that, because of their greater access to resources, tubewell owners will be able to extract a surplus from water sales—raising the prospect of 'water lords' emerging. But others (notably Shah 1993; Wood 1995) find that in most cases water markets are competitive, or at least are contestable in the sense that alternative suppliers could enter the market. This prevents sellers from charging monopoly prices. Furthermore interlinked relationships between neighboring farmers influence transactions, as do local customs (Kolavalli and Chicoine 1989; Meinzen-Dick 1996; Wood 1995).

This paper examines the implications of water rights for the operation of groundwater markets in Pakistan, with particular reference to their impact on equity, agricultural productivity, and incomes. It also explores the potential for shared tubewell ownership to provide small farmers with a stronger claim on groundwater resources. The analysis is based on a study of groundwater markets in villages in two districts of Pakistan: Faisalabad District, in the heart of the canal-irrigated plains of Punjab, and Dir District, in the hilly areas of the Northwest Frontier Province. It combines household survey data on agricultural production and operation of water markets from 1991–92 with information on current and historic statutory and customary water rights (Alderman and Garcia 1993; Meinzen-Dick 1996).

Irrigation and Water Rights

Although water in the Indus basin is all linked hydrologically, pluralism is apparent at two levels: multiple, overlapping water sources, as well as multiple, overlapping legal and normative repertoires that apply to water from each source. These have important implications for the way in which water is managed, and the distribution of benefits.

Canal Irrigation

The Indus Basin Irrigation System (the world's largest contiguous irrigation system) provides water to over 15 million hectares of farmland, in an arid and semiarid climate where agricultural production depends on irrigation. Over 80 per cent of the gross cropped area is irrigated, and produces over 90 per cent of the total value of agricultural production.

The state holds the rights to water in this public irrigation system. Access to water from the canals is tied to ownership of land in the command area. Water is allocated according to a rotational water delivery pattern, called *warabandi*, which provides turns to farmers in fixed proportion to their landholdings. Thus owning or renting irrigated land entitles the farmer to a fixed turn of irrigation flow during a rotation cycle, to be used only on that land.

Statutory water rights to surface irrigation have changed relatively little from the Canal and Drainage Act of 1873. The principle of that act, and subsequent surface irrigation management, is to distribute scarce water over as large an area as possible. But the opportunities for more intensive agriculture which have come in the wake of the 'green revolution' and increasing population pressure in Pakistan have created strong demands for more water and more flexibility of deliveries. The low water availability and rigid allocation pattern of the *warabandi* system limits the productivity of surface irrigation and public tubewells, a limitation which is especially apparent in comparison with groundwater irrigation from private wells, where farmers have more control of water timings (Renfro and Sparling 1986). Furthermore, the *warabandi* deliveries are not even reliable because of problems with operation and maintenance of the public systems, especially in the tail end of the canal system.

Groundwater Irrigation

Groundwater has historically been very important for irrigation, as well as most other water uses in the predominantly arid and semiarid climate of Pakistan. With the development of the large-scale Indus Basin Irrigation System, canals eclipsed aquifers as the main source of water. Far from being a valuable resource, groundwater became a problem for irrigation in many canal-irrigated areas because seepage and percolation from canal irrigation caused water tables to rise within the crop root zone, leading to widespread waterlogging and salinity. In order to deal with the problem, the government developed the salinity control and reclamation programs (SCARP) between the 1950s and 1980. They used public tubewells to provide vertical drainage, pumping groundwater to be mixed with canal irrigation supplies. Because the public tubewells were tied to the same rigid *warabandi* as public canal systems, this use of groundwater did not increase flexibility of irrigation. Moreover, public tubewells experienced serious problems with unreliable deliveries of irrigation water and rising operation and maintenance expenses. As a result, the government has now closed down or transferred most public tubewells to farmers, except in areas with very saline groundwater.

The introduction of mechanized electric and diesel pumps dramatically reduced the costs of lifting groundwater. With growing demand for water and limited surface supplies, since the 1970s groundwater irrigation has been the most rapidly-growing source of irrigation. By the early 1990s it served approximately 25 per cent of the irrigated area, and provided over 36 per cent of the irrigation water available at the farm gate (Pakistan, Ministry of Food, Agriculture and Cooperatives 1991). Much of this is under private control. There are now over 374,000 private tubewells in Pakistan, compared to 16,000 public tubewells (Pakistan, Ministry of Food, Agriculture and Livestock 1994).

The new technologies opened up new possibilities, and contributed to the expansion of private groundwater irrigation. Groundwater has shifted from being a negative environmental externality to being a valuable resource. But the increase in pumping also created new externalities: instead of rising water tables, in many areas withdrawals now exceed recharge, lowering water tables and increasing pumping costs. In the prime agricultural province of Punjab as a whole, withdrawals exceed groundwater recharge by an estimated 27 per cent (NESPAK 1991). In this context, the allocation of this increasingly scarce resource becomes particularly critical for the productivity and equity of agricultural production.

Groundwater rights are not as clearly defined as rights to surface water. According to state law, groundwater belongs to the owner of the land over it.[1] In practice this is impossible to monitor. Under the old technology of manual lifts, the low extraction rate effectively limited the ability to draw water from under others' land. Newer tubewell technology with mechanized pumps pulls water from a wider area around the well, which does not respect land ownership boundaries.

Thus, water in the aquifer is effectively an open access resource, and it is ownership of the well itself that determines access to groundwater. Previously, water from the public tubewells was mixed with canal water, and allocated according to the *warabandi* rules. However, this now applies only in areas of saline aquifers, where the groundwater has a negative, rather than positive value. Under most private wells, individual well owners control the water that can be pumped from their well.

Groundwater may also be controlled by a group of farmers who share the investment in the well, as well as the benefits of the groundwater that comes from it. There is a longstanding tradition of shares in wells in Pakistan, which dates to the precolonial era. According to one British colonial official writing on customary law: 'So important are the rights in wells, usually hereditary, following the same law as the right in the soil, that a complete statement of the sub-division of property in each well forms part of the settlement record' (Tupper 1881, Vol. III: 179, quoted in Gilmartin).

Because of the high cost of installing wells and pumping devices, private groundwater development may leave out small or poor farmers who are unable to make the necessary investment. At present, only 6 per cent of farmers in Pakistan own tubewells. On the other hand, widespread private ownership could lead to over-investment in wells and pumpsets, and can contribute to over-exploitation of the aquifers.

Institutional arrangements are therefore required if access to groundwater is not to be limited to a relatively small number of well owners. Public tubewells provide one approach, which allows the government to regulate both the extraction rate and distribution of the groundwater, but the record of performance of public tubewells has not met expectations. By contrast, private ownership of tubewells embodies greater incentives for improved performance, but creates greater difficulties in monitoring and controlling overall extraction rates. Shared tubewell ownership creates a common property among a group of owners and reduces the investment costs for each owner.

Under individual private well ownership, water markets have emerged as one institution for increasing access to groundwater. While groundwater markets are not officially recognized, the sale of water from private tubewells is a growing form of water allocation. Yet these informal markets do not function as classic markets, with prices reflecting the full scarcity value of water. The remainder of this paper examines the operation of water markets in two cases, analyzes the ways in which they may be influenced by water rights, and explores the alternative of joint tubewell ownership to provide small farmers with control over the resource.

Operation of Water Markets in Faisalabad and Dir Districts

Information from farmers in two study areas permits a more detailed examination of relationships between access to water, land tenure, agricultural production and other factors. What are the differences between pump owners and other farmers? How do the rights created by private or joint ownership of a tubewell affect reliability of access to water? How do agricultural production and gross earnings relate to access to water?

Within the two study areas, Faisalabad represents an area of relatively intensive agriculture, with canals providing the sole source of irrigation to about half the cultivated area, conjunctive use of surface and groundwater on a third of the area, and groundwater as the sole source on the remainder (Punjab, Bureau of Statistics 1988). Groundwater use in the district is less than recharge, but there are some problems with groundwater salinity. Annual rainfall is under 500 millimeters, so agriculture requires irrigation. The major crops grown in Faisalabad are wheat, sugarcane, cotton, rice, and maize.

Dir District has a hilly terrain. With higher annual rainfall (averaging 1,364 millimeters), the area is less dependent than Faisalabad District on irrigation. The main sources of irrigation are small-scale surface systems, with some tubewells. The major crops are wheat, tomato, onion, and maize.

Characteristics of Buyers and Sellers

The average farm size of sample farmers in Faisalabad is 3.6 hectares. Most farm households own at least some of their own land, but 18 per cent are tenants. In Dir, the average farm size is smaller (2.1 hectares). A third of the families are tenant farmers, and patron–client relationships between landlords and tenants are stronger. The Gini coefficients[2] for land ownership are quite high: 0.73 in Faisalabad and 0.76 in Dir. However, inequality of incomes is not as great (0.40 and 0.31 for Faisalabad and Dir, respectively) because income sources are diversified to include livestock, non-farm income, and remittances (Alderman and Garcia 1993).

The survey of groundwater use among sample farmers indicates that the South Asian pattern of tubewell owners having larger landholdings, found in much of Pakistan, holds also in the study areas. Farmers who own tubewells also own significantly[3] more land than either groundwater purchasers or non-users of groundwater, though their operational holding sizes are not significantly larger than water buyers (Table 9.1). Nearly one-third of water buyers and non-users of groundwater are landless tenants, whereas all tubewell owners own at least some land. Water buyers are from significantly younger households than those of tubewell owners, on average, indicating that they may not be as well established. When land is divided among sons, the eldest may keep the tubewell, and others purchase from him or other surrounding farmers.

Well owners may sell water, but this is not a primary enterprise in the study areas. Only nine of 29 sample well owners reported selling water, and even those who sold water remain farmers first, selling surplus water only after meeting the needs of their own crops (see also Strosser and Kuper 1994). The well owners tend to be bigger farmers, and they have more of a stake in ensuring production on their own land than in selling water to others. This is linked to both the price and productivity of purchased groundwater.

Price of Groundwater

The cost of purchased groundwater was not much higher than the cost of pumping for well owners, which indicates that those who sell do not extract much rent from the water. There are three main types of informal contracts for groundwater. The first uses a flat charge per hour of pumping that ranges from Rs 14 to Rs 80 per hour, depending on the pump type, capacity, and location. The second is a 'buyer brings fuel' arrangement in which the buyer supplies the diesel and motor oil for the pump, and pays Rs 4 to Rs 6 per hour to the well owner, which is explained as a charge to cover the wear and tear on the engine. Well owners with diesel pumps are apparently only recovering their own costs under either arrangement. Strosser and Kuper (1994) report that the buyer-brings-fuel sales in their study areas do not include a charge for wear and tear on the engine. In such situations, sellers do not even recover their maintenance and depreciation costs. A third arrangement is sharecropping

Table 9.1: Average Characteristics of Sample Tubewell Owners, Water Buyers

Characteristics	Tubewell Owner	Tubewell Water Buyer	Non-User of Groundwater	Total Sample
Land owned (acres)	8.21	3.46	4.64	4.83
	(5.85)	(6.56)	(7.89)	(7.43)
Operational holding (acres)	7.72	6.04	5.93	6.20
	(5.47)	(5.16)	(7.66)	(6.83)
Percent pure tenants	0	33	31	27
	(0)	(48)	(46)	(0.45)
Percent owner-tenants	13	13	16	15
	(34)	(34)	(37)	(0.36)
Age of household head	59.50	50.13	56.51	55.29
	(13.31)	(14.25)	(13.44)	(13.93)
Sample size	24	45	108	117

Source: Meinzen-Dick 1996.

Note: Figures in parentheses are standard deviations.

for water, with up to a third of the water user's produce going to the well owner. If the water seller was also the user's landlord, the combined share for land and water was up to half the produce.

This sample is not large enough to determine the effect of different ecological and socioeconomic conditions on the cost of private tubewell water.[4] However, it is notable that under any type of contract the price of water does not vary over the course of a season to reflect changes in its scarcity and value.

Reliability of Access

The advantage of groundwater for agricultural production does not lie in its inherent water quality. Because of salinity problems with groundwater, canal water is better for cultivation. It is the ability to match irrigation deliveries to crop needs under private tubewells that has the most positive effect on productivity. In contrast to rigid (though often unreliable) *warabandi* rotation schedules, farmers with tubewells can irrigate their fields more frequently during periods of peak demand throughout the year (except during periods of mechanical breakdown). Even considering breakdowns, tubewell owners reported that pump or engine failures made groundwater unavailable for an average of 1–2 weeks per season, which is still better than the reported unavailability of canal water for an average of 4–5 weeks per season.

Private tubewells offer more reliable irrigation services than public sources such as canals and government tubewells. However, the reliability is lower for water purchasers than for farmers with their own wells because tubewell owners sell surplus water only after meeting the needs of their own crops. Water markets provide purchasers access to groundwater, but not control over the resource. Shortages of groundwater or energy supplies are not shared equally between owner and purchaser, but rather reduce groundwater availability to purchasers first.

To examine the effect of differential control over the resource, the survey asked tubewell water sellers and purchasers whether water was always available when requested, as an indicator of reliability.[5] Over half (56 per cent) of the buyers reported that they could not always get water when they needed it during periods of peak demand, and 22 per cent reported problems during periods of electricity shortage. Not surprisingly, sellers were less likely to report that they did not always supply water when requested.

What influences the reliability of purchased irrigation water? A logistic regression analysis of reliability as a function of tubewell characteristics (source of power, diameter, and depth), buyers' characteristics (land ownership, age), relationship between buyer and seller (relative, landlord), and regional dummy variables (Jaranwala village, Dir District) indicates that the type of tubewell and status of the buyer (indicated by land ownership and age) had a significant effect (Meinzen-Dick 1996). Buying from an electric tubewell gives less reliable access because the pumps are more susceptible to power outages. Larger-capacity tubewells are more reliable, but deeper tubewells are not—perhaps because they are located in groundwater-scarce areas. Those buyers who own more land and have older heads of households have significantly more reliable access to purchased tubewell water. Thus, the small farmers from young households, who are less likely to be able to own tubewells, also face the most precarious access to tubewell water through private groundwater markets.

Farmers in Dir were significantly more likely to have reliable supply. This may be because the demand for groundwater is not as great in Dir, but it may also reflect the fact that many farmers in Dir buy water from their landlords (though buying from close relatives or landlords did not show a significant effect on reliability, after controlling for district). Another possible factor is the prevalence of sharecropping for water in Dir. Under this arrangement, the water sellers have an incentive to supply tubewell water in an adequate and timely manner because they have a stake in the outcome of the crop, and a share in the risk if the water supply does not meet crop needs. It is noteworthy that sharecropping for tubewell water is practiced under the cultivation of crops such as tomatoes, onions, or rice, which are sensitive to moisture stress at critical periods, but not for wheat or less water-sensitive crops. Similar findings on sharecropping for moisture-sensitive crops in Gujarat suggest that risk-sharing is a significant consideration in the choice of contract and timeliness of irrigation service (Aggarwal 1996b).

Impact on Production

Irrigation improves agricultural productivity by reducing crop risks and increasing yields, but the extent of these effects depends on how closely supplies match crop water requirements. Farmers assured of good water supplies often use higher levels of inputs, and may switch to more profitable, but water-sensitive crops. Thus, the control farmers have over water is likely to be related to the size of the 'irrigation surplus' (Shah 1993). A number of studies have shown that farmers purchasing groundwater have higher productivity than those using only public canal or public tubewell supplies in Pakistan, but tubewell owners had the highest levels of productivity (Freeman et al. 1978; WAPDA 1980). Renfro (1982: 83) concludes that, in comparison with water purchasers, 'obviously actual sampled tubewell owners can exert more control over water supplies with favorable impacts on productivity.'

This same pattern is found in the study areas of Faisalabad and Dir. A linear regression analysis of household gross margins[6] as a function of season, household size, tenure, landholding, tractor ownership, soil salinity, and district provides an estimate of the effect of water control on the irrigation surplus (Table 9.2). Gross margins are higher in kharif (winter season) than in rabi (summer monsoon season), in part because of the higher water availability and cropping intensity in kharif. Soil salinity reduces total income from cultivation because yields are lower on saline fields, and farmers switch to less profitable, salinity-tolerant crops. There is a gross margin of approximately Rs 650 per acre (US$64 per hectare), after other factors are controlled for. Neither household size, tenancy, nor the dummy variable for Dir District have a significant impact on gross margins. Tractor ownership has a substantial impact. Like tubewell ownership, tractor ownership gives farmers greater control over the timing of agricultural operations which, in turn, increases returns to cultivation.

The estimated effects of canal irrigation alone and purchased tubewell water alone were not statistically significant. This is not to say that canal irrigation alone does not increase profitability compared to rainfed cultivation. However, the variability of gross margins among those sample farmers using only canal sources is too high for the coefficient to be significant. The few farmers dependent on purchased tubewell water alone, without canal sources, also face highly variable returns from production. By contrast, water from farmers' own tubewells alone (without canal irrigation) has a significant effect of almost Rs 5,000.

Table 9.2: Household Gross Margins Per Season Regression Model

Independent Variables	Coefficient	Standard Error	T Statistic	Variable Mean
SEASON	−1813.61*	1109.41	−1.64	0.49
HHSIZE	7.10	154.12	0.05	3.48
TENURE	−336.54	1194.66	−0.28	0.45
SALINITY	−3483.46**	1793.54	−1.94	0.14
LANDSIZE	653.69**	90.36	7.23	6.82
TRACTOR	9946.28**	2515.10	3.96	0.07
DIR	−288.82	1580.61	−0.11	0.47
CANALONLY	2315.23	1603.18	1.44	0.41
BUYTONLY	2277.10	3761.10	0.61	0.03
OWNTONLY	4959.79**	2476.14	2.00	0.10
CANALBUYT	6190.24**	2206.98	2.81	0.23
CANALOWNT	13853.20**	3704.35	3.74	0.04
(Constant)	−191.56	2282.84	−.08	

Adjusted R Square = 0.37.
Number of Observations = 329.
Source: Meinzen-Dick 1996.
Notes: *Significant at 0.10 probability level.
**Significant at 0.05 probability level.
HH Size—Household Size; DIR—Dir District; CANALONLY—Canal water only; BUYTONLY—Purchased tubewell water only; OWN-TONLY—Own tubewell water only; CANALBUYT—Canal + purchased tubewell water; CANALOWNT—Canal + own tubewell water.

Access to purchased tubewell water in conjunction with canal irrigation has a stronger effect than own tubewell water only (Rs 6,190), but the effect of own tubewell water plus canal access had more than twice as great an effect as any other type of irrigation (Rs 13,853). This indicates particularly high returns to tubewell owners in areas with conjunctive use. Water purchasers, who have less control over tubewell applications, do not benefit as much from use of groundwater.

In sum, well owners tend to be bigger farmers, and they have more of a stake in ensuring production on their own land than in selling water to others. Prices paid for water seem close to costs for pump owners, suggesting tubewell owners are not gaining large rents from selling water. Access to tubewell water through groundwater markets can be precarious, since tubewell owners irrigate their own fields first. Water buyers benefit from groundwater, but not as much as tubewell owners. Water markets do provide access to groundwater, but the data from this study indicate that the degree of control over water and consequent benefits for agricultural production are substantially higher for tubewell owners than for the generally smaller and poorer farmers who depend on buying water.

Water Rights and Water Market Operation

To what extent can the behavior of informal water markets in Pakistan be explained in terms of water rights? The answer is far from clear—as, indeed, the rights to groundwater are far from clear. There is a range of overlapping legal and normative repertoires which may apply (Benda-Beckman et al. 1997); including statutory laws such as the Canal and Drainage Act; religious laws based on Islamic tradition; rights based on inheritance and relationship; and norms regarding behavior towards neighbors and kin. Statutory law gives rights to groundwater to the owner of overlying land. This would imply that well owners could sell water, but it is conceivable that farmers with land near a well could claim that the groundwater was pulled from under their land, and hence they have a right to it. However, verification is a problem because of unobservability, and therefore the statutory law is unenforceable. Islamic law forbids the sale of water, especially surplus water, but definitions of 'surplus' water are somewhat vague (Wescoat 1995). While water confined in a reservoir or vessel can become private property, it is unclear whether a well constitutes such a vessel. There also may be other bases for non-owners of wells to assert a claim on groundwater, especially where there is common descent from the original well owner (e.g., where land has been partitioned between brothers, leaving the well on the land of one).

The limits on the price in informal groundwater markets could therefore be seen as reflecting limits on private 'ownership' of groundwater, and an acknowledgment of the implicit claims of neighboring farmers to water from a tubewell. If tubewell owners are not seen as the owners of the water, the transaction would be more the rental of tubewell equipment (akin to tractor rental), rather than sale of water (see Palmer-Jones 1994; Saleth 1994). However, Shah (1994) suggests that this is mostly an academic distinction, and in interviews farmers did not conceptually distinguish between the two.[7] Nevertheless, given the evasiveness of definitions of rights to groundwater, it would be worth pursuing local perception of water rights, and their consequences for groundwater sales.

As Spiertz points out in this volume (Chapter 6), legal pluralism shows the importance of examining the various types of interests in water (and land), the types of social relationships connected with these interests, and the social institutions and normative frameworks which are involved. In the case of localized groundwater markets in Pakistan, sales are not between anonymous buyers and seller, but are frequently embedded in kinship, neighbor, and patron–client relationships.

Under conditions prevailing in the study areas, as in most of Pakistan, tubewell irrigation water is not a commodity which can be transported far from the source to the area of application. Conveyance losses between the tubewell and the field restrict purchasers to buying from tubewells located in close proximity of their fields (and restricts sellers to those within a limited radius of the well). Many buyers therefore have only one or two potential sources, whereas sellers may have a dozen or more potential clients, in addition to the needs of their own land. Sales are limited to close neighbors (who are also often relatives), and there are repeated interactions between buyer and seller over the course of many years—not only on water transactions, but many in many other ways. Therefore, there may be an implicit payment for water in obligations to provide labor, other forms of reciprocity, or even intangible, social rewards.

Norms regarding relationships between neighbors offer a more likely explanation for why farmers do not adjust water prices to capture the scarcity value of water. Analyzing groundwater markets in Bihar, Wood (1995) explains that a fixed price reduces transaction costs, and it avoids perceptions that a seller is profiting from the misfortunes and water needs of the buyer (who is often a neighbor, or relative, or both). Maximizing profits from water sales can result in the loss of reputation and goodwill, and cost the seller more in the long run.

This is especially true in Pakistan, where *izzat*, or honor, is a prized commodity. Providing water to others can earn *izzat*, but charging prices in excess of what is locally sanctioned would result in the loss of *izzat*. Although Islamic laws are rarely mentioned as factors affecting water markets, the norms on charging are consistent with Islamic hadiths, or traditions: well owners do not profit from the sale of 'surplus' water, but are under no obligation to cut back on their own water use (especially in periods of scarcity or peak demand) in order to provide water to others. Vander Velde (personal communication, 1996) reports that farmers in Pakistan persistently assert 'that water cannot and will not be denied anyone facing disaster (i.e., actual loss of crop).' For well owners to assert this norm and ask only a 'reasonable' price to cover their costs is important for preserving *izzat*, and a local reputation as a good Muslim.

While the norm of providing water to anyone facing disaster is widely held, it is not always followed, especially if it would involve putting the well owners' crop at risk. In Pakistan, as in Bihar, 'the notional existence of such a general price does not translate into economic entitlement for those prepared to pay the price. Such families can be, and often are, denied the use of a pumpset (Wood 1995: 29).' Instead of scarcity pricing in these informal water markets, groundwater becomes a rationed commodity, and purchasers are limited in their access not by price but by other, less explicit, barriers. The limited access in times of scarcity reflects the subordinate rights of purchasers.

Joint Tubewells as Alternatives to Water Markets

Neither public (canal or tubewell) nor private (tubewell) water supply systems adequately meet the needs of small farmers for reliable water under their control. Joint tubewell ownership provides an alternative means of access to groundwater for small farmers.

In the study areas, joint well ownership is especially prevalent in Jaranwala (one of the villages in the Faisalabad District), where canal irrigation was not available. The lack of alternative irrigation supplies has pushed these farmers to purchase tubewells, and joint investment among up to 12 farmers has enabled even small farmers in this village to own at least a partial share of a well.

Jointly-owned wells are still compatible with water markets. Water can be made available to non-owners, though usually at a different cost than to owners. Shared ownership allows more options for siting the tubewells where they can tap good quality groundwater and are able to serve the maximum number of farmers, usually near the head of a watercourse (Gill 1994).

A major advantage of joint tubewell ownership is that it enables the smaller farmers to gain stronger rights to the groundwater. Thus, ownership of wells, and hence control of groundwater resources, is shared more equitably instead of a few large farmers becoming de facto owners of the resources. The value of this ownership right in giving farmers a claim on water when supplies are scarce is seen in Jaranwala. In that area, where alternative water supplies are unavailable, farmers prefer owning at least a stake in a tubewell to depending on purchases from someone else.

The major disadvantage of joint tubewell ownership lies in the social transaction costs, which are higher than for sole ownership. Farmers must negotiate with each other for making the initial purchase and deciding where to locate the tubewell. Then agreements must be reached for how to share water, expenses, and maintenance responsibility on an ongoing basis. Aggarwal's (1996a) study of group wells in Andhra Pradesh, India, found that in existing group wells, everyday allocation of water could be managed by simple rule of thumb, but mobilizing resources for maintenance and expansion was more difficult. If such investment is difficult for existing groups, the obstacles to organizing for the initial investment in a new group would be even greater. This would be especially problematic in areas with limited traditions of cooperation, or where hierarchical patron–client ties are stronger than horizontal patterns of cooperation, as in many areas of Pakistan (see Byrnes 1992; Merrey 1979).

Furthermore, the water sharing arrangements may restrict the degree to which a farmer has control over the use of the tubewell. Strosser and Kuper (1994) found that, while sole owners of tubewells in their study area had a higher cropping intensity and larger areas under the main crops (wheat and cotton) than other farmers, tubewell water purchasers and tubewell shareholders had similar cropping intensities and areas under wheat and cotton, suggesting that tubewell water purchasers and tubewell shareholders face irrigation services of similar quality.

Examination of gross margins from agricultural production in Faisalabad and Dir indicates that shareholders in tubewells do receive higher returns than water purchasers. These economic gains appear to be related to greater control over the well and groundwater resources. However, further research with a larger sample of sole and joint tubewell owners is required to determine how much water control each type of farmer is able to exercise, and the consequent impact on productivity and incomes.

In many cases, tubewell groups have formed spontaneously, often between relatives with adjoining land. There have also been government programs to promote group tubewells, notably through the On-Farm Water Management (OFWM) Program. The original emphasis of OFWM organizational efforts was on formation of Water Users' Associations (WUAs) to upgrade, maintain, and distribute water at the watercourse level of the canal systems. OFWM has worked with a number of WUAs, providing equipment, technical, and organizational assistance. Gill (1994) reports that one such collective tubewell served 95 farmers, and provided water at a lower cost than the state tubewell and individual tubewells in the vicinity. Ali and Mirza (1994) argue that joint tubewell ownership can provide an economic interest to strengthen group activity under formal WUAs for surface irrigation. However, the sustainability and replicability of such government-initiated efforts needs to be carefully examined, especially where the cost of the tubewells are borne by the government.

Promoting joint tubewell ownership among small farmers requires more than subsidizing wells or providing technical assistance for groups of farmers. What is required is attention to ways to facilitate cooperation, both for initial investment and ongoing operation. Steenbergen (1995) notes that the emergence of institutions to collectively manage groundwater resources cannot be assumed. The Dutch-assisted PATA project in the Northwest Frontier Province has employed organizers who mobilize collective action for a number of activities, including joint wells. The full procedures for developing such systems have also been documented and disseminated through manuals and videos (PATA Project 1994). Further studies of the history of formal and informal joint tubewell groups would be valuable in this regard. This should include information on how they came together, what arrangements have been reached for sharing of water and expenses; disputes which have arisen, and mechanisms for conflict management. Evidence of optimal group size, landholding distribution, and mechanisms for reducing social transaction costs can assist in promoting joint tubewells to increase small farmers' access to and control over vital groundwater resources.

Defining water rights from shared tubewells is particularly important. While rights to groundwater may be difficult to establish, quantify, or enforce, shares in the water extracted from the well are somewhat easier to define. Ali and Mirza (1994) cite examples of tubewell groups on watercourses which have set up *warabandi* schedules for use of tubewell water. Some of these schedules even make provisions for load shedding, breakdowns, or other contingencies. Organizers under the PATA project encouraged new well groups to record the rights of all members on official stamp paper and to register this paper with the tahsildar (a sub-district representative of the Revenue Department, who also keeps land records).

Conclusion

Rights to groundwater in Pakistan are not set in stone; rather, they are much more fluid, and subject to negotiation. The resource itself has changed, from being absolutely scarce before the development of the Indus Basin canal irrigation system, to being an abundant nuisance, to once again being scarce relative to the growing demand for water. In the process, the institutions for managing groundwater have evolved, from community management through shares in wells, to public management to deal with the negative externalities of waterlogging, to private management. Water taken from tubewells is controlled by the owner of the well, which in practice means that most groundwater is controlled by larger landowners who have the resources to sink tubewells. The evolution of institutions to manage increasingly scarce groundwater equitably and sustainably is a major challenge for the years ahead.

Water markets are one such institution that allows other farmers to purchase groundwater. They have evolved spontaneously, and are now a major means of spreading access to groundwater. Evidence from study areas in Faisalabad and Dir districts indicates that in these informal exchanges, well owners do not extract a large 'rent' for the water resource. The implicit rights of adjacent farmers to groundwater from a tubewell, based on statutes, Islamic hadiths, and inheritance may play a role in limiting the price of groundwater, but it is likely that repeated interactions among neighbors play a greater role. However, water purchasers cannot always obtain access to groundwater, especially at times of peak demand, when tubewell owners use much of the well's capacity for their own fields. This subordinate right and unreliability of access limits agricultural productivity for those who must depend on water from other people's wells.

Shared tubewells provide an alternative means for small farmers to obtain access to groundwater. While joint ownership of irrigation infrastructure is likely to provide them stronger rights to the resource, it also entails higher transaction costs. The need for farmers to cooperate in initial investment, allocating and distributing the water, and in maintaining and expanding the system provides a significant barrier to the creation of common property groundwater resources, even among small groups at the local level. However, as fresh groundwater resources become scarce, institutional mechanisms for sharing the resource are likely to become increasingly important to ensure the productivity and equity of resource management.

Notes

1. This is consistent with English common law traditions of land ownership extending from the center of the earth to the heavens—a static concept that does not easily accommodate a flowing resource (Scott and Coustalin 1995: 840).
2. The Gini coefficient is a measure of inequality, with a value of 0 where resources are equally distributed to each household, and a value of 1 where all resources are concentrated in one household.
3. Significance in this paper refers to statistical significance. For more information on the magnitude of effects, see Table 9.1 and Meinzen-Dick 1996.
4. Unfortunately, much of the information on the price of purchased tubewell water comes from water buyers, rather than from the sellers.

There are thus not enough data on tubewell operations costs and water delivery rates to determine the profit margin for water sales or the exact price per unit water pumped.

5. It may be argued that, if particular farmers know they cannot purchase water at certain times, their supply is still reliable. In practice, farmers do not know with certainty whether they will or will not be able to get water at a given time; hence, it is unreliable.

6. The gross margin is computed by deducting all cash input costs (including the costs of irrigation) from gross crop revenues. This indicates the returns to land, family labor, and own capital. Rental payments for land have not been deducted from the gross margins, to ensure comparability between land owners and tenants.

7. Based on extensive IIMI research, Vander Velde (personal communication, 1996) also finds no evidence 'that anyone other than the land owner is entitled to the water in the sense of owning it. In fact, ... that right can be a specific factor in lending land for use as security against a loan, something that is done surprisingly frequently—the borrower lends the land and the water right (surface as well as groundwater) to the lender for the specific length of the loan. Lenders are sufficiently secure in this right to invest in tubewell development and to carry on intensive irrigated cropping for the period of the loan, too. So if there was not some kind of legal/customary security here, it's doubtful a lender would risk BOTH the amount of the loan and the cost of tubewell development in such a transaction.'

References

Aggarwal, Rimjhim M. 1996a. *Possibilities and limitations to cooperation: Lessons from the case of group owned wells in India.* Working Paper, Dept. of Agriculture and Resource Economics, University of Maryland, College Park, Md., U.S.A.

———. 1996b. *Risk sharing and transaction costs in groundwater contracts: Evidence from rural India.* Working Paper 96–17. Dept. of Agriculture and Resource Economics, University of Maryland, College Park, Md., U.S.A.

Alderman, H. and **M. Garcia.** 1993. *Poverty, household food security, and nutrition in rural Pakistan.* Research Report No. 96. Washington, D.C.: International Food Policy Research Institute.

Ali, A. and **A.H. Mirza.** 1994. Water user's associations as a mechanism to link agriculture and irrigation at the grassroots. In *Institutional reforms to* accelerate irrigated agriculture, Vol. 2: Special studies, 1–27. Islamabad: John Mellor Associates and Asianics Agro-Development International.

Barah, B.C. 1992. Emergence of groundwater market and ecological impact on the drought prone areas. Paper presented at the International Conference on Prospects of Chinese Agricultural Development in the 1990s, August 20–25, Beijing, China.

Benda-Beckmann, Franz von, Keebet von Benda-Beckmann, and **H.L. Joep Spiertz.** 1997. Local law and customary practices in the study of water rights. In *Water rights, conflicts and policy*, ed. Rajendra Pradhan, Franz von Benda-Beckmann, Keebet von Benda-Beckmann, H.L. Joep Spiert, Shantam S. Khadka and K. Azharul Haq, 221–42. Proceedings of a workshop held in Kathmandu, Nepal, January 22–24, 1996. International Irrigation Management Institute: Colombo, Sri Lanka.

Byrnes, Kerry J. 1992. *Water user's associations in World Bank-assisted irrigation projects in Pakistan*. World Bank Technical Paper No. 173. Washington, D.C.: World Bank.

Easter K. William, Mark Rosegrant, and **Ariel Dinar**, eds. 1998. *Markets for water: Potential and performance*. Boston, Mass.: Kluwer Academic Publishers.

Freeman, David M., Max K. Lowdermilk, and **Alan C. Early.** 1978. *Farm irrigation constraints and farmers' responses: Comprehensive field survey in Pakistan*. Fort Collins, Colo.: Colorado State University Press.

Gill, Mushtaq Ahmad. 1994. Sustainability of water users' associations as groundwater irrigation managers: A case study under on-farm water management. In *Farmer management of groundwater in Asia: Selected papers from a South Asian regional workshop*, ed. M.D.C. Abhayaratna, Douglas Vermillion, Sam Johnson, and Chris Perry, 153–60. Colombo, Sri Lanka: International Irrigation Management Institute.

Gilmartin, David. 1997. The irrigating public: The state and local management in colonial irrigation. In *State, Society and the Environment in South Asia*, ed. Stig Toft Madsen. London: Curzon Press.

Janakarajan, S. 1994. Trading in groundwater: A source of power and accumulation. In *Selling water: Conceptual and policy debates over groundwater markets in India*, ed. M. Moench, 47–58. Gujarat, India: VIKSAT, Pacific Institute, Natural Heritage Institute.

Kahnert, F., and **G. Levine**, ed. 1993. *Groundwater irrigation and the rural poor: Options for development of the Gangetic basin*. Washington, D.C.: World Bank.

Kolavalli, Shashi and **David L. Chicoine.** 1989. Groundwater markets in Gujarat, India. *Water Resources Development* 5 (1): 38–44.

Meinzen-Dick, Ruth S. 1996. *Groundwater markets in Pakistan: Participation and productivity*. Research Report 105. Washington, D.C.: International Food Policy Research Institute.

Moench, Marcus, ed. 1994. *Selling water: Conceptual and policy debates over groundwater markets in India.* Gujarat, India: VIKSAT, Pacific Institute, Natural Heritage Institute.

Merrey, Douglas J. 1979. *Irrigation and honor: Cultural impediments to the improvement of local level water management in Punjab, Pakistan.* Water Management Technical Report No. 53. Water Management Research Project, Engineering Research Center. Fort Collins, Colo.: Colorado State University.

NESPAK (National Engineering Services Pakistan). 1991. Contributions of private tubewells in the development of water potential. (Field Report). Pakistan: Government of Pakistan, Ministry of Planning and Development, Planning and Development Division.

Pakistan, Ministry of Food, Agriculture and Cooperatives. 1991. *Agricultural statistics of Pakistan 1990–91.* Islamabad: Government of Pakistan.

Pakistan, Ministry of Food, Agriculture and Livestock. 1994. *Agricultural statistics of Pakistan 1992–93.* Islamabad: Government of Pakistan.

PATA Project. 1994. *Land and water use programme.* Scheme development guide book. Saidu Sharif, Pakistan: PATA.

Punjab, Bureau of Statistics. 1988. *Punjab development statistics.* Lahore, Pakistan: Government of Punjab.

Renfro, Raymond Z.H. 1982. Economics of local control of irrigation water in Pakistan: A pilot study. Fort Collins, Colo.: Colorado State University.

Renfro, Raymond Z.H. and **Edward W. Sparling.** 1986. Private tubewell and canal water trade on Pakistan Punjab watercourses. In *Irrigation investment, technology, and management strategies for development,* ed. K. William Easter, 193–210. Boulder, Colo.: Westview Press.

Rosegrant, Mark W. and **Hans P. Binswanger.** 1994. Markets in tradable water rights: Potential for efficiency gains in developing-country water resource allocation. *World Development* 22 (11): 1613–25.

Saleth, R. Maria. 1994. Groundwater markets in India: A legal and institutional perspective. In *Selling water: Conceptual and policy debates over groundwater markets in India,* ed. M. Moench, 59–71. Gujarat, India: VIKSAT, Pacific Institute, Natural Heritage Institute.

Scott, Anthony and **Georgina Coustalin.** 1995. The evolution of water rights. *Natural Resources Journal* 35 (4): 821–979.

Shah, Tushaar. 1993. *Groundwater markets and irrigation development: Political economy and practical policy.* Bombay, India: Oxford University Press.

———. 1994. Groundwater markets: An overview and new questions. In *Selling water: Conceptual and policy debates over groundwater markets in India,* ed. M. Moench, 3–9. Gujarat, India: VIKSAT, Pacific Institute, Natural Heritage Institute.

Steenbergen, Frank van. 1995. The frontier problem in incipient groundwater management regimes in Balochistan (Pakistan). *Human Ecology* 23 (1): 53–74.

Strosser, Pierre and **Marcel Kuper.** 1994. *Water markets in the Fordwah/Eastern Sadiqia area: An answer to perceived deficiencies in canal water supplies?* IIMI Working Paper No. 30. International Irrigation Management Institute. Colombo, Sri Lanka.

Tupper, C.L. 1881. *Punjab customary law.* 3 Vols. Calcutta: Government Printing Press.

WAPDA (Water and Power Development Authority). 1980. *Private tubewells and factors affecting current rate of investment.* Lahore, Pakistan: WAPDA, Economic Research Section, Planning and Development Division.

Wescoat, James L., Jr. 1995. The 'right of thirst' for animals in Islamic law: A comparative approach. *Environment and Planning D: Society and Space* 13: 637–54.

Wood, Geof D. 1995. *Private provision after public neglect: Opting out with pumpsets in North Bihar.* Occasional Paper 01/95, Center for Development Studies, University of Bath, Bath, U.K.

Wood, Geof D. and **Richard Palmer-Jones.** 1990. *The water sellers: A cooperative venture by the rural poor.* West Hartford, Conn.: Kumarian Press.

10

Nature's Bounty or Scarce Commodity: Competition and Consensus Over Groundwater Use in Rural Bangladesh

SYED ZAHIR SADEQUE

Conflicts are emerging amongst groundwater users in the context of declining water tables during the dry season in Bangladesh. Despite seemingly abundant water, increasing use of deep water table extracting technologies for irrigation takes water away from shallow hand pumps used for domestic water supply. This causes a seasonal crisis affecting millions of people dependent upon hand pumps. Because groundwater rights are not clearly defined, no one is sure how to deal with the growing problem. As well-endowed farmers with tubewells draw down groundwater while non-irrigating households usually depend upon shallow handpumps for domestic water, control over groundwater becomes an issue of access to improved technologies. This study explores these issues in two low water table areas and examines how it affects people's lives. In the absence of clear water rights, new forms of cooperation are emerging, as well as possible confrontation between groundwater irrigators and others.

Introduction

Jobeda Khatun, a widow about 40 years old, lives with three of her children, a son aged 20, and two daughters aged 17 and 13. Ten years ago when her husband was still alive and they had a reasonable income, they installed a hand tubewell on their homeplot. This privately owned well serves about six households in a cluster. Like many other hand tubewells in the village, their pump becomes inoperative during the dry months of February–April. Jobeda and her daughters scramble for water during these three months. They must go 500 meters away to collect water from the nearest 'Tara' pump. As they are adult women, local customs do not allow her or her daughters to venture out and collect water from the deep tubewell far away in the fields. Besides, the deep tubewell is seldom operated during daylight hours, and as a landless non-agricultural household they are least favored in receiving deep tubewell water. Jobeda asks why they should be deprived of water that is everyone's right. The deep wells are drawing their share of water for the benefit of the rich, who have farmland. Jobeda feels doubly deprived. They are functionally landless, with only a tiny homeplot shared with other kin members. As landless households they do not reap the benefits of agricultural modernization (irrigation being a very visible symbol), while even for domestic needs their hand tubewell does not yield water during the dry season due to the operation of mechanized deep tubewells.

This paper explores emerging conflicts over water, like that shown here, which influence the lives of rural villagers in Bangladesh. The first section discusses the growth of groundwater scarcity in a country where water has usually been abundant or in excess. The second section outlines the inadequacy of legal foundations to regulate rights to groundwater. Rapid appraisal studies, described in the third section, look at these issues in the more detailed context of two localities, and describe emerging informal rules and arrangements governing groundwater access.[1] The final sections present conclusions, issues for further research and potential policy responses to improve water rights and groundwater resource management.

Proliferating Pumps and Declining Groundwater

Bangladesh is a densely populated country of over 120 million people living within an area largely formed by the floodplain and delta of two major river systems of South Asia, the Brahmaputra (called Jamuna in Bangladesh) and the Ganges (for most part called Padma in Bangladesh). Average annual rainfall ranges from 1,500–5,000 millimeters. Monsoon rainfall is concentrated from June to September. The remaining eight months receive 15–20 per cent of the annual rainfall. There is a distinct hot and dry period during March–May, when water shortages are acute in parts of the country. This is also the period of winter rice cultivation, requiring constant irrigation, which further compounds water scarcity.

Since its emergence as an independent country in December 1971, Bangladesh has always faced problems in meeting its food needs. The Fourth Five-Year Plan (1990–95) stated that to achieve food self-sufficiency the country needs to transform the agricultural sector from 'rainfed to irrigated agriculture' (Bangladesh 1990). Groundwater-based minor irrigation has been the mainstay of increasing rice production. Success in moving towards rice self-sufficiency brings new challenges for agriculture and public policy (Goletti 1994), including coping with increasing competition for groundwater resources.

The availability of groundwater is dependent on groundwater storage, usage, and annual recharge from rainfall, rivers and flooding. Considering the soil characteristics, high rainfall and flow of surface water from a very large catchment area, Bangladesh is generally endowed with good but uneven groundwater resources. The hydrogeological conditions allow extraction of groundwater cheaply with simple technologies almost everywhere in the country. In terms of water table there are four major types of area, as Map 10.1 shows:

- Shallow water table areas (SWT) where water is available within 7 meters, and so accessible using surface, suction pumps;
- Low water table areas (LWT) where water is available below 7 meters;

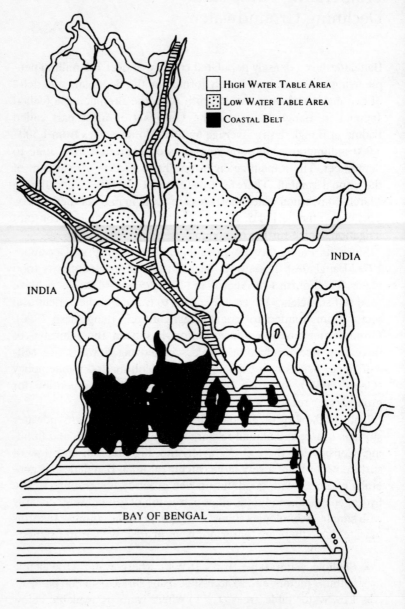

High Water Table Area
Low Water Table Area
Coastal Belt

INDIA

INDIA

BAY OF BENGAL

Map 10.1: Hydrogeological Areas

- Coastal saline area where water at shallow depth is saline; and
- Hilly terrains of the Chittagong Hill Tracts.

In the early 1980s, shallow water tables underlay about 75 per cent of the country, and around 8 per cent of the country had low water table areas. The coastal saline area and Chittagong Hill Tracts are rather static, although, due to upstream withdrawal of surface water by India during the dry months, salinity is increasing in the coastal areas of Bangladesh. The coastal saline area and Chittagong Hill Tracts use various deep tubewells and other technologies for extracting groundwater.

In the shallow water table area, common No. 6 suction hand-pumps extract drinking water, while mechanized shallow pumps draw water for irrigation. Hand tubewells mostly lie in homestead plots which are on average over one meter above the crop field level. In the low water table area, deepset handpumps supply drinking water, while mechanized deep tubewells irrigate crops. The required depth of these tubewells is considerably more than 7 meters and varies according to soil conditions and water table. Farmers buy tubewells individually or form a group to buy one. Shallow tubewells usually have a capacity of a half cusec (cubic foot per second), and the deep tubewells are typically two cusec in capacity. Such deep tubewells can irrigate about 25 hectares of rice land. Deep tubewells cause temporary drawdown of the water table in adjoining areas, and lower the overall level of the aquifer.

Beginning in 1986, the Government of Bangladesh-UNICEF Rural Water Supply and Sanitation Program has started sinking a new lift mode pump, locally known as 'Tara pump.' The Tara pump is a manual lift mode pump rather than the prevalent suction mode technology, and can lift water from as deep as 15 meters below the surface. For the low water table areas this is the appropriate pump for drinking water supply. As a technology it is well proven and accepted. However, Tara pumps are still not widely available, and they are usually 5–6 times more expensive than ordinary hand tubewells. Although manufactured by the private sector, they are still available only through the public sector distribution system.

The government has been active in the provision of water for all purposes, with varying levels of involvement. Until recently, the government has taken a major responsibility to provide improved drinking water supplies. In the rural areas, this has changed considerably, as individuals are installing and operating No. 6 hand-pumps in increasing numbers (Sadeque and Turnquist 1995). Despite the impressive private sector participation in shallow water table areas, other areas still depend upon government provision of water supply and the available technologies are more expensive. Beneficiary contributions for government-installed wells remain limited to only a small down payment at installation, and responsibility for minor repairs.

Mechanized pumping for groundwater irrigation, although introduced by government, has become almost totally privatized. After the deregulation of the minor irrigation sector, privatization of existing equipment and liberalization of sales of pumps in the late 1980s, the sector began witnessing a phenomenal growth in the number of mechanized pumps.

The availability of groundwater in most areas has resulted in the proliferation of tubewells for pumping both drinking and irrigation water. Currently there are over 2.5 million handpumps in operation, less than one-third of which are government-owned and the rest are privately owned. An estimated half a million shallow tubewells, and nearly 35 thousand deep tubewells, are currently in operation for irrigation purposes. The shallow tubewells, due to their low cost, are increasing rapidly. Although the more expensive deep tubewells registered a slower growth, the member of shallow tubewells grew by 40–50 thousand each year during the 1990–95 period.

Seasonal lowering of groundwater level caused by increasing groundwater development runs the risk of periodic tubewell failure due to large annual variability in rainfall and groundwater levels. The main irrigation season in Bangladesh comes during the months of February to May, when the water table is at its lowest, and precipitation is minimal. It is during this period that the mechanized irrigation pumps are increasingly viewed as competitors to handpumps providing drinking water. This crisis has exacerbated in recent years as irrigation coverage has increased dramatically, further lowering the groundwater level.

Typically, in the low water table areas, ordinary No. 6 handpumps become inoperative during the dry months when the water table recedes below 7 meters. Large-scale introduction of deep tubewells and shallow tubewells has exacerbated water table recession during the dry months. More and more traditional low-cost hand tubewells (HTW) are rendered inoperative, particularly in the relatively drier northwest and highly irrigated central region of the country. The National Water Plan reported results from several tests showing the adverse effects of irrigation abstraction upon the hand tubewells in the northwestern districts (Bangladesh 1991: Vol. 1). Hydrographic data indicates a slow but consistent decline of groundwater over the years, which is more than the seasonal drawdown (Bangladesh 1991).

The low water table area is increasing rapidly and is likely to cover around 50 per cent of the country by the year 2000 (DPHE 1995). Government agencies like the Department of Public Health Engineering (DPHE) and Bangladesh Water Development Board (BWDB) monitor groundwater through wells. They have developed comprehensive data bases on groundwater levels over the last decade. Contour maps and hydrographic charts show the declining groundwater table. Figure 10.1 compares the low water table and shallow water table areas over the projected years. From a mere 8 per cent of the country in 1980, the low water table area increased to 15 per cent in 1988. It was forecasted to increase to 40 per cent in 1995 and over 50 per cent by 2000 (DPHE 1995).

A recent DPHE-UNICEF study investigated the declining water level in 386 *thanas* (county-like administrative units) out of a total 486 *thanas* of the country. Table 10.1 shows the comparative scenario of this study. The expanding low water table area and shrinking shallow water table area are evident as well.

Table 10.1: Number of *Thanas* Under Shallow and Low Water Table Areas

	1995	*2000*	*2010*	*Future Development*
SWT	196	159	131	113
LWT	152	189	217	235
Subtotal	348	348	348	348
Outside Study	138	138	138	138
Total *Thana*	486	486	486	486

The National Water Plan (NWP) accepted the seasonal failure of handpumps, and concluded that only deep tubewells could realize complete development of agricultural potential (Bangladesh 1991:

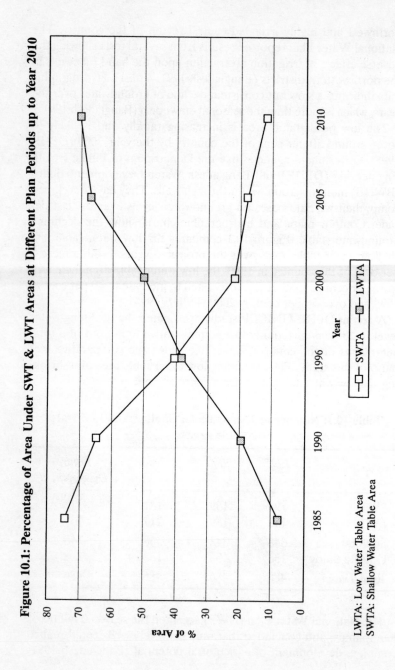

Figure 10.1: Percentage of Area Under SWT & LWT Areas at Different Plan Periods up to Year 2010

LWTA: Low Water Table Area
SWTA: Shallow Water Table Area

10–71). The NWP was more concerned with the availability of irrigation water than with domestic requirements. However, the implications are quite dramatic for rural water supply options in Bangladesh. Based on the current drinking water needs, 400,000 hand tubewells would need to be replaced by Tara pumps in the low water table area by the year 2000, to ensure the current level of access. The cost implications would be stupendous. At current prices, estimated cost of the hardware required for this replacement alone would be at least US$500 million.

Withdrawal of an increasing amount of water in upstream countries and the sinking of ever increasing numbers of mechanized tubewells has lowered groundwater levels in the dry season. In the competition for groundwater, simple, low-cost technologies like hand tubewells, used mostly for drinking and other domestic uses, lose out. The perception of affected people of the low water table areas as victims of water deprivation is becoming marked, with acrimony towards irrigation.

Groundwater Policies and Regulation

Historically, rights and ownership of groundwater have never been a serious issue. Surface water was regulated by authorities even prior to the arrival of British colonialists in the 18th century. Under the Irrigation Act of 1876, plans for diversion or use of surface water which would change the existing natural flow required notification to government. This was intended to allow the affected people to propose alternative arrangements or make claims for compensation (Khan and Khan 1987). Similar issues with amendments were included in subsequent surface water regulations of 1952 and 1983. The principal laws regulating water resources are the Bengal Irrigation Act, 1876, Bangladesh Irrigation Water Rate Ordinance, 1983, East Bengal Embankment and Drainage Act, 1952, State Acquisition and Tenancy Act, 1950 and Groundwater Management Ordinance, 1985, subsequently held in abeyance. The Irrigation Acts were designed to determine levies for water rates, while the Embankment and Drainage Act defined the construction, operation and maintenance of embankments and drainage structures.

The State Acquisition and Tenancy Act of 1950 recognized State ownership of subsoil resources, in theory dissipating the ambiguity on the control and ownership of subsoil water stemming from English Common Law tradition. Although State ownership of groundwater became recognized with that Act, it was never applied accordingly. So in practice, the legal framework for control and ownership of groundwater is still held under Common Law traditions, leaving the scope of regulation ambiguous. Municipal areas have laws regulating sinking of mechanized deep wells. Individuals or groups outside the municipal areas can sink deep wells for irrigation or any other industrial purposes. Water sales by farmers and groups are often carried out to increase the command area of irrigation wells.

The Groundwater Management Ordinance of 1985 was an attempt to regulate the fast growing minor irrigation sector. The purpose was to address siting, installation, and spacing of minor irrigation equipment, including shallow and deep tubewells. It was promulgated during the heyday of regulation in the economy when agricultural development, like other sectors of the economy, was led by parastatal corporations. However, the ordinance met with severe resistance once it was promulgated. It was never acted upon seriously, as deregulatory moves were already underway. The parastatal entrusted with its implementation (Bangladesh Agricultural Development Corporation, BADC) was itself being downsized, completely surrendering the irrigation-related responsibilities to the private sector.

Several government agencies under different ministries deal with water issues. Their mandates are different and therefore the priorities they set out often conflict. Planning and management of water resources under such conditions are therefore for obvious reasons rather disjointed, disregarding critical factors. Surface water is under the ministry of irrigation and water resources. Groundwater activities are carried out and monitored by individuals, the water resources ministry, the ministry of environment, and agencies under the local government ministry.

The need for a comprehensive survey of water resources and their development strategies has been enunciated by the government since 1990 (NWP 1990, 1991; Bangladesh Water and Flood Management Strategy 1995). The National Water Plan of 1990, 1991; and the Bangladesh Water and Flood Management Strategy, as well as the Five-Year Development Plans, address the important issues as part of water resource management strategy. As often is the case, the strategy and plan documents contain all the right rhetoric, but are rarely put to use when water related activities are undertaken. Lack of a single institutional focus and mechanism, and the absence of a comprehensive policy binding on all, causes an ad hoc approach in the sector. Consequently the planners and managers of water resources operate with a segmented approach and are target-oriented. Efforts are usually disjointed and supply driven, which are usually detrimental to the national interest and ignore such important principles as water balance, conjunctive use of surface water and groundwater, and efficient utilization of a unitary economic resource.

None of these ordinances or strategy papers adequately address the question of water rights and allocation principles. The overriding concern with water in Bangladesh centers on flooding and water management issues. Due to the historic abundance of both surface and groundwater, and absence of major conflicts over control of the resource, water rights and allocation principles have not yet been accorded priority. However, with declining water tables, and more and more localized conflicts arising in rural areas over the use of groundwater, it is time that planners and administrators dealing with water consider revamping the existing regulations to recognize water rights of individuals, communities and sectors.

Various principles may apply to groundwater management. Water is both a public and private good, and therefore the allocation system must take into account the needs of all users, particularly the poor. It is also an economic and a scarce commodity, which suggests that its use should be determined by opportunity cost pricing. However, that should not ignore such basic needs as access to safe drinking water, sanitation and hygiene practices. As water is an essential resource with wide ranging uses, its development and management should involve all users and beneficiaries.

Open access resources are often overexploited, as rights and allocation principles are often not clearly defined and enforced. This contrasts with cases where communal properties have been managed over generations with traditional rules governing use and methods to deal with abuses. The erosion of common property resources, and impacts on the sustenance of poor households are well-recognized phenomena in Bangladesh. Flood control embankments and other infrastructures seriously affect the income, nutrition, and employment opportunities of poor households and fisherfolk communities in the flood plains (Sadeque 1992). Unlike forests and pastures, groundwater has not been a common property resource for communities to regulate in the past. In comparison to the surface water of rivers, whose use faces some regulation in terms of diversion or lessening of flow as well as controls on fishing rights, groundwater resource is still very much in a laissez-faire state. Introduction of new technologies, in the form of pumps, has changed the possibilities for access to groundwater. Because of the lack of clearly defined rights and rules governing its use, groundwater is an open access resource, available to anyone with the technology to extract it.

Competition over groundwater resources is forcing communities and authorities to think about instituting better regulations on the use of groundwater. A technocratic and regulatory approach would favor zoning and regulatory control. However, people and communities are also beginning to develop local-level controls and self-management of this critical resource. What remains to be analyzed is whether these local controls are an equitable and sustainable alternative to the technocratic administrative controls which have been conceived in the past.

Multiple Use of Water: The Bone of Contention

In the low water table area of northwest Bangladesh (Rajshahi, Naogaon, Chapai Nawabganj and Natore Districts), increasing irrigation activity has severely affected drinking water supply abstracted from hand tubewells. A rapid appraisal during the first week of April 1996 gathered information in two localities of the northwestern low water table area. Both village communities are typical of Bangladesh.

Ilisha Bari, of Chandipur union in the Sadar *thana* of Naogaon District, is a community of 130 households and over 800 people. It is 8 kilometers away from the district town and is connected to it by a paved road. Most households (50 per cent) are engaged in agricultural activities. The rest are mainly involved in wage labor (25 per cent), weaving, pottery and other handicrafts (10 per cent), and others are self-employed and professionals. Other than ponds there are no sources of surface water in the village.

Hatgovindpur village, of Mohanpur union in the Godagari *thana* of the Rajshahi District, is more agrarian in occupational composition. The total population is approximately 900 and there are 125 households. Over 60 per cent are either farmers who own their land or are sharecroppers. The rest are wage laborers and self-employed. The village is fairly remote, 9 kilometers from the *thana* (subdistrict) headquarters, connected by a partly paved road. It has no surface water sources other than ponds within the homestead area. Both the villages have over 15 hand tubewells for drinking water. The government-UNICEF Rural Water Supply and Sanitation (RWSS) Program recently installed two or three Tara pumps in each village. Deep tubewells have been in operation since the early 1980s in each of the villages for Boro rice cultivation during dry months. Land ownership is skewed: over 40 per cent people are functionally landless, having no agricultural land of their own.

Methodology

Rapid appraisals conducted intensive field study for two days in each community. Social maps of the villages recorded *para* (neighborhoods), roads, groves, crop fields, and tubewells. Homesteads are clusters of houses of same lineage, or individual nucleus. A checklist of important issues centering around domestic water requirements, fetching, access to tubewells and safe water, tubewell functioning, perceptions regarding water rights and policies governing water use, risks, and hedging against constraints was developed to guide interviews. Interviews were held with hand tubewell owners/caretakers, women users, Tara pump caretakers, and deep tubewell operators/managers. Focus group discussions were held with women from poor households having no irrigated land, households with irrigated land, and Tara pump allottee groups. Information collected through interviews and discussions was cross-checked and is summarized in the following sections.

Impact of Declining Groundwater on Drinking Water Supply

Over the years, winter (Boro) rice has become a critical source of food and income for the study villages. Farmers in the area used to grow a single rainfed crop. With the introduction of deep tubewells they now grow two crops a year. Due to its higher productivity and less uncertainty, Boro rice has become the major harvest for the villagers. Each year beginning in January–February, the irrigation pumps on the deep tubewells start functioning and the hand tubewells start running dry, as the water table recedes well below their suction capacity. The entire population of both the villages begins their vigil for collecting drinking water. The few Tara pumps in their village are their only option. These pumps are built with a capacity to supply water to about 10–15 households. But during this long 3–4 month period they are always in operation as more and more people start accessing water from these pumps. The government RWSS program provides these pumps to groups of 10 households. The caretakers (the household that organizes the signature collection of allottees and usually pays the contribution sum), who are the de facto owners of the pump, institute new rules for the use of the pumps during this period. As they (caretakers) are also responsible for maintenance, the extra pressure on the pumps becomes a source of irritation for them.

Previous studies on access and equity issues of public hand tubewells have also noted that the caretaker households control access to tubewells, as well as making rules about non-owner's access (Sadeque and Turnquist 1995). Religious and cultural norms preclude total exclusionary tactics by the controlling household, but restrictions of various sorts are placed by the caretaker family, especially at times of crisis, such as:

- The caretaker family has the right to jump the queue.
- Families related to caretakers have better, often unrestricted access.
- Complete restriction on taking water for domestic purposes other than drinking and cooking.
- Low caste people are tactfully discouraged.
- Restrictions on the pretext that children are careless users.
- Restrictions on account of privacy of the caretaker family.

The Tara pumps were meant for tiding over the lean period, but a set of rules now restricts their use. This is contrary to the intention behind their installation. As they are limited in number, and the only ones to operate during the dry season, the allottee group, fearing that overuse by non-members may reduce their intake or break down the pump, are instituting restrictions on use of the pumps. A general note of discouragement hangs over non-allottees.

Restrictions on the volume of water for domestic use affect the lives of people in more than one way. People's health and hygiene suffers most, as a sufficient quantity of safe water is not available. In the study area prevalence of various skin diseases was noticed, with women and children being the worst sufferers, as bathing water is scarce. Children do without bathing for consecutive days. Adult men bathe in ponds, which usually have a couple of feet of muddy water. In a country where the monsoon season (June–September) brings an enormous amount of rain and a third of the country is regularly inundated, scarcity of water for bathing is a tragedy.

As the Tara pumps are meant for drinking water and are situated in homestead clusters, they are favored as the source of drinking water during the dry months. However, people sometimes secure drinking water from deep tubewells irrigating the field crops. Deep tubewells are not a favored source because they are further away from homesteads, and women and children are the principal carriers of water. Although the capacities of the deep tubewells are far greater and users need not touch the machines to collect water, they are nonetheless not that convenient or easily accessible by people.

Deep tubewells are now mostly private, owned by those who bear the costs associated with their sinking and operation. Therefore, public welfare at private cost has become problematic. Increased power costs and uncertainty of electrical power availability have further compounded the problem. For the farming community of these low water table areas, winter rice cultivation has become increasingly critical for household food security. High input prices now mean that cultivating minor crops has become unprofitable and the only alternative is irrigation-based cereal production, although the sustainability of rice monoculture is questionable.

Irrigating households feel that as they are the ones paying for the irrigation pumps and their maintenance, they should have exclusive rights to the water. To discourage others from carrying water from the pumps and to minimize evaporation losses, deep tubewells are often run at odd hours like late at night. Such restrictions affect non-irrigating households, as irrigation pumps are often the only running water source in many neighborhoods. The restrictions on fetching water from deep tubewells imposed by the physical and technical aspects of the wells, as well as by the operators and managers include:

- Non-irrigating households are least favored in collecting deep tubewell water.
- Women cannot bathe in the open area of the crop field.
- Washing cannot be carried out at the deep tubewell pump site.
- Physical limits on carrying water from distant crop field.
- Operation of deep tubewells at odd hours (usually late evenings).

Dry season water shortage is a phenomenon that people in low water table areas will have to live with. Respondents in the study area see a causal link between the operation of deep tubewells and the lowering of water tables. Those without access to technologies to extract water from lower water tables argue that the deep tubewells are sucking water from the reach of public handpumps, and non-irrigating households are suffering. They feel that for a natural resource like water, exclusionary policies are unjust, and the expansion of groundwater-based irrigation is contributing to their misery. Restrictions on the use of irrigation pump water by non-irrigating household, as referred to earlier, make things even more difficult. The idea of water as a natural resource for the benefit and sustenance of everyone is engraved in the perception and world view of the rural inhabitants who are feeling the erosion of their right to this resource. People voiced their concern in this vein, regarding the nature of this 'God given resource,' or natural resource in academic lexicon. They point out that access to deep water table extracting technology by some is making the resource (water) alienable.

Relatively well-to-do households have a somewhat different experience. For example, Lutfunnesa, aged around 45 is a homemaker in a joint family household, where her husband, Emajuddin Pramanik is the eldest brother. His two other brothers are also part of this joint family. Emajuddin and his younger brother Tasir jointly manage their family farm of around 15 acres, while his youngest brother is a migrant worker in Saudi Arabia. They are all married and have around a dozen children between them. They have over five acres of land under the deep tubewell command area. They also have a hand tubewell on their homeplot that was provided by the government which they, as the caretaker family, look after (and effectively control). It also runs dry during the dry months. Lutfunnesa sends their young children, and their only live-in servant, to fetch water from their deep tubewell. They get unrestricted access to the deep tubewell, but often face difficulties as the deep tubewell is seldom operated during daytime hours. They are affected by the lowering of the water table, but in the interest of their field crops they are not complaining. They would eventually like to have a Tara pump on their homeplot, as they feel that the deep tubewell is for irrigation and people should not use its water for domestic purposes. Currently they also procure water from a Tara pump in the village, and are on good social terms with the caretaker of that pump.

In spite of the competition over groundwater resources for irrigation and drinking water supply and the conflicts and resentments arising out of it, there is evidence of consensus in sharing this finite resource as well. In both Ilisha Bari and Hatgovindpur, we came across several examples of self-management in sharing this common resource. Water is a critical life support resource and that is well recognized. Providing water to the thirsty is a cherished virtue and important sign of piety in Islam. Culturally, water is synonymous with life for all communities, and therefore access cannot be denied. In both the villages and also in the surrounding area, people can obtain some water fairly easily, securing a pitcher or two of deep tubewell water. But under drought-like conditions, people are often encouraged to bring in an equal amount of surface water (available in ponds, ditches, and canals). This is becoming more of a norm in certain areas, where the irrigation command area is extensive and the lowering water table affects all tubewells. This exchange practice, although not highly discriminatory, is a real threat to public health. Carrying muddy water from ditches runs the risk of contaminating the water pitchers carrying drinking and cooking water. As the incidence of water borne diseases is very high during this period, public health experts see further deterioration of health conditions due to this practice.

Another type of cooperation that is emerging in the area is operation of the deep tubewells in the early morning hours. Usually the pumps run during evening hours to minimize evaporation losses, which also partly holds for early morning hours. Running the pumps early in the morning accommodates the peak water use time for rural households, and many households collect water from deep tubewells at that time. However, it is only possible to carry a limited amount of water from distant crop fields. People are allowed to bathe next to some deep tubewells (usually washing clothes with soap is not allowed), but only men and children can take advantage of this.

Some of these cooperative arrangements were beginning to emerge in the late 1980s when regulatory steps to control siting and installation of tubewells (Bangladesh Groundwater Management Ordinance 1985) were in the process of implementation and regulation was at its highest level. People realized that negotiation was better than having controls imposed by central and distant authorities which might not be in the interest of either party. Additionally, regulations would result in bureaucratic control and therefore encourage corruption.

Technologies are not scale neutral, nor are they gender neutral. Agricultural modernization programs in developing societies have never quite come to terms with this issue. Irrigation water and the emerging water markets are often no exception to this problem. We have already noted how women suffer due to lack of access to clean water during the lean period. They are the prime users and collectors of water. Improved technologies for harnessing water from deeper levels have thus disproportionately affected them. Access to technologies is likely to create new configurations in the sharing of benefits. Those excluded from the technology are likely to lose out and differentiation may increase at a brisker pace. The opportunities in drinking water supply on the other hand are quite promising to bypass these problems. The higher value and low volume of drinking water makes an ideal case for self-management and decentralization of services, but dealing with drinking water cannot be done in isolation from the use of irrigation technologies.

Conclusions and Scope for Future Research

Groundwater is neither under complete state authority nor purely in the private domain. It is now increasingly being used for productive purposes (mainly irrigation) and is coming under intense competition with other uses, i.e., drinking, domestic use, and fisheries. Narrow sectoral development approaches exacerbate the conflicts arising out of competing use of this resource, while the absence of a comprehensive water policy furthers the sub-sectoral target orientation to maximize their development.

The lessons from our rapid appraisal suggest that there are points of conflict as well as consensus in sharing the resource. People who lack ownership or control over the required technology for abstracting deeper water (deep tubewell and Tara pumps) have no control rights and have limited ability to harness the resource. As a result they face real constraints in accessing safe water for domestic purposes during the four dry months of February–May. Poor women, children, and vulnerable groups outside the allottee group of Tara pumps suffer the most from the shortage of domestic water supply. Due to their limited social network and linkage they are often not in a position of strength to negotiate water from groups who have access to it. Therefore, the emerging informal rules over the harvest of groundwater resources are affected by existing power relations in the society.

This raises the question of unequal access to a shared resource, related to access to improved and more expensive technologies. The deprived community here becomes the victim of conventional exploitative development (CED) of natural ecosystems (Regier et al. 1989). Groundwater becomes available only to people having deep tubewell technologies, and increased exploitation deprives others from tapping it with cheaper existing technologies. Individual welfare is subject to subtractability by others who have access to technology. This brings in the question of equity and adverse effect upon users of hand tubewells arising out of unregulated use of water. The mitigation measures of such CED activity must be found in an approach where points of conflicts are resolved equitably, and preferably with the participation of all stakeholders at the local level. Under such an arrangement, resources can be sustainably utilized with due consideration to welfare issues and consensus forged among all users, with local-level informal rules. Newer sets of rules may be developed to deal with the use of groundwater. There are numerous examples of self-regulation and cooperation in water use during the lean period, a few of which were reported in this study. Such attempts may resemble what is broadly known as reform sustainable redevelopment (RSR), as explained by Regier et al. (1989).

While policies and regulations may be developed at the central government level, due consideration from the perspectives of all stakeholders is a critical need in order to formulate principles that are equitable and generally acceptable to all. Certain critical resources have multiple uses and the user groups have different interests. When the resource in question is governed by guidelines and priorities of several different entities, conflicts are bound to arise. It is no wonder that usage practices are often conflicting, given different institutional control of this resource, along with the private sector as an important actor. In turn, this results in different bases for negotiation and rule making.

In the case of groundwater in Bangladesh, the rights and allocation principles are still not well-defined. Historically they were never developed because of the abundance of water and unavailability of technologies that could radically alter the water balance, like the new deep tubewells. It is apparent that with increasing demand on groundwater use, policies and maybe some form of regulation is needed to deal with the emerging conflicts. As the conflict over water rights is still in an embryonic form, this is perhaps the opportune moment to concentrate on this issue and come up with equitable water rights acceptable to all stakeholders.

The choices left are several. Self-management for consensus as cited earlier is an option. Self-regulation as a common-property resource, rather than imposed controls is another. Basin-wide management, integrating use rights of different groups, is another option. However, we know little about these issues and these options constitute the core scope for future research.

Emerging Policy Responses

Seasonal drawdown of water table in the low water table areas has become a reality, and so have the problems associated with it. To ensure the sustainability of the claimed almost universal coverage of safe drinking water (stated to be 97 per cent in 1995, by UNICEF), certain actions and policy responses are needed.

Foremost of these is a clear enunciation of water use priorities and declaration of a comprehensive water policy. Any future statement on this must depart from the conventional thinking of target fixing and supply-driven response. The economic value of water must be given due consideration in the policy statement, but community participation and special attention to the needs of women, children and vulnerable groups must also be given priority in tandem with economic valuation. They need not be mutually exclusive, as numerous examples of water delivery system around the world testify (Narayan 1995). Technology choice, demand preference, and opportunity for appropriate capacity building at the user level and institutional level also should be looked at in developing the policy statement.

Short- and medium-term recommendations to deal with the seasonal water scarcity in the low water table area are:

- Investigate possibilities of group ownership of Tara pumps as opposed to the present system of allotment to groups who contribute only a nominal sum. This will lessen the subsidy burden for the government (currently approximately 85 per cent) and allow for wider distribution with the same government resources, as well as ownership of the program by the beneficiary group.
- Although the Tara pumps are manufactured by the private sector they are distributed only by the government. Initiatives for their private sector distribution should be encouraged. NGOs and nationalized commercial banks may consider providing micro loans for the purchase of Tara pumps. This must be complemented with improved capacity-building for operation and maintenance, developing a private-sector marketing strategy for the hardware and spares, and monitoring the pumps' social acceptability.
- Cost sharing should replace the current flat contribution for hand tubewells (including the more expensive ones). This, along with the earlier recommendations on Tara pump distribution policy, is likely to support gradual replacement of ordinary hand tubewells by Tara pumps in the low water table area.
- Water sharing for domestic purposes should be formalized for all deep tubewells used for irrigation. Irrigation pumps are still the cheapest source of water. Each deep tubewell owner might construct a small overhead tank and a few pipe connections at the site for the benefit of ordinary hand tubewell users during the dry season. Given the relatively small volume of water for domestic uses compared to irrigation, sharing of groundwater

during the lean period should be accepted by the irrigators, especially if they are made aware of how their use of this finite and unitary resource subtracts from the welfare of others.

- Policy support for changes in cropping pattern should be seriously considered. Crops requiring less water can reduce the drawdown in marginally low water table areas. It is also critical to reverse the present unsustainable rice monoculture and improve nutrition.

- Finally, long-term investment projects, with support from international donor financing, may be considered for replacing the hundreds of thousands of ordinary hand tubewells with Tara pumps. However, increased cost sharing and beneficiary participation in operation and maintenance, along with private sector options, must be ensured for the investment project to materialize.

Note

1. The author wishes to acknowledge the support of Mr A. Motaleb, Project Coordinator, Department of Public Health Engineering—Handpump Training and Monitoring Project (DPHE-HTMP) in conducting the field study.

    The research for this paper was conducted during 1995–96, before the arsenic contamination in goundwater was comprehensively detected and publicized. However, despite the changed circumstances, the main contention of the paper still holds. Ensuring supply of safe drinking water in rural Bangladesh has limited options other than groundwater, which is free of bacterial contamination, the major cause of infant mortality and morbidity of all age cohorts in Bangladesh. Among the various options, recent advances in developing simple and cost-effective arsenic filters hold the greatest potential for ensuring safe water supply in rural Bangladesh. However, groundwater irrigation is lowering groundwater levels, compounding problems for simple low cost drinking water pumps.

References

Ali, Mohammad, George E. Radosevich, and **Akbar Ali Khan** (eds.). 1987. *Water resources policy in Asia*. Rotterdam: A.A. Balkema.

Bangladesh. 1990. Fourth five-year plan. DPHE (Department of Public Health Engineering), official reports. Dhaka, Bangladesh.

Bangladesh. 1991. *National water plan.* 1990. Dhaka, Bangladesh. UNDP—The World Bank.

DPHE (Department of Public Health Engineering). 1995. Official Report. Dhaka, Bangladesh.

Goletti, Francesco. 1994. *The changing public role in a rice economy approaching self-sufficiency: The case of Bangladesh.* Research Report 98. Washington, D.C.: International Food Policy Research Institute.

Government of Bangladesh and The World Bank. 1995. *Bangladesh water resources and flood management strategy.* Dhaka, Bangladesh.

Khaleque, Kibriul. 1984. Prospect of social forestry in the Garo villages of Madhupur. University of Dhaka. Mimeo.

Khan Amjad Hossain, M.D. and **Akbar Ali Khan.** 1987. Surface water strategy, policies and laws in Bangladesh. In *Water resources policy in Asia*, ed. Mohammad Ali, George E. Radosevich, and Akbar Ali Khan, 267–84. Rotterdam: A.A. Balkema.

Narayan, Deepa. 1995. The contribution of people's participation, evidence from 121 rural water supply projects. ESD Occasional Paper Series No. 1, The World Bank, Washington D.C.

Regier, H.A., R.V. Mason, and **Fikret Berkes.** 1989. Reforming the use of natural resources. In *Common property resources*, ed. Fikret Berkes, 111–26. London: Belhaven Press.

Sadeque, Syed Zahir. 1992. Capture fisheries and other common property resources in the flood plains of Bangladesh. *Journal of Social Studies* 55: 20–34. Center for Social Studies, University of Dhaka.

Sadeque, Syed Zahir and **Susan Turnquist.** 1995. Handpump financing issues in Bangladesh: An exploratory study. Regional water and sanitation group—South Asia. The World Bank, Dhaka.

11

Farmers, Factories and the Dynamics of Water Allocation in West Java

GANJAR KURNIA, TETEN W. AVIANTO,
AND BRYAN RANDOLPH BRUNS

Competition between rice farmers and textile factories south of Bandung illustrates how water use rights and water allocation are changing in the context of dynamic economic and social conditions. Although law and regulation appear to offer the farmers a better bargaining position than factories in terms of getting water, the trend of Indonesian development policy and economic considerations gives factories the advantage. Examining the dynamics of water management institutions illuminates challenges to common property institutions, and clarifies questions faced by current efforts to improve the performance of water management institutions in Indonesia and elsewhere.

Introduction

Water, which began as a natural resource that could be obtained easily in West Java, has become a problem. The high pressure of human population, together with rapid development, causes increasing needs for water. Water has become a scarce resource, an economic commodity which has a very strategic position, and increasingly becomes a 'serious business' (Bloomquist 1992). For the island of Java, overall water usage is slightly over half the dependable flow (Soenarno 1995). In some basins, such as Ciliwung, demand already exceeds available flows and transfers are made from the Citarum and Ciujung-Ciliman basins.

Water shortages, which initially only arose among farmers within an irrigation system or between systems, now become conflicts between various needs. This is occurring even though on average, West Java has abundant rainfall of about 400 centimeters per year. With irrigation, farmers in many areas have been able to grow three crops a year. Water usage for irrigation in West Java has reached 26 billion cubic meters per year, or about 43 per cent of the available potential (Affandi 1996).

Rapid growth is increasing the water needed for industry and for urban areas, including flushing rivers and urban drainage canals. Industrial demand is estimated to increase from 9 cubic meters per second in 1995 to 27 cubic meters per second in the year 2000, and to 107 cubic meters per second in 2015 (Affandi 1996). Between now and the year 2015, it is estimated that 200,000 hectares in West Java will be converted from rice fields to other uses. Reducing the irrigated area does not mean that the need for water will decline. The level of water per hectare needed for household or industrial use in the areas which have changed function is estimated to be larger than that needed for a comparable area under irrigation.

Water quality is also important. For example, south of the city of Bandung, factory waste has already polluted some water which irrigates farmers' rice fields. The problem is to protect the availability of water, whether in quantity, or quality for various needs, especially for those who are economically or socially considered to be under-privileged, the farmers who depend on agriculture.

This paper looks at how increasing competition for water is affecting irrigation and water resource management, focusing on parts of the province of West Java. The paper draws on research on changes in rural water resource management, conducted by the Center for Development Dynamics at Padjadjaran University in Bandung, West Java with support from the Ford Foundation. Other parts of the research are looking at crop diversification and rural–urban migration. This paper draws on cases which examined competition between agricultural, industrial and municipal water use. The first part of the paper discusses competition for water between farmers and factories in the Ciwalengke irrigation system, illuminating some of the processes at work. Analysis of the regulatory framework for water rights in the second part of the paper shows problems and opportunities for helping farmers secure their rights to use water.

Competition between Irrigation and Factories in Ciwalengke

The Ciwalengke irrigation system in the Bandung District of West Java was built in 1942. The Wangisagara Dam diverts water from the Citarum River (Map 11.1). About 6,500 households in five villages grow two or three crops of rice a year, on about 2,100 hectares of land irrigated by the system. Farmers also grow cucumber, chili, soybeans, longbeans, corn, peanuts, and onions, mainly during the dry season. Staff from the local branch of the Provincial Water Resources Service operate the dam and manage the main and secondary canals. Farmers are responsible for distributing water within tertiary areas.

Ever since the 1940s there have been textile factories in the area, which used traditional weaving machines. Since the mid-1980s, the textile factories in Majalaya introduced a printing process which needs water in large quantities. Besides using groundwater, factories take water from the Ciwalengke irrigation system, from both secondary and tertiary canals. Today 31 textile factories use water from the Ciwalengke irrigation system. They are concentrated in the middle of the system.

Theoretically the flow of water available in Ciwalengke, 1,534 liters per second, is enough for irrigation and industry. According to official figures, irrigation needs 824 liters per second and industry 233 liters per second. In reality, downstream of the factories some rice fields lack water in the dry season. Approximately 109 hectares are left fallow, which never happened before the factories began taking water from the irrigation system.

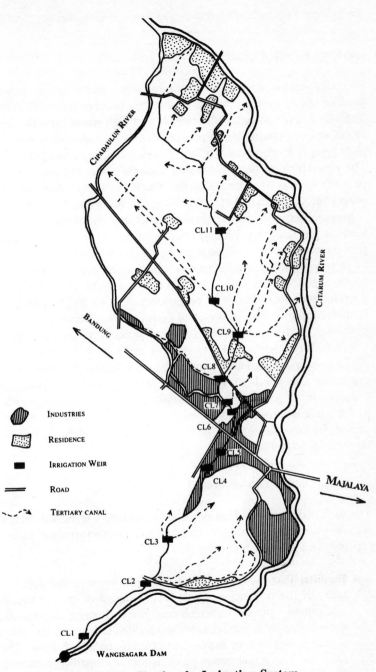

Map 11.1: Ciwalengke Irrigation System

Declining Water Quality

Factories release wastewater containing dyes and other materials used in textile printing. Water quality has become more alkaline. The waste contains suspended solids, and high water turbidity can cause sedimentation, block photosynthesis in water, and reduce plant growth. Factory wastes affect biological oxygen demand (BOD). The polyester printing process increases the water temperature to between 40 and 70 degrees Celsius. The water temperature affects other characteristics of water chemistry, including dissolved oxygen.

Measurements of water quality found that the textile industry waste is not good for fish and plants. Interviews with farmers and government officials indicate that production in rice fields polluted by factory waste decreases from seven tons per hectare to four or five tons per hectare. Some fields do not even yield. When the production level decreases or when production is no longer possible, farmers stop growing crops on the polluted land. Because of these problems, fields may be converted from agriculture to other uses.

The factory waste has also caused the mass death of fish belonging to farmers, a particular problem since Majalaya is famous as a center for fish ponds in West Java. Factory wastes have polluted groundwater in some villages and adjoining fields. This makes wells in some areas unusable for domestic water supply during the dry season. In some cases the groundwater is so polluted that it cannot be used for irrigating crops.

How Factories Acquire Water

The variety of methods factories use for acquiring water illustrates the complexity of the situation faced by farmers, factories and agencies involved in water management.

- **Permits:** Factories formally obtain permits from the government of the province of West Java. Control of ground water assessment, ground water abstraction and waste disposal is determined by Regional Law No. 3/1988. Generally, the Provincial Mines Agency issues the permit on behalf of the governor, based on a recommendation from the Bupati (the district head) after a technical recommendation from the local section of the Provincial Water Resources Service. In Ciwalengke all factories have this permit.

- **Adding intakes:** Informally there is a tendency for factories to take more water than their permits allow. Some factories install additional, unauthorized inlets in tertiary and even secondary canals. Sometimes these are installed like ordinary intakes. Others are hidden below regular intakes or concealed in inconspicuous locations.

- **Pumping:** In principle, water intake based on permits is controlled by the diameter of the inlet pipe. By attaching a pump, the flow can be greatly increased. The excess water taken by factories can be seen in the flow of water remaining after the last inlet for the factory, which often does not leave enough water for downstream factories and rice fields.

- **Buying and renting fields:** When there is lack of water, irrigation is rotated by turns between industry and rice fields. When a factory needs water, but has used its turns, the industry may look for water from the nearest rice fields. Factories buy fields or rent them from farmers to acquire access to water. Such paddy fields act as water reserves for factories. Some of these fields are left fallow. Others are planted, but agreements with farmers give factories priority for taking water during times of need. These transactions are accepted locally as a means of transferring water use rights, even though there is no basis for such transfers in the formal legal system.

- **Cooperation with farmers:** Textile factories give assistance to farmers, particularly in upstream areas, which may keep them from objecting to water taken by factories. Upstream farmers close to the factories' intakes benefit, while more distant downstream farmers suffer the impact of water scarcity. There is also a case where industry 'helped' to improve drainage for the farmers' rice fields—which was also used by the industry to dump wastes.

- **Taking water out of turn:** When there is lack of water (in the dry season) in the Ciwalengke irrigation system, factories and farmers are supposed to take turns, that is from 6:00 A.M. to 4:00 P.M. for factories and from 4:00 P.M. until 6:00 A.M. for farmers. In reality, factories always need water to maintain continuity of production, so besides buying or renting fields, factories sometimes continue to take water out of turn.

In sum, factories use a range of legitimate, informal and illegitimate means to obtain water. The outcome is that factories obtain the water they need, but downstream fields often lack water during periods of shortage.

From Competition to Conflict

Competition for water has sometimes caused farmers to lose crop production and earnings. Open conflict has happened not just between farmers and individual textile factories but also among farmers themselves. The farmers in the Ciwalengke irrigation system have visited the factories to discuss their problems, and have also held large demonstrations. At times farmers have made efforts to get water by force, by damaging irrigation checkdams and other structures.

Institutional capacity to respond to farmers' concerns has been limited. Farmers made accusations that the irrigation officials collaborated with the industries in manipulating irrigation rules. Local staff of the Provincial Water Resource Services (PWRS) feel unable to take strong action against the factories. The irrigation unit complained that permits for taking water were issued by another agency without the PWRS' recommendation (by the Mining Department acting on behalf of the governor). Even in the case where fields owned by a retired senior official in district government were affected, his influence was not sufficient to prevent problems.

Today, in the Ciwalengke irrigation system, there are five water users' associations (WUAs, known as P3A 'Mitra Cai'), established according to government procedures. Officially, their activities are limited to distributing water among farmers. Only one WUA is active. Irrigation operation and maintenance activities in other parts of the system are done by the village administration (by the head of the village economic development section and other village officials). Even for an active WUA, when there is a problem between farmers and factory, it is handled by the village administration.

Industrial development has increased land prices and the local cost of labor. The land price is so high that if a household sells land and puts the money in the bank, the interest is greater than what they can earn from farming. In this context, many farmers, suffering from lost production and insecurity of water supplies, feel they have no choice but to sell their land.

The existence of the factories in Ciwalengke can be considered to be a catastrophe and a blessing. The factories create shortages of water and declines in water quality. On the other hand, farmers' children who do not wish to follow their parents' footsteps in farming can work in the factories. This combination of interests within households keeps the situation from polarizing into a simple conflict between farmers and factories. Farmers show a clear acceptance and concern for the factories' need for water, and the jobs which the factories provide.

However, much of the factory employment does not benefit farmers. In total, the 31 factories in the Ciwalengke irrigation system employ about 4,500 people, a majority of whom come from outside the area. Employment of local people in factories can be a problem. As an example, in the first stage before a factory was built in one location, there was a written agreement that the factory would recruit up to 60 per cent of workers from local residents. In reality only a small number of the local residents were hired. The fact that a large number of outside workers were accepted while the local workers were not may create conflicts in the future. With the addition of these newcomers, housing and other facilities need to be increased. To fulfill that demand, more land was converted from agriculture.

In this dilemma between the benefit and catastrophe due to the industry, some farmers proposed a solution to save their irrigation and let the industry run smoothly. The idea is to pump the Citarum, Cipadung, and Cirosea Rivers to irrigate rice fields, while the Ciwalengke River would be used by industry. This proposal has been discussed with factory owners, but there is no consensus on whether this approach will be implemented. There are questions about what role the factories would play in buying pumps and paying for operating costs. This approach would help improve rice production, but would not solve the problem of pollution from wastewater disposed by the factories. The record of factories in not fully complying with previous agreements, and evading regulatory requirements, raises questions about whether they will fulfill commitments even if an agreement is reached. Conversely, from the factory owners' point of view, it is not clear whether such an agreement would solve water conflicts and prevent future complaints from farmers about water availability.

Water Rights and the
Bargaining Position of Farmers

From Ciwalengke, there is an image that farmers and the agricultural sector in general have a weak position in getting water security. The strong economic and political position of factory owners plays a major role. The direction of development towards industrialization frequently causes the agricultural sector to be defeated. However, the situation is also shaped by the regulatory framework, and by the limitations in the ability of farmers to obtain legal recognition and protect their rights to use water for irrigation.

Water Resources Regulation

Indonesia's Constitution defines Indonesia as a state based on law. Legal concepts and doctrines play a major role in how the government acts and conceives of itself. However, as Satjipto Rahardjo (1994: 494) argues 'The legal sector is stratified, with the modern legal system in a thin layer at the top and the age-old structure, processes and practices forming the substantial component.' Water allocation takes place within this context of a state very concerned with the formal apparatus of legal regulation, but often with a weak capacity to implement regulations, especially amidst dynamic economic change.

In principle the government has full authority to regulate water resources. The Constitution states that the government controls Indonesia's lands, waters, and all the natural resources contained in them. Law No. 11/1974 on water, Article 3 (paragraphs 2 and 3)[1] makes clear that water and water resources are included in the natural resources controlled by the government, with the powers shown below.

Paragraph 2: State control as referred to in paragraph (1) of this article shall empower the government to:

(a) manage and develop the utilization of water and water resources;

(b) authorize or license water users on the basis of the relevant general and project plans and in accordance with corresponding regulations;

(c) regulate, authorize, or license the utilization, purpose of use, and supply of water and water resources;

(d) regulate, authorize, or license the exploitation of water and, water resources; and

(e) to determine and regulate legal acts and the relationships among individuals and/or corporations in respect of water and or water resources uses.

Paragraph 3: The provisions of paragraph (2) above of this Article shall be subject to the existing rights of the local *adat* (traditional) communities in so far as such rights are not contradictory to the national interest.

Government Regulation No. 22/1982 on Water Resources Administration states that people have the right to water for daily needs, and requires licenses for all other uses. Government Regulation No. 23, 1992 on Irrigation gives the Minister of Public Works, and provincial governors, authority to regulate water use, including determining which areas are to be irrigated in which seasons. Water licensing requirements are set out in an Ordinance of the Minister of Public Works (No. 49/PRT/1990). Permits are issued to factories, such as in Ciwalengke, as well as regional water supply utilities. However, permits are not required for irrigation and other rural water use. Indonesia's legal framework has elements which constitute a basis for regulating water use, but these are not yet systematically implemented so as to form an integrated system of water rights. Efforts are currently being made to develop such a water use rights system (Bawayusa 1994, Ramu and Soediro 1996).

Regulation of water allocation could be considered to be implicit in the process by which irrigation systems are built and operated. The criteria for designing irrigation systems specify that impact on the water balance for the river basin should be taken into account during design. Provincial and basin water resources management committees are being established, based on Ordinance of the Minister of Public Works No. 67/Prt/1993. These committees may offer a forum for broader discussion of the impact of new construction, as well as water allocation. However, these committees have not yet begun to play a significant role.

The committees which have been set up are almost completely composed of government officials from various agencies. In some cases the list of members specifies a government-sponsored farmers' organization as a representative of farmer concerns, and regional chambers of commerce as representatives of business interests. Pilot efforts are currently underway to explore how federations of water user associations can be organized to incorporate more effective representation of farmers. Systematic procedures for public consultation in planning of basin water allocation have not yet been formulated or institutionalized.

These water resources management committees are being established to help the governor in carrying out water allocation according to the relevant sections of Government Regulation No. 22/1982 which cover:

- determining the priority sequence of water and/or water resources utilization planning;
- determining the priority sequence of water usage or water resource utilization within the protection, development and utilization plan;
- regulating water and/or water resources utilization;
- regulating the discharge system of waste water and other waste materials;
- regulating the construction of irrigation and other structures at water sources; and
- settling other problems which may arise.

For irrigation activities, the government each year decrees cropping patterns specifying which areas are allocated sufficient water in which season to irrigate rice, which areas are allocated sufficient water for less water-intensive crops, such as soybeans, peanuts or corn, and which areas will not be irrigated. This system is used to regulate water use, contribute toward achieving the goal of national rice self-sufficiency, and discourage continuous cropping of rice which contributes to pest problems. Formally, regulation of cropping patterns applies to all agricultural land, though enforcement is more effective in large, lowland irrigation systems operated by the government than in small, farmer-managed schemes in upland areas.

In 1992 Parliament enacted a law which says that farmers should have greater freedom to choose their own crops. However, implementing regulations for this legislation have still not been developed.

At present, government regulation of cropping patterns continues. Government decisions also specify times and locations for drying out the irrigation system for maintenance. Farmers' scope for resisting government decrees is limited, particularly in lowland areas where agriculture depends on large scale irrigation systems.

A water use right is at most implicit in the cropping pattern decrees, and limited to cropping seasons within a single year. This provides little security for farmers' access to water. Even where licenses are issued for other uses, their duration is usually only for a few years. This uncertainty means that farmers and others lack secure incentives to invest in agricultural development.

Water permits and use rights in irrigation do not provide any legal basis for transferring rights between users. Such transfers may occur informally, as they do in Ciwalengke. At the local level, purchase or rental of land may be viewed as a legitimate and equitable way of transferring water rights. Unlike customary water rights in Balinese *subaks*, there is no traditional or legally recognized way to transfer water use rights separately from land.

In government-managed irrigation systems, the PWRS is responsible for acquiring and delivering water. The government is responsible for managing water distribution down to and 50 meters beyond tertiary outlets. Farmers are responsible for distribution within tertiary areas. Farmers are informed about the official cropping patterns, and may be informed about rotational distribution during periods of shortage. Generally they have little information on what they can expect and lack clear communication channels for pursuing their access to water. Water distribution schedules and quantities are supposed to be posted on signboards at division structures and outlets, but visits to sites reveal that these often go unused.

The government is now implementing reforms to institute irrigation service fees in government-managed irrigation systems. These reforms are supposed to establish greater accountability for the provision of irrigation services. Water user associations, WUA federations, and deliberative bodies of government officials and WUA representatives at the district level are intended to provide channels for farmers to have a greater voice in irrigation decisions. Greater transparency and accountability in water distribution, about when and how much water farmers can expect to receive, are among the reforms being introduced. In some cases, this includes installation of new measuring structures at the boundaries between water user associations and between WUA federations. Pilot projects have achieved notable successes in improving irrigation services in some sites, as well as mobilizing high levels of fee payment. Current efforts to rapidly expand irrigation service fees to new areas have emphasized collection of fees. By comparison, the associated institutional reforms to improve accountability and communication seem neglected, even though they are essential to achieving improvements in irrigation operation and maintenance—which are the basic reason for instituting irrigation service fees and related management reforms.

Legally, water is controlled by the government, so the government has a central position in managing water. There is scope for taking local concerns into account. Regulations do make provisions for such things as determining the priority scale in water usage and water resource in accordance with the people's need in every place and condition (Section 13 Regulation No. 11/1974); adapting to urgent/emergency interest (Section 14); and taking notice of the local people's tradition (Sections 3, 17, 20).

In principle, farmers have some opportunities for taking part in decisions. Planning for the officially determined cropping patterns is supposed to include initial consultation with farmer groups about their cropping preferences. Farmers may be invited to attend sessions of the irrigation committee to provide information (Article 35 of Government Regulation No. 23/1982). As mentioned above, recent regulations regarding provincial water resources management committees state that 'in doing their duties, the provincial water management committee may invite groups or individuals to attend relevant meetings or sessions to gain additional data or information needed (Article 4 paragraph 8, Ministerial Ordinance Department of Public Work No. 671/PRT/1993). So far, little use has been made of these mechanisms for participation.

Enforcement of regulations is a major issue. Most disputes that cannot be resolved by the parties involved are dealt with by administrative authorities. The law plays a significant role as it guides the actions of these officials, providing a framework for considering the claims of those involved in water conflicts. Few conflicts are taken to court, particularly in rural areas. The ability of courts in Indonesia to impose their judgments on other parts of the government has been limited. Rural people often lack confidence in courts as equitable forums for obtaining justice. Recently some judges have shown more boldness in handing down decisions, even if they conflict with government policies. In the case of forest concessions, activists have used court cases to challenge current practices. The courts have not yet played a significant role in water resource conflicts, but constitute one alternative for the future, particularly if the judicial system continues further in the direction of greater independence and effectiveness.

Priorities in Water Allocation

The 1974 Law on Water Resources Development lists various needs to be considered in formulating water allocation according to priorities. Government Regulation No. 22. on Water Resources Management makes clear that drinking water has the first priority in water allocation. Beyond this the government has authority to determine priorities according to the needs of the people, at the time and conditions prevailing. There is little explanation of how different priorities are to be integrated. The government does have the authority to override existing rights in the event of an emergency. It is unclear how to set priorities between new uses and existing uses. It is not clear whether there is any firm legal basis for recognizing prior rights, even though officials may pragmatically recognize such rights in practice. The national 1974 Law ranks needs as follows:

A. a. Drinking water
 b. Domestic use
 c. National defense and security
 d. Religious purposes
 e. Municipal uses, for instance fire prevention, flushing, watering plants.
B. a. Agriculture
 b. Animal husbandry
 c. Plantations
 d. Fisheries
C. a. Energy
 b. Industry
 c. Mining
 d. Water transport
 e. Recreation

West Java Provincial Regulation No. 18 of 1989 states that the main priority for water usage is drinking water which comes straight from the source. Priority order is decided based on water usage and/or water supply in the water resource. This provincial regulation shows an indication that the priority scale may be operationally adapted according to needs in the field. The process of giving water licenses is carried out based on these criteria. Based on such regulations, the government's chance to take sides with anyone, including farmers, seems to be wide open.

What happens if downstream there is an irrigated rice field, and then there is a demand for 'higher priority' domestic use upstream? This has occurred where luxury 'villas' and housing complexes have been built upstream of agricultural areas. In existing regulations, it is unclear how the conflicting priorities of existing uses and new 'higher priority' uses are to be managed.

Similar issues exist where utilities seek water for urban areas. For example, the water of the Cisangkuy River in the Bandung District has long been used to irrigate rice fields. Near the top of the watershed, a reservoir stores water and then releases it to generate electricity, regulating the flow of the river. The Ciherang dam is one of a series of dams along the river. A short ways upstream of the Ciherang dam, a weir diverts water to be piped to the city of Bandung. Another utility serving suburban areas in Bandung district has an intake nearby. In 1994 the Bandung Regional Water Enterprise added a second pipe, which could have doubled the amount of water taken from the river. This was discussed with the PWRS, but irrigators were not consulted or informed about plans for the new intake.

The PWRS operates the Ciherang dam and other major dams along the river, except the reservoir which is operated by the National Electric Enterprise. PWRS has official responsibility for water resources management. It experiences significant problems in obtaining information about the reservoir operation, even though this crucially affects the availability of water in the basin. Similarly, information is difficult to obtain about the actual amounts of water diverted by the water utilities, although the amounts officially allocated are clearly specified. In these circumstances it is difficult for the PWRS to fulfill its responsibilities in water allocation. Opportunities for farmers and water users to participate in the process of water allocation are limited or nonexistent.

The Ciherang irrigation system now suffers from an increasing shortage of water. Irrigation officials have sought to maintain service through more intensive management, and assert that the irrigated area has been kept the same. Information from farmers suggests that as much as 700 hectares in the Ciherang irrigation system can no longer be cultivated during the third season.

The government may take sides in disputes and sometimes does not act in accordance with the priorities as stated in official regulations. Various agencies within the government have different priorities and interests. If confronted face to face with the water need for industry, which officially is the third priority (after agriculture), the agriculture sector sometimes has to yield. Farmers downstream in the Ciwalengke irrigation system are such a case. If we see only the economic aspect, the 'benefit' or 'value added' in the industrial sector generally is much higher than the agriculture sector However, many people depend on agriculture for their livelihoods, and so depend on protecting the supply of irrigation water.

Land-use Planning

Coordination is needed not just for water permits but also for planning land use and issuing building permits. Indonesia is in the process of establishing a system of spatial land-use planning. Areas have been divided into zones according to suitable land-uses. Among other things, this is intended to protect fertile agricultural land and keep it from being converted to other uses. Much land around urban areas in West Java and other provinces is rapidly being converted to factories, housing developments and other uses. So far, land-use planning and building permit requirements have had only limited effectiveness in channeling development in less disruptive directions.

There is a long-standing system for requiring building permits. Before building permits are issued, neighboring landowners are supposed to be informed. This would give them a chance to object if they think they would be hurt, for example by blockage of a canal. These legal requirements seem to be frequently ignored in practice.

An extreme example of this is in the Leuwikuray irrigation system, recently rehabilitated in 1989, in which only a small portion of the command area is still irrigated. In this and other cases, construction for housing and factories has blocked canals, denying those further down the canals access to water. Construction of walls to enclose private property has resulted in canals being blocked, or access closed off even if canals keep flowing. Surprisingly, developers seem to have been able to easily take over canals and adjoining land which legally are state property, without paying any compensation.

By making the need for 'water' one of the key considerations in land-use planning, the position of the agricultural sector and farmers could be better guaranteed. Water needs for other sectors would need to be considered in the same way. One consequence from the implementation of decisions in land-use planning is that these should be linked with the procedures for giving permission to obtain water.

Regulation No. 22/1982, Article 18, gives another means to protect rights to water, including the compensation when the water is used by another. The section mentions that: 'A person who owns a piece of land is not in his right to cause damage to the natural flow of water so it damages a neighbor.' The legal penalty for those who break this regulation is specified in Regulation No. 11/74, Section 15. The maximum penalty is imprisonment for two years or a fine of up to 5 million rupiah (about U.S.$2,200 in 1996) for those who purposefully do not take part in the effort to conserve land, water, water resources, and irrigation. Farmers in Ciwalengke could ask for monetary compensation for pollution damage. Article 6 of Government Regulation No. 4/1982 on major rules in maintaining the environment states that 'whoever damages or pollutes the environment will be responsible for paying compensation.'

In theory, legal mechanisms exist which could help farmers protect their interests. In practice these legal mechanisms are often weak or irrelevant. The government lacks the capacity to enforce regulations on its own. The weakness of civil society means that there are few local groups to assist enforcement by providing countervailing pressure against better connected industrial and urban interests. Farmers often are unaware or unable to use existing regulations and legal mechanisms to resist changes which threaten their livelihoods. The lack of well-educated farmers and of alternative patrons make farmers depend on the local government as a guarantor. However, factories give more benefit, particularly in taxes, to the local government than farmers.

Recent changes toward greater openness in the media, despite problems and setbacks, indicate increasing scope for various groups to voice their claims and press for responses. Land disputes are receiving increasing attention in the media. Students and other groups have become more assertive about assisting farmers and others to defend their access to land. Similar dynamics could develop in the case of access to water, especially if formal institutions continue to perform poorly in providing secure access to water.

WUA and Strengthening Farmers' Bargaining Position

Existing water user associations only have formal responsibility for distributing the available supply of irrigation water among their members as efficiently as possible, to serve tertiary units in large irrigation systems and village irrigation (locally-managed) systems. In practice, farmers may act to protect their access to water, and consider that they should have rights to use water, but these rights are not yet clearly recognized by the formal legal system. Government guidelines related to WUAs emphasize effectiveness in internal operation and maintenance. But what is the use of effectiveness if there is no water? The strategic role of WUAs in the future is not only as a legal institution which could make contracts with outsiders. More important is how to enable an organization to represent all the farmers to secure access to water for their land.

The Minister of Interior has issued an instruction that clarifies the procedures through which WUAs can obtain status as legal bodies. As the necessary legislation is passed by district assemblies, WUAs can obtain full legal standing to enter into contracts and to go to court to protect their interests. Legal status offers a clearer basis for WUAs in farmer-managed irrigation systems to obtain water use rights, if water licensing is implemented for irrigation.

For government-managed systems, the PWRS might hold licenses for the systems it operates, with WUA holding some management responsibilities for tertiary, and possibly also secondary, canal areas. Within government-managed irrigation systems, greater accountability for water delivery would make WUAs more useful to their members in securing access to water. Many formal water user associations have been established in connection with irrigation development projects, but usually quickly become inactive. More fundamental reorientation in approaches to WUA development may be needed to make them effective in serving farmers' needs (Bruns and Helmi

1996). Current approaches to WUA development emphasize establishing formal organizations complying with government guidelines, rather than optimizing the social capital of existing local institutions, which often rely on village government (Bruns 1992). WUAs may also have more potential to develop as viable enterprises, which can mobilize adequate resources and serve the interests of their members, if they can engage in other economic activities, not being confined to internal operation and maintenance (Goldensohn et al. 1996; Helmi 1996).

Economic and social changes in rural areas are reshaping the problems and opportunities affecting irrigation management institutions. Women have always played a major part in agriculture, but traditional gender roles gave men a greater role in irrigation management and other village 'public' affairs. Where men go away to work, women are having to take increasing responsibility for irrigation management. Increasing absentee ownership also means bigger gaps between landowners and cultivators, and greater difficulties in communicating with absentee landowners. Migration, agricultural diversification and other economic changes are increasing the cost of labor, and the opportunity cost of farmers' time. Both local institutions and government models for irrigation management have relied on mobilization of quasi-voluntary local labor from water users, for maintaining canals, distributing water, attending meetings, and filling leadership roles. Observations in the field, and analysis of social dynamics, suggest that local irrigation management may shift increasingly towards a contractual basis, carried out by paid specialists rather than part-time volunteers.

There frequently is a lack of coordination between WUAs in different villages. Sometimes a policy carried out by one WUA or village upstream disadvantages farmers downstream. In Ciwalengke, because of the lack of coordination between WUAs, there are WUAs that have their own policies, which are beneficial when seen from one WUA's interest, but when seen in terms of other WUAs are disadvantageous, particularly where upstream WUAs tolerate and benefit from excessive abstraction of water by factories, creating problems for downstream areas. Federations of WUAs could provide a more effective forum for finding and implementing solutions to such conflicts.

Federations of WUAs within irrigation systems are being formed as part of the introduction of irrigation service fees in government-managed irrigation systems. One example of water allocation by irrigators' organizations along a river is seen in the case of '*subak-agung*' in Bali, discussed further in the chapter by Nyoman Sutawan in this volume. *Subak-agung* combine different irrigators' associations into a federation. *Subak-agung* can act not just to distribute water between irrigation systems but also to represent farmers in dealing with other parties, including the government, to protect the rights of farmers. This can be used as an example and further developed in other areas, including West Java.

Conclusion

Growing competition for water threatens rural livelihoods. The interests of rural people often lose out to the stronger political and economic power of industry and cities. The case of Ciwalengke shows a variety of problems emerging as factories seek to acquire more water. Even though the flow is considered to be adequate, it turns out to be inadequate given all the means factories employ to acquire water. Crop yields are reduced, and fields are fallowed or sold for lack of water. Furthermore the water disposed from factories has polluted the irrigation system. Existing procedures for issuing permits lack adequate coordination between relevant agencies. Joint usage by farmers and factories taking water directly from the irrigation canals does not work out according to the regulations. For the time being the low level of enforcement which exists provides only very limited water security for these farmers, in terms of both quantity or quality.

Existing laws and regulations in Indonesia are important as they guide the actions and decisions of government agencies and administrative authorities in dealing with water conflicts, even though the courts themselves are not yet a major factor in water resource management. Various laws and regulations do exist which could be used to enable legal institutions to more effectively assist rural people in securing their access to water. Since most problems will still be negotiated outside of court, dispute resolution could be enhanced by facilitators, suitable forums and training in negotiation skills.

By overemphasizing the orientation of development policy towards industrialization, water for farmers and agriculture may be lost. The legal security of 'water use rights' for farmers needs to be clarified. Water use rights, in the form of permits, need to be issued for agriculture and other rural uses, not just for factories and municipal water supplies. These should recognize the customary rights established by farmers' historic use. In allocation of basin water resources, prior usage should create a use right which cannot simply be ignored by later users with a 'higher' priority.

Transactions between farmers and factories to transfer water show that water is already being treated as a tradable commodity. More explicit recognition of farmers' water rights, individually and collectively, would give farmers a more even basis for negotiating water allocation with the irrigation agency, factories and any other users sharing the resource. Demand from other users is rapidly increasing and there will be continuing pressure to reallocate water from agriculture to other uses. The diversity of ways in which factories go about acquiring water in Ciwalengke, including various agreements with individual farmers and groups, helps show why simply forbidding water transfers is unlikely to be successful. Instead the need is for arrangements within which farmers can better defend their interests, including receiving adequate compensation when their water is shifted from irrigation to meet other needs.

The responsibilities of water users associations should go beyond distributing water within tertiary areas. Despite their weak position and lack of formal rights, farmers already do act collectively to defend their access to water. The position of WUAs needs to be improved, as an institution which can represent farmers facing the outside world, including forming federations of WUAs. Water user associations and WUA federations would provide a constructive means for organizing farmer involvement as stakeholders in water resource management. Development of a better system of water use rights and stakeholder participation in basin water management would help empower farmers to secure their access to irrigation water.

Note

1. Translations of Water Law No. 11/1974 and Government Regulation No. 22/1982 are based on translations included in Ramu (1994), with some modifications by the authors.

References

Affandi, Apun. 1996. Farmers water rights: Seminar proceedings. Centre for Development Dynamics, Padjadkaran University, Bandung.

Bawayusa, Made. 1994. Survey report on water use right system and practices in the sub-basin of Cisanggarung and Cisadane Rivers, West Java, Indonesia. Pertemuan pembahasan panitia pelaksana tata pengaturan air dan unit pengelola sumberdaya air di tingkat satuan wilayah sungai (Discussion meeting on water allocation implementing committees and water resources management units at the river territory level.) Cipanas, September 14–15, 1994. Directorate General of Water Resources Development, Ministry of Public Works.

Bloomquist, William. 1992. *Dividing the waters: Governing groundwater in Southern California*. San Francisco, Calif.: ICS Press.

Bruns, B. 1992. Just enough organization: Water users associations and episodic mobilization. *Visi: Irigasi* (6): 33–41.

Bruns, Bryan and Helmi. 1996. Participatory irrigation management in Indonesia: Lessons from experience and issues for the future. Background Paper for the National Workshop on Participatory irrigation Management, November 4–8, 1996, Jakarta, Indonesia, International Network for Participatory Irrigation Management, World Bank Economic Development Institute, and the United Nations Food and Agriculture Organization.

Goldensohn, Max, Honorato Angeles, Sigit Arif, Gillian Brown, Upendra Gautam, Kapila Goonesekera, Leo Gonzalez, Helmi, Tariq Husain, A. Saleemi, and **K.K. Singh**. 1996. *Participation and empowerment: An assessment of water user associations in Asia and Egypt*. Irrigation Support Project for Asia and the Near East, Arlington, Virginia.

Helmi. 1996. Irrigation systems management in transition: A study of irrigation institutions and the development of water users' associations with reference to systems turnover programme in Indonesia. Ph.D. Dissertation, Wye College, University of London.

Rahardjo, Satjipto. 1994. Between two worlds: Modern state and traditional society in Indonesia. *Law and Society* 28 (3): 493–502.

Ramu, K.V. and **S.H. Soediro.** 1996. Formal water use rights system for Indonesia. Paper presented at the joint seminar on optimization of water allocation for sustainable development. Jakarta, January 16–17. DGWRD-JICA-INACID.

Ramu, K.V. 1994. Basin water resources management, the Indonesian approach: A collection of papers. Regional training course on integrated river basin management (jointly organized with the United Nations

Environment Program). Directorate General of Water Resources Development, Ministry of Public Works, Republic of Indonesia.

Soenarno. 1995. Alat kebijakan untuk mewujudkan sikap hemat air irigasi (Policy instruments for shaping attitudes to conserve irrigation water). Prosiding loka karya hemat air irigasi (kebijakan, teknik, pengelolaan dan sosial budaya). (Proceedings of a workshop on conserving irrigation water: Policies, Technical Issues, Management, and Culture), ed. Ganjar Kurnia. Centre for Development Dynamics, Padjadjaran University, Bandung.

12

Negotiation of Water Allocation among Irrigators' Associations in Bali, Indonesia

NYOMAN SUTAWAN[1]

When previously separate irrigation systems were combined to share new permanent weirs built by the Bali Irrigation Project, there was a strong need to negotiate water allocation among the irrigators' associations. A research team from Udayana University motivated the combined subaks *to organize themselves into federations, called* subak-gede. *Along the course of the river, downstream irrigator's associations often lacked water, especially during the dry season. The research team also motivated the* subaks *and* subak-gede *along river courses to organize themselves into a larger federation called* subak-agung. *This paper describes federation and negotiation amongst competing groups of* subaks, *with special reference to water allocation and distribution, cropping patterns, and planting schedules.*

Introduction

Subaks are socio-religious agricultural communities in Bali dealing with matters related to water management and crop production, particularly rice. They are characterized by (*a*) common source of irrigation water; (*b*) availability of one or more rice field temples (*bedugul*); and (*c*) autonomy in handling their own affairs such as managing its own budget, written or unwritten bylaws (*awig-awig*) and in making contacts with other institutions. *Subak* autonomy has legally been recognized by the government as stated in Article 14 of the Local Government Regulation of Bali Province No. 02/PD/DPRD/1972 on irrigation. Among the many studies with relevant information are Geertz (1980); Pitana (1993); Sushila (1992); Sutawan (1992); and Sutawan, et al. (1984, 1990); for a description on *subak-gede* see Sushila (1984) and Sutawan et al. (1986).

In some cases, several *subaks* unite into a single body called *subak-gede* for coordination purposes. *Subak-gede* is defined here as an inter-*subak* coordinating body or a federation of *subaks*. Each may have its own intake or weir along one or more river courses, or a federation of *subaks* may share a common intake or weir. The term *subak-gede* was known even during the period of Dutch occupation, but it is not known how *subak-gedes* were originally formed. A federation of irrigation systems along one or more river courses including at least one *subak-gede* is called a *subak-agung*—a term recently introduced by the Udayana research team.

Subaks fulfill the design principles that characterize long-enduring, self-organized irrigation institutions as conceptualized by Ostrom (1992). *Subaks* have clearly defined boundaries. They have rules specifying the distribution of the water share based on various factors accepted or agreed upon by the farmers concerned. The rules may be adjusted and modified according to the changing conditions based on a consensus of all the *subak* members concerned. Any member of the *subak* can monitor rule violations such as water stealing and cropping schedules. Bylaws, written or unwritten, specify sanctions to anyone violating the rules. It is the *subak* head's responsibility to solve any internal conflicts such as water stealing, but if he is unable to overcome the problem the case is forwarded to a local official with jurisdiction over irrigation matters, the *sedahan*. If the *sedahan* cannot implement a resolution, he can take it to the *sedahan agung*. Although legal recognition of *subak* is limited, they have autonomy in handling their own internal affairs. Nested enterprises are seen in the sub-division of *subaks* into smaller units called *tempek*, which in many cases have internal autonomy as signified by a common rice field temple shared by the members of the *tempek* or its own budget which is managed without the intervention of the *subak*. Formation of federations, *subak-gede*, and *subak-agung*, further extends the principle of nested enterprises. While many of these design principles have been identified in numerous other locally-managed irrigation systems, few systems have offered the opportunity to study the process and outcomes of interactions between different irrigation systems as they form federations of individual systems (as described in this chapter).

Prior to the 1920s, the *subak* members diverted river water by constructing a weir, irrigation tunnels, canals, and other irrigation structures without any assistance from the government. Probably the only assistance they got was the issuance of approval by the king to divert water for irrigation. The irrigation system was managed by the *subak* members completely on a self-help basis. Water allocation and distribution among members of the same *subak* was based on the proportional *tektek* principle.

Government assistance to *subak* began around 1925. Since then it tended to increase gradually, but after the setting up of the Bali Irrigation Project (BIP) in 1979 it increased rapidly. Many irrigation systems, each of which previously had their own intakes, have now been physically integrated into single irrigation systems sharing a new common permanent weir, usually with a total command area of at least 150 hectares. The purpose of combining systems has generally been to pursue technical economies of scale. However, many of these irrigation systems are not functioning according to the initial plan. The newly-integrated systems mainly benefit the upstream *subaks* whereas the downstream ones keep drawing water from their previous intakes. This situation can create jealousy on the part of the downstream *subaks* and thus may become a source of conflict. There is a strong need to negotiate water allocation among the related *subaks* within the irrigation system that integrates several previously independent intakes, especially because the related *subaks* were not involved in the preparation phase of the project.

This paper describes the process of negotiation among competing groups of *subaks*, with special reference to water allocation and distribution, cropping patterns, and planting schedules. It moves from micro (intra-*subak*) to macro (river basin) scale of negotiations. The second section briefly introduces *subak* water management, water shares, distribution methods, and division structures. Negotiation of water allocation among *subaks* sharing new intakes is then discussed.

The fourth section illustrates the process of negotiation about using river water to benefit all related *subaks* along a river course. The conclusions of the paper are presented in the final section.

Water Allocation and Distribution

Factors Determining Water Allocation

The water shares received by individual members of the *subak* are measured in *tektek*, a volume of water flowing through an inlet of a specified depth and width, which varies from *subak* to *subak*. The use of *tektek* as a measurement of water allocation of individual members within a *subak* seems to be the result of a long process of negotiations and renegotiations by trial and error. In many cases *tektek* are not exactly proportional to the size of the landholdings. The size of rice land receiving one *tektek* varies both among *subaks*, and within individual *subak*. In some places, it ranges from 0.20– 0.60 hectare within the same *subak*. In others, the range is between 0.30–0.80 hectare. This fact may lead one to believe that irrigation water is not equitably allocated, especially if equity is perceived as receiving equal amounts of water per unit area. Balinese farmers say that water is equitably allocated if one or more of the following factors has been considered and accepted through consensus by all farmers concerned:

- initial investment of labor and other contributions such as money and materials provided by the farmer for construction of the irrigation system;
- soil condition, with land of higher porosity usually entitled to receive an extra share of water;
- the distance of the farmers' plot from the intake, to compensate for the loss of water along the irrigation canals and ditches due to seepage, percolation, and evaporation;
- the position and role of the farmer in the *subak* organization, i.e., the *subak* head and other *subak* officials may receive an extra share of water;
- transaction of water rights that may increase or decrease a farmer's water share while the size of land being irrigated remains the same.

Transfers of water shares among members of a *subak* are reported to *subak* leaders because the shares determine the rights and duties of the respective *subak* members. In the case of a new member, the transfer needs permission from the *subak* leaders, and the new member is required to pay a certain amount of money to the *subak*.

A change in the size of rice land of an individual member being irrigated does not necessarily change the water share. For example, a farmer may have converted dry land to wet paddy fields or vice-versa. If one *tektek* formerly supplied 0.40 hectare, but then another 0.30 hectare of dry land was opened and converted into new rice land, the water allocation does not change unless an additional share was purchased.

The duties and responsibilities to be performed by the individual members of the *subak* are closely related to their water shares. A member receiving two *tektek*s of water must contribute twice as much maintenance labor. However, there are exceptions to this rule: the extra share of water received by the *subak* official (if any) is exempt from additional contribution of labor, money and other materials. The same applies to the extra share given to the individual member as compensation for soil porosity, seepage, percolation and evaporation. By customary law, extraordinary *subak* members such as the priest and the head of the village community are generally exempt from the routine work of the *subak*.

Methods of Water Distribution

Water distribution is practiced by the following methods:

- **Continuous flow:** The water is allowed to flow freely from the intake at the weir/dam through primary, secondary, and then tertiary canals and finally to the individual water inlet. This method is usually practiced in *subaks* with adequate water supply.
- **Rotational arrangement within one paddy season:** Where water is relatively scarce or inadequate, the *subak* area is divided into two or three groups such as head, middle, and tail. The head gets water first, then after three to four weeks of land preparation, the water is given to the middle and at last after

the middle finishes land preparation, the tail-end receives water.

- **Water distribution based on crop rotation:** The *subak* is again divided into groups. During the rainy season, all groups may grow paddy simultaneously. After the harvest, the first group may grow paddy for a second time, but the others must grow secondary (non-paddy) crops. For the next crop season the first group must grow secondary crops while the rest may grow paddy. Water priority is given to the group whose turn it is to grow paddy.

Design of Water Division Structures

Division structures made of wood (e.g., coconut trunks) or concrete control flows into smaller canals. The division structures are more than a technical means of distributing water: they embody the water shares that have evolved in the system through years of negotiation (see Ambler 1990). One *tektek* of water must flow through an opening at the division structure with a specified depth and width, which varies from *subak* to *subak*. If, for example, a group of farmers receives a total of 10 *tekteks* whereas another group receives 20 *tekteks*, then the proportion of the opening should be one is to two.

Subaks presently use three models of division structures. The first is the traditional model called *numbak*, in which the openings of the division structure are placed in a straight line, having an equal surface without any sluice gate (straight line model). The second model is known as *ngerirun*, recently introduced by the BIP (Bali Irrigation Project). The *ngerirun* model places one of the openings in the same direction as the main stream whereas the rest are placed perpendicular to it (perpendicular branching model). This model takes two forms: equal surface of openings without sluice gate and unequal surface of openings equipped with sluice gate. Many farmers were not satisfied with the *ngerirun* model for various reasons and consequently in many places they have modified and even reconstructed them to be more like the traditional model. *Subaks* rejected the *ngerirun* model for several reasons. It failed to distribute water equitably. Its narrow openings were easily clogged by debris and this put farmers getting water from the left or right of the structure at a disadvantage. It required additional labor and cost for maintenance. Furthermore, the embankment was easily damaged because during times of abundant water supply the water often overflowed the canal due to the narrow openings (Sutawan 1991).

The third model, called a combined model, was introduced by the BIP around 1985–86 as a result of the *subaks'* rejection of the *ngeri-run* model. The combined model modified the traditional division structure by equipping it with sluice gates, and the surfaces of the openings were made unequal. The *subaks* were also dissatisfied with this model, and have modified or even totally reconstructed the newly introduced division structures. *Subaks* replaced the combined structures with the *numbak* model, putting a piece of wood block on the openings with the lower surface so that all openings have equal surfaces, or built a *numbak*-type structure upstream without dismantling the combined structure. The main reasons for rejection were that the unequal surface of the openings was considered to be unfair by the farmers getting water from the opening with higher surface, and the sluice gates were difficult to operate and were an additional burden for the farmers (Sutawan 1991). Changing the proportioning devices under the BIP was more than a simple technical intervention: it also affected water rights of the members. Because the external actors in the BIP did not take this into consideration, the physical changes were rejected.

Negotiation among *Subaks* Sharing a Common Intake

In contrast to the well-established proportional water rights allocated among members of a *subak*, inter-*subak* water rights are not as well established. This has become an important issue as *subaks* are made to share common diversion structures. The Sungsang Irrigation System, integrating two *subaks* and their respective intakes, illustrates how the irrigation water has been reallocated through intensive dialogue and negotiation among the related *subaks*. These irrigation systems are located downstream on the Ho River in the Tabanan Regency, as Map 12.1 shows.

The Sungsang Irrigation System combined two previously independent *subaks*—Sungsang Subak (290.6 hectares) and the Blumbang Subak (190.8 hectares)—each obtaining water from its own

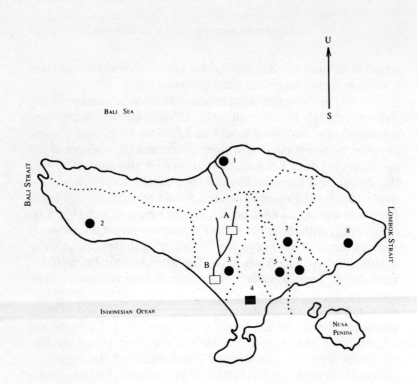

········· BORDER OF REGENCY

■ PROVINCIAL CAPITAL

● REGENCY CAPITAL

□ LOCATION OF IRRIGATION SYSTEMS UNDER STUDY

1 SINGARAJA

2 NEGARA

3 TABANAN

4 DENPASAR

5 GIANYAR

6 KLUNGKUNG

7 BANGLI

8 AMLAPURA

A PENEBEL IRRIGATION SYSTEM

B SUNGSANG IRRIGATION SYSTEM

Map 12.1: The Location of the Irrigation Systems Under Study on the Map of Bali

intake along the Ho River (Sutawan et al. 1989). The intake of Sungsang Subak is located about 2,700 m downstream from the intake of Blumbang Subak. A new permanent weir was built about 200 m downstream from the former Blumbang intake, replacing the old intake, and both *subaks* were integrated to become a single irrigation system. The construction of the new system was completed in 1984–85. The layout of the Sungsang Irrigation System is shown in Map 12.2.

For more than three years after the completion of the project, the new system did not function according to the initial plan. The water was only used by the Blumbang Subak, whereas the Sungsang Subak relied on its previous intake for its water source. Both *subaks* remained socially independent from each other. The new system merely benefitted the upstream Blumbang Subak. This situation occurred because the project did not involve the related *subaks* in the decision-making process.

In order for the costly project to benefit both *subaks*, the Udayana research team in collaboration with Section of Water Resources Development, Bali Provincial Office of Public Works under the sponsorship of the Ford Foundation has been able to motivate both *subaks* to form a federation. With this federation, the Sungsang Irrigation System becomes not only an integration of the physical system alone, but also an integration of the social system.

At the beginning, the idea of establishing a *subak-gede* was rejected by both *subaks*, especially by the upstream *subak* for the following reasons: (*a*) according to the farmers from the Blumbang Subak the water entering the structure dividing water between the Blumbang Subak and the Sungsang Subak is quite inadequate if used by both *subaks*, particularly during dry season; (*b*) leaders of both *subaks* thought that each *subak* might lose its autonomy as a result of the *subak-gede* formation; (*c*) Sungsang Subak preferred to have its intake upgraded by the government rather than being integrated with Blumbang Subak into a single irrigation system; (*d*) the creation of the *subak-gede* was thought to bring an additional burden to the existing *subaks'* officials in terms of time, labor and money; and (*e*) Blumbang Subak was reluctant to share water with Sungsang Subak because the division structure is located on a steep slope and the Sungsang canal is much lower than the Blumbang canal so it would be disadvantageous for the Blumbang Subak.

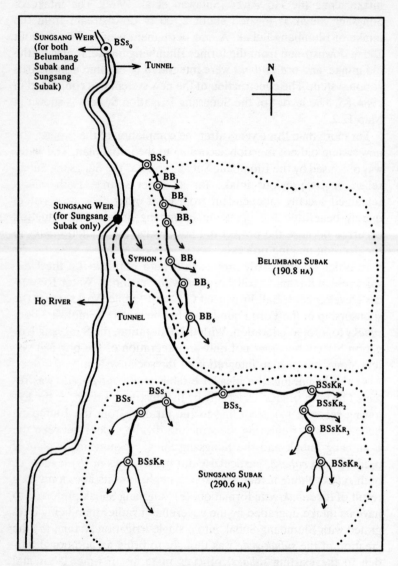

Map 12.2: Layout of Sungsang Irrigation System, Tabanan Regency

In spite of the negative reaction of both *subaks* to the idea of a *subak-gede* formation, the Udayana research team tried very hard to explain the importance of the federation and continued to encourage them to organize themselves under one coordinating body without necessarily losing the autonomy of the existing *subaks*. In a number of meetings involving both *subaks'* officials and also attended by heads of related agencies, the team emphasized that the government has spent a lot of money to build the Sungsang Weir for the benefit of both *subaks*, and since water will become increasingly scarce in the future, it is necessary for both *subaks* to cooperate and help each other.

Unexpectedly, a few weeks after the meeting with the team, both *subaks*, probably convinced about the importance of coordination, worked hand in hand to do minor repairs along the main canal of the Sungsang Irrigation System. The main canal had many leaks so that the water loss was considerable (about 43 per cent and 71 per cent during the dry season and wet season respectively).

The research team organized another meeting similar to previous meetings. Through a long dialogue the related *subaks* finally agreed to organize themselves under a federation which was expected to function as a coordinating body without sacrificing the autonomy of the existing *subaks*, subject to the following conditions: (*a*) the government should repair and improve the irrigation facilities such as the primary canal and the secondary canals as well as the water division structures which were built by the BIP but were not functioning properly or were in bad condition; (*b*) the old intake of the Sungsang Subak should be upgraded by the government and should be permitted to keep functioning since there are no *subaks* further downstream, and the water entering the BSs_1 is not enough for both *subaks*; and (*c*) the Sungsang Subak should be given a definite water share through the BSs_1 after it has been changed to the traditional model of division structure.

Both *subaks* also agreed to assign the head of Sungsang Subak and the head of Blumbang Subak as the persons responsible for organizing further meetings to discuss and formulate the draft proposal for the rehabilitation of irrigation structures previously built by the BIP. In preparing the proposal they would be assisted by the research team and the technical staff from the Bali Provincial Office of Public Works.

It was proposed that the division structures built by the BIP should be changed to the traditional model usually used by the *subaks*. The proportion of the openings at BSs$_1$ should be made one is to two for the Sungsang Subak and the Blumbang Subak respectively and its sluice gate should be removed or should not be used any more. The primary canal's leaks should be sealed, and the canal's width enlarged from 1.5 m to 2.0 m so that water loss due to overflows could be avoided.

The government, i.e., the Bali Provincial Office of Public Works accepted the above proposals and requirements, but not all of the proposed rehabilitations were realized since funds were limited. Recognizing this situation, the *subaks* showed their willingness to reconstruct the remaining water division structures located on the secondary canals on a self-help basis.

Both *subaks* agreed to name the federation 'Subak-gede Tirta Nadi', and elected officials for the newly formed *subak-gede*. Many of the agreements related to the federation have been written in the bylaws of the *subak-gede*. Some of the important points of consensus reached by the *subak-gede* which were incorporated in the bylaws and which have been successfully implemented include:

- the Sungsang Subak must get one-third of the water flowing through the primary canal of the Sungsang Irrigation System because the Sungsang Subak still uses its former intake after it has been upgraded by the government.
- water borrowing among the two *subaks* is possible through consensus.
- the cropping pattern for both *subaks* remains unchanged, namely paddy–paddy–*palawija* (secondary crops). Blumbang Subak should plant first, and then, three to four weeks later, Sungsang Subak.
- both *subaks* should be responsible for the maintenance of the 2,200 m primary canal. One-third should be the responsibility of the Sungsang Subak and the remaining two-thirds should be the responsibility of the Blumbang Subak, and likewise for repair costs.

Negotiation Along a River Course

Many *subaks* in the Tabanan Regency draw water for irrigation from the Ho River. Two main problems could be identified in relation to the use of water by the *subaks* along the Ho River: the lengthy procedure of water borrowing among weirs; and the uncoordinated cropping pattern and planting schedule. The federation of the *subaks* along a whole river course was expected to play a role in coordinating water use, cropping patterns, planting schedules and other activities of common interest to the *subaks* within the watershed. The Udayana research team has succeeded in motivating the *subaks* along the course of the Ho River to organize themselves under a larger federation (*subak-agung*) involving the related *subaks* and the *subak-gedes* (see Sutawan et al. 1991).

There are 13 weirs along the main course of the Ho River (35.5 km): six government-built and seven *subak*-built weirs. Of the six government-built weirs, four are integrations or unifications of several *subak*-built weirs. The names of the weirs and their locations along the main course of Ho River can be seen in Map 12.3.

Water Borrowing

The *subaks* within the Gadungan-Lambuk Irrigation System have usually had a shortage of water, especially during the dry season. They frequently needed to request additional water from the upstream weirs. In some cases, the downstream *subaks* are not allowed to borrow or request additional water from the upstream ones. In some other cases, even though water borrowing is permitted, there was a lengthy procedure to get permission, involving various government officials up to the Regency (*kabupaten*) level. Downstream *subaks* had to wait for almost two weeks until they received additional water, and often the water arrived too late to prevent crop failure in part of the downstream *subaks*. The *subaks* within the Gadungan-Lambuk Irrigation System proposed that such a time consuming procedure should be simplified through negotiations within the *subak-agung*.

Planting Schedules

Before the introduction of new rice varieties around 1968–69, the cropping pattern was paddy–paddy–*palawija*/fallow. All farmers planted paddy at the same time at least within the same *subak*. After

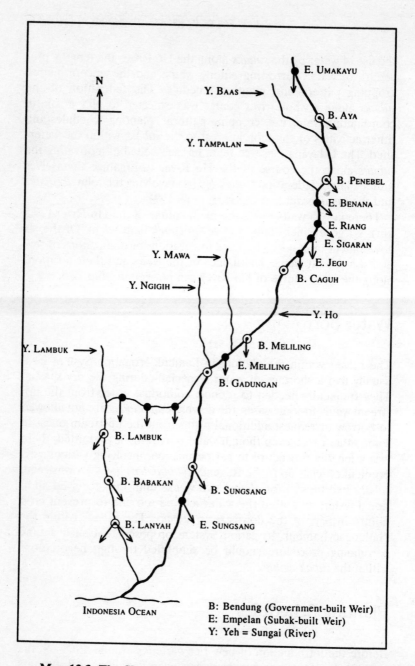

Map 12.3: The Sketch of River Courses and the Position of Intakes Along Ho River

1968–69, however, the *subaks* planted paddy all year round—sometimes, depending upon the availability of water, even three times a year without being interrupted by fallow or *palawija*. The farmers of the same *subak* were allowed to grow paddy whenever they liked without restriction (irregular planting time). As a result, crop damages or harvest failures often occurred due to pest attacks, such as happened in 1975. The bitter experience of the 1975 crop failure compelled the government at the Regency level in 1983 to instruct the *subaks* not to grow paddy all year around, but rather to go to the traditional cropping pattern of paddy–paddy–*palawija*/fallow.

The phenomenon of the pest population explosions in Bali is due to the disruptions of cropping patterns and planting schedules that accompanied the introduction of new rice varieties. Lansing (1991) argues this was related to the disappearance of the water temples' practical role in water management. From his investigation on irrigation systems that lie between the Oos and Petanu Rivers in south-central Bali and employing an ecological simulation model he concluded that coordination of cropping patterns by the *subak* temples produced the highest yields by striking an optimum balance between water stress and pest damage. The dates of temple ceremonies are fixed based on Balinese calendar. Even now, the rituals are still performed by the *subaks* in Bali irrespective of the rice varieties planted. However, due to the shorter growing period of the crop concerned, the rituals no longer coincide with the stage of rice growth.

One way to reduce the risk of crop damage due to pest infestation is to regulate planting within a *subak* to occur almost simultaneously. Within the larger area, slight variations in planting times are needed to render a temporally more or less uniform harvest, followed by a region-wide period of fallow (staggering along a river course). Although each *subak* has already arranged the planting schedule based on consensus, the planting schedule for all the *subaks* along the Ho River had not yet been coordinated. Therefore, for more efficient use of the river water and for pest control, there was a need to coordinate planting schedules among *subaks* along the river course.

Forming the Federation

In an effort to motivate the *subaks* along the course of Ho River to form an inter-*subak* federation, the research team organized a sequence of meetings. A field worker was assigned for each research site to help prepare or arrange the meetings, and to document the process as well as the outcome of field activities related to the action research. First, a few meetings were held within each *subak* or *subak-gede*, then three meetings were conducted involving all *subaks* and all *subak-gedes* along the Ho River. Along the Ho River there are five inter-*subak* federations (*subak-gedes*) and four single (independent) *subaks*. In all about 15 meetings were conducted. For the single *subak* only the *subak* officials, and for the federations only the *subak-gede* officials, were invited to the meetings. Each meeting took two to four hours. Besides the *subak* and *subak-gede* officials, the research team also invited the water inspector, *sedahan*, the agricultural extension worker, and the heads of related government agencies at the Regency level to attend the meetings.

The meetings were held at the respective *subak* hall except for larger meetings, such as inter-*subak*/*subak-gede* meetings, which were held at the nearby village hall, and at the nearby elementary school in the afternoon. During the meetings, particularly for the first meeting, the researchers only explained the purpose of the meeting and asked the opinions of the *subak* or *subak-gede* officials with regard to some important issues. After that, the head of the *subak*/*subak-gede* was asked by the researchers to lead the meeting. During the inter-*subak*/*subak-gede* meetings they were encouraged to appoint one of their officials to lead the proceedings. The field worker patiently pushed the head of each *subak*/*subak-gede* to organize a meeting within its own area of jurisdiction; to be attended at least by the officials of the related *subaks* for the case of *subak-gede* and by the majority of the *subak* members for the case of the single *subak*.

In organizing the *subak-gede* as well as the *subak-agung* the Udayana research team employed a participatory approach. The farmers were not treated just as a source of data, but were allowed to make the decisions. The role of the researchers in organizing the *subak-gede*/*subak-agung* was limited to that of facilitator and motivator, and there were many chances for intensive dialogue among the participants of the meetings.

All of the *subaks* agreed to organize themselves under one coordinating body in the form of a *subak-agung*, i.e., a federation of irrigation systems along the river course in which at least one of the irrigation systems has a form of *subak-gede*. Through intensive dialogues, participants of the intra-*subak* as well as inter-*subak* meetings finally reached the following important agreements:

- to form a federation to be named 'Subak-agung Yeh Ho';
- all *subaks* should provide information about the cropping patterns and the planting schedules being practiced in their own respective areas, to be used as reference for formulating the cropping pattern and planting schedule arrangements for the whole irrigation system within the federation;
- the time-consuming procedure of water borrowing should be simplified;
- both *subak*-built weirs should be made permanent and equipped with sluice gates by the government;
- an interim official of the federation should be assigned to prepare the draft of the bylaws concerning the cropping pattern, planting schedule, and water borrowing procedures;
- the head of the interim officials should be chosen from among the heads of *subaks* in the middle section of the river, for easier communication;
- the Umakaya Weir should not be included in the federation because of its remote upstream location and because its command area is only five hectares.

The *Subak-agung* of Yeh Ho with the total area of 5,134 hectares and 11,428 farmers was inaugurated on 30 April, 1991 by the Head of the Tabanan Regency. The federation has been able to formulate a number of issues through consensus to be incorporated in the bylaws of the federation. Some of the agreements which are related to the cropping pattern, planting schedule and water borrowing are:

- the cropping pattern to be adopted shall be twice paddy and once *palawija*/fallow in a year. Growing paddy continuously without interruption with other crops or fallow shall be considered as violating the rules and therefore shall be fined according to the consensus of *subak-agung* officials;
- water borrowing procedures among weirs along the course of the Ho River shall not be through the Office of *Sedahan-agung* anymore, but just through the head of *subak-agung* in coordination with the water inspector or weir keeper(s);

- for the purpose of achieving a more equitable use of water along the watershed, the whole area of the *subak-agung* of Yeh Ho shall be grouped into three groups;
- the definite time schedule of planting for each group mentioned above shall be decided by consensus through the meetings of *subak-agung* officials. Group I will plant first, to be followed by group II and finally by group III.

Most of the agreements mentioned above, which have been incorporated in the bylaws, have been successfully implemented without difficulty. The most significant positive change observed since the establishment of the *subak-agung* along the Ho River has been simpler, less bureaucratic procedures for water borrowing. The farmers from the downstream *subaks* for whom lack of water was a problem, especially during the dry season, are now satisfied because the process for requesting additional water goes directly to the head of the *subak-agung* rather than laboriously via the *sedahan-agung* (Sutawan et al. 1995a).

In addition to the *subak-gede* and *subak-agung* on the Ho River described above, the research team from Udayana University was involved in the formation of similar organizations on the Buleleng, Banyamula, and Nagka Rivers. Because these were participatory processes, with farmers themselves identifying key concerns and issues, there is no single prescription. However, concerns regarding water sharing arrangements, planting schedules, and responsibility for operation and maintenance were recurring themes in many of the cases. Which *subaks* should be included in the federations becomes a critical factor because it affects the allocation of water between individual systems. This is seen most clearly in *subak-gede* that share a common diversion weir, but also in *subak-agung*, where common membership gives *subaks* a stronger claim to a share of water, or to borrow extra water when the resource is scarce.

Because the water rights of *subaks* had not been established as clearly as the rights of individual members within the *subaks*, there was considerable negotiation over the allocation of river water, including not only the proportion of flows, but also the timing, procedures for borrowing water in exceptional times, consideration of seepage and return flows, and even, in one case, allowance for non-agricultural water needs (such as washing, bathing, and cattle). Incorporating agreements reached on these issues into the bylaws of the federations, written by the members themselves, helped in clarifying expectations.

For the purpose of establishing *subak-gede* and/or *subak-agung* elsewhere in Bali the Udayana research team disseminated their experience to the staff of the irrigation agencies in Bali through a training course. Training was conducted by the Udayana research team between the end of December 1993 and August 1994. There were 24 participants in the training course comprising of two water inspectors and one technical staff member from each irrigation agency at the Regency level. Through this training, five *subak-gedes* were established by the participants (see Sutawan et al. 1995b). According to a staff member from the Water Resource Development of the Department of Public Works, Bali Province, the new federations have succeeded in performing many of the agreements as set out by the *subaks* concerned. However, in order to verify the success of the implementation, continuing impartial field visits should be conducted for evaluation.

Conclusion

Combining different weirs into a single larger permanent weir is a complex undertaking, for it is not just unifying a number of irrigation systems in the sense of the physical system alone, but also in the sense of a social system. The failure of externally-developed projects to address water rights directly, or to involve existing *subaks*, led to some of the projects not being fully functional. The experience of negotiating water utilization described in this paper, both among *subaks* sharing a common intake as well as among *subaks* along a river course, indicates that an inter-*subak* federation or coordinating body can play a significant role in minimizing conflict among water users and help formulate better arrangements concerning water allocation and distribution, cropping patterns and planting schedules that are more acceptable to all *subaks* concerned.

The initial establishment of such federations has involved some form of intervention from outside the *subak*, such as a university, a research institution, or even a non-government organization. However, the intervention should adopt a participatory approach by encouraging intensive dialogue among the related *subaks* concerned so that the federation may become functional and beneficial for all water-users. It is quite possible that if these newly-built federations, both *subak-gede* and *subak-agung*, operate well and play the roles as expected by the farmers concerned, neighboring *subaks* having similar problems may also be eager to establish a federation. By learning from those already established as introduced and motivated by the researchers, such federations may spread spontaneously without any external catalyst. Perhaps as the availability of water worldwide becomes increasingly scarce, the establishment of inter-system federations along a water course, such as the *subak* in Bali, can be implemented elsewhere.

Note

1. The author is grateful to Bryan Bruns for his extensive comments on this paper, and to Crispin Jones for making the English readable.

References

Ambler, John S. 1990. The influence of farmer water rights on the design of water-proportioning devices. In *Design issues in farmer-managed irrigation systems*, ed. Robert Yoder and Juanita Thurston, 37–50. Colombo, Sri Lanka: International Irrigation Management Institute.

Geertz, Clifford. 1980. Organization of Balinese Subak. In *Irrigation and Agricultural Development in Asia*, ed. E. Walter Coward, Jr., 70–90. Ithaca, N.Y.: Cornell University Press.

Lansing, J. Stephen. 1991. *Priest and programmers: Technologies of power in the engineered landscape of Bali*. Princeton, N.J.: Princeton University Press.

Ostrom, Elinor. 1992. *Crafting institutions for self-governing irrigation systems*. San Francisco, Calif.: ICS Press.

Pitana, I. Gede, ed. 1993. *Subak-system irigasi tradisional di Bali* (Subak-traditional irrigation system in Bali). Denpasar, Bali: P.T. Upadasastra.

Sushila, Jelantik. 1984. Perkembangan subak-gede di Kabupaten Tabanan. (The development of subak-gede in the Tabanan Regency). Denpasar, Bali: Bagian Pengairan Dinas Pekerjaan Umum Propinsi Bali. Office of Public Works, Bali Province. Mimeo.

Sushila, Jelantik. 1992. Subak: System irigasi di Bali (Subak: Irrigation system in Bali). In *Irigasi di Indonesia-dinamika kelembagaan petani (Irrigation in Indonesia-farmers institution dynamics)*, ed. John S. Ambler. Jakarta: Penerbit LP3ES.

Sutawan, Nyoman. 1991. Traditional versus modern: Issue on design of division structures in Bali Irrigation Upgrading Programs, *Agriculture International* 1 (1) (March): 62–64.

———. 1992. Pengelolaan irigasi secara swadaya: Kasus Subak Timbul Baru di Kabupaten Gianyar Bali. (Irrigation management on a self help basis: a case of the Timbul Baru Subak in the Gianyar Regency). In *Irigasi di Indonesia: Dinamika kelembagaan petani (Irrigation in Indonesia: Farmers institution dynamic)*, ed. John S. Ambler, 238–59. Jakarta: Penerbit LP3ES.

Sutawan, Nyoman, Made Swara, Nyoman Sutjipta, Wayan Suteja, and **Wayan Windia.** 1984. Studi perbandingan subak dalam system irigasi non-PU dan subak dalam system irigasi PU: Kasus Subak Timbul Baru dan Subak Celuk Kabupaten Gianyar (A comparative study of jointly-managed subak and farmer-managed subak: The case of the Celuk Subak and the Timbul Baru Subak in the Gianyar Regency). Denpasar: Universitas Udayana. Mimeo.

Sutawan, Nyoman, Made Swara, Wayan Windia, I. Gede Pitana, and **I. Wayan Sudana.** 1986. Studi mengenai subak-gede: Suatu wadah koordinasi antar subak di Bali (A study on subak-gede: An inter-subak coordinating body in Bali). Denpasar-Bali: Universitas Udayana. Mimeo.

Sutawan, Nyoman, Made Swara, Wayan Windia, and **I. Wayan Sudana.** 1989. Laporan akhir pilot proyek pengembangan sistem Irigasi yang menggabungkan beberapa empelan/subak di Kabupaten Tabanan dan Buleleng (Final report on pilot project for the development of irrigation systems integrating several intakes/subaks in the Regencies of Tabanan and Buleleng, Bali Province). Denpasar-Bali: Universitas Udayana. Mimeo.

Sutawan, Nyoman, Made Swara, Wayan Windia, Wayan Suteja, Nyoman Arya, and **Wayan Tjatera.** 1990. Community-based irrigation system in Bali-Indonesia. In *Irrigation management in Asia*, ed. W. Gooneratne and S. Hirashima. New Delhi: Sterling Publishers.

Sutawan, Nyoman, Made Swara, Wayan Windia, Gde Sedana, I. Gusti Made and **Putu Marjaya.** 1991. Laporan akhir penelitian aksi pembentukan wadah koordinasi antar system irigasi (subak-agung) di Wilayah Kabupaten Tabanan dan Buleleng, Propinsi Bali (Final report on action research on the establishment of irrigation systems federation along the river course in the Regencies of Tabanan and Buleleng, Bali Province). Denpasar-Bali: Pusat Penelitian Universitas Udayana. Mimeo.

Sutawan, Nyoman, Made Swara, Wayan Windia, Wayan Suteja, I. Wayan Sudana, and **Ketut Swamba.** 1995a. Hasil pemantauan pelaksanaan awig-awig Subak-agung Yeh Ho Kabupaten Tabanan dan Subak-agung Gangga Luhur Kabupaten Buleleng Propinsi Bali (Evaluation on the implementation of the by-laws of inter-subak federations in the Regencies of Buleleng and Tabanan). Denpasar-Bali: Universitas Udayana. Mimeo.

———. 1995b. Laporan pelaksanaan pelatihan cara-cara pembentukan wadah koordinasi antar system irigasi pada aliran sungai bagi petugas CDPU kabupaten seluruh Bali (Report on the conduct of training on how to organize inter-system federations along the river courses for staff of irrigation agencies at the Regency level in Bali). Denpasar-Bali: Universitas Udayana. Mimeo.

13

Acequias and Water Rights Adjudications in Northern New Mexico

NORTHERN NEW MEXICO LEGAL SERVICES

New Mexico is heir to an irrigation system that was developed in North Africa, taken to Spain by the Moors, imported to the Americas by Spanish invaders, interacted with Pueblo Indian irrigation customs, and codified into the Anglo-American legal structure of the state. The community ditches, acequias, *have existed in rural parts of the state for hundreds of years. The New Mexico State Engineer's Office, and on occasion the U.S. federal government, have initiated adjudications to judicially establish ownership of water rights on various river systems and to quantify and prioritize those rights. Northern New Mexico Legal Services acts as advocates to assist acequia associations in preserving their water rights during the course of the adjudication, works with the community members to make the legal process understandable so that they will have a meaningful voice in the adjudication, and more generally works toward making the adjudications as inclusive and participatory as possible.*

Introduction

Since the invasion of what is now New Mexico by the Spanish in the 16th century, there has been an ongoing struggle for the most valuable resource in the high desert territory—water. Native American tribes and Pueblos and rural Hispanic farmers shared this precious gift for centuries, but the increasing demand on a limited water supply caused by urbanization, industry, and tourism in the 20th century has resulted in continuing disputes, controversy, and litigation.

Northern New Mexico Legal Services (NNMLS) is a non-government organization primarily funded by the federal government to provide civil legal advice and representation to the 96,000 eligible poor persons living in the northern half of the state.[1] NNMLS' staff of 20 serves over 4,000 clients per year. Since the inception of the program, over 30 years ago, protection of traditional land and water rights has been one of our priorities.

Northern New Mexicans live in a high desert environment. NNMLS s clients irrigate at elevations of 2,300 meters and higher. They depend on the spring runoff from the melting snow in the surrounding mountains, and on the summer rains, to provide water for their orchards and crops during the growing season, which lasts from May or June until September. Annual rainfall in northern New Mexico averages only 35 centimeters per year, but varies widely. In 1995 runoff was at 180 per cent of normal, while runoff in the first half of 1996 was only 40 per cent of normal.

The water rights work conducted by NNMLS involves dynamic interaction among several elements. First is the law, which defines the rights of individual water users or claimants. Second are the practices and procedures of a state agency, in this case, the New Mexico State Engineer's Office (SEO), whose task it is to implement and interpret the law. The third, and most crucial element, is the client, who claims a right to use water. The degree to which a traditional water user is able to participate effectively in the process of establishing a water right is determined by the resources available to the client. These resources include familiarity with the law, or with the agency's procedures, and access to technical, academic, financial, and legal support. NNMLS itself can be considered a fourth element in the interaction, in its role as a broker. This is important, because in many cases, the poor are excluded from access to state law and state agencies.

The following discussion will, by means of a composite example combining common elements of real cases, examine the process of establishing a traditional water user's right to use that water. Subsequent sections briefly describe NNMLS activities in strengthening *acequia* organizations, and discuss controversies about transferability of water rights.[2]

Adjudications—An Example

In September of 1991, José Rios, a 70 year old man who has a sixth grade education and is more fluent in Spanish than in English, received a 35-page packet of papers from the New Mexico State Engineer's Office at his home in rural northern New Mexico. The cover letter informed him that he had been joined as a defendant in a lawsuit which was the general water rights adjudication dealing with all water right claims in the Gallinas River drainage (see Map 13.1). Included in the packet were a Supplemental Complaint, the state's Motion to Joint Parties Defendant & Minute Order, a Summons, an Offer of Judgment, and a Notice and Receipt of Summons & Supplemental Complaint and Explanation.

The Summons advised him that unless he served and filed a responsive pleading or motion, the state would apply to the court for the relief demanded in the Supplemental Complaint. The Offer of Judgment offered to recognize his right to divert public surface water from the stream system for irrigation purposes and indicated a priority date, identified the source of the surface water, the point of diversion (El Porvenir, the name of his *acequia*), the amount of his acreage, and the amount of water he would be entitled to per acre per year.

What to do? In order to protect his water rights, this client would need to be familiar with a number of terms and their legal consequence. He knew what an *acequia* was, he had been cleaning it every spring since he was a child, and used it to irrigate his garden and alfalfa crop.

Acequias are community-run ditches or irrigation systems whose genesis is in arid north Africa and whose use was carried by the

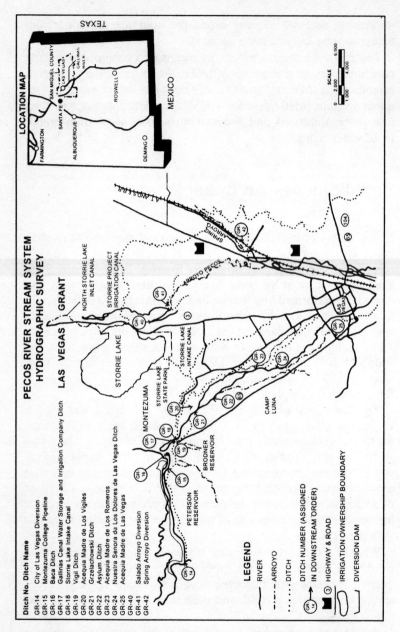

Ditch No. Ditch Name

GR-14   City of Las Vegas Diversion
GR-15   Montezuma College Pipeline
GR-16   Baca Ditch
GR-17   Gallinas Canal Water Storage and Irrigation Company Ditch
GR-18   Storrie Lake Intake Canal
GR-19   Vigil Ditch
GR-20   Acequia Madre de Los Vigiles
GR-21   Grzelachowski Ditch
GR-22   Asylum Ditch
GR-23   Acequia Madre de Los Romeros
GR-24   Nuestra Senora de Los Dolores de Las Vegas Ditch
GR-25   Acequia Madre de Las Vegas
GR-40
GR-41   Salado Arroyo Diversion
GR-42   Spring Arroyo Diversion

PECOS RIVER STREAM SYSTEM
HYDROGRAPHIC SURVEY

LEGEND

⎯⎯⎯ RIVER
⎯··⎯·· ARROYO
········ DITCH

GR
14   DITCH NUMBER (ASSIGNED
     IN DOWNSTREAM ORDER)

▬▬▬ HIGHWAY & ROAD

⎱⎰ IRRIGATION OWNERSHIP BOUNDARY

◥◣ DIVERSION DAM

Map 13.1: Upper Pecos River Stream System, adapted from Hydrographic Survey, Gallinas River Section, 1991

Moors to Spain a thousand years ago and by the Spanish to the Americas 500 years ago. The *acequias* in northern New Mexico were constructed by Spanish and Mexican settlers long before New Mexico became part of the United States. Once a land grant was given, collective construction of a ditch was essential to provide a source of irrigation in the high desert terrain.

But, Mr Rios asked, 'what is a stream adjudication?' Because NNMLS staff had learned that the state was sending similar packets to some 1,200 water rights claimants in the area, we were able to place announcements in the local newspaper and on the Spanish-language radio station advising irrigators of community education meetings at which NNMLS staff would answer that and other questions.

Under New Mexico law, an adjudication is a lawsuit brought by the state, and occasionally by the federal government, to determine who has water rights on a particular stream, and the extent or amount of their water rights. A water right does not exist on a piece of land until water has been put to 'beneficial use,' that is, until someone begins to use it regularly for irrigation. For example, because Mr Rios irrigated from an unlined ditch that had been in continuous use since the Spanish or Mexican period, he should be entitled to a water right bearing a priority date in the 18th or 19th century. The priority date is of particular importance because New Mexico law recognizes the doctrine of prior appropriation which gives priority for water use to those with the earlier dates. Simply stated, that doctrine permits persons with the oldest water rights to prevent users with 'junior priority dates' from irrigating during water shortages.

By statute, adjudications are initiated, '... in order that the amount of unappropriated water subject to disposition by the state ... may become known.' In other words, the state starts the lawsuit so that it may determine what unowned water exists, if any. In some cases, the state of New Mexico pursues adjudications on specific streams where there is a legal obligation to deliver water downstream to another state, such as Texas or Arizona, or to another country, specifically, Mexico. If New Mexico is faced with a dry-year situation in which these downstream obligations can only be met by curtailing some of the use within New Mexico, the listing of adjudicated owners and their priorities would be used to determine which users water supply would get curtailed.

The statutes further provide that a final decree '...shall in every case declare, as the water right adjudged to each party, the priority, amount, purpose, periods and place of use, and as to water used for irrigation, ... the specific tracts of land to which it shall be appurtenant.' These elements of a water right were what Mr Rios was advised of in his Offer of Judgment. Of course, this offer from the state was based on its interpretation of the facts and might differ from what occurred on the ground. The state relied on aerial photographs and field checks to create hydrographic survey maps from which it determined its offer to Mr Rios. Although these maps were not sent out with the packets containing the offers, NNMLS staff had copies of the hydrographic maps at the community meetings and taught Mr Rios and his neighbors how to locate their tracts of land and to identify which parcels were shown to have irrigation rights and which were not.

Water rights in New Mexico are subject to forfeiture and reversion to the state if a parcel is not irrigated for four years unless circumstances beyond the control of the owner cause the non-use. Because our maps had been color-coded to show the state's reason for an offer of 'no water rights' on one of Mr Rios' parcels, he was able to explain that he had not irrigated that part of his land because the *acequia* that provided water to that land had been blocked at the headgate by a powerful land owner who diverted all the water for his own use. Later, in negotiations with the state, NNMLS staff would be able to use this information to convince the SEO that Mr Rios had a legal excuse for not irrigating his parcel of land and that he was entitled to an Amended Offer of Judgment recognizing his right to irrigate the land that had lain fallow for a number of years because of the actions of his upstream, powerful neighbor. Without this, the powerful upstream farmer would have not only taken Mr Rios' water for the past few years, but also deprived him of his right to water in the future. Rather than just legally confirming existing patterns of access to water, adjudication thus incorporates procedures to identify how water should be distributed in terms of historic claims.

Negotiation sessions were based on an agreement between NNMLS and the SEO in which the state agreed not to apply to the Court for default judgments after 30 days, but rather attempt to resolve disputes based on evidence developed by the *acequia* members and NNMLS staff. Contrary to popular belief, negotiation or 'settling

Figure 13.1: The Water Rights Adjudication Process

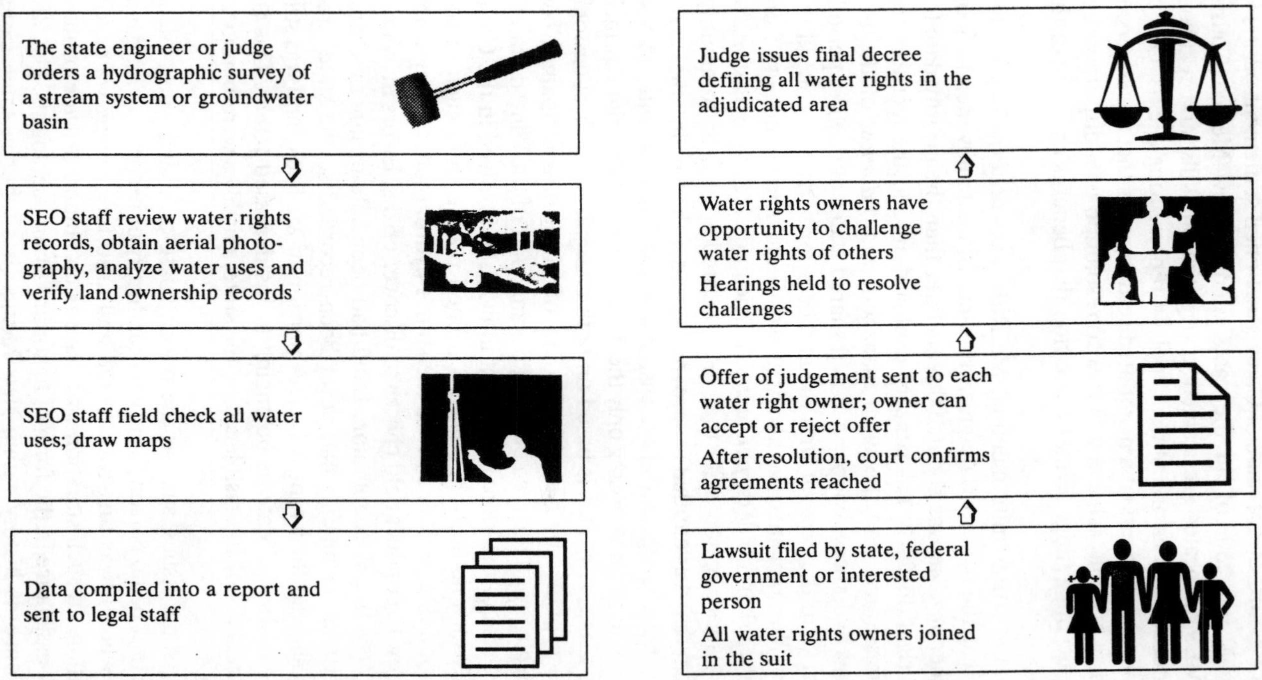

The state engineer or judge orders a hydrographic survey of a stream system or groundwater basin

⇨

SEO staff review water rights records, obtain aerial photography, analyze water uses and verify land.ownership records

⇨

SEO staff field check all water uses; draw maps

⇨

Data compiled into a report and sent to legal staff

⇨

Lawsuit filed by state, federal government or interested person

All water rights owners joined in the suit

⇨

Offer of judgement sent to each water right owner; owner can accept or reject offer

After resolution, court confirms agreements reached

⇨

Water rights owners have opportunity to challenge water rights of others

Hearings held to resolve challenges

⇨

Judge issues final decree defining all water rights in the adjudicated area out of Court' or obtaining a Court-sanctioned settlement occurs in over 90 per cent of all the cases filed in New Mexico Courts. NNMLS advocates are trained in negotiation skills, and regularly use negotiation as one of their tools in representing clients. One of the obvious benefits of a negotiated settlement is that the adversaries may actually achieve a 'win-win' resolution of a dispute rather than having a judge render a decision that benefits only one of the parties.

At the community meeting, Mr Rios was concerned about the fact that the priority date given to some of his family members on another *acequia* was about 100 years later than the priority date for his irrigation ditch. His concern centered around the fact that the commissioners and the ditch managers, *mayordomos*, of the two ditches had always cooperated and shared water during dry periods rather than the *acequia* with the earlier priority date getting all the water. We explained to him that we would need affidavits from member-shareholders, *parciantes*, particularly elderly irrigators, to demonstrate to the SEO that there existed a local or community custom that was entitled to recognition under the law. In other cases courts have recognized these customary principles for water allocation, rather than imposing only the 'first in time, first in right' principles of state law. This is based on both recognition of local custom, and acceptance by New Mexico law of Mexican and Spanish law which governed the area before it became part of the United States.

Because of the large number of individuals involved in the Gallinas River adjudication, NNMLS trained people from each of the irrigation ditches how to read the state's hydrographic survey maps and how to conduct field checks to discover errors. Errors in ownership were the most common. Land had been sold or inherited and the proper documents had never been recorded so the state's records showed the wrong owner. A portion of Mr Rios' land was still indicated by the state as belonging to his deceased father. Due to the enormity of the task faced by the state, mistakes were bound to occur.

For some issues, such as the priority date of an irrigation ditch, there may be no person living who can testify or prepare an affidavit as to when it was first constructed and used for carrying water for irrigation. In such situations, we have been able to provide professional assistance in the form of historians or archaeologists. Usually this concerns history within New Mexico itself, but in some cases

Mexican lawyers and historians have also testified about relevant principles and precedents, historically under Spanish law and in current practice in Mexico. Academic experts can research archives and scholarly works to establish the dates of settlement for a specific village, or can date the materials used in the construction of a church or other original structure. Although the state routinely uses historians in determining its offered priority dates, our experts often have additional access to old family documents such as land grant papers, deeds, marriage or birth certificates, or other writings of historical value that may serve to establish an earlier priority date.

The field checks conducted by NNMLS staff and by trained community members helped assure that, when the final decision regarding a person's water rights was made, either through negotiation or by the Court, the *parciante*'s version of the facts would be taken into account and the process would be more inclusive than it had been prior to involvement of the NNMLS Program. For Mr Rios that meant that the Amended Offer of Judgment from the SEO properly listed him as the owner of the land which he did, in fact, own and that his right to irrigate the land which he had been prevented from using was recognized.

Organizational Development

New Mexico has approximately 1,000 *acequia* associations, mostly located in the north-central parts of the state. A second component of NNMLS' water rights work is assisting *acequias* and *acequia* associations to conform their internal structures to the requirements of the state or funding sources.

The governing body of *acequias* typically consists of three commissioners, who are elected by the *parciantes* (members), and who, in turn, appoint a *mayordomo*.[3] It is the *mayordomo*'s responsibility to assure that water is distributed to the *parciantes* on an equitable basis.

Acequia associations are recognized by New Mexico statute as forms of local government, self-governing subdivisions of the state.[4] *Acequia* associations are corporate bodies, with the legal power to control the affairs of the ditch or *acequia*, including acquiring and holding property and water rights. *Acequias* have the power to assign tasks and assess fees from members, to acquire land and easements for rights-of-way, to enter into contracts, to borrow money, to sue and be sued in court. Their water rights and land are protected from loss through adverse possession; even if for some reason they cannot or do not exercise their right, it still legally remains theirs.

The legitimacy of *acequias* has been recognized since the adoption of the Water Law of 1907, which was enacted while the area was still a territory of the United States and had not yet become a state. *Acequias* are required to adopt bylaws, hold annual meetings, and elect officers. They must prepare bylaws rules and regulations in accordance with state law and give a copy to each water right owner. In many cases there can be a significant gap between formal legal requirements and local practice. In law voting is to be done according to the amount of the voter's water right or interest in the ditch, but voting is often done on a simpler, one person-one vote, basis. Regulations specify that officers are to be elected every two years, on specific dates, but this is often handled in accordance with local customs, even though these do not precisely follow legal stipulations.

In order to qualify for funding from other sources, *acequias* may need to incorporate as non-profit organizations, to obtain tax-exempt or charitable tax status. As they deal with the state or other entities, they need to develop budgets, write proposals, draft contracts for services, and submit project reports. NNMLS assistance in these areas permits these community ditch associations to expand their resources and to develop the skills necessary to access other resources.

New Mexico has several regional associations of *acequias*. These associations have helped to lobby for legislation to assist with repairs and improvements, particularly after flood damage, as well as protecting *acequias'* water rights. An *acequia* commission, composed of members appointed by the governor, advises on priorities for rehabilitation funding and has the duty of facilitating communication between local *acequias* and the state or federal government, and reviewing plans or legislation which might affect *acequias*. For rehabilitation and improvement, associations are eligible for grants from the state and federal government. The state also makes loans for construction and rehabilitation and grants to assist with the costs of water rights adjudication suits.

Water Rights Transfers

Another aspect of NNMLS water rights work involves assisting communities who wish to protest the proposed transfer of water rights. These cases touch upon the most fundamental change that the American legal system brought to water rights in New Mexico. Water was converted from a community-owned and managed resource to an individual property right. It is completely foreign to the Spanish and Mexican legal view of *acequia* water rights that an irrigator who no longer wants to irrigate land along the *acequia* could permanently dry up that land and move the water right to a different community many kilometers away. Water rights were seen as belonging to the land, to the *acequia* or to the community, not as individually-owned property. It was the community that labored together to construct the *acequia*, so the benefits of that labor were supposed to remain with the community.

Under New Mexico law, however, each *acequia* member owns his or her own water right, in an amount proportional to the amount of irrigated land that he or she owns. That right is considered severable from the land and movable to a new location, in a process known as a transfer. The state may permit a transfer of water rights to change the point of diversion or place of use or purpose of use of water unless the transfer is protested. Notice of the proposed transfer advising the public of its right to protest must be published in a newspaper of general circulation prior to issuance of the permit. The protest can be lodged by an *acequia* association, a city or county, or other affected water users. Once a protest is filed, the applicant (the person requesting the transfer permit) must prove at an administrative hearing before a hearing officer of the SEO that the proposed transfer will (*a*) not impair the rights of other water users, (*b*) is not contrary to the conservation of water, and (*c*) is not detrimental to the public welfare.[5]

Before NNMLS involvement with water rights transfers, the SEO had a practice of routinely permitting transfers, via 'dedications,' without requiring publication or the opportunity for protest, based on a promise by the applicant to later acquire water rights, in an amount equal to its proposed use, and retire them from use. These applied to both surface and groundwater rights, which are managed as a single resource, and to conversion from surface rights to groundwater rights. The applicant would keep its promise to the state, because it could usually find people willing to sell their water rights. For example, a tourist development upstream could get a permit to divert water and assure the state that it would later dedicate the appropriate amount of water to the state. This process prevented the possibility of any protest.

This 'dedication' process was questioned by us and by other supporters of traditional water users, because we saw it as a means of preventing our clients from exercising their constitutional right to due process of law. Through 'dedications,' transfers could be approved by the state without anyone having the opportunity to show that the proposed transfer would adversely affect the quantity or quality of their water supply, would waste water, or would be against the public interest. Eventually, the attorney general of New Mexico issued an opinion agreeing with our position. This forced the SEO to abolish the practice which had even been questioned by some of its own legal staff. This is a clear example of how traditional water users, through legal resources available to them, can change an agency's interpretation of the law and its procedures for implementing that law.

That a proposed transfer is contrary to the public welfare is a recognized legal reason that can prevent a transfer.[6] It is this basis for protesting a water transfer which most clearly pits traditional water use against commercial use. An attorney from NNMLS represented *acequia* associations who were protesting a transfer of water for a proposed condominium and golf course development. In this case, individual *parciantes* were bound together by the threatened 'development' in their community. The 'public interest' argument was that the transfer would contribute to the destruction of the entire *acequia* culture in this rural community. Although the SEO hearing officer decided to permit the transfer, his decision was overridden by the state engineer who agreed with our position. In subsequent cases, NNMLS has hired historians and cultural anthropologists to prepare reports and to testify regarding the value of traditional rural culture, and to confirm the negative impact that transfers to commercial water use would have.

Although it is generally accepted that these negative effects will occur, many transfer applicants argue that the benefits of the new use will outweigh these negative impacts, and that therefore the transfer should be approved by the state. Since there is literally no more unallocated surface water for new uses in New Mexico, the only way any new water use can occur is by purchasing an existing water right, discontinuing its current use, and transferring it to a new use. This results not only in a greatly increased demand for *acequia* water rights, but also in a great deal of political pressure brought to bear on the State Engineer's Office to approve transfers. Cultural and community values are pitted in this way against conventional notions of economic development.[7]

The Future

Increasing urbanization, combined with industrial and recreational development, have accelerated the demand and competition for this resource, water. Amongst our predominantly Hispanic clients, there is an expression *'Agua es vida'*—'Water is life.' Since World War II, northern New Mexico has experienced a shift from small subsistence farms to a wage-labor economy in which there is diminished interest in agricultural pursuits. Young people are drawn to the cities and their elders, who can no longer work the land, are tempted to sell their water rights to developers. Is the *acequia* way of life, which has survived for hundreds of years in New Mexico, an anachronism? Is the family farm doomed to extinction?

Those *parciantes* who recognize the value of the *acequia* culture want to develop methods of keeping water in their communities, and of adapting their farming practices to a money economy. With them, we are exploring concepts such as water leasing, a process by which a *parciante* who no longer wishes or is unable to use water can rent or lease the right to a neighbor. In that way, the water right is not lost through forfeiture, the owner of the water right receives compensation, and the water remains in beneficial use in the community. The four-year forfeiture provision can also be avoided by leasing the water right to a beneficial user on a different *acequia* on the same stream. At the end of the lease period, the owner, if circumstances have changed, can again use the water.

Rural economic development is necessary to make the family farm economically viable and attractive. Cooperatives and the raising of specialty crops such as flowers, berries, or chillies are ideas which we are beginning to investigate with our clients. We may have successfully protected their right to use the water, but they must develop crops and marketing techniques to adapt to today's economic realities.

What we have begun debating and asking is why *acequias* are only viewed as a source of water rights to be bought out, rather than as stakeholders who should be participating as partners in economic development that is consistent with cultural and community values. In other words, rather than the transfer process being conducted in this divisive win–lose manner, we could be considering water reallocation proposals that actually solve more than one problem at once. The person wanting the water could work in partnership with the ones having the water so that the economic benefits occurred steadily over time instead of only once. Jobs or revenue from the new use of water might be made available to the members of the community. The new economic activity itself could be located in the community whose water was wanted. With such options the state could accomplish several goals at once: (*a*) it would still satisfy the needs of the buyer or lessor, (*b*) it would have a reallocation of water that is much less controversial for the state engineer to decide and much more in conformity with the way the people of northern New Mexico view water, and (*c*) because it would provide a stream of benefits to the community rather than a lump sum payment, it might do more about the problem of rural poverty and economic development in northern New Mexico than is accomplished with one-time-one-person buyouts of water rights.

To us, these alternative choices have clearly different public welfare implications. We can envision these alternative choices, but we will not actually see them come about until stakeholders, including legislators, *parciantes* and others in the state rethink the status quo in terms of how to pursue transfers and how the state should decide on transfer proposals.

Conclusion

The Gallinas adjudication, which was initiated more than four years ago, is still active. Although Mr Rios has received an acceptable

Amended Offer of water rights, he still does not have a judgment from the Court confirming that offer. The wheels of bureaucracies and justice turn slowly. We feel that we have helped to change the process so that it is more participatory and inclusive, so that factual and legal determinations are not made by default. NNMLS has informed and trained the community in many of the aspects of the adjudication process and has also helped to establish an informal network of informed community leaders who can share their knowledge and experiences. Uncertainties about funding mean there are no guarantees that NNMLS will be able to continue its activities on this issue. It is our hope that we will leave, as our legacy to the traditional water users of New Mexico, communities who know how to address the water rights problems that they may confront, how to adapt to changing social and economic situations, and how to access the resources needed to support their struggle.

Notes

1. NNMLS work on water rights has been expanded with assistance from the Ford Foundation, which has helped to support much of the work discussed in this chapter.
2. For further information, see Ebright 1997.
3. For a description of the operation of *acequias*, see Crawford 1988.
4. Information on the legal status of *acequia* associations is based on a brochure prepared by the State Engineer Office (SEO) 1991.
5. Despite these provisions, New Mexico is still quite market-friendly for water transactions, with relatively low administrative and transactions costs for trades, even compared to other states in the United States (Johnson et al. 1981).
6. For further discussion of transfers see Parden 1989.
7. Water rights transfers in the western United States and their impact on public welfare have been the subject of extensive discussion. For discussions of New Mexico, including references to the larger literature see DuMars and Minnis (1989) and Parden (1989). As noted by Parden, water conflicts in northern New Mexico were the subject of the popular novel and film, *The Milagro Beanfield War* (Nichols 1974).

References

Crawford, Stanley. 1988. *Mayordomo: Chronicle of an acequia in northern New Mexico.* Albuquerque, N.M.: University of New Mexico Press.

DuMars, Charles T., and **Michele Minnis.** 1989. New Mexico water law: Determining public welfare values in water rights allocation. *Arizona Law Review* 31: 817–39.

Ebright, Malcolm. 1997. *Land grants and lawsuits in northern New Mexico.* Albuquerque, N.M.: University of New Mexico Press.

Johnson, Ronald N., Micha Gisser, and **Michael Werner.** 1981. The definition of a surface water right and transferability. *Journal of Law and Economics* 24 (October): 273–88.

Nichols, John. 1974. *The Milagro beanfield war.* New York: Holt, Rinehart and Winston.

Parden, Shannon A. 1989. Note: The Milagro beanfield war revisited in Ensenada Land and Water Association v. Sleeper: Public welfare defies transfer of water rights. *Natural Resources Journal* 29: 861–76.

SEO (State Engineer Office). 1987. Water rights adjudication. (information sheet). Santa Fe, New Mexico.

———. 1991. *Acequias.* Santa Fe, New Mexico.

14

Negotiating Water Rights:
Implications for Research
and Action

BRYAN RANDOLPH BRUNS
and RUTH S. MEINZEN-DICK

Capacity for negotiation can and should be improved, building on experience and techniques from participatory irrigation management and alternative dispute resolution. Reforming water rights should be approached as a negotiated process, in contexts such as development projects, formalizing rights, basin management, or intersectoral transfer. Research is needed to better understand multiple, conflicting claims to water, and the problems and opportunities for improving water allocation.

Introduction

The preceding chapters have shown a variety of ways in which rights to water are negotiated and renegotiated in response to increasing competition. They illustrate the pluralism of contesting claims, among irrigators, between those using water in different sectors, and between local or customary rights and national law. Disputants shop among different forums in pursuit of solutions which will best serve their interests. Agency procedures shape how diverse concerns can be heard and integrated into decisions regarding water allocation. If supportive conditions and institutions are available, then negotiation among stakeholders can contribute to more equitable and efficient solutions to water conflicts.

This concluding chapter explores implications for practice, policy and research. One of the lessons of this book is that contexts are different, and uniform prescriptions will not fit well anywhere. This chapter does not attempt to provide detailed guidelines, but rather suggests directions for negotiating water rights in different contexts, and offers references to further resources. The first section reviews ways to improve capacity to negotiate water allocation. The following sections discuss issues for research and action in four key contexts: renegotiating rights during project intervention, formalizing water tenure, developing basin governance institutions, and coping with demands for intersectoral transfer.

Improving Negotiation

Most disputes about water are not resolved by courts, nor by technocrats. They are worked out by the parties involved, sometimes with the help of outsiders. A persistent theme in this book and in much of the literature on water conflicts concerns the advantages of agreements negotiated among disputants, rather than decisions imposed by a court, agency or other outside source. This allows participants to use their own detailed knowledge and creativity to craft solutions suited to their particular concerns, not just formal criteria accepted in law or recognized by outside officials. For example, in Burkina Faso (Chapter 3), local forums were adapted to explicitly include women producers, whom project officials had initially excluded; in Kirindi Oya (Chapter 4) introduction of a 'late *maha* crop' created new flexibility to adjust seasonal water allocation to actual rainfall.

Substantial opportunities exist for improving the processes through which negotiations occur, by improving agency procedures, enhancing the negotiating capacity of water user associations, agencies and other stakeholder organizations, and providing third-party assistance for conflicts which disputants have been unable to solve by themselves. Negotiated approaches use and enhance the social capital of organizations and networks in civil society.

Scoping

Questions such as: who are the stakeholders, which forums are appropriate, how should issues be framed and how to best facilitate negotiation, can be the agenda of an initial participatory scoping process devoted to assessing the issues and stakeholders involved. Where this prepares for subsequent negotiation, it forms a distinct stage of prenegotiation. Prenegotiation may be particularly important where there are large cultural differences, little mutual understanding, and no shared agenda (Rothman 1995).

Barbara van Koppen's study of rice valley improvement in Burkina Faso in Chapter 3 showed both what could happen when primary stakeholders, women cultivating rice, were ignored. Assessment of who the main stakeholders are should clarify who has the greatest interest in solving a particular problem, and who might block a solution unless they have been involved in forming a consensus.

Current thinking tends to focus on watersheds as 'natural' units. However, problems and solutions may cover a 'problemshed' with a different geographic scale and different scope of participants. Water scarcity may only be critical in a particular sub-basin. In some areas, such as Java, irrigation development has created complex hydrological linkages moving water back and forth across 'natural' basin boundaries. People outside a watershed may have strong concerns, for example about recreation and environmental issues, which need to be represented if an acceptable solution is to be formulated.

The cases in this book support the argument that in almost all cases water rights already exist, in some form or other. Local water rights may be informal. Legal pluralism may be explicitly recognized in law to some degree. Furthermore, different laws may be inconsistent, and different agencies may have conflicting interpretations of the same set of laws. In almost all cases there are claimants who need to be heard, whether based on their formal legal standing, customary rights, or for the pragmatic reason that seeking their consent is likely to work better than trying to ignore or override their claims.

How stakeholders will be represented is a key question in preparing for negotiation. Organization of water user associations has created groups which may be able to represent farmers. Federations, such as discussed in Chapter 11, can bring together different WUAs, while still allowing those at the local level to have their voice heard. Efforts to organize negotiation are likely to bear more fruit where negotiation will respond to urgent threats already recognized by farmers, and offer, not imposition of one-sided sacrifices or mitigation of losses, but the prospect of genuine gains for farmers.

Increasing demand from different water users enlarges the scope of those concerned. Local uses for domestic water, livestock and other non-irrigation needs require stronger efforts to involve women and other stakeholders, besides the male irrigators who are typically the focus of irrigation organization (Meinzen-Dick 1997). Negotiations between different users in a basin become multiparty, with heterogeneous participants. Negotiations bring together strangers, people who may have had little or no previous contact. Cultural differences may complicate negotiation (Faure and Rubin 1993). Small-scale cultivators in upper watersheds may differ ethnically from more commercialized farmers in lowland areas. Government bureaucrats, from irrigation agencies or water supply utilities, have to expose their discussions to farmers and local leaders, as well as industrialists from the private sector. Capacity to identify and involve stakeholders is critical for creating the conditions for effective negotiation.

Convening Forums

Earlier chapters illustrated negotiating forums, ranging from informal interaction among users, the silent dialogue of opening and closing outlets, to court proceedings and formal meetings between bureaucrats and farmers. Convening stakeholders is one of the options with the greatest potential for improving water allocation. As earlier chapters have shown, disputants choose between various forums for pursuing their interests in disputes. New forums create new possibilities.

For participation in irrigation design, having a series of meetings has been critical for going beyond a simple one- or two-way exchange of information to broad participation, joint problem solving, and consensus. The basic workshop structure of small group discussions and plenary sessions can be productive with all kinds of participants. A stakeholder workshop could last for a single day, or a participatory planning process could cover a series of meetings over many months. Conducting such activities requires preparation and skills in facilitation. Watershed management efforts in the United States have found it useful to appoint a coordinator for those tasks (Natural Resources Law Center 1996). The payoff lies in more directly enabling stakeholders to share their perspectives, assess their own problems, and build institutional capacity.

Ad hoc groups, such as a task force with members from different stakeholder groups, may help formulate options for solving water resource problems. Citizen's advisory panels (CAPs) have served in other fields as a structure for systematic consultation. Involvement of senior managers who are willing to listen and respond is usually crucial for such CAPs to be effective (Cohen 1997). Depending on the purpose, relying on the initiative of volunteers may suffice, or members may be nominated by various stakeholder groups. A panel or other forum might be convened and given authority by an official agency, but this also could be initiated by a university, nongovernment organization, or local citizens group.

Facilitating Negotiation

Informal mediation of various sorts is common. Friends, neighbors, and religious leaders can help, particularly when conditions become so hostile that direct discussion between the disputants is not productive. Mediators do not have the power to make and enforce decisions, but instead try to ease communication and facilitate agreement. Mediators can offer different perspectives and help to suggest new options for solutions. They can convene meetings, identify needs for technical analysis and otherwise aid dispute resolution. Professional mediators may be useful, particularly if conflicts are intense and specialized facilitation skills are needed.

Experience in promoting participation in irrigation shows the value of community organizers who facilitate local participation (Manor et al. 1990). The difficulties of irrigation agencies in funding and institutionalizing positions for irrigation organizers (Bruns 1993) suggest that the priority should be on building the capacity of community organizations, agency staff, and other stakeholders to negotiate, rather than relying primarily on external facilitators. Experienced farmer leaders and other resource people may be recruited to act as advisors or consultants (N. Pradhan and Yoder 1989; U. Pradhan 1994). Where there are substantial needs, training programs can provide a systematic approach to improving the capacity of participants to deal with water allocation and rights.

Alternative dispute resolution (ADR) techniques open many options besides seeking solutions from a court or other external authority. Negotiated approaches have been applied to many water conflicts in western United States, particularly for Native American water rights (see Checchio and Colby 1993; Folk-Williams 1988 among others). However, '[t]here has been almost no systematic application of dispute resolution principles to water conflicts in Asia and the Near East' (Bingham et al. 1994: vii; see also Dinar and Loehman 1995; Stanbury and Lynott 1993, and, for a dissenting emphasis on the uniqueness of conflict resolution in different domains, Dunlop 1995). Action research would be useful in applying these techniques in developing countries, and documenting the effects of cultural or other contextual factors, along with the outcomes.

Interest-based negotiation can help shift the focus away from fixed bargaining positions, towards a creative search for solutions that satisfy underlying interests (Fisher and Brown 1988; Fisher and Ertel 1995; Fisher et al. 1991; Fisher Kopelman and Schneider 1994). Focusing on problems, not personalities, can offer more space for finding solutions. Power is not only a matter of wealth and authority, instead power for each party depends crucially on their best available alternative to a negotiated agreement. Reframing problems in new, mutually acceptable terms is often a key to generating creative solutions. Disputants can craft mutually beneficial 'win-win' solutions (Reck and Long 1989), escaping the assumption that conflict is a zero-sum situation where whatever one side wins must come from what the other side loses. Interest-based negotiation is one of several systematic approaches to negotiation which may be introduced through facilitators, training, and other means (Edelman and Crain 1993; Karrass 1992; Lewicki et al. 1996; Nierenberg 1981).

Arbitration is a more effective and attractive option where the legal system provides power to enforce the arbitrator's judgments.

Where courts are inaccessible or distrusted, local leaders, religious figures, government administrators, and others may play quasi-judicial roles as arbitrators, making decisions even if they are not formally empowered to act as judges (Engel 1978). In the same way that litigants may prefer to settle out of court, a parallel dynamic may work in a quasi-judicial context. Stakeholders in a water conflict may prefer to negotiate their own solution rather than having one imposed by a government authority. Such negotiations occur 'in the shadow of the law' (Mnookin and Kornhauser 1979, cited in Gilson and Mnookin 1995). They are often heavily influenced by how laws define the situation, and by the potential for authorities to help enforce an agreement. As with 'settling out of court,' the threat that the authority will impose a decision nobody likes, if disputants cannot agree among themselves, may provide a crucial impetus to formulating a negotiated solution.

Fact-finding

A key technique in promoting productive negotiation is to get the parties involved in identifying which facts they can agree on. This highlights areas of agreement and conflict. It may reveal where further technical analysis would be welcomed. Experience with participation in irrigation design has shown that the changes important to farmers are often very minor from a technical point of view, for example adjusting a canal alignment to run along a property boundary or siting a structure a few meters up or downstream. In other cases, information on how much water is available with what reliability is critical. Clarifying the technical questions at issue may similarly help to simplify finding solutions to water allocation conflicts in at least some cases.

Technical knowledge is an important collective good which may not be adequately produced unless there is government intervention or successful cooperation among users to sponsor relevant research (as seen in Guillet's case from Spain). In Chapter 4, Brewer argued that the main role played by the irrigation agency was as a source of technical advice. In his study of groundwater management in southern California, Bloomquist (1992) concluded that technical analysis by the state government made a crucial contribution to the success of user efforts to manage the groundwater resource.

The case study by Northern New Mexico Legal Services showed how fact-finding can include a variety of sources of information such as oral histories and archival research to identify historical water rights. Analysis of the relative opportunity costs of water for farmers and other users may clarify the potential space for satisfactory win-win agreements. Analysis of return flows may delimit how much water remains available for transfer without impacting third parties. Simulation models can synthesize complicated information about the hydrological interrelationships for use by agencies, or others, such as a stakeholder advisory panel. Alternative scenarios can be modeled, while recognizing the limitations of simulation and the need for judgments which go beyond technical considerations.

Where disputants distrust agency expertise, it may be essential to provide them with the resources needed to recruit their own experts, hold meetings, and otherwise prepare themselves to negotiate. This means putting money in their hands. Participation in irrigation management has often relied on uncompensated efforts of local leaders. While such voluntary efforts may still be crucial for larger problems, there is also a greater need for specialized expertise. If local organizations lack the financial capacity to hire experts themselves, then providing funding for fact-finding and other activities may be essential to make negotiation possible.

Implementing Agreements

In traditional irrigation systems it is common to find that downstream users can only enforce their 'water rights' by sending people to close and guard each and every gate or outlet between their fields and the headworks. Implementation arrangements need to be considered from the beginning of negotiation. In Chapter 7, Pradhan and Pradhan illuminated the variety of stratagems the farmers of Yampa Phant used in their quest to acquire water and legitimate water rights. This kind of contested context is where implementation usually occurs.

The transfer of authority to sanction violators is one of the characteristics which distinguishes genuine empowerment for local resource governance from more diffuse 'participation.' Consensus may be essential for reaching agreement, but settlements which rely only on consensus for enforcement may be fragile. Implementation is often a continuing process of negotiation, albeit one where the range of disagreement has been narrowed.

Devising agreements which can be implemented is the crux of successful negotiation. Although irrigation schemes and watersheds commonly have very different boundaries than administrative units, agreement of administrative authorities is likely to be essential to mobilizing resources and enforcing agreements. Brewer's analysis of seasonal allocation in Sri Lanka identified several characteristics which contributed to creating workable agreements: simplicity, flexibility, expert advice, and a forum with stakeholder participation and authority. In disputes about Native American water rights in western United States, negotiation has provided a valuable alternative to litigation. However, agreements have depended heavily on the willingness of the federal government to fund new supplies or other compensation (McCool 1993; Folk-Williams 1988).

Limits of Negotiation

Experience during irrigation construction has shown that even when thorough efforts are made to ensure full participation during design, some people are still left out, or choose not to take part. However, once construction starts, some of them become concerned, once they see that things are really happening and their interests are affected. Realistically, negotiated approaches to water allocation need to accept the incompleteness of participation, and the likelihood that new claims will be raised later on.

Negotiation cannot solve every problem. If some disputants believe they will be better off suing in court, directly influencing decision-makers, or otherwise pursuing non-negotiated solutions, then it may not even be possible to 'bring everyone to the table.' Negotiation is likely to be most relevant when parties are willing to listen to each other and make trade-offs among multiple goals (Shabman and Cox 1995). As discussed earlier, various methods can help facilitate negotiation and overcome obstacles (see also Arrow et al. 1995; Susskind 1996; Ury 1991), but they will not always succeed. Negotiation is not the only choice, but it is an option that should be available in various negotiating contexts, such as the four contexts discussed in the following sections of this chapter.

Renegotiating Rights

Old Rights Versus New Rights

Water resources development projects restructure local water rights, and risk undermining existing water allocation institutions or missing opportunities to improve equitable access to water, unless water rights are explicitly renegotiated. Intervention often represents an attempt, overt or hidden, to reform local water rights. Research, including the cases discussed in this book, has highlighted the risks of ignoring existing water rights, or attempting unilateral expropriation and transfer within water resources projects (Pradhan and Pradhan in this volume, Pradhan et al. 1997). Well-intended but poorly designed intervention intended to expand access to water may produce results which are not only inequitable, but counterproductive (Benda-Beckmann et al. 1997; Coward 1986).

Where water rights are unclear and contested between old and new users, developing satisfactory institutions and allocation rules can be a difficult, lengthy, and highly conflictual process, as Brewer discussed in chapter 4. If improved infrastructure means that those near the head end of the canal have no further need and commitment to share water with those downstream, then access to water could end up even worse than before intervention (Ostrom 1995; c.f. Sutawan in this volume). Those who lose rights may have the power to later reassert their rights and exclude others from any improved access, especially once the special outside attention accompanying project intervention is gone. Even if expropriation 'succeeds' in reallocating rights it may destroy the institutional foundations for subsequent management or productivity of the system, as seen in van Koppen's case from Burkina Faso. However, allowing existing users to monopolize windfall gains of improved supplies may also be highly inequitable, helping only those who are already better off. State or external assistance can provide leverage for negotiating access to water for the poor, especially if this could potentially make everyone better off, and expanded access would strengthen the economic justification for investments.[1]

Renegotiating Rights

Explicitly renegotiating water rights during project planning appears to be one option for dealing with the dilemma between respecting the rights of existing water users and providing access to new users. A key issue is likely to be definitions of 'equity,' including how much weight is given to historic use, past and current investment, and future needs. In practical terms there is a need for policies and procedures which analyze existing local principles and practices for allocating water (including contested claims) and to support negotiation of agreements which secure access to water for both existing and new users. In some cases, such as the in the chapter on Burkina Faso, and similar to studies discussed by Coward (1990) and Gerbrandy and Hoogendam (1996) there may be a well-worked out system of local rights, which establishes a clear foundation for intervention. However, as Pradhan and Pradhan argued for the case in Nepal, and as in Sengupta's discussion of Bihar, local water rights may be disputed or ambiguous, making negotiation essential, but complex. Figuring out ways to understand and negotiate rights, and better understanding the factors which influence what is and is not feasible in the way of expanding and reforming access to water, should be a high priority for research. This is linked to a larger research agenda concerning the problems which can accompany decentralization, going beyond simplistic views of homogeneous 'communities' to address the distribution of decentralized power and benefits between poor people and local élites, or more abstractly, tensions between equity and local control.

Separating Water and Land

Separating water rights from land creates the possibility of allocating water, and the ensuing project benefits, to people rather than to land (Chopra et al. 1988; Patel-Weynand 1997; Wood et al. 1990). If allocation on principles beside land is to be accepted as part of state-supported projects then policies may need to be changed. While much research has been done on traditional share systems, it would be useful to know more about what happens when share systems are introduced or incorporated as part of project intervention (Wilkins-Wells 1996). Farmers may resist reforms separating land and water, as threats to local control, smallholder cultivation systems and communal regulation of land and water tenure, especially if communal rights are to be privatized and made transferable (Guillet 1998; Maass and Anderson 1978; and Guillet 1999).

Rights and Water Quality

The cases in this volume have shown that water rights are rarely defined in terms of simple volumes of water, but usually include consideration of timing and a range of conditionalities. What has been less commonly addressed are issues of water quality in the definition of rights. Yet as municipal, industrial, and agricultural uses all put growing amounts of contaminants into the water, quality issues become increasingly important (as seen in Chapter 11). Negotiation is likely to be at least as important in defining and refining water quality rights. For example, in one basin stakeholder meeting in Tamil Nadu, India, the Vaigai Washermen's Association representatives argued that they had a historical right to clean water from the Vaigai River, and that their reputation for high-quality laundry services was being threatened by pollution from textile factories (Ashok Subramanian, personal communication). However, monitoring and enforcing water quality standards agreed upon often requires technical expertise, either from a state agency or other regulatory body.

Water Tenure

Strengthening Rights

Access to water is crucial to the livelihoods of individuals, households and communities, and is threatened in many contexts. Strengthening rights to use water represents one way of building assets, control over valuable resources. There are increasing pressures for governments (or self-governance institutions) to more systematically recognize and formalize water rights. However expanding formal water rights is only one of several ways to try to strengthen rights to water or reform water allocation institutions. A legal pluralist perspective helps clarify how access to water is shaped not just by formal rights in state law, but by 'rights' as they are defined in local contexts, diverse principles, rules, and practices concerning who should receive how much water, when and where. The capacity to defend rights against competing claimants is essential for rights to be meaningful (as noted by Pradhan and Pradhan in Chapter 7).

Much more could be done to recognize and strengthen the capacity of the organizations and institutions through which water allocation currently occurs. Federations, forums, and other new institutional arrangements for governing water allocation can be developed, without necessarily requiring formalization of rights. Research and action is needed to explore such approaches, as alternatives or complements to formalizing rights.

Advantages and Disadvantages of Formalization

As shown by experience with formalizing land tenure, formal rights by themselves may be neither necessary, nor sufficient, to secure access to resources. Depending on the circumstances, formalization may do more harm than good. Research has shown that titles and private ownership often do not improve tenure security, especially where indigenous property rights institutions are strong (Bruce 1993; Place and Hazell 1993). Formal registration procedures are vulnerable to manipulation and abuse, especially by those who are better educated, richer and more powerful, although measures can be taken to improve accessibility. Research should assess the relative advantages and disadvantages of formalization, compared to other approaches to resource management.

Wholesaling Water

'Wholesaling' of water to user associations which would then handle retail distribution to individual users might create a clearer form of water right than most irrigators in government-managed systems currently enjoy in South and Southeast Asia. However, agencies usually lack the level of control over water delivery which is presumed in recommendations for wholesaling. Simply switching from individual fee collection to bulk volumetric sales, which is sometimes what is meant by wholesaling, is not sufficient to improve either the water rights or the efficiency of water use (Meinzen-Dick and Mendoza 1996). Successfully shifting to a wholesaling approach would require not just transferring responsibility to user groups at the tertiary or secondary level, but improving the capacity of the agency and user organizations to negotiate allocation and to distribute water accordingly.

Transforming Rights

Strengthening of formal water use rights systems is being considered or attempted in many countries of South and Southeast Asia. Inventorying or formally registering existing rights invokes complex questions about the plurality of claims. Rights may be inadvertently or deliberately transformed in the process of being systematically recorded (Coward 1990; Sengupta in this volume). Implicit or explicit use or control rights of secondary water users (i.e., those besides the main irrigation or industrial uses, such as fishers, herders, or a range of domestic water users) are too easily overlooked or brushed aside. Research can help to clarify the diversity of claims which exist, and options for better accommodating diverse claims within more formalized water rights systems.

To the extent that formal law defines and regulates water differently, then there is the risk that valuable aspects of existing allocation institutions may be 'lost in translation.' There are important choices in how formal rights are defined, for example whether water rights are proportional or volumetric, tied to land or separable, and held by individuals or by collective organizations such as a WUA (Bruns 1998; Rosegrant and Binswanger 1994).

General principles of good governance also apply, such as: involvement of stakeholders, transparency, accountability, requirements for public notice, public hearings, means for challenge or comment, and provision for appealing disputes to higher levels. There is no uniquely best way to go about inventorying or formalizing rights. Registering rights based on 'customary' practice is desirable as a general principle. However, as discussed earlier, local rights may be complex and contested, so this may not be just a matter of documenting existing rights, but instead, in at least a significant portion of cases, a process may be needed for negotiating formal rights. If formalization is applied selectively, for example in specific basins, research can help clarify where it might or might not be worthwhile.

Efforts are also be needed to build the capacity of individuals (or organizations holding rights) to defend their rights. Participatory procedures can enable water resource users to take part in gathering and utilizing information about water allocation (Sowerwine et al. 1994). The work of Northern New Mexico Legal Services assisting *acequia* irrigators, who in principle hold very senior water rights, is an example of the challenges poor farmers and farming communities face in defending their rights during complex, costly, and lengthy water rights adjudication procedures. In essence, establishing formal rights is a process of renegotiating rights amidst competing claims. Much needs to be learned about how to best do this, and when it may be preferable to wait or pursue alternative approaches rather than forcing formalization of water tenure.

Basin Governance

As competition for water grows, irrigators must look outward, beyond the boundaries of their schemes, to deal with strangers in basin water allocation. The scale and scope of problems for water resources governance expands across geographic, administrative and social boundaries. One of the key tasks of governance is to create an institutional framework within which strangers can peacefully agree to cooperate and coordinate their actions (North 1990). Relying on government agencies alone to allocate water in basins may fail to respond to the interests and priorities of water users, as well as incurring high transactions costs compared to having users cooperate to reach and implement decisions. At the same time, negotiations between users will have to be conducted within a framework of broader regulation. Developing better approaches requires finding effective combinations of self-governance, state regulation, and market principles (Dudley 1992; Meinzen-Dick and Rosegrant 1997; Picciotto 1995).

Enabling Self-governance

Numerous studies have documented the capacity of irrigators' organizations to manage irrigation within individual schemes. Much less research has been done on how to accommodate other water uses within irrigation systems, or manage between systems. It would help to know much more about the extent to which coordination already occurs, even if informally or ad hoc, as well as what problems and opportunities are created by greater user involvement in basin governance. Sutawan's chapter showed how negotiating water rights between groups was a feasible, but complex, process. In practical terms, action research is needed on how to form or strengthen federations, basin management bodies or other institutions, and how users can best be represented.

More ambitious than just incorporating users in agency procedures for basin water allocation is the question of whether governance of basins or sub-basins can be primarily handled by users. Groundwater management in southern California (Bloomquist 1992) offers one of the few well-studied examples of how such problems have been resolved in the context of self-governance. Multiple, sometimes overlapping units, public, private and user-controlled, cooperated in a 'polycentric' pattern of governance, emphasizing horizontal coordination rather than vertical hierarchy. Representative basin governance organizations exist in many countries, such as France, Spain, and Chile among others, although apparently with stronger technical agency roles. As countries throughout Asia and other regions seek to develop basin-level water institutions (see Arriens et al. 1996), it would be useful to know more about what affects their performance.

Institutional change is an evolutionary process, involving incremental changes and learning from trial and error (Bloomquist 1992; Ostrom 1990). Efforts to improve basin water management may be more fruitful if they start from urgent problems and build from there to evolve institutional capacity rather than trying to establish a comprehensive framework. It may be better to conceive of reform in terms of punctuated institutional coevolution, rather than gradual refinement of regulations within an equilibrium condition. Research and pilot activities can develop institutions, which then might be drawn upon in responding to crises, rather than assuming that change will mainly occur within a top-down process of carefully deliberated policy reform.

Intersectoral Transfer

Alternatives to Expropriation

As cities grow they look for more water. Reallocating water from agriculture often appears to be the easiest source of additional supplies, especially if augmenting supplies through storage dams is deterred by high economic, social, and environmental costs. Efforts to reallocate water may be justified in terms of the higher economic value of municipal and industrial uses, increasing efficiency, and legal priority for 'drinking' water.[2] In such circumstances, can farmers and others in rural areas defend their access to water? If farmers give up water to others, can they receive adequate compensation? What will happen to other customary water users, such as fishers, livestock keepers, gardeners, or domestic users, whose claims based on customary or religious rights may be harder to document? How can water be assured for environmental needs, to protect instream flows and water-based habitats?

In most countries of South and Southeast Asia, the state asserts formal ownership of water, and so in theory has authority to reallocate water. Even without legal authority for expropriation, industries rely on their economic and political power to obtain water from farmers, legitimately and illegitimately, as in the case discussed by Kurnia, Avianto and Bruns. Institutional frameworks for carrying out transfer through voluntary agreements among users are usually nonexistent. Since agriculture typically uses over 70 or 80 per cent of current supplies, it appears almost inevitable that other needs will be met by transfer from agriculture to other users when new supplies cannot be developed. The question is how this process will occur, whether it will be dominated by expropriation, or whether institutional innovations can allow transfers to occur through negotiation of mutually satisfactory agreements.

Water Acquisition

Unless efforts are made to improve procedures for water transfer there is a risk of repeating the history of problems in land acquisition and resettlement for storage dams and other water resources projects.[3] Many governments and international agencies are now putting in place better procedures for land acquisition, such as carefully reviewing alternative solutions, minimizing impacts, and recognizing indigenous ownership, informal tenure and other rights which were often neglected in the past. Procedures for compensation and other assistance seek to involve affected persons in planning, and move from an emphasis on only cash compensation toward ensuring that those affected are at least as well off after the project as before. More attention is needed to applying similar principles where projects seek to acquire water currently used by farmers.

Defending Access

Expropriation of water, transfer with little or no compensation to those who lose water, threatens rural livelihoods. Farmers may be in a weaker political and economic position than urban interests, but are still not lacking means to resist having their water taken away. The much higher economic value of water in non-agricultural uses, and the relatively small size of such new demands compared with the large volumes currently used in agriculture, creates at least the possibility for win-win agreements for water transfer. Leasing and other innovative institutional arrangements could provide attractive alternatives to selling rights or having them expropriated (Moore 1997). Technical measures to increase the productivity of water in agriculture can help ensure that existing users are not adversely affected. Research is needed on what is currently happening in terms of intersectoral transfer, and what constructive examples exist for managing transfer. In addition to more conventional research approaches, much could be learned through action research working with communities whose access to water is threatened.

Water Markets

Water markets are emerging in many areas, even in the absence of legal legitimization, and sometimes deliberately avoiding formal regulation (Shah 1993). Informal trading of water, spot markets, may evolve spontaneously without requiring formal water rights. Informal markets can provide substantial, although unequal, benefits in expanding access to the resource (Meinzen-Dick in this volume). Permanent trading of water rights, crossing beyond local boundaries, is only likely to be feasible where such rights are recognized in state law (Easter et al. 1998).

Establishing tradable water rights and water markets is advocated as one way of dealing with the need to reallocate water, allowing it to occur through voluntary transactions (Rosegrant and Binswanger

1994; Rosegrant and Gazmuri Schleyer 1994). Tradable rights encourage shifting water to those able to pay the most, strengthening incentives for economic efficiency. Establishing tradable water rights and markets is likely to increase, not decrease the need for negotiation. The common pool characteristics of surface and ground water resources, difficulty in exclusion and rivalry in consumption, mean that the issue is not one of being able to simply privatize water, but of finding effective combinations of market mechanisms, state regulation, and self-governance institutions. Trading water itself requires negotiation, which often cannot treat water as a generic commodity, but must deal with the location-specific characteristics of supply and demand, i.e., there usually is a high degree of asset specificity (Williamson 1996), and bilateral monopoly (Alston 1978).

If water user associations hold rights, they are likely to require internal negotiation to agree on any transactions. Trades may affect irrigation organizations, surrounding communities which lose water, downstream users, and other third parties (Ingram and Oggins 1992). Better empirical information on the impacts of transfers could clarify debates which are often based on ideology and preconceptions (Young 1986). Requirements to ensure instream flows for aquatic habitats now have a major influence in U.S. water resource management[4] and environmental impacts of development are receiving increasing attention in many countries. Therefore, strengthening negotiation capacity, and formalizing rights compatible with existing local allocation practices, are likely to be essential prerequisites for any attempt to establish water markets. If the gains from reallocating water are limited, and permanent transfers infrequent, then one option is to create a legal framework enabling transfer, without requiring the establishment of the institutional apparatus for full-fledged water markets. Research on transformations in water rights as water markets emerge, and the implications of policy reforms to create tradable rights, is a priority for further study, as well as looking at the transaction costs of establishing water markets compared with other approaches for managing intersectoral transfer.

Water Rights and Civil Society

Water rights institutions are part of a larger institutional framework. Several authors in this book have noted the interrelationship between water rights negotiation and the strength or weakness of courts as means for managing conflicts. Collective action by farmers is affected by the extent to which farmers are already formally organized, and the extent to which laws and agency practice recognize and support such organization, or not. These are just two examples of how water allocation, and the possibilities for improving allocation, may be affected by the social capital of existing institutions and the relative development of civil society.

Community Capacity

Empowering communities to negotiate their rights to water raises serious challenges. Research is needed to escape myths, trying to clarify, empirically and conceptually, what shapes the community's capacity to deal with threats, whether from outsiders seeking to exploit disadvantages of poor information, economic or political weakness, and discourses dominated by legal-bureaucratic conceptions; or from leaders and other élites who may use their roles to pursue private interests in ways which sacrifice the concerns of others in the community. If negotiators act as agents for communities, will they adequately represent the interests of those they are supposed to serve? How do women, the landless, or marginalized ethnic groups gain a voice—either directly or through negotiators? A shift to negotiated approaches brings new demands on institutions for collective action, focusing on external relations across boundaries. Formalizing water tenure raises issues similar to those concerning efforts to privatize fisheries, rangeland or forests. If rights are made transferable will they quickly be lost to wealthy outsiders, or sustainably managed to local advantage? Should rights be held individually, or collectively as common property? Can communities cope with speculators? What factors affect the capacity of communities to deal with markets for resource rights?

Conclusion

The kinds of conflicts over water allocation examined in this book will become more prevalent in the years ahead. Addressing these through negotiated approaches that take into account the plurality of claims on water resources is more complex than imposing (or attempting to impose) allocation by the state, but in the long run the negotiated approaches are likely to be more effective and equitable. Negotiation will not solve all conflicts, but much more should be done to improve the capacity to negotiate, and to make sure that negotiation is available as an option.

Building Capacity to Negotiate

Policies for decentralization, stakeholder participation, and strengthening civil society institutions in governance, including in natural resource management, are creating conditions which favor increased emphasis on negotiated approaches to water allocation. Institutional innovation is needed to strengthen the capacity of water user organizations, government agencies and other stakeholders to pursue negotiated solutions. Forums need to be created and strengthened which can deal with the scope and scale of water conflicts. More effort should be made to strengthen negotiating skills, applying and adapting available techniques. Research and applied activities also need to look at the limitations of negotiated approaches.

Understanding Legal Pluralism

Attempts to reform water rights are likely to fail unless grounded in an adequate understanding of and respect for how water allocation is practiced at the local level. Concepts of legal pluralism offer a fertile source of ideas about how state and local law interact, and how disputes are negotiated. Legal pluralism provides a useful set of conceptual tools for study beginning from people's everyday experience, how they conceive of water, rights to water, and related social institutions and interests. Research drawing on these ideas can clarify the factors shaping processes and outcomes of renegotiating rights, appropriate ways to strengthen water tenure, how to make new organizations and institutions accessible and effective, and how local institutions for regulating resource rights respond to the opportunities and threats of markets. For example, studies of who uses which forums could help identify ways to make forums (including negotiation, courts, agency decision-making) more accessible to those currently excluded.

Action Research

Learning process approaches to pilot experiments played a crucial role in devising new methods for improving participation in irrigation, combining insights from researchers and practitioners, and linking field experiments with policy reform. Action research approaches offer the most promising directions for learning and institutional innovation in water allocation. Renegotiating rights as part of water development projects requires explicitly creating agreements about rights which often have only been dealt with implicitly. Consideration about formalizing water rights should be linked to field studies and pilot activities to clarify the advantages and disadvantages of formalization, as part of a larger set of institutional options for strengthening rights, involving stakeholders, and resolving disputes. Where formalization seems desirable or inevitable, there is a need to learn how to make formalized tenure appropriately compatible with existing practices, equitably accessible, and defensible. Basin management institutions need to learn how to make participation efficient and worthwhile for stakeholders, working across geographic, administrative, and cultural boundaries. Action research, by university researchers or NGOs, helping communities defend their access to water could yield many lessons about better institutions for managing water allocation.

Notes

1. For example, an action research project to rehabilitate tanks in Tamil Nadu, India included the negotiation of an expanded set of water shares in the tank, with the additional shares (and representation on the committee to go along with the shares) going to low-caste groups who previously had been excluded (see Mosse 1995).
2. Whereas many analyses of 'intersectoral' allocation tend to equate rural communities with irrigation, and urban areas with domestic and industrial uses, the case studies from West Java (Chapter 10) and Bangladesh (Chapter 9) show that there can be a wide range of irrigation, domestic, and even industrial water uses within rural areas. Similarly, periurban and urban agriculture can use significant amounts of water for horticultural production.

3. In a number of well-publicized cases, when land was appropriated for dams and submerged areas, local residents were given compensation based on externally-imputed prices, and compensation was only given to those with formal documentation of land ownership. The local, national, and international opposition to such policies has made many governments reluctant to develop new water projects with storage dams. Ironically, this has created more pressure for appropriation of water from farmers who have irrigation—often with similarly inadequate compensation policies.
4. See White, Valdez and White (1980) on negotiation of instream flows.

References

Alston, Richard M. 1978. Commercial irrigation enterprise: The fear of water monopoly and the genesis of market distortion in the nineteenth century American West. New York: Arno Press.

Arriens, Wouter Lincklaen, Jeremy Bird, Jeremy Berkhoff, and **Paul Mosely.** 1996. *Towards effective water policy in the Asian and Pacific region: Proceedings of the regional consultation workshop.* 3 vols. Manila: Asian Development Bank.

Arrow, Kenneth J., Robert H. Mnookin, Lee Ross, Amos Tversky, and **Robert B. Wilson,** eds. 1995. *Barriers to conflict resolution.* New York: W.W. Norton.

Benda Beckmann, Keebet von, Mirjam de Bruijn, Han van Dijk, Gerti Hesseling, Barbara van Koppen, and **Lyda Res.** 1997. *Women's rights to land and water. Literature review.* The Hague: The Special Program Women and Development, Department of International Cooperation, Ministry of Foreign Affairs, The Government of The Netherlands.

Bingham, Gail, Aaron Wolf, and **Tim Wohlgenant.** 1994. *Resolving water disputes: Conflict and cooperation in the United States, the Near East and Asia.* Washington, D.C.: USAID Irrigation and Support Project for Asian and Near East.

Bloomquist, William. 1992. *Dividing the waters: Governing groundwater in Southern California.* San Francisco, Calif.: Institute for Contemporary Studies.

Bruce, John. 1993. Do indigenous tenure systems constrain agricultural development? In *Land in African agrarian systems*, ed. Tom J. Bassett and Donalt E. Crummey, 35–56. Madison, Wisc.: University of Wisconsin Press.

Bruns, Bryan. 1993. Promoting participation in irrigation: Reflections on experience in Southeast Asia. *World Development* 21 (11) (November): 1837–1849.

Bruns, Bryan. 1998. Water rights questions. Presented at the Tenth Afro-Asian Regional Conference of the International Commission for Irrigation and Drainage, Bali, Indonesia, July 19–24, 1998.

Chopra, Kanchan, G.K. Kadekodi, and **M.N. Murthy.** 1988. Sukhomajri and Dhamala watersheds in Haryana. A participatory approach to development. Delhi: Institute of Economic Growth.

Checchio, Elizabeth, and **Bonnie Colby.** 1993. Indian water rights: Negotiating the future. Water Resources Research Center, University of Arizona, Tucson.

Cohen, Nevin. 1997. Implementing community advisory panels: Essentials for success. *Interact: The Journal of Public Participation* 3 (1): 30–37.

Coward, E. Walter, Jr. 1986. Direct or indirect alternatives for irrigation investment and the creation of property. In *Irrigation investment, technology and management strategies for development,* ed. K.W. Easter, 225–44. Boulder, Colo.: Westview Press.

Coward, E. Walter, Jr. 1990. Property rights and network order: The case of irrigation works in the Western Himalayas. *Human Organization* 49 (1): 78–88.

Dinar, Ariel, and **Edna Tusak Loehman,** eds. 1995. *Water quantity/quality management and conflict resolution: Institutions, processes and economic analysis.* Westport, Conn.: Praeger.

Dudley, Norman J. 1992. Water allocation by markets, common property and capacity sharing: Companions or competitors. *Natural Resources Journal* 32 (Fall): 757–778.

Dunlop, John T. 1995. The creation of new processes for conflict resolution in labor disputes. In *Barriers to conflict resolution,* ed. K. Arrow, R.H. Mnookin, L. Ross, A. Tversky and R. Wilson, 274–90. New York: W.W. Norton.

Easter, K. William, Mark W. Rosegrant, and **Ariel Dinar,** eds. 1998. *Markets for water: Potential and performance.*

Edelman, Joel, and **Mary Beth Crain.** 1993. *The tao of negotiation: How to resolve conflict in all areas of your life.* London: Piatkus.

Engel, David M. 1978. *Code and custom in a Thai court: The interaction of formal and informal systems of justice.* Tucson, Ariz.: University of Arizona Press.

Faure, Guy Olivier, and **Jeffrey Z. Rubin,** eds. 1993. *Culture and negotiation: The resolution of water disputes.* Newbury Park, Calif.: Sage Publications.

Fisher, Roger, and **Danny Ertel.** 1995. *Getting ready to negotiate: The getting to yes workbook.* New York: Penguin Books.

Fisher, Roger, Elizabeth Kopelman, and **Andrea Kupfer Schneider.** 1994. *Beyond Machiavelli: Tools for coping with conflict.* Cambridge, Mass.: Harvard University Press.

Fisher, Roger, and **Scott Brown**. 1988. *Getting together: Building relationships as we negotiate*. New York: Penguin Books.

Fisher, Roger, **William Ury**, and **Bruce Patton**. 1991. *Getting to yes: Negotiating agreement without giving in*, 2nd ed. New York: Penguin Books.

Folk-Williams, John A. 1988. The use of negotiated agreements to resolve water disputes involving Indian water rights. *Natural Resources Journal* 28 (1) Winter): 63–103.

Gerbrandy, Gerban, and **Paul Hoogendam**. 1996. The materialization of water rights: Hydraulic property in the extension and rehabilitation of two irrigation systems in Bolivia. In *Crops, people and irrigation: Water allocation practices of farmers and engineers*, ed. G. Diemer and F.P. Huibers, 53–72. London: Intermediate Technology Publications.

Gilson, Ronald J. and **Robert H. Mnookin**. 1995. Cooperation and competition in litigation: Can lawyers dampen conflict. In *Barriers to conflict resolution*, ed. Kenneth J. Arrow, Robert H. Mnookin, Lee Ross, Amos Tversky, and Robert B. Wilson, 184–211. New York: W.W. Norton.

Guillet, David. 1999. Water demand management and farmer managed irrigation systems in the Colca Valley of Southwestern Peru. In *Globalization and the rural poor in Latin America: Crisis and response in campesino communities*, ed. W. Loker. Boulder, Colo.: Lynn Rienner.

Guillet, David. 1998. Rethinking legal pluralism: Local law and state law in the evolution of water property rights in Northwestern Spain. *Comparative Studies in Society and History* 40 (1): 42–70

Ingram, Helen, and **Cy R. Oggins**. 1992. The public trust doctrine and community values in water. *Natural Resources Journal* 32 (Summer): 515–537.

Karrass, Chester L. 1992. *The negotiating game: How to get what you want*. Revised ed. New York: Harper Collins.

Lewicki, Roy J., **Alexander Hiam**, and **Karen Wise Olander**. 1996. *Think before you speak: The complete guide to strategic negotiation*. New York: John Wiley and Sons.

Maass, Arthur, and **Raymond L. Anderson**. 1978. *...And the desert shall rejoice: Conflict, growth and justice in arid environments*. Cambridge, Mass.: MIT Press.

Manor, Shaul, **Sanguan Patamatamkul**, and **Manuel Olin**, eds. 1990. *Role of social organizers in assisting farmer managed irrigation systems*. Proceedings of a regional workshop held at Khonkaen, Thailand, May 15–29, 1989. Colombo, Sri Lanka: International Irrigation Management Institute.

Martin, Edward D. and **Robert Yoder**. 1987. Institutions for irrigation management in farmer-managed systems: Examples from the hills of Nepal. IIMI Research Paper No. 5.

McCool, Daniel. 1993. Indian water settlements: The prerequisites of successful negotiation. *Policy Studies Journal* 21 (2): 227–42.

Meinzen-Dick, Ruth S. 1997. Valuing the multiple uses of irrigation water. In *Water: Economics, management and demand*, ed. Melvin Kay, Thomas Franks and Laurence Smith, 50–58. London: E & FN Spon.

Meinzen-Dick, Ruth S. and **Meyra Mendoza.** 1996. Alternative water allocation mechanisms: Indian and international experiences. *Economic and Political Weekly* 31 (13): A25–30.

Meinzen-Dick, Ruth S., and **Mark W. Rosegrant.** 1997. Alternative allocation mechanisms for intersectoral water management. In *Strategies for intersectoral water management in developing countries—challenges and consequences for agriculture*, ed. Jurgen Richter, Peter Wolff, Hubertus Franzen, and Franz Heim, 256–73. Feldalfing, Germany: Deutsche Stiftung für internationale Entwicklung.

Mnookin, R., and **L. Kornhauser.** 1979. Bargaining in the shadow of the law: The case of divorce. *Yale Law Journal* 88: 950–97.

Moore, Deborah. 1997. Environment, equity and efficiency: Global challenges for the 21st century. *Common Property Resource Digest* 1 (43): 7–9.

Mosse, David. 1995. Local institutions and power: The history and practice of community management of tank irrigation systems in south India. In *Power and participatory development: Theory and practice*, ed. Nici Nelson and Susan Wright, 144–156. London: Intermediate Technology Publications.

Natural Resources Law Center. 1996. *The watershed source book: Watershed-based solutions to natural resource problems*. Boulder, Colo.: University of Colorado School of Law.

Nierenberg, Gerard I. 1981. *The art of negotiating*. New York: Pocket Books.

North, Douglass C. 1990. *Institutions, institutional change and economic performance*. New York: Cambridge University Press.

Ostrom, Elinor. 1990. *Governing the commons: The evolution of institutions for collective action*. Cambridge, U.K.: Cambridge University Press.

Ostrom, Elinor. 1995. Constituting social capital and collective action. In *Local commons and global interdependence: Heterogeneity and cooperation in two domains*, ed. R.O. Keohane and E. Ostrom, 125–60. London: Sage.

Patel-Weynand, Toral. 1997. Sukomajri and Nada: Managing common property resources in two villages. In *Natural resource economics: Theory and application in India*, ed. J. Kerr, D. Marothia, C. Ramasamy, K. Singh, 363–74. New Delhi: Oxford IBH.

Picciotto, Robert. 1995. *Putting institutional economics to work: From participation to governance*. Washington, D.C.: The World Bank.

Place, Frank, and **Peter Hazell.** 1993. Productivity effects of indigenous land tenure systems in Sub-Saharan Africa. *American Journal of Agricultural Economics* 75: 10–19.

Pradhan, Rajendra, K.A. Haq, and **Ujjwal Pradhan.** 1997. Law, rights and equity: Implications of state intervention in farmer managed irrigation systems. In *Water rights, conflict and policy*, ed. Rajendra Pradhan, Franz von Benda-Beckmann, Keebet von Benda-Beckmann, H.L. Joep Spiertz, S. Khadka, and K. Azharul Haq, 93–110. Colombo, Sri Lanka: International Irrigation Management Institute.

Pradhan, Naresh and **Robert Yoder.** 1989. Improving irrigation system management through farmer-to-farmer training: Examples from Nepal. IIMI Working Paper No. 12. Sri Lanka: IIMI.

Pradhan, Ujjwal. 1994. Farmer-to-farmer training as a way of assistance to the farmers on the improvement of irrigation systems. In *From farmers' fields to data fields and back: A synthesis of participatory information systems for irrigation and other resources*, ed. Jennifer Sowerwine, Ganesh Shivakoti, Ujjwal Pradhan, Ashutosh Shukla and Elinor Ostrom, 187–98. Proceedings of an International Workshop held at the Institute of Agriculture and Animal Science, Rampur, Nepal, March 21–26, 1993. Colombo, Sri Lanka: IIMI and Institute of Agriculture and Animal Science: Rampur, Nepal.

Reck, Ross R., and **Brian G. Long.** 1989. *The win-win negotiator: How to negotiate favourable agreements that last*. New York: Simon and Schuster.

Rosegrant, Mark W. and **Hans P. Binswanger.** 1994. Markets in tradable water rights: Potential for efficiency gains in developing country water resource allocation. *World Development* 22 (11): 1–11.

Rosegrant, Mark W. and **S. Renato Gazmuri Schleyer.** 1994. *Tradable water rights: Experiences in reforming water allocation policy*. Washington, D.C.: Irrigation Support Project for Asia and the Near East.

Rothman, Jay. 1995. Pre-negotiation in water disputes where culture is core. *Cultural Survival Quarterly* 1995 (Fall): 19–22.

Shabman, Leonard A., and **William E. Cox.** 1995. Conflict over eastern U.S. water transfers: Toward a new era of negotiation? In *Water Quantity/ Quality Management and Conflict Resolution*, ed. A. Dinar and E.T. Loehman, 189–201. Westport, Conn.: Praeger.

Shah, Tushaar. 1993. *Groundwater markets and irrigation development: Political economy and practical policy*. Bombay, India: Oxford University Press.

Sowerwine, Jennifer, Ganesh Shivakoti, Ujjwal Pradhan, Ashutosh Shukla, and **Elinor Ostrom**, eds. 1994. *From farmers' fields to data fields and back: A synthesis of participatory information systems for irrigation and other resources*. Proceedings of an International Workshop held at the Institute of Agriculture and Animal Science, Rampur, Nepal, March 21–26, 1993. Colombo, Sri Lanka; Kathmandu, International Irrigation Management Institute, Institute of Agriculture and Animal Science.

Stanbury, Pamela and **Jana Lynott.** 1993. Irrigation management and conflict resolution. Research and Development Bureau, Office of Economic and Institutional Development. USAID.

Susskind, Lawrence, and **Patrick Field.** 1996. *Dealing with an angry public: The mutual gains approach to resolving disputes*. New York: Free Press.

Ury, William. 1991. *Getting past no: Negotiating with difficult people.* London: Business Books Limited.

White, Mary Ray, Felix D. Valdez, and **Michael D. White.** 1980. *Instream flow negotiation: Review of practices.* Washington, D.C.: Fish and Wildlife Service, U.S. Department of Interior, FWS/OBS-80/53.

Wilkins-Wells, John. 1996. *Irrigation enterprise management practice study.* Fort Collins: Colorado State University and U.S. Bureau of Reclamation.

Wilkins-Wells, John. 1996. Legal and policy considerations in the promotion of common property organizations (water users associations) in low income nations. Berkeley, Calif. Paper presented at the Sixth Conference of the International Association for the Study of Common Property.

Williamson, Oliver E. 1996. *The mechanisms of governance.* New York: Oxford University Press.

Wood, Geof, D., Richard Palmer-Jones; with **Q.F. Ahmed, M.A.S. Madal,** and **S.C. Dutta.** 1990. *The water sellers: A cooperative venture by the rural poor.* Hartford, Conn.: Kumarian Press.

Young, Robert A. 1986. Why are there so few transactions among water users? *American Journal of Agricultural Economics* 68 (5): 1144–51.

About the Editors and Contributing Authors

Editors

Bryan Randolph Bruns is a consulting sociologist based in northern Thailand, helping people and organizations to improve participation, communication and service delivery in rural development. He specializes in participatory learning and action for water resource management, including farmer-managed irrigation development, irrigation management turnover, water user association development, and public participation in basin water management. He holds a Ph.D. in Development Sociology from Cornell University. Dr Bruns has worked extensively in Southeast Asia, and has published articles and contributed to international conferences dealing with participatory approaches to irrigation and water resource management.

Bryan Bruns
Consulting Sociologist
C-723 Lanna Condo, T. Pa Tan
Chiang Mai 50300 Thailand
Email: BryanBruns@compuserve.com
www.BryanBruns.com

Ruth S. Meinzen-Dick is a Research Fellow in the Environment and Production Technology Division at the International Food Policy Research Institute, Washington, where she works on water resource management and factors that contribute to effective local organizations, and where she is also coordinator of the CGIAR System-Wide Initiative on Property Rights and Collective Action. She holds a Ph.D. in Development Sociology from Cornell University and has worked extensively in South Asia and southern Africa. Dr Meinzen-Dick has published a number of articles as also co-edited books on irrigation management in India, Zimbabwe, and Pakistan besides a World Bank Technical Paper on user organizations for water resource management.

Ruth Meinzen-Dick
International Food Policy Research Institute
2033 K St. NW
Washington D.C. 20006
Email: r.meinzen-dick@cgiar.org

Contributing Authors

Teten W. Avianto is a researcher working on hydrological and ecological aspects of water allocation, at the Centre for Development Dynamics, Padjadjaran University, in Bandung, West Java, Indonesia. He holds an Engineer's degree in Agricultural Technology from Padjadjaran University. He is currently an Associate of the Leadership for Environment And Development (LEAD) Programme (*http://www.lead.org*), sponsored by Rockefeller Foundation; and he is a student in the Development Studies Graduate Programme of the Bandung Institute Technology. He has worked extensively as a consulting hydrologist in tropical forest areas of Indonesia. He received an award as a finalist in the Indonesian Young Researcher Selection in 1997, based on research at the site described in the chapter he co-authored for this book.

Teten W. Avianto
Padjadjaran University
Center for Development Studies
Jalan Dipati Ukur No. 35
Bandung 40192
Indonesia
E-mail: teten@indo.net.id
http://www.ypb.or.id/teten

Jeffrey D. Brewer is a social scientist with the International Water Management Institute (formerly the International Irrigation Management Institute), Colombo, Sri Lanka. He holds a Ph.D. in Cultural Anthropology from the University of California, Los Angeles. He has worked extensively in South and Southeast Asia, Latin America, and the Middle East on issues and projects concerned with irrigation and agricultural management and development. He has published papers on several aspects of irrigation water management and other subjects.

Jeffrey D. Brewer
International Water Management Institute
P.O. Box 2075
Colombo
Sri Lanka
Email: J. Brewer@cgiar.org

David Guillet is Professor in the Department of Anthropology at Catholic University. His specialties include ecological anthropology, natural resource management, and common property. He has carried out research in the Andean countries, India and Spain and since 1991 has been directing a long-term study, sponsored by the National Science Foundation, of irrigation in northwestern Spain. He is the author of *Covering Ground: Communal Water Management and the State in the Peruvian Highlands* (University of Michigan, 1992).

David Guillet
Department of Anthoropology
Catholic University of America
Washington D.C. 20064
U.S.A.
Email: guillet@cua.edu

Ganjar Kurnia is head of the Center for Development Dynamics, Padjadjaran University, Indonesia. He is lecturer as well in the graduate and post graduate field of sociology at the same university. Ganjar Kurnia achieved DEA in Sociology and Economics of Community and post graduate studies in Rural Sociology from University of Paris X Nanterre. His bachelor's degree is from Padjadjaran University, Department of Agricultural Social Economics, with additional training in demography. He has attended international seminars and workshops in the field of irrigation, and conducted research on irrigation, demography, and other development affairs.

Ganjar Kurnia
Padjadjaran University
Center for Development Dynamics
Jalan Dipati Ukur No. 35
Bandung 40192
Indonesia
Email: pdpunpad@melsa.net.id

Northern New Mexico Legal Services (NNMLS) is a nongovernment organization primarily funded by the Federal government to provide civil legal advice and representation to the 96,000 eligible poor persons living in the northern half of the state. NNMLS' staff of 20 serves over 4,000 clients per year. Since the inception of the program over 30 years ago, protection of traditional land and water rights has been one of the organization's priorities.

Northern New Mexico Legal Services
805 Early Street
P.O. Box 5175
Santa Fe, NM 87502
U.S.A.
Email: hn1547@handsnet.org

Rajendra Pradhan, a Kathmandu based anthropologist with varied research interests, is currently affiliated with Legal Research and Development Forum (FREEDEAL), a Nepalese research and training NGO. He has studied religion among the Newars of Kathmandu, the care of the elderly in a Dutch village, and food beliefs and practices in southern Nepal. For the past several years he has been directing research on water rights in Nepal, especially in farmer managed irrigation systems. He recently co-edited a book on water rights in Nepal and India (*Water Rights, Conflict and Policy* 1997), and is working on another book.

Rajendra Pradhan
Kathmandu, Nepal
G.P.O. Box 10447
Kathmandu
Nepal
Rajendra@freed.wlink.com.np

Ujjwal Pradhan is a program officer for water resources development and policy with the Ford Foundation's New Delhi office. Formerly he was social scientist and Head of the Nepal Country Program of the International Irrigation Management Institute (IIMI). In 1990–91 he served as an institutional development specialist with Euroconsult for the World Bank-funded Irrigation Service Fee Project based in Jakarta, Indonesia. He has a doctorate in Development Sociology, with a focus on Agriculture and Natural Resource Sociology from Cornell University. His doctoral dissertation dealt with property rights and relations and state intervention in irrigation in Nepal.

Ujjwal Pradhan
Ford Foundation
55 Lodi Estate
New Delhi 110003
India
Email: U.Pradhan@fordfound.org

Syed Zahir Sadeque is a Sociologist, currently working at the International Center for Integrated Mountain Development, Kathmandu, Nepal. He has taught sociology in universities in Bangladesh, worked as National Consultant for Agriculture Sector Team of CIDA, as a Program Specialist for USAID Mission in Dhaka, and as the Team Leader of UNDP/World Bank Water and Sanitation Programme in Bangladesh. He has also undertaken several concurrent consulting assignments for UNDP, IIMI/ADB, Ford Foundation and others in Bangladesh. His research interests are agriculture, natural resources, community participation, social assessment and soundness procedures in project design and monitoring-evaluation. He holds a Ph.D. in Development Sociology from Cornell University (1986).

Sayed Zahir Sadeque
International Centre for Integrated Mountain Development,
4/80 Jawalakhel
G.P.O. Box 3226
Kathmandu
Nepal
Email: Sadeque@icimod.org.np

Nirmal Sengupta is a Professor at Madras Institute of Development Studies. He has a M. Stat., Dip. in Econometrics and Planning and Ph.D degrees, and has worked in different capacities in the Bihar State Planning Board, India; National Institute of Rural Development, Hyderabad, India, Netherlands Ministry of Cooperation, UNDP and FAO. Other books include *Managing Common Property: Irrigation in India and Philippines* and *User-Friendly Irrigation Designs*.

Nirmal Sengupta
Madras Institute of Development Studies
79 Second Main Road
Gandhinagar
Chennai 600 020
India
Email: ssmids@ren.ren.nic.in

H.L. Joep Spiertz was Senior Lecturer of Agrarian Law and Legal Anthropology at the Agricultural University Wageningen, The Netherlands. His teaching and research dealt with the issues of regulation and the significance of law for the problems of equitable access to and sustainable use and management of natural resources. He carried out legal anthropological research on adat law on Bali, and published a number of articles, and co-edited books on the social scientific study of law and the theoretical and methodological aspects of the study of property and water rights within farmer-managed irrigation systems in Indonesia, Sri Lanka and Nepal.

Nyoman Sutawan is a Professor of Agricultural Socio-economics in the Department of Socio-economics/Agribusiness, Faculty of Agriculture of Udayana University, Denpasar-Bali. He has been involved in considerable action research on irrigation *subaks*, including the work presented in this volume.

Nyoman Sutawan
Jalan Morotai No. 39
Denpasar 80114
Bali, Indonesia
Fax/phone: 62-361-232154
Email: sutawan@denpasar.wasantara.net.id

Barbara van Koppen is coordinator of the Gender and Water Programme of the International Water Management Institute. She has done research in Burkina Faso and Bangladesh, and in other African and Asian countries, on poverty alleviation and gender in irrigation. She is author of a book with Simeen Mahmud on *Women and water-pumps in Bangladesh: The impacts of participation in irrigation groups on women's status* and has published in several international journals. Before joining IWMI she worked as a lecturer/ researcher at Wageningen Agricultural University, The Netherlands; as a technical assistant in irrigation projects in Burkina Faso; and as an action-researcher with Dutch farm women. She holds a Ph.D. in Gender and Irrigation from Wageningen Agricultural University.

Barbara van Koppen
International Water Management Institute
P.O. Box 2075
Colombo
Sri Lanka
Email: b. vankoppen@cgiar.org

Douglas L. Vermillion obtained his Ph.D. in Development Sociology from Cornell University in 1986. His thesis involved a detailed field investigation into the emergence of socially-recognized water rights among farmers in two transmigration settlements in north Sulawesi, Indonesia. From 1986 until 1998, he has been a research scientist for the International Irrigation Management Institute (IIMI). During this time he worked for four years in Indonesia on field studies about constraints to irrigation management performance in public irrigation systems in Java, and directed a study about the small-scale irrigation turnover program. At the IIMI headquarters in Colombo, Sri Lanka, he directed a comparative research program on the transfer of irrigation management from government agencies to water users associations. This involved IIMI studies on the structure, process and impacts of irrigation management transfer in the USA, Sri Lanka, India, Pakistan, Sudan, Indonesia, China, Mexico and Colombia. At present, Dr. Vermillion lives with his family in Spokane, Washington, USA. He is working on a book and doing consulting work on irrigation management in developing countries.

Douglas Vermillion
4318 South Hogan St.
Spokane, Washington 99203
U.S.A.
Email: dvermillion@compuserve.com

Index